Toward An Anthropological
Theory of Value

Toward An Anthropological Theory of Value

The False Coin of Our Own Dreams

David Graeber

palgrave

TOWARD AN ANTHROPOLOGICAL THEORY OF VALUE
Copyright © David Graeber, 2001. All rights reserved. No part of this book
may be used or reproduced in any manner whatsoever without written per-
mission except in the case of brief quotations embodied in critical articles or
reviews.

First published 2001 by PALGRAVE™
175 Fifth Avenue, New York, N.Y. 10010 and
Houndmills, Basingstoke, Hampshire, England RG21 6XS.
Companies and representatives throughout the world.

PALGRAVE is the new global publishing imprint of St. Martin's Press LLC
Scholarly and Reference Division and Palgrave Publishers Ltd. (formerly
Macmillan Press Ltd).

ISBN 0-312-24044-9 (cloth)
ISBN 0-312-24045-7 (paperback)

Library of Congress Cataloging-in-Publication Data
Graeber, David
Toward an Anthropological Theory of Value: The False Coin of Our Own
Dreams
      p.   cm.
   Includes bibliographical references and index.
   ISBN 0-312-240449 – ISBN 0-312-24045-7 (alk. paper)
   1. Values.   2. Anthropology—Philosophy.   3. Social values.
4. Ceremonial exchange.   I. Title.
GN469.5.G73   2001
303.3'72—dc21
                                                                200121794

A catalogue record for this book is available from the British Library.

Design by Letra Libre, Inc.

First edition: December 2001
10 9 8 7 6 5 4 3 2 1

Printed in the United States of America.

Contents

The belief of all, faith, is the effect of the need of all, of their unanimous desires. Magical judgment is the object of a social consent, the translation of a social need. . . . It is because the effect desired by all is witnessed by all that the means are acknowledged as apt to produce the effect. It is because they desired the healing of the feverish patients that sprinklings of cold water and sympathetic contact with a frog seemed to the Hindus who called on the Brahmins of the Atharva-veda sufficient antagonists to third- or fourth-degree fever. In short, it is always society that pays itself in the counterfeit money of its dreams.

—from Marcel Mauss and Henri Hubert, *Mana and Magic*
(1904, trans. Loic Wacquant)

Acknowledgments

It feels a little silly writing acknowledgements for a book like this, an intellectual project at least fifteen years in the making. The logical thing would perhaps be to thank everyone I've ever known, because you never know where your ideas really came from. There are two names though that I really ought to mention: my oldest friend, Stuart Rockefeller, an intellectual companion since high school, and Nhu Thi Le, whose mind for the last six has touched everything mine has. Any idea you read in here might very well actually have been invented by one of them; in many cases, perhaps most, they are really joint projects that all three of us, and probably others, are equally responsible for. (Except for the parts that are just dumb: I had nothing to do with those!)

Aside from that I must acknowledge the professors and staff and students of the anthropology department of the University of Chicago when I was there, who produced an environment that actually encouraged people to think for themselves and experiment with ideas, something surprisingly rare in academia; my fellow workers at Crerar; my colleagues and students at Haverford, NYU, and Yale; and my comrades in the direct action movement here and abroad who give me hope for humanity, and with whom I have spent so many pleasant hours tearing down walls. Oh, and my parents, who made me who I am.

And my brother Eric. And Kristi Long, the best editor who ever lived, and everyone at Palgrave (except whoever it was who made me switch around the title).

A Few Words by Way
of Introduction

When I originally set out to write this book, the goals I had in mind were relatively modest. I was interested, first of all, in making a contribution to anthropological theories of value. Many anthropologists have long felt we really should have a theory of value: that is, one that seeks to move from understanding how different cultures define the world in radically different ways (which anthropologists have always been good at describing) to how, at the same time, they define what is beautiful, or worthwhile, or important about it. To see how meaning, one might say, turns into desire. To be able to do so promises to resolve a lot of notoriously thorny problems not only in anthropology but also in social science more generally. I wanted to see if I could map out at least the outlines of such a theory and also, to relate them to certain ideas about wealth and power and the nature of money that I had first set out in an essay several years before (Graeber 1996).

In the course of writing, however, something started happening. The more I wrote, the more I was forced to confront the fact that my own assumptions and priorities were in many ways diametrically opposed to much of what now stands as common wisdom in the social sciences—or at least those disciplines (sociology, anthropology, history, cultural studies, etc.) that see themselves as most politically engaged. As I found myself increasingly obliged to clarify points of difference, I realized the book was turning into something much more ambitious: in some ways, it was acquiring the qualities of political tract, or at least, an extended reflection on the relation between disciplines like anthropology and politics.

The standard history—the sort of thing a journalist would take as self-evident fact—is that the last decades of the twentieth century were a time when the American left largely retreated to universities and graduate departments, spinning out increasingly arcane radical meta-theory, deconstructing everything in sight, as all around them, the rest of the world became increasingly conservative. As a broad caricature, I suppose this is not entirely inaccurate.

But recent events suggest there might be very different ways to tell this story. The last several years have seen the rapid growth of new social movements— particularly, movements against neoliberalism (in the United States referred to as "free market" ideologies)—in just about every corner of the world, including, somewhat belatedly, the United States itself. Yet the so-called academic left in America has played almost no role in this; in fact, many of its presumed members seem only vaguely aware that such movements exist. Perhaps this is not all that surprising: neoliberalism itself remains a subject on which modern critical meta-theory has never had very much to say.

But why is that? It seems to me that in a surprising variety of ways, this critical theory actually anticipated neoliberal arguments. Take, for example, the concept of "postmodernism." Now, admittedly this is a somewhat tricky one because there were never many scholars willing to actually call themselves "postmodernists." But in a way, this was precisely what made the term so powerful: "postmodernism" was not something anyone was proposing but a fait accompli that everyone simply had to accept. From the '80s on, it has become common to be presented with a series of arguments that might be summarized, in caricature form, as something like this:

1. We now live in a Postmodern Age. The world has changed; no one is responsible, it simply happened as a result of inexorable processes; neither can we do anything about it, but we must simply adopt ourselves to new conditions.
2. One result of our postmodern condition is that schemes to change the world or human society through collective political action are no longer viable. Everything is broken up and fragmented; anyway, such schemes will inevitably either prove impossible, or produce totalitarian nightmares.
3. While this might seem to leave little room for human agency in history, one need not despair completely. Legitimate political action can take place, provided it is on a personal level: through the fashioning of subversive identities, forms of creative consumption, and the like. Such action is itself political and potentially liberatory.

This is, as I say, a caricature: the actual arguments made in any particular theoretical tract of the time were usually infinitely more complex. Still, they almost invariably did share some version of these three themes. Compare them, then, to the arguments that began to be promulgated in the '90s, in the popular media, about a phenomena referred to as "globalization":

1. We now live in the age of the Global Market. The world has changed; no one is responsible, it simply happened as the result of inexorable

processes; neither can we do anything about it, but we must simply adopt ourselves to new conditions.

2. One result is that schemes aiming to change society through collective political action are no longer viable. Dreams of revolution have been proven impossible or, worse, bound to produce totalitarian nightmares; even any idea of changing society through electoral politics must now be abandoned in the name of "competitiveness."

3. If this might seem to leave little room for democracy, one need not despair: market behavior, and particularly individual consumption decisions, *are* democracy; indeed, they are all the democracy we'll ever really need.

There is, of course, one enormous difference between the two arguments. The central claim of those who celebrated postmodernism is that we have entered a world in which all totalizing systems—science, humanity, nation, truth, and so forth—have all been shattered; in which there are no longer any grand mechanisms for stitching together a world now broken into incommensurable fragments. One can no longer even imagine that there could be a single standard of value by which to measure things. The neoliberals on the other hand are singing the praises of a global market that is, in fact, the single greatest and most monolithic system of measurement ever created, a totalizing system that would subordinate everything—every object, every piece of land, every human capacity or relationship—on the planet to a single standard of value.

It is becoming increasingly obvious that what those who celebrated postmodernism were describing was in large part simply the effects of this universal market system, which, like any totalizing system of value, tends to throw all others into doubt and disarray. The remarkable thing is that they failed to notice this fact. How? And why has it been so difficult for them to come up with a way to criticize a system that would seem to fly directly in the face of everything they are calling for?

Probably the reason is because those who used terms like "postmodernism" did not, in fact, see themselves as calling for anything. They were not writing manifestos for a postmodernist movement. They thought they were simply describing something that was already taking place, inexorably, through the movement of one or another sort of structural force. And in this their attitude was, again, merely an exaggerated version of a much more common one. This, I think, is the best explanation for the current paralysis. To put it bluntly: now that it has become obvious that "structural forces" alone are not likely to themselves produce something we particularly like, we are left with the prospect of coming up with some actual alternatives. Even aside from the always-daunting fact that this would mean deciding who "we" are, it would require a massive change of theoretical habits. It would mean accepting that people, as part of social movements of one kind or another, might be capable of affecting the course of history in a significant way. That alternatives can indeed be created, and not just come about. That would in turn mean having to give some serious thought to what role intellectuals can legitimately play in this process, and how they might do so without fomenting the kind of stupid sectarian dogmatism we've so often ended up fomenting in the past. My own experience over the last year working with the Direct Action Network suggests that on a lot of these questions, the activists are way ahead of us.

Obviously, this book is not itself an attempt to answer these questions. It is, as I say, a book that I wrote largely in order to work out some problems in anthropological theories of value. Still, it strikes me that if one is looking for alternatives to what might be called the philosophy of neoliberalism, its most basic assumptions about the human condition, then a theory of value would not be a bad place to start. If we are not, in fact, calculating individuals trying to accumulate the maximum possible quantities of power, pleasure, and material wealth, then what, precisely, are we? The first three chapters of the book are an effort to survey how social theorists have dealt with such questions in the past, the dead ends that they have tended to run into, and also, how many of most apparently innovative recent theorists have tended to recycle these same old dilemmas—without, for the most part, realizing they were doing so. It ends with a suggestion for one possible way out, starting from what I call the "Heracleitian tradition," one that sees what seem to us to be fixed objects as patterns of motion, and what seem to be fixed 'social structures' as patternings of action. Value, I'll suggest, can best be seen in this light as the way in which actions become meaningful to the actor by being incorporated in some larger, social totality—even if in many cases the totality in question exists primarily in the actor's imagination. This argument turns on a rather idiosyncratic reading of the ideas of Karl Marx.

The second half of the book focuses more on two themes, exchange, and social creativity. It begins with an essay originally entitled "Beads and Money: Notes Toward a Theory of Wealth and Power" (Graeber 1996), which asks why it is that objects chosen as currencies (beads, shells, gold, silver, etc.,) so often consisted of things that were otherwise used only as objects of adornment; it goes on to explore several detailed ethnographic case studies, ranging from a chapter on wampum in the seventeenth century American northeast, to a return to the French anthropologist Marcel Mauss' famous examples of Trobriand, Maori, and Kwakiutl "gift economies," and finally, some material drawn from my own work on magic and royal ritual in the Merina kingdom in Madagascar. Over the course of it I try to tease out and further develop some of Mauss' less well-known ideas, and in particular his belief in the role anthropology could play in the development of revolutionary theory. In many ways, Mauss serves as a perfect complement to Marx: while one dedicated himself to a thorough critique of capitalism, the other was ultimately interested in bringing the fruits of comparative ethnography—the only discipline capable of addressing the full range of human possibilities—to bear on envisioning possible alternatives to it. Each approach has its dangers if taken too far. If one takes up the Maussian project with too much uncritical enthusiasm, one ends up with a naive relativism utterly blind to power. But if one is too rigorous and single-minded about one's critical project, one can easily slip into a view of social reality so cynical, of a world so utterly creased with power and domination, that it becomes impossible to imagine how anything could really change—and this is, I argue, precisely what began to happen when critical theory was pushed too far in the '70s and '80s, and opened the way for the neoliberal backlash to be found in so many strains of postmodernism.

I did not write this book just for anthropologists. I like to think that it might be of some interest to social theorists in general, and in particular those currently struggling, like me, with how to relate theory to a sense of political engagement. In the final analysis, it is a plea, as the Zapatistas like to say, "for humanity, and against neoliberalism": an attempt at least to begin to imagine what a humanistic social science—one that does not, in so doing, abandon everything that is genuinely valuable in the notion of "science"— might actually be like.

Chapter 1 ⧈

Three Ways of Talking about Value

If one reads a lot of anthropology, it is hard to escape the impression that theories of value are all the rage of late. One certainly sees references to "value" and "theories of value" all the time—usually thrown out in such a way as to suggest there is a vast and probably very complicated literature lying behind them.[1] If one tries to track this literature down, however, one quickly runs into problems. In fact it is extremely difficult to find a systematic "theory of value" anywhere in the recent literature; and it usually turns out to be very difficult to figure out what body of theory, if any, that any particular author who uses the term "value" is drawing on. Sometimes, one suspects it is this very ambiguity that makes the term so attractive.

What I'd like to do in this chapter is offer some suggestions as to how this situation came about. I think it has something to do with the fact that anthropology has been caught in a kind of theoretical limbo. The great theoretical dilemmas of twenty years ago or so have never really been resolved; it's more like they were shrugged off. There is a general feeling that a theory of value would have been just the thing to resolve most of those dilemmas, but such a theory never really materialized; hence, perhaps, the habit of so many scholars acting as if one actually did exist.

It will become easier to see why a theory of value should have seemed to hold such promise if one looks at the way the word "value" has been used in social theory in the past. There are, one might say, three large streams of thought that converge in the present term. These are:

1. "values" in the sociological sense: conceptions of what is ultimately good, proper, or desirable in human life
2. "value" in the economic sense: the degree to which objects are desired, particularly, as measured by how much others are willing to give up to get them

3. "value" in the linguistic sense, which goes back to the structural linguistics of Ferdinand de Saussure (1966), and might be most simply glossed as "meaningful difference"

When anthropologists nowadays speak of "value"—particularly, when they refer to "value" in the singular when one writing twenty years ago would have spoken of "values" in the plural—they are at the very least implying that the fact that all these things should be called by the same word is no coincidence. That ultimately, these are all refractions of the same thing. But if one reflects on it at all, this is a very challenging notion. It would mean, for instance, that when we talk about the "meaning" of a word, and when we talk about the "meaning of life," we are not talking about utterly different things. And that both have something in common with the sale-price of a refrigerator. Now, putting things this way raises obvious objections. A skeptic might reply: it may well be that all these concepts do have something in common, but if so, that "something" would have to be so utterly abstract and vague that pointing it out is simply meaningless. In which case the ambiguity really *is* the point. But I don't think this is so. In fact, if one looks back over the history of anthropological thought on each of the three sorts of value mentioned above one finds that in almost every case, scholars trying to come up with a coherent theory of any one of them have ended up falling into terrible problems for lack of sufficient consideration of the other ones.

Let me give a brief sketch of these histories, one at a time:

I: Clyde Kluckhohn's value project

The theoretical analysis of "values" or "systems of values" is largely confined to philosophy (where it is called "axiology") and sociology (where it is what one is free from when one is "value-free.") It is not as if anthropologists haven't always used the term. One can pick up a work of anthropology from almost any period and, if one flips through long enough, be almost certain to find at least one or two casual references to "values." But anthropologists rarely made much of an effort to define it, let alone to make the analysis of values a part of anthropological theory. The one great exception was during the late 1940s and early '50s, when Clyde Kluckhohn and a team of allied scholars at Harvard embarked on a major effort to place the issue of values at the center of anthropology. Kluckhohn's project, in fact, was to redefine anthropology itself as the comparative study of values.

Nowadays, the project is mainly remembered because it managed to find its way into Talcott Parson's *General Theory of Action* (Parsons and Shils 1951), meant as a kind of *entente cordiale* between sociology, anthropology, and psychology, which divided up the study of human behavior between

them. Psychologists were to investigate the structure of the individual personality, sociologists studied social relations, and anthropologists were to deal
with the way both were mediated by culture, which comes down largely to
how values become esconced in symbols and meanings. Kluckhohn's main
anthropological work had been among the Navaho, but he conceived the notion of doing a comparative study of values that focused on the county of
Rimrock, New Mexico (1951b, 1956; Vogt and Albert 1966), which was divided between five different communities: Navaho, Zuñi, Mormon, Texan,
and Mexican-American. Its existence, Kluckhohn thought, provided as close
as one could get in anthropology to a controlled experiment: a chance to see
how five groups of people with profoundly different systems of value adapted
to the same environment. He sent off five students, one to study each (and
in fact quite a number of the next generation of American anthropologists
were involved in the Rimrock study at one time or another), while he remained behind at Harvard, leading a seminar on values and working out a
succession of working papers that aimed to define the terms of analysis.

So what, precisely, are values? Kluckhohn kept refining his definitions.
The central assumption though was that values are "conceptions of the desirable"—conceptions which play some sort of role in influencing the
choices people make between different possible courses of action
(1951a:395). The key term here is "desirable." The desirable refers not simply to what people actually want—in practice, people want all sorts of
things. Values are ideas about what they *ought* to want. They are the criteria
by which people judge which desires they consider legitimate and worthwhile and which they do not. Values, then, are ideas if not necessarily about
the meaning of life, then at least about what one could justifiably want from
it. The problem though comes with the second half of the definition: Kluckhohn also insisted that these were not just abstract philosophies of life but
ideas that had direct effects on people's actual behavior. The problem was to
determine how.

Of course when one speaks of values in the traditional sense, this is not
so difficult. By this I mean, in the sense in which one might say that the
Navaho community in Rimrock places a high value on something it calls
"harmony," or the Texan, on something it calls "success." Normally "value
analysis," such as it is, consists of identifying such terms and interpreting
them, figuring out precisely what "harmony" or "success" means to the people in question, and placing these definitions in a larger cultural context.
The problem though is that such terms tend to be highly idiosyncratic.
Kluckhohn was interested in the systematic *comparison* of values.

In order to compare such concepts, Kluckhohn and his disciples ended up
having to create a second, less abstract level of what he called "value orientations." These were "assumptions about the ends and purposes of human

existence," the nature of knowledge, "what human beings have a right to expect from each other and the gods, about what constitutes fulfillment and frustration" (Kluckhohn 1949:358–59). In other words, value orientations mixed ideas of the desirable with assumptions about the nature of the world in which one had to act. The next step was to establish a basic list of existential questions, that presumably every culture had to answer in some way: are human beings good or evil? Should their relations with nature be based on harmony, mastery, or subjugation? Should one's ultimate loyalties be to oneself, to a larger group, or to other individuals? Kluckhohn did come up with such a list; but he and his students found it very difficult to move from this super-refined level to the more mundane details of why people prefer to grow potatoes rather than rice or prefer to marry their cross-cousins—the sort of everyday matters with which anthropologists normally concern themselves.

At this point the story takes on something of the color of tragedy. Almost everyone involved felt that the Rimrock study was a failure; in writing up their conclusions, the fieldworkers found it almost impossible to develop common terms. Even while Kluckhohn's disciples—notably philosopher Edith Albert—were continuing to pour out essays gushing with scientific confidence in the late '50s and early '60s, Kluckhohn himself seems to have spent the last years of his life plagued by a sense of frustration, an inability to find the breakthrough that would make a real, systematic comparative study of values possible—or anyway, to relate it properly to action (Albert 1956, 1968, Kluckhohn 1951a, 1961, F. Kluckhohn and Strodtbeck 1961). It was all the more frustrating because Kluckhohn saw his project in many ways a last-ditch effort to rescue American anthropology from what almost everyone perceived as the theoretical doldrums. Where British anthropologists had always conceived their discipline as a branch of sociology, the North American school founded by Franz Boas had drawn on German culture theory to compare societies not primarily as ways of organizing relations between people but equally, as structures of thought and feeling. The assumption was always that there was, at the core of a culture, certain key patterns or symbols or themes that held everything together and that couldn't be reduced to pure individual psychology; the problem, to define precisely what this was and how one could get at it. One is left with a strange, rather contradictory picture, since this was also the time when Boasian anthropology was at the height of its popular influence and academic authority, flush with Cold War money, at a time when their books were often read by ordinary Americans, but at the same time, was burdened with a growing feeling of intellectual bankruptcy. Kluckhohn's effort to reframe anthropology as the study of values could be seen as a last-ditch effort to salvage the Boasian project; it is nowadays seen as yet another dead end. The consensus of those who even bother to talk about the episode (Edmonson 1973, Dumont

1982), though, is that there was nothing inherently wrong with the project itself: rather, it failed for the lack of an adequate theory of structure. Kluckhohn wanted to compare systems of ideas, but he had no theoretical model of how ideas fitted together as systems. In his last few years he became increasingly interested in the idea of borrowing models from linguistics, but the tools then available were simply not up to the challenge. His critics seem to imply that if he or his project had lasted a few more years, until structuralist models burst on the scene in the late '60s, everything might have been different.

Be this as it may, the project had no intellectual successors. This is not to say, of course, that anthropologists no longer talk about "values." Some regional subdisciplines are veritably obsessed with particular values (especially those dealing with regions without too much elaborate social structure, such as clans or lineage systems): most notoriously the anthropology of the Mediterranean, which has been for most of its history focused on "honor." But there has been next to nothing on "values" in general. This is true even of scholars working in Kluckhohn's own intellectual tradition. Some of the most influential American cultural theorists of the '60s and '70s—I am thinking here especially of Clifford Geertz and David Schneider—were in many ways continuing in it, but they moved in very different directions.

In a way this is rather too bad. For all its sterility in practice, there is something appealing about Kluckhohn's key idea: that what makes cultures different is not simply what they believe the world to like, but what they feel one can justifiably demand from it. That anthropology, in other words, should be the comparative study of practical philosophies of life. Actually the closest parallel to it in the social sciences was probably Max Weber's comparative study of world religions, which also was concerned with delineating a limited number of possible ways for thinking about the meaning of human existence and then trying to understand the implications for social action of each. It's possible that his work may even be due for something of a revival: there have been some recent efforts, for example by Charles Nuckolls (1999), to integrate such value analysis with psychological approaches in anthropology. But for present purposes, the important thing is that the first great effort to come up with an anthropological theory of values ran most definitively aground; and that anthropological concerns with such issues started developing, in the '60s, in two opposite directions: one that looked to economics, the other, to linguistics.

II: the maximizing individual

Practically from the beginnings of modern anthropology, there have been efforts to apply the tools of microeconomics to the study of non-Western societies. There are several reasons it seemed an obvious thing to do. First, because (apart from linguistics) economics has always been the social science that could make the most plausible claim that what it was doing was anything like a natural science; it has long had the additional advantage of being seen as the very model of "hard" science by the sort of people who distribute grants (people who themselves usually have some economic training). It also has the advantage of joining an extremely simple model of human nature with extremely complicated mathematical formulae that non-specialists can rarely understand, much less criticize. Its premises are straightforward enough. Society is made up of individuals. Any individual is assumed to have a fairly clear idea what he or she wants out of life, and to be trying to get as much of it as possible for the least amount of sacrifice and effort. (This is called the "mini/max" approach. People want to minimize their output and maximize their yields.) What we call "society"—at least, if one controls for a little cultural "interference"—is simply the outcome of all this self-interested activity.

Bronislaw Malinowski was already complaining about this sort of thing in 1922, in what is arguably the first book-length work of economic anthropology: *Argonauts of the Western Pacific.* Such a theory would do nothing, he said, to explain economic behavior in the Trobriand Islands:

> Another notion which must be exploded, once and for ever, is that of the Primitive Economic Man of some current economic textbooks . . . prompted in all his actions by a rationalistic conception of self-interest, and achieving his aims directly and with the minimum of effort. Even *one* well established instance should show how preposterous is this assumption. The primitive Trobriander furnishes us with such an instance, contradicting this fallacious theory. In the first place, as we have seen, work is not carried out on the principle of the least effort. On the contrary, much time and energy is spent on wholly unnecessary effort, that is, from a utilitarian point of view. (Malinowski 1922:60)

Malinowski takes up the example of the attitude Trobriand men have toward their yam gardens: the endless energies they pour into vying to make their garden the most tidy and attractive (effort that is in strictly "economic" terms entirely useless). The whole point of gardening was to show off how much effort a man could sink into it; as a result, half the yields ended up rotting for lack of anyone to eat them. What's more, those that were eaten were not eaten by the gardener himself:

> The most important point about this is, however, that all, or almost all the fruits of his work, and certainly any surplus which he can achieve by extra effort, goes not to the man himself, but to his relatives-in-law. Without enter-

ing into details . . . it may be said that about three quarters of a man's crops go partly as tribute to the chief, partly as his due to his sister's (or mother's) husband and family (Malinowski 1922:60–61).

In other words, rather than "economizing" their efforts, Trobriand men are actively trying to perform unnecessary labor; then they give the products away to their sister's families. There's not even any direct reciprocity involved, since the man's own family is fed not by his sister's family but the brothers of his own wife.

Such examples could be multiplied endlessly, and, in the early days of anthropology, they were. It didn't make much difference. Every decade or so has seen at least one new attempt to put the maximizing individual back into anthropological theory, even if economic theory itself usually ends up having to bend itself into ribbons in order to do so.

In fact, the effort to reconcile the two disciplines is in many ways inherently contradictory. This is because economics and anthropology were created with almost entirely opposite purposes in mind. Economics is all about prediction. It came into existence and continues to be maintained with all sorts of lavish funding, because people with money want to know what other people with money are likely to do. As a result, it is also a discipline that, more than any other, tends to participate in the world it describes. That is to say, economic science is mainly concerned with the behavior of people who have some familiarity with economics—either ones who have studied it or at the very least are acting within institutions that have been entirely shaped by it. Economics, as a discipline, has almost always played a role in defining the situations it describes.[2] Nor do economists have a problem with this; they seem to feel it is quite as it should be. Anthropology was from the beginning entirely different. It has always been most interested in the action of those people who are *least* influenced by the practical or theoretical world in which the analyst moves and operates. This was especially true in the days when anthropologists saw themselves as studying savages; but to this day anthropologists have remained most interested in the people whose understanding of the world, and whose interests and ambitions, are most different than their own. As a result, it is generally carried out completely without a thought to furthering those interests and ambitions. When Malinowski was trying to figure out what Trobriand gardeners were trying to accomplish in acting as they did, it almost certainly never even occurred to him that whatever that was, reading his book might make them better able to accomplish it. In fact, when an anthropologist discovers that anyone is using anthropological texts in this way—say, as a guide for how to perform their own rituals—they are usually quite disturbed.

Economics, then, is about predicting individual behavior; anthropology, about understanding collective differences.

As a result, efforts to bring maximizing models into anthropology always end up stumbling into the same sort of incredibly complicated dead ends. The classic case studies of economic anthropology, for instance—Franz Boas' reports on the Kwakiutl potlatch (1897, etc.) or Malinowski's on Trobriand kula exchange (1922)—concerned systems of exchange that seemed to work on principles utterly different from the observers' own: ones in which the most important figures seemed to be not so much trying to accumulate wealth as vying to see who could give the most away. In 1925, Marcel Mauss coined the phrase "gift economies" to describe them.

Actually, the existence of gifts—even in Western societies—has always been something of a problem for economists. Trying to account for them always leads to some variation of the same, rather silly, circular arguments.

Q: If people only act to maximize their gains in some way or another, then how do you explain people who give things away for nothing?
A: They are trying to maximize their social standing, or the honor, or prestige that accrues to them by doing so.
Q: Then what about people who give anonymous gifts?
A: Well, they're trying to maximize the sense of self-worth, or the good feeling they get from doing it.

And so on. If you are sufficiently determined, you can always identify *something* that people are trying to maximize. But if all maximizing models are really arguing is that "people will always seek to maximize *something,*" then they obviously can't predict anything, which means employing them can hardly be said to make anthropology more scientific. All they really add to analysis is a set of assumptions about human nature. The assumption, most of all, that no one ever does anything primarily out of concern for others; that whatever one does, one is only trying to get something out of it for oneself. In common English, there is a word for this attitude. It's called "cynicism." Most of us try to avoid people who take it too much to heart. In economics, apparently, they call it "science."[3]

Still, all these dead ends did produce one interesting side effect. In order to carry out such an economic analysis, one almost always ends up having to map out a series of "values" of something like the traditional sociological sense—power, prestige, moral purity, etc.,—and to define them as being on some level fundamentally similar to economic ones. This means that economic anthropologists do have to talk about values. But it also means they have to talk about them in a rather peculiar way. When one says that a person is choosing between having more money, more possessions, or more prestige, what one is really doing is taking an abstraction ("prestige") and reifying it, treating it as an object not fundamentally different in kind from jars of spaghetti sauce or ingots of pig iron. This is a peculiar operation, because in fact prestige is not an object that one can dispose of as one will, or even, really, consume; it is rather an attitude that exists in the minds of other people.[4] It can exist only within a web of social relations. Of course, one might argue that property is a social relation as well, reified in exactly the same way: when one buys a car one is not really purchasing the right to use it so much as the right to prevent others from using it—or, to be even more precise, one is purchasing their recognition that one has a right to do so. But since it is so diffuse a social relation—a contract, in effect, between the owner and everyone else in the entire world—it is easy to think of it as a thing. In other words, the way economists talk about "goods and services" already involves reducing what are really social relations to objects; an economistic[5] approach to values extends the same process even further, to just about everything.

But on what basis? In reality, the only thing spaghetti sauce and prestige have in common is the fact that some people want them. What economic theory ultimately tries to do is to explain all human behavior—all human behavior it considers worth explaining, anyway—on the basis of a certain notion of desire, which then in turn is premised on a certain notion of pleasure. People try to obtain things because those things will make them happy or gratify them in some way (or at least because they think they will). Chocolate cheesecake promises pleasure, but so does the knowledge that others do not consider you obese; rational actors regularly weigh one against the other. It is this promise of pleasure economists call "value."

In the end, most economic theory relies on trying to make anything that smacks of "society" disappear. But even if one does manage to reduce every social relation to thing, so that one is left with the empiricist's dream, a word consisting of nothing but individuals and objects, one is still left to puzzle over why individuals feel some objects will afford them more pleasure than others. There is only so far one can go by appealing to physiological needs.[6] In the end, faced with explaining why in some parts of the world most people are indifferent to the pleasures of chocolate cheesecake but excited by those of salted prune drinks, or why in others obesity is considered attractive, economists, however begrudgingly, usually admit they do have to bring some notion like society or culture back in.

It was just these kind of issues that lay behind the Formalist-Substantivist debate that preoccupied economic anthropology in the 1960s (Polanyi 1957, 1959, 1968; Dalton 1961, Burling 1962, Cook 1966, etc.). Nowadays, most consider this debate to have been rather pointless—and indeed, the theoretical basis of both positions has been largely discredited—but the basic issues have never, really, been resolved. Let me provide a rapid summary.

The terms "formalism" and "substantivism" were actually both invented by Hungarian economist Karl Polanyi. Polanyi's most famous work, *The Great Transformation*, was an account of the historical origins, in eighteenth and nineteenth century England, of what we now refer to as "the market." In this century, the market has come to be seen as practically a natural phenomenon—a direct emanation of what Adam Smith once called "man's natural propensity to truck, barter and exchange one thing for another." Actually, this attitude follows logically from the same (cynical) theory of human nature that lies behind economic theory. The basic reasoning—rarely explicitly stated—runs something like this. Human beings are driven by desires; these desires are unlimited. Human beings are also rational, insofar as they will always tend to calculate the most efficient way of getting what they want. Hence, if they are left to their own devices, something like a "free market" will inevitably develop. Of course, for 99% of human history, none ever did, but that's just because of the interference of one or another state or feudal elite. Feudal relations, which are based on force, are basically inimical to market relations, which are based on freedom; therefore, once feudalism began to dissolve, the market inevitably emerged to take its place.[7]

The beauty of Polanyi's book is that it demonstrates just how completely wrong that common wisdom is. In fact, the state and its coercive powers had everything to do with the creation of what we now know as "the market"—based as it is on institutions such as private property, national currencies, legal contracts, credit markets. All had to be created and maintained by government policy. The market was a creation of government and has always remained so. If one really reflects on the assumptions economists make about human behavior, it only makes sense that it should be so: the principle of maximization after all assumes that people will normally try to extract as much as possible from whoever they are dealing with, taking no consideration whatever of that other person's interests—but at the same time that they will never under any circumstances resort to any of the most obvious ways of extracting wealth from those towards whose fate one is indifferent, such as taking it by force. "Market behavior" would be impossible without police.

Polanyi goes on to describe how, almost as soon as these institutions were created, men like Smith, Malthus, and Ricardo appeared, all drawing analogies from nature to argue that these new forms of behavior followed inevitable, universal laws. It is the study of these laws that Polanyi refers to as economic "formalism." Polanyi is perfectly willing to admit that formal methods are appropriate for understanding how people will behave within such a market. But in most societies, such institutions did not exist; one simply cannot talk about an "economy" at all, in the sense of an autonomous sphere of behavior that operates according to its own internal logic. Rather, one has to take what he calls a "substantive" approach and examine the actual process through which the society provides itself with food, shelter, and other material goods, bearing in mind that this process is entirely embedded in society and not a sphere of activity that can be distinguished from, say, politics, kinship, or religion.

The Substantivist school of economic anthropology (its chief exponent was Polanyi's student, George Dalton) was thus basically empirical. One takes a given society, looks at how things are distributed, and tries to understand the principles. The main result was a list of new forms of exchange and distribution, all of which did not seem to operate on principles of economic maximization, to add to the gift economies with which anthropologists were already familiar. These included the notion of redistributive economies, the phenomena of ports of trade (neutral enclaves in which merchants of different countries could do business according to pre-established exchange rates: [Polanyi, Arensberg and Pearson 1957]), the notion of spheres of exchange (Firth 1959, Bohannon 1955, 1959; Bohannon and Bohannon 1968), and Marshall Sahlins' spheres of sociability (Sahlins 1972).

All this was a definite contribution to human knowledge. The problem was the overall theoretical armature. It is one thing to say "societies" have different ways of distributing goods. It is another to explain what particular members of the society in question think they're doing when they give gifts, or demand bridewealth, or exchange saffron for ivory in a port of trade. This is precisely what their opponents were quick to point out. Because almost immediately, the Substantivist challenge was met by a counter-offensive by self-proclaimed Formalists (for example, Burling 1962, Cook 1966). Formalists claimed that Polanyi had misunderstood what economics was actually about. It did not depend on the presence or absence of something called "the economy." Economics was concerned with a certain type of human behavior called "economizing." People economize when they make choices between different uses for scarce resources in an attempt to minimize their outputs and maximize rewards. (Yes, they said, this did involve some a priori assumptions about human nature, but everyone has to work from *some* assumptions: the ultimate test is whether the resulting theories produce results.) The point of social science is not comparing different forms of social system but understanding what motivates human beings to act the way they do.

Here they did have a point. For the most part, Substantivists didn't try to explain anything; they just created taxonomies. Insofar as they did invoke a larger theory, it was generally some variant on Durkheimian functionalism. Where economists saw the shape of society largely as the outcome of individual decisions, Functionalists represented society as an active force in its own right—even, as something close to a conscious, purposive agent, though its only purpose seems to be a sort of animalistic self-preservation.

For a Durkheimian, economic institutions can be seen as a means of social integration—one of the ways society creates a network of moral ties between what would otherwise be a chaotic mass of individuals—or, if not that, then at least the means by which "society" allocates resources. The obvious question is *how* "society" motivates people to do this. Without some theory of motivation, one is left with a picture of automatons mindlessly following whatever rules society lays down for them, which at the very least makes it difficult to understand how society could ever change.

Of course, the Formalists, as I have already noted, could not do much better. They were working with tools originally designed to predict individual behavior in a market setting; by twisting them around, they could sometimes predict the behavior of individuals in other cultures but not the values that motivated them, or, for that matter, the shape of society as a whole. At their most ambitious, a Formalist might try to demonstrate how, if one starts with a collection of people living in, say, Baluchistan, and a scattershot collection of "values" (food, sex, prestige, not being tortured in hell for all eternity, etc.,) one could then show how the existing shape of Baluchi society emerged as the result of the strategies people adopted to secure them. This is pretty much what Frederick Barth proposed anthropologists should do, calling his approach Transactionalism (1966; cf. Kapferer 1976). Transactionalism was probably the most ambitious attempt to apply the principles of formal economics to anthropology, and it caused something of a stir in the late 1960s. The obvious question though, was—even if it was possible to create a model that would thus generate the entire Baluchi lineage system or the structure of a West African kingdom from the right collection of values—what would be the point? What would one then know that one had not known before one started? The result would not even be an historical reconstruction, but a purely logical model that need have nothing to do with the actual historical origins of the societies in question.

Most anthropologists nowadays would wonder what the point is in even going into all this; the Substantivist-Formalist debate is considered definitively passé. But there is a point. It seems to me that these basic issues have never been resolved. Those who start by looking at society as a whole are left, like the Substantivists, trying to explain how people are motivated to reproduce society; those who start by looking at individual desires end up, like the Formalists, unable to explain why people chose to maximize some things and not others (or otherwise to account for qestions of meaning). In fact, though scholars have drifted off to other concerns, the same problems keep re-emerging. As we shall see, a lot of what passes for the newest and most refreshing poststructural theory nowadays is largely warmed-over Transactionalism, minus the fancy economic formulae, with some even fancier linguistic formulae pasted on instead.

III: Structuralism and linguistic value

Linguists have long been in the habit of speaking of the meaning of a word as its "value." From quite early in the history of anthropology, there have been efforts connect this usage to other sorts of value. One of the most interesting can be found in Evans-Pritchard's *The Nuer* (1940:135–38): a discussion of the "value" of the word *cieng*, or "home." For a Nuer, Evans-Pritchard notes, the "value" of this word varies with context; a speaker can use it to refer to one's house, one's village, one's territory, even (when speaking to a foreigner) Nuerland as a whole. But it is more than a word; the notion of "home," on any of these levels, also carries a certain emotional load. It implies a sense of loyalty, and that can translate into political action. Home is the place one defends against outsiders. So we are talking about value in the sociological, "values" sense as well. "Values," Evans-Pritchard says, "are embodied in words through which they influence behavior" (135). Or, alternatively, the notion of "home," when it serves to determine who one considers a friend, and who an enemy, in the case of potential blood-feuds, "becomes a political value" as well. Note here how "value" slips back and from from "meaning" to something more like "importance": one's home is essential to one's sense of oneself, one's allegiances, what one cares about most in life.

This was a fascinating start, but it never really went anywhere. When a contemporary anthropologist speaks of the value of words, instead, they are almost invariably referring back to the ideas of Ferdinand de Saussure, founder of modern, structural linguistics.

In his *Course of General Linguistics* (1916 [1966]), Saussure argued that one could indeed speak of any word as having a value, but that this value was essentially "negative." By this he meant that words take on meaning only by contrast with other words in the same language. Take for example the word "red." One cannot define its meaning, or "value," in any given language, without knowing all the other color terms in the same language; that is, without knowing all the colors that it is not. We might translate a word in some African language as "red," but its meaning (or value) would not be the same as the English "red" if, say, that other language does not have a word for "brown." People in that language might then be in the habit of referring to trees as red. The most precise definition of the English "red," then, would be: the color that is not blue, not yellow, not brown, etc. It follows then that in order to understand the "value" of any one color term one must also know those of all the others in that language: the meaning of a term is its place in the total system.[8] Saussure's arguments of course had an enormous impact on anthropology, and were the most important influence on the rise of Structuralism—which took off from Saussure's suggestion that all systems of meaning are organized on the same principles as a language, so that technically, linguistics should be considered just one sub-field of an (as yet non-existent) master discipline that he dubbed semiology, the science of meaning.[9]

As these examples suggest, Saussure's approach was more about vocabulary than grammar, more about nouns and adjectives than verbs. It was concerned with the objects of human action more than with the actions themselves. Not surprising, then, that those who tried to follow Saussure's lead and actually create this non-existent science tended to be most successful when exploring the meaning of physical objects (Barthes 1967; Baudrillard 1968; Sahlins 1976). Objects are defined by the meaningful distinctions one can make between them. To understand the meaning (value) of an object, then, one must understand its place in a larger system. Just as the value of "red" is determined negatively, by all the other colors it is not, if one were to analyze the meaning of, say, a turtleneck worn underneath one's jacket, one must examine the full set of other things one person *might* be wearing: that is, wearing a turtleneck means that one is *not* wearing a shirt and tie beneath one's jacket, but that neither is one wearing a T-shirt, or nothing at all. Again, the meaning of one element makes sense only in terms of its contrast with other possible elements within the same system. This is a crucial consideration, because it means nothing can be analyzed in isolation. In order to understand any one object, one must first identify some kind of total system. This became the trademark of Structuralism: the point of analysis was always to discover the hidden code, or symbolic system, which (language-like) tied everything together.

Almost inevitably, though, the question became how to connect this sort of value to value in either of the other two senses. In the early days, when Structuralism was a new idea that seemed to offer resolutions for almost any outstanding problem in social theory, it seemed self-evident that it should be possible to do so. Hence Marshall Sahlins (former Substantivist, newfound Structuralist) concluded his famous analysis of the Western clothing system in *Culture and Practical Reason* (1976) by suggesting that one could only understand economic value, too, as the product of meaningful distinctions. To understand why people want to buy things, he said, we have to understand the place that thing has in a larger code of meaning.

> Production for gain is the production of a symbolically significant difference; in the case of the consumer market, it is the production of an appropriate social distinction by way of concrete contrast in the object. The point is implicit in the apparent ambiguity of the term "value," which may refer to the price of something or the meaning of something (as the differential concept of a word), or in general to that which people hold "dear," either morally or mon-

etarily. Anthropologists, incidentally, are quite familiar with this ambiguity, if not always entirely conscious of it, since many adopt it to illustrate the universality of rational economic behavior—even where market exchange is specifically absent. The people are nevertheless economizing their resources: it's just that they are interested in "values" other than the material—brotherhood for example (1976:213–14).

So, value in each sense is ultimately the same, just as the Formalists were often forced to admit. Things are meaningful because they are important. Things are important because they are meaningful.

Sahlins goes on to observe that Saussure himself made a similar analogy, and suggests the passage in which he does so should be the basis for any future economic anthropology. To understand the value of a five-franc piece, Saussure had written, one must be able to understand (a) something different with which it can be "exchanged," i.e., a loaf of bread, and (b) something similar to which it can be "compared," i.e., a one franc piece, or other denominations of money.

> In the same way a word can be exchanged for something dissimilar, an idea; besides, it can be compared with something of the same nature, another word. Its value is therefore not fixed so long as one simply states that it can be "exchanged" for a given concept, i.e., that it has this or that signification: one must also compare it to similar values, with other words that stand in opposition to it (Saussure in Sahlins 1976: 214–215).

Perhaps the best one can say about this passage is that in the flush of enthusiasm that often follows the discovery of powerful new techniques for understanding reality—such as Structuralism was in the '60s and '70s—there is good reason to put common sense on hold and see how far these techniques can take you. Still, this seems to be the point at which they reached their limits. I mean, really: what does it mean to say that when you use a word, you are "exchanging" it for a concept? In what way does this really resemble paying a shopkeeper for a loaf of bread? Most of all, what sort of "comparison" are we really talking about here? After all, when one observes that a loaf of bread costs five francs, and a steak-frites costs twenty, one is not simply observing that the bread and steak-frites are *different*. One is more likely to be emphasizing the fact that one is worth *more*. This is why one can say an element of evaluation is involved. This is also precisely what makes money unique—that it can indicate exactly how much more one is worth than the other[10]—and precisely what Saussurean models cannot account for. The latter provides a way to understand how the world is divided up, how objects are grouped into categories based on their differences with other sorts of object—and Sahlins is of course right when he says that in a consumer society, marketing is often a matter of creating symbolic distinctions between products that are otherwise virtually identical, like two different brands of corn flake or detergent—but this in itself does not explain why people are willing to spend money on them. People do not buy things simply because they recognize them as being different than other things in *some* way. Even if they did, this would do nothing to explain why they are willing to spend more on certain things than others.

On Structuralism, the results are by now more or less in. The general consensus is that its greatest weak point is evaluation. Many have pointed out for example that Structuralist literary critics have often provided brilliant analyses of the formal principles underlying a novel or a poem, discovering all sorts of hidden patterns of meaning, but that they provided no insight at all into whether the novel or poem in question was any good. Similarly, Structuralist approaches in anthropology—as exemplified in the works of Claude Levi-Strauss (1949, 1958, 1962, 1966)—tend to focus on how members of different cultures understand the nature of the universe, and for this they can be remarkably revealing; but the moment one tries to understand how, say, one thing is seen as better—preferable, more desirable, more valuable—than another, problems immediately emerge. As a result, the great dilemma of Structuralism has been how to move on from understanding people's passive contemplation of the world (Geertz's "cerebral savage"), to their active participation in it.[11]

Actually, no one has done more than Marshall Sahlins toward thinking a way out of this box, often with spectacular results (Sahlins 1981, 1985, 1988, 1991). So perhaps I am not being especially fair to him in singling out this one, very early, text. But it's also true that since, he has tended to abandon talk of value entirely. The only author who has made a consistent effort to develop a theory of value along Structuralist lines is Louis Dumont (1966, 1971, 1982, 1986). His work thus deserves more detailed consideration.

Dumont is of course best known for having been almost single-handedly responsible for popularizing the concept of "hierarchy" in the social sciences. His notion of value, in fact, emerges directly out of his concept of hierarchy.

Classical Structuralism, according to Dumont, was developed as a technique meant to analyze the formal organization of ideas, not values. Carrying out a structural analysis means, first, identifying certain key conceptual oppositions—raw/cooked, pure/impure, masculine/feminine, consanguinity/affinity, etc.—and then mapping out how these relate to one another, say, within in a series of myths or rituals, or perhaps an entire social system. What most Structuralists fail to realize, Dumont adds, is that these ideas are also "values." This is because with any such pair of terms, one will be considered superior. This superior term always "encompasses" the inferior one. The notion of encompassment is in turn the key to Dumont's notion of hierarchy. One of his favorite illustrations is the opposition of right and left. Anthropologists having long noted a tendency, which apparently occurs in the vast majority of the world's cultures, for the right hand to be treated as somehow morally superior to the left (Hertz 1907, Needham 1973). In offering a handshake, Dumont notes, one must normally extend one hand or the other. The right hand put forward thus, in effect, represents one's person as a whole—including the left hand that is not extended (Dumont 1983, see Tcherkezoff 1983.) Hence, at least in that context, the right hand "encompasses" or "includes" the left, which is also its opposite. (This is what he calls "encompassing the contrary.") This principle of hierarchy, he argues, applies to all significant binary oppositions—in fact Dumont rejects the idea that two such terms could ever be considered equal, or that there might be any other principle of ranking, which as one might suspect has created a certain amount of controversy, since it pretty obviously isn't true.[12]

So: meaning arises from making conceptual distinctions. Conceptual distinctions always contain an element of value, since they are ranked.[13] Even more important, the social contexts in which these distinctions are put into practice are also ranked. Societies are divided into a series of domains or levels, and higher ones encompass lower ones—they are more universal and thus have more value. In any society, for instance, domestic affairs, which relate to the interests of a small group of people, will be considered subordinate to political affairs, which represent the concerns of a larger, more inclusive community; and likely as not that political sphere will itself be considered subordinate to the religious or cosmological one, where priests or their equivalents represent the concerns of humanity as a whole before the powers that control the universe.[14] Perhaps the most innovative aspect of Dumont's theory is the way that the relations between different conceptual terms can be inverted on different levels. Since Dumont developed his model in an analysis of the Indian caste system, this might make a good illustration. On the religious level, where Brahmans represent humanity as a whole before the gods, the operative principle is purity. All castes are ranked according to their purity, and by this standard Brahmans outrank even kings. In the subordinate, political sphere in which humans relate only to other humans, power is the dominant value, and in that context, kings are superior to Brahmans, who must do as they say. Nonetheless Brahmans are ultimately superior, because the sphere in which they are superior is the most encompassing.[15]

None of this, of course, applies to contemporary Western society, but according to Dumont, the last three hundred years or so of European history have been something of an aberration. Other societies ("one is almost tempted to say, 'normal ones'") are "holistic," holistic societies are always hierarchical, ranked in a series of more and more inclusive domains. Our society is the great exception because for us, the supreme value is the individual: each person being assumed to have a unique individuality, which goes back to the notion of an immortal soul, which are by definition incomparable. Each individual is a value unto themselves, and none can be treated as intrinsically superior to any other. In most of his more recent work in fact (Dumont 1971, 1977, 1986) Dumont has been effectively expanding on Polanyi's arguments in *The Great Transformation,* arguing that it was precisely this principle of individualism that made possible the emergence of "the economy."

One could go further. In France, there is by now a Dumontian school of anthropology, largely made up of his devoted students, and its approach to traditional, non-Western societies (normal, hierarchical ones that is) is in many aspects a new form of Substantivism. If anything, it is more radical than the original in its uncompromising rejection of anything that smacks of methodological individualism.[16] The main difference is that it has tossed out the functionalist assumption that economic institutions act to integrate society, and put in its place the Saussurean notion that you have understand a total system of meaning in order for any particular part of it to make sense. Either way, it means that the first step in analysis is to identify some totality. The Dumontians call their project one of "comparing wholes," by which they mean not so much symbolic systems as societies taken as totalities structured around certain key values. (Or, as Dumont puts it, "ideas-values.")

Note how even in Dumont's original analysis of India, the use of the term value covers quite a range. Purity, for example, is clearly a value of the "cultural values" variety with which Kluckhohn concerned himself, a conception of what people should want to be like; power, on the other hand, seems more like one of the values Formalists came up with when trying to account for what people actually seem to want, even if they don't necessarily admit to it.[17] The claim is that both are ultimately "ideas-values" that can be analyzed in Saussurean terms, as part of an overall system of meaning.

The best illustration of how all this works itself out in practice can be found in a book called *Of Relations and the Dead* (1994), co-written by four of Dumont's students: Daniel de Coppet, who worked among the 'Aru'Aru in the Solomon Islands (1969, 1970, 1982, 1985, 1992), Cecile Barraud in the Moluccan village of Tanebar-Evav (1979), Andre Iteanu among the Orokaiva of Papua New Guinea (1983a, 1983b, 1990), and Robert Jamous among the Berbers of the Moroccan Rif. The idea of the book is to compare each society as a total system.

In every case, the societies turn out to be structured around two or three key values. The highest is the one that defines its members' place in the cosmos as a whole. So among Jamous' Berbers, while important men spend much of their time defending and increasing their honor through various forms of aggressive exchange, ranging from dramatic gift-giving to the exchange of violence in blood-feuds, honor is not the highest value. The highest is *baraka,* which can roughly be translated divine grace and is immanent in the holy men who resolve feuds and generally mediate human relations with God. In Barraud's Moluccan village, life is taken up in a series of marital exchanges, but this takes place on what is ultimately a lower level of value called *haratut*—roughly, island society in relation to its own divine ancestors—while the most important level is that of *lor,* or "law," in which the society of both living and dead is bound to other societies. The two Melanesian cases are even more complicated, since the values are not named—the authors make the interesting (and profoundly structuralist) suggestion that key values receive names only when a society is aware that other societies with different values exist. When it does not, members of that society will not distinguish the nature of their social order from the nature of the cosmos as a whole, and the values are seen as inhering in the very fabric of reality. Among the 'Aru'Aru, for example, the three key values are embodied in three basic constituents of every human being: body, breath, and ancestral "image" (the last is the only element to survive a person's death). These in turn correspond to the three most important objects of exchange: taro, pork, and shell money. According to De Coppet, 'Aru'Aru ritual life is largely made up of an intricate web of exchanges, in which taro, pork, and shell money change hands as a way of building up and breaking down human personae, creating new ones with marriages or dissolving them in funerals, and, on the highest level, reproducing the relations between human beings and their ancestors.

In societies such as these, the authors argue, it is utterly absurd to talk about individuals maximizing goods. There are no individuals. Any person is himself made up of the very stuff he exchanges, which are in turn the basic constituents of the universe.

They also admit that all four societies have their "great men"—Melanesian "big men," Bedouin "men of honor," important lineage heads in the Moluccas—and that these are always, those who have achieved mastery of that society's most important form of exchange. But the values they are trying to maximize are never the ultimate values of that society. Always, there are two levels, so that while on the lower one, the "values" involved may resemble the sort a Transactionalist might come up with—"honor," "power," wealth, etc.—on the most important level they are more values in Kluckhohn's sense, ideas about what is ultimately important in life. So, they note, from the point of view of society, great men only exist in order to sponsor certain forms of cosmological ritual—ritual that in turn serves to reproduce society as a whole, along with its key values. While this somewhat contradicts Dumont's own statements that the value he is dealing with has nothing whatever in common with the economic sort (economists look at preferences; hierarchical values are about intrinsic superiority), it means that this model does embrace all three of the main ways of talking about value; though strictly subordinating one to a synthesis between the two others. As for why great men perform these rituals: well, this is not for the purpose of self-aggrandizement, but simply because they believe it is the right thing to do.

More than any other approach, the Dumontians provide the promise of a grand synthesis of theories of value—in their case, through a sort of supercharged Substantivism. The question: at what cost? In order to do so, they have had to make a strict division between "modern" societies, in which people are individuals and seek economic values, and "holistic" ones, in which they do not. Hence there is a fundamental break between the sort of society in which most anthropologists live and the sort they study. Second, they reintroduce all the notorious problems of functionalism. For example, to speak of societies as "wholes" does seem to imply there are clear borders between them, and they exist in relative isolation.[18] Examining history shows this is very rarely the case. Even more, it becomes almost impossible to see how these societies can ever change. In fact, one of Dumont's most notorious arguments is that the Indian caste system *cannot,* by definition, change. Its structure is fixed; therefore, it can either continue, or it can collapse and be replaced by an entirely different system: like a chair eaten away by termites, it will maintain the same form until it falls apart (1970:219). These are the main reasons why anthropologists rejected functionalism to begin with.

conclusions

At this point, the reader should at least have some idea of the history the term "value" evokes. It is a term that suggests the possibility of resolving ongoing theoretical dilemmas; particularly of overcoming the difference between what one might call top-down and bottom-up perspectives: between theories that start from a certain notion of social structure, or social order, or some other totalizing notion, and theories that start from individual motivation. Reconciling the two has been a perennial problem for social theory.

Of course, there are those who would question whether there's much of a point in grand theory to begin with. Some scoff at the very notion, arguing that all anthropology really has to offer to the world is ethnography, the description of other societies and other ways of life. There is no doubt that this is a very important part of what we do: keeping a record, one might say, of cultural and social differences, a compendium of what being human has meant, in different times and places (and hence, perhaps of human possibilities). It is hard to deny that if anyone is reading our books, say, two hundred years from now, this is what they're most likely to be looking for. The conventional reply is that every ethnography always implies a theory. Since even the most apparently bland and factual descriptions turn out to be based on all sorts of a priori assumptions about what is important and relevant, and these, on what human beings, or human society, are fundamentally about, the real choice then is between thinking about such questions explicitly, or leaving them implicit—in which case, one will inevitably end up drawing on one's own culture's unstated folk beliefs. The usual result is one or another sort of economism. And the more one deals with human motivations, the more of a problem this becomes. A more recent variant of this attitude, that it's the "grand" part of "grand theory" that's objectionable, has—as we'll see in the next chapter—resulted in much the same problems.

Economics, of course, has a very clear notion of what it is trying to do, and of what constitutes a successful analysis (does it or does it not predict what happens?). One way to look at the history of anthropological theory is to ask the same question. What is it anthropologists in any given period were trying to figure out? The discipline has clearly gone through stages in this regard. At all stages one gathered data. But for a nineteenth century evolutionist, for instance, the point of gathering the data about a particular society was to determine where it stands in a grand historical series, and to discover how its existence might reveal something about the universal history of mankind. For a functionalist, it was a matter of showing how a given practice or institution contributed to social stability (which did carry with it the tacit but rarely stated assumption that without such institutions society would collapse into some kind of Hobbesian chaos). For a structuralist, the point of analysis was to show how social forms were made up of symbolic elements that hang together as a total system of meaning. For all, however, the ultimate point was the same: to delineate some kind of logically coherent system, which meant moving away from individual action—and, in doing so, left the empty space into which economistic theories were always trying to crawl.

By the early '80s, there was a general consensus that this was the great problem of the day: how to come up with a "dynamic" theory of structuralism, one that could account for the vagaries of human action, creativity, and change. The way it was usually phrased was as a matter of moving from *langue* to *parole*, from language ("the code" of meaning, however conceived) to speech. It was at this point that value really came to the forefront of intellectual debate. For reasons that should be obvious by now, a theory of value seemed to be just what was needed to bridge the gap: to bring together society and human purposes, to move from meaning to desire.

It is interesting that in these arguments, virtually no one mentioned the legacy of Kluckhohn. His work was considered definitively outdated. If anything, this shows the extent to which structuralism really has come to set the terms of debate. However primitive the models Kluckhohn actually produced, he did at least open up the possibility of looking at cultures as not just different ways of perceiving the world, but as different ways of imagining what life ought to be like—as moral projects, one might say. This was so far from the approaches most theorists were starting from that it seemed utterly irrelevant.

Anyway, all this perhaps provides an explanation for both the continued popularity of the term "value," and the lack of a concrete theory behind it. Anthropology didn't really resolve the dilemmas of the early '80s. For the most part, it just skipped over them. The discipline moved on to other issues: concerning the politics of ethnographic fieldwork, memory, the body, transnationalism, and so forth. Structuralism faded out of prominence, then gradually came to seem ridiculous; theories that concentrated on power (Foucault) or practice (Bourdieu) largely replaced it; there was (and is) a general feeling that the debate was over. Hence, the tendency to act as if such a theory does, in fact, exist.

As we will see in the next chapter, though, most of the new theories that seem to have made the old arguments irrelevant are, at least in many of their aspects, little more than retooled versions of the same old thing. Nor do I think that ignoring the problem is necessarily the best way to make it go away.

Chapter 2 ▨

Current Directions
In Exchange Theory

S o far, I've described how the term "value" held out the promise of re-solving some of the outstanding theoretical problems in anthropology, notably the clash between functionalism and economism, which took its clearest and most vitriolic form in the arguments between Formalists and Substantivists in the 1960s. I've also suggested that, common wisdom to the contrary, these issues are not really all that dead. At the same time that Dumont's school has been leading an explicit effort to revive something along the lines of Polanyi's substantivism, many post-structuralists—usually much less explicitly—have ended up reproducing most of the same assumptions about the world as economic Formalism. A brief survey of the current state of exchange theories should help make clear how much the same old dilemmas keep spinning endlessly around.

In this chapter, then, I'm going to take that history up to the present, and provide at least a brief summary of the main existing theories of value. I'll start with a brief account of the rise of Marxism and critical theory, then consider the return of economizing models (my main examples will be Pierre Bourdieu and Arjun Appadurai), and, after a glance at the work of Margaret Weiner, a more detailed consideration of an alternative approach, which I'll call Neo-Maussian, which has come to its most brilliant fruition in the works of Marilyn Strathern, but which in many ways is simply a revival of the Saussurean approach.

the Marxist moment and its aftermath

If in the 1960s the most spectacular arguments were between Formalists and Substantivists, by the '70s, the great debate was between Structuralists and

Marxists. Since both sides introduced some radically different perspectives into anthropology, it is perhaps not all that surprising that both sides assumed older debates were simply irrelevant.

For most of this century, there was no such thing as Marxist anthropology. This was because if one wanted to be an orthodox Marxist, one had to stick to the evolutionary scheme developed by Morgan and Engels in the middle of the nineteenth century, which held that all societies must pass through a fixed series of stages: from primitive matriarchy to patriarchy, slavery, feudalism, and so on, in strict order of succession. Since it soon became apparent that this was not true, anthropologists with Marxist sympathies were left with the choice of either violating the party line, or writing nonsense. Most avoided introducing Marxist theory into their work at all (usually a good idea anyway in pre-war Western universities, where Marxists were often persecuted). The real break only came in the 1960s, when Louis Althusser, in France, developed—and even more important, managed to legitimate—a more flexible set of terms, centering on the idea of a "mode of production," Marxist anthropology suddenly became possible.[1] The groundwork was laid by French anthropologists like Claude Meillaisoux and Maurice Godelier, but their ideas soon spread to England and America as well. The most important thing Marxist approaches introduced was a focus on production. From a Marxist perspective, both Formalists and Substantivists had entirely missed the point, because all their debates had been about distribution and exchange. To understand a society, they argued, one must first of all understand how it continues to exist—or, as they put it, "reproduces" itself—by endless creative activity.

This was quite different from functionalism. Functionalists begin with a notion of "society," then ask how that society manages to hold itself together. Marxists start by asking how what we call "society" is continually being re-created through various sorts of productive action, and how a society's most basic forms of exploitation and inequality are thus rooted in the social relations through which people do so. This has obvious advantages. The problem with the whole "mode of production" approach, though, was that it was developed to analyze societies with a state: that is, in which there is a ruling class that maintains an apparatus of coercion to extract a surplus from the people who do most of the productive work. Most of the real triumphs of the MoP approach—I am thinking, for example, of Perry Anderson's magisterial "Passages from Antiquity to Feudalism" (1974a) and "Lineages of the Absolutist State" (1974b)—deal with outlining the history of different modes of production, many of which can coexist in a given society; the way in which the dominant one provides the basis for a ruling class whose interests are protected by the state; the way that modes of production contain fundamental contradictions that will, at least in most cases, ultimately drive them to turn into something else. Once one turns to societies without a state, it's not clear how any of these concepts are to be applied.

One thing Marxism did introduce was a series of powerful analytical terms—exploitation, fetishism, appropriation, reproduction . . . —that everyone agreed Marx himself had used brilliantly in his analysis of Capitalism, but that no one was quite sure how to apply outside it. Different scholars would use these terms in very different ways and then would often end up quarreling, quoting canonical texts at each other, arguing over what Marx had "really meant" in them. This tendency (and the specialized jargon itself) quickly gave Marxism a somewhat hermetic quality that played a large part in limiting its appeal to outsiders. After a fairly brief spurt of interest in the '70s, Marxism in anthropology—at least in the English-speaking world[2]—soon found its place mainly as a technique for understanding capitalism itself and the different ways in which indigenous people have come into relation with it.

All this might make it seem that Marxism has not had an enormous impact on anthropology. But this is true only in the most superficial, institutional sense. In a deeper one, its influence was overwhelming. This is because Marxism in many ways became the inspiration for a whole series of new approaches—I'll refer to them, for shorthand purposes, as "critical theory"—that beginning in the 1960s transformed most anthropologists' ideas about what their discipline was ultimately about. For most of this century, anthropology has been determinedly relativistic. Since the time of Boas, it had become almost an item of faith that moral judgments had no place in it: since cultural standards were ultimately arbitrary, who were we to apply Western standards to people who did not share them? Marxism was obviously nothing if not critical; but it also took those very Western cultural standards as the ground of everything it wished to criticize. It had been developed as a technique for exposing the workings of a system of inequality and injustice within the analyst's own society, so as to contribute to the dissolution of that society, and the creation of a radically different one. If a Marxist criticized non-Western social orders, it was not because it was different from his or her own, but largely to the degree it was *similar*.[3] So too with the other critical approaches that emerged at the same time: the most important being feminism, whose impact on anthropology and on intellectual life in general is likely to be even more enduring than Marxism itself. So too with other disciplines like semiotics and cultural studies. All were part of a broad left turn in academic life that probably peaked in the late '70s (just before politics everywhere started veering to the right), but that permanently altered the basic terms of intellectual debate, ensuring that most academics now think of themselves as political radicals, even if as time has gone on it has reduced many to producing what seem like ever more fervent position papers for a broader political movement that does not, in fact, exist.

Now, Marx himself did develop a theory of value. In *Capital,* and elsewhere, he argued that the value of commodities is derived from the human labor that went into producing them, but that this fact tends to be forgotten when the object is bought and sold on the market, so that it seems that its value somehow arises naturally from the qualities of the object itself. This is of course a very famous argument that has generated a vast literature. But there were few explicit attempts to see how it might be applied to noncapitalist systems, or if indeed it could be.[4]

Common wisdom has it that where '60s debates were mainly about exchange and '70s ones about production; in the '80s the focus shifted to consumption. This is not entirely untrue. While the interest in the cultural meanings of consumption goes back at least to the work of Baudrillard (1968, 1972, 1976), there has since the '80s been a blossoming of theory that presents consumption as a form of creative self-expression. Its most insistent advocate is the British anthropologist Daniel Miller (1987, 1995). Actually, Sahlins' work on commodities stands at the beginnings of the same tradition, and insofar as such people deal with "value" as an issue they do so largely in the same sense of a Saussurean code. But this same period has also seen the emergence of at least two approaches to exchange, both, in their own ways, rising in reaction to Marxism. One—the one that generally accompanies the "creative consumption" literature—is a kind of curious revival of economic formalism, though now, with pretensions to science largely stripped away. The other—which I've labeled "Neo-Maussian"—is perhaps more interesting.

But first things first.

I: the return of economic man

This is hardly the place to launch into a history of poststructuralism, but there are a few points that I should probably have to cover in order to ensure that what follows makes any sort of sense. It's actually rather difficult to pick out any single theme uniting the works of the various authors (Foucault, Derrida, Bourdieu, Deleuze and Guattari, Lyotard . . .) normally brought together under this rubric. But if there is one, it is the urge to shatter totalities, whatever these may be, whether "society," "symbolic order," "language," "the psyche," or anything else. Instead, Poststructuralism tends to see reality as a heterogeneous multiplicity of "fields," "machines," "discourses," "language games," or any of a dozen other cross-cutting planes, plateaus, and what-have-you, which—and this is crucial—do not form any sort of overarching structure or hierarchy. Rather than contexts encompassing one another, as in Dumont, one has a mosaic of broken surfaces, and on each surface, a completely different game played by a different set of rules. Moreover, post-structuralists usually insist that one cannot even talk about individuals moving back and forth between these surfaces; rather, the players (or "subjects") are constructs of the game itself; effects of discourse, and our sense that we have a consistent self, largely an illusion. Ultimately, language speaks us. Where previous debates asked whether one should begin with society or the individual, here both society *and* the individual shatter into fragments. We seem to have left such debates as Formalism versus Substantivism altogether in the dust. But here appearances turn out to be a bit deceptive.

Within each plane, or game, or field, the picture usually looks strikingly familiar. There are a bunch of individual players (or, occasionally, collective ones) competing with or otherwise attempting to dominate or impose their will on the others.

There's no room here to go case by case, but it might be useful to start with an example from Pierre Bourdieu. This is for two reasons. First, because Bourdieu is the theorist considered to have gone the furthest in actually reconciling structuralism and theories of human action. His notion of habitus, of symbolic systems that can be absorbed and endlessly reproduced without the actor ever being aware she is doing so, is justly famous. Second, because his approach to economic action is so explicitly formalist.

Consider his reinterpretation of Mauss' essay on the gift. On the first page of this essay, Mauss defines gifts as "prestations which are in theory voluntary, disinterested and spontaneous, but are in fact obligatory and interested" (1927:1). Just as in our own society, there is often a pretense of pure generosity when one first gives a gift, though in reality the receiver is expected to return something of equal or greater value later on. Hence a gift can often be a challenge, and the recipient, profoundly humiliated if he cannot produce a suitably generous response. Nonetheless, Mauss' ultimate point is that the "interest" involved need have nothing to do with making a profit—or even scoring a moral victory—at anyone's expense. Gifts act as a way of creating social relations. They create alliances and obligations between individuals or groups who might otherwise have nothing to do with one another. Functionalist theorists (Polanyi himself, among others) immediately swept up this notion because it corresponded so perfectly to their assumptions. Exchange was first and foremost a way of achieving social integration. For some, it became the very glue that held society together.[5] If anything, this held even more for Structuralists: Claude Levi-Strauss (1949) extended the argument further by suggesting that the institution of marriage, in any society, should be considered the exchange of women between groups of men, which again functioned to create a network of alliances.

Bourdieu, in his ethnographic study of the Kabyle of Algeria (1977), manages to take a radically different turn on the gift by returning to the pretense of generosity. Often, he notes, all that makes gift exchange different from simple barter is the lapse of time between gift and counter-gift. It's this delay that makes it possible to pretend each is simply an act of generosity, of denying any element of self-interested calculation. This sort of subterfuge, he suggests, is typical of traditional societies, which unlike ours do not recognize an explicit field of economic activity.

A rational contract would telescope into an instant a transaction which gift exchange disguises, by stretching it out in time; and because of this, gift exchange is, if not the only mode of commodity circulation practiced, at least the only mode to be fully recognized, in societies which, because they deny 'the true soil of their own life,' as Lukacs puts it, have an economy in itself and not for itself. Everything takes place as if the essence of the "archaic" economy lay in the fact that economic activity cannot explicitly acknowledge the economic ends in relation to which it is objectively oriented: the "idolatry of nature" which makes it impossible to think of nature as a raw material or, consequently, to see human activity as *labour,* i.e., as man's struggle against nature, tends, together with the systematic emphasis on the symbolic aspect of the activities and relations of production, to prevent the economy from being grasped as an economy, i.e., as a system governed by the laws of interested calculation, competition, or exploitation (Bourdieu 1977:171–72).

Notice what is happening here. Bourdieu starts with an argument reminiscent of Karl Polanyi. In traditional societies like the Kabyle, the economy is not a sphere unto itself; rather, it is embedded in social relations.[6] But where Polanyi's "economy" was just a society's way of providing itself with food and other necessities, Bourdieu's definition is strictly Formalist: it is a matter of self-interested calculation, making rational decisions about the allocation of scarce resources with the aim of getting as much as possible for oneself. In real, "objective" terms, he argues, economizing—or something very much like it—is always going on. It's just that where there is no market, everyone goes to enormous lengths to disguise this fact. This endless labor of camouflage is such a burden—often it takes up as much time as that invested in economic activity itself—that it tends to dissolve away immediately as soon as a market economy is introduced, whereon the hidden reality of calculated self-interest is openly revealed.

What one has, then, in a traditional society, is one that is dominated by an overt morality which can never really be put into practice: people are aware of the existence of self-interested calculation, they uniformly disapprove of it in principle, yet it is nonetheless the basis of everything they do. The result is a sort of across-the-board principle of Sartrean bad faith.[7]

Bourdieu ends up rehearsing all the usual economizing arguments. When people act in ways that seem economically irrational, this is only because the values they are maximizing are not material. "Practice never ceases to conform to economic calculation even when it gives every appearance of disinterestedness by departing from the logic of interested calculation (in the narrow sense) and playing for stakes that are non-material and not easily quantified" (1977:177) Therefore we must

> extend economic calculation to all the goods, material and symbolic, without distinction, that present themselves as rare and worthy of being sought after in a particular social formation—which may be 'fair words' or smiles, handshakes or shrugs, complements or attention, challenges or insults, honour or honours, powers or pleasures, gossip or scientific information, distinction or distinctions, etc. (1977:178).[8]

In Kabyle society, though, these ultimately boil down to two forms of "capital," as Bourdieu calls it: economic capital (land, domestic animals . . .) and "symbolic capital" (family honor and prestige). In a society without a self-regulating market, it's the latter that's more generally useful, because one can use honor to get wealth much more easily than the other way around.

On some level, what Bourdieu is saying is undeniably true. There is no area of human life, anywhere, where one cannot find self-interested calculation. But neither is there anywhere one cannot find kindness or adherence to idealistic principles: the point is why one, and not the other, is posed as "objective" reality. This is where Bourdieu is at his most poststructuralist. Every field of human endeavor, he argues, is defined by a set of competitive strategies. If it is customary to give gifts, then gift-giving will be part of those strategies. Therefore, the motives of the giver are unimportant. You might be a kind and decent person motivated only by the desire to help a friend, but objectively that doesn't matter, because in the overall structure of the situation, gifts are always part of a game of dominance, an attempt to accumulate symbolic capital and gain an advantage over the other party; this is how everyone else will perceive your actions, and this will be their real meaning. (To suggest otherwise would be to fall into the trap of "subjectivism.") Note how closely this position echoes that of economics. There, too, the assumption is that "objective" or "scientific" analysis means trying to cut through to the level on which you can say people are being selfish, and that when one has discovered this, one's job is done.

Now, it's one thing to find this attitude among conservative economists; quite another to find it at the heart of critical theory. Even more in Pierre Bourdieu, a social theorist who has, more than any I can think of, dedicated himself to exposing structures of privilege and exploitation even within the academic world (at no little personal cost). No one could doubt his own integrity and good intentions. Why, then, his insistence on discounting the importance of integrity and good intentions in human affairs?

I suspect it emerges from a flaw in the very project of critical theory. When Marxism, semiotics and the rest burst on the academic scene in the 1960s and '70s, they were seen above all as ways to probe beneath the surface of reality. The idea was always to unmask the hidden structures of power, dominance, and exploitation that lay below even the most mundane and ordinary aspects of daily life. Certainly such things are there to be found. But if this is *all* one is looking for, one soon ends up with a rather jaundiced picture of social reality. The overall effect of reading through this literature is remarkably bleak; one is left with the almost Gnostic feeling of a fallen world, in which every aspect of human life is threaded with violence and domination.[9] Critical theory thus ended up sabotaging his own best intentions, making power and domination so fundamental to the very nature of social reality that it became impossible to imagine a world without it. Because if one can't, then criticism rather loses its point. Before long, one had figures like Foucault or Baudrillard arguing that resistance is futile (or at least, that organized political resistance is futile), that power is simply the basic constituent of everything, and often enough, that there is no way out of a totalizing system, and that we should just learn to accept it with a certain ironic detachment. And if everything is equally corrupt, then pretty much anything could be open for redemption.[10] Why not, say, those creative and slightly offbeat forms of mass consumption favored by upper-middle class academics?

Of course, I am describing intellectual trends now as if they existed in a vacuum. In reality, the story is probably more one of the dissolution of the vast social movements in the '60s (except for feminism), the political rout of the left beginning in the early '80s, and the global rise of neoliberal ideologies. Not that this existed in isolation from intellectual trends either—one might well argue that the rise of neoliberalism (essentially, the exact thing Polanyi was arguing against fifty years ago) has been made possible by the failure of the left to come up with plausible alternatives—but this would take the argument way beyond the scope of this book. For now, suffice it to say that post-structuralism opened up yet another space into which the maximizing individual could crawl.

Finally, now, we can return to value.

Appadurai's "politics of value"

If there is one essay that has the most influence on the way anthropologists nowadays talk about value, it is certainly Arjun Appadurai's "Commodities and the Politics of Value" (1986), the introduction to a volume called *The Social Life of Things*. Phrases from this essay—"regimes of value," "tournaments of value," "the politics of value" itself—have been cited and repeated endlessly ever since. This makes it all the more important to ask exactly what sort of value Appadurai was talking about. The essay is well worth a second look.

Appadurai begins by talking about the term "commodity," which Marx, among others, applied to objects produced in order to be sold on a commercial market. This emphasis on production, he notes, arises from Marx's belief that value arises from human labor; the problem with this formulation, though, is that it makes commodities essentially a capitalist phenomena, typical of some societies and not others. Anthropologists would do better, he suggests, to forget Marx's approach entirely and look instead to those developed by Georg Simmel in *The Philosophy of Money* (1907).

Value, according to Simmel, is not rooted in human labor, nor does its existence depend on any larger social system. It arises from exchange. Hence, it is purely an effect of individual desire. The value of an object is the degree to which a buyer wants it. It is measured by how much that person is willing to give up in order to get it.

Like Marx, Simmel was thinking mainly of how things work in a market economy. But Appadurai insists that, unlike Marx's, his model can be easily be applied even where formal markets don't exist. In every society, there is at least some form of exchange. Therefore there's no reason to think of "commoditization" as a purely capitalist phenomena. Any object becomes a commodity when one thinks of it primarily as something one could acquire in exchange for something else, or that one would be willing to give up in order to get something one desires more.

> This means looking at the commodity potential of all things rather than searching fruitlessly for the magic distinction between commodities and other sorts of things. It also means breaking significantly with the production-dominated Marxian view of the commodity and focusing on the total trajectory from production, through exchange/distribution, to consumption (1986:13).

Now, it must be admitted that this approach does have its advantages. These are the usual advantages of a formalist approach. It allows the analyst to skip past the problem of social totalities, structures of meaning, and the like and focus on individual actors and their motivations. Alternatively, as Appadurai suggested, we could look at the history of an individual object: to follow its "life history" as it moves back and forth between different "regimes of value" (1986:5, 14–15). This latter was one of the most bold and exciting proposals in the essay, and it has been endlessly cited ever since, as has the phrase "regimes of value" itself. The latter is certainly evocative. But given Appadurai's endorsement of Simmel, it is hard to see what he could actually mean by it.

What does it mean to say an object passes back and forth between "regimes of value?" Could we be talking about the way the same object—say, a rocking chair—might be sold as merchandise in a retail outlet, then gradually acquire sentimental value as a family heirloom, and then, after many years, end up for sale once again? Apparently not. If "value" is simply the measure of someone else's desire to acquire the chair, "sentimental value" is ruled out. It's true that, in a companion essay, Igor Kopytoff (1986, cf. Bloch and Parry 1989:12–16) does argue that there are two sorts of value: objects can be valued either as commodities, which can be compared to other objects, or as "unique" objects that cannot. This would seem to include unique heirlooms, but it's hard to see how a "regime" of value could arise out of a system that does not allow comparison of any kind. What, then? Perhaps one might be talking about different *kinds* of exchange: say, the chair might be at one point given as a gift, at another, sold at auction? No again, because Appadurai argues it is wrong to make any strict distinction between gifts and other sorts of commodity. Here, he refers to Bourdieu's analysis, noting that what anthropologists have referred to as "gift exchange" is not simply generosity but, like commodity exchange, a matter of self-interested calculation (1986:12; c.f. also Carrier 1990, 1991).

Actually, Appadurai takes the argument much further than Bourdieu ever did. The classic distinction between commodities and gifts is that while commodity exchange is concerned with establishing equivalencies between the value of objects, "gifts" are primarily about relations between people. Bourdieu, despite one reference to gift-giving as a "mode of commodity circulation," never really contradicts this. When he writes about the exchange of gifts between Algerian peasants, he treats it not primarily as a way of acquiring things but as a way of accumulating "symbolic capital": of establishing one's honor, or generosity, or of putting a rival to shame. Appadurai, on the other hand, ends up writing as if all exchanges are simply about *things* and have nothing to do with making, maintaining, or severing social relationships.[11] Insofar as goods affect relations between people—insofar as society and culture come in at all—he is left only with the domain of consumption: and indeed much of the essay is concerned with how consuming of goods involves sending and receiving social messages. Hence, Appadurai's "politics of value" largely comes down to the story of how various elites try to control and limit exchange and consumption, while others (almost always popular forces) try to expand it, and with the social struggles that result. "Regimes of value," in turn, are the outcome of such struggles: the degree to which these elites have succeeded in channeling the free flow of exchange, or, alternately, to which existing cultural standards limit the possibilities of what can be exchanged for what.

The rejection of Marx, the emphasis on self-interested strategies, the glorification of consumption as creative self-expression—all this was entirely in keeping with the intellectual trends of the mid '80s. But it also serves as an object lesson about why, when one catches a wave, one might do well to think about where it is ultimately heading. Because the end result is anthropology as it might have been written by Milton Friedman. As James Ferguson (1988) has pointed out, there is a reason why Simmel is the darling of modern-day free market Neoliberals. Appadurai leaves one with an image of commerce (self-interested, acquisitive calculation) as a universal human urge, almost a libidinal, democratic force, always trying to subvert the powers of the state, aristocratic hierarchies, or cultural elites whose role always seems to be to try to inhibit, channel, or control it.[12] It all rather makes one wish one still had Karl Polanyi (1944) around to remind us how much state power has created the very terms of what is now considered normal commercial life.

One could, of course, argue that all this is beside the point. The real importance of Appadurai's essay was the liberating effect it had on other scholars (Thomas 1991:28): providing a charter, as it were, to examine how objects can move back and forth between different cultural worlds and thus to ask a whole new series of questions about colonialism, tourism, collecting, trade, and so on. There is certainly something to this. Many—perhaps most—of the anthropologists who have borrowed Appadurai's terminology drop the blatantly economistic elements anyway: when someone like Brad Weiss (1996) refers to "regimes of value," he obviously means something very different than Appadurai himself. In this way, Appadurai clearly has done us all a service. But theory does make a difference. Let me take one example. Both Appadurai's essay and Kopytoff's emphasize the possibility of writing the "social biography of a thing"; but both also define their terms in such a way that it becomes impossible to consider that an object's biography could *itself* contribute to its value.[13] The result is a purely methodological suggestion, and while there's undoubtedly a certain charm to the fantasy that one could reconstruct, say, the entire history of a well-traveled cassette or handgun or pair of tweezers, it would be a little like producing a list of everyone who's ever sat on a certain park bench: in the end, you have to wonder what was supposed to be the point.

This is worth considering, because the other major new approach to value of material objects that came out around the same time—Annette Weiner's writings on "inalienable possessions" (1985, 1992, 1994)—takes exactly the opposite direction.

parenthetical note: Annette Weiner on inalienable objects

The term "inalienable" is derived from Mauss' essay on the gift: in it, Mauss suggested that gifts are in a certain sense "inalienable" (*immeuble*), because even after they have been given away, they are still felt in some sense to belong to the giver. If nothing else, they continue to carry with them something of his or her personality. What, Weiner asks, would a theory of value look like if it were to take this phenomenon as its starting point? It would certainly look very different from the one found in Appadurai and Kopytoff. Heirlooms, for instance, would not be valuable just because (as Kopytoff would have it) they are "unique," but rather, because of their specific histories. Recognizing this in turn could help resolve some of the more confusing aspects of Kopytoff's essay: for example, the way he suggests that in many traditional societies, varieties of goods are ranked by their "degree of singularity," rather as if some objects could be more unique than others. Really, what one is talking is the object's capacity to accumulate a history: hence, in our society at least, there are artifacts that are truly unique (the Hope diamond, Monet's water lilies, the Brooklyn Bridge), and then, just below them in value, a class of "collector's items" (ancient Greek coins, Miro prints, first-edition Silver Surfer comic books). These are not quite unique, but they have a rarity that derives from their historical origins; what's more, when they circulate, they almost invariably accumulate a further history in the form of a pedigree of former owners—which then in turn tends to further enhance their value. In any society, one should probably be able to map out at least a rough continuum of types of objects, ranked according their capacity to accumulate history: from the crown jewels at the top, to, at the bottom, such things as a gallon of motor oil, or two eggs over easy.

Weiner notes that in many of the societies discussed by Mauss (the Maori, the Kwakiutl, the Trobriand Islanders), the most famous heirlooms do indeed have their own names and "biographies," which includes their origins, past owners, people who had tried or succeeded to win or recover them. It would seem, then, that circulation can actually enhance an object's value. But by fixing on the notion of "inalienability" Weiner ends up pulling things in exactly the opposite direction. If an object's identity is permanently attached to that of one, original owner, circulation cannot do this (see Weiner 1976:180–83).

Hence, the main thrust of *Inalienable Possessions* is to propose the existence of something Weiner calls "transcendent" or "absolute" value. Weiner is thinking most of all of ancient treasures, here, which are often also badges of office that not only establish a holder's name and position but ground it in the doings of gods or ancestors from the beginnings of the world. The objects that most embody transcendent value—say, Australian tjuringas, the crown jewels of England—no one would ever give away. Still, they can be lost, stolen, forgotten, or destroyed. Preserving them is thus an achievement, the maintenance of an image of eternity (1992:8–12). Their value, then, is measured in the fear of loss. In many societies, there is a complex game of strategies going on in which others are constantly trying to get hold of the heirlooms that ultimately guarantee another's historical identity and thus the authentication of their claims to status and authority. In other words, everyone is actually trying to ensure their most valuable heirlooms *do not* circulate. This might seem about as far as one can go from Simmel's position, that value is a product of exchange. But in many ways, we are simply dealing with a mirror image. Rather than value being the measure of how much one would like to acquire something one does not possess, in Weiner, it becomes the measure of how little one would wish to give up the things one does. Objects of transcendent value are simply the very last things one would be willing to part with.[14]

So far, then, it's hard to see how we have made a whole lot of progress since the '60s. Weiner's work points in all sorts of interesting directions, but she often seems trapped between creating a mere mirror-image of economism, or alternately (as in her notion of "reproduction": Weiner 1978, 1980, 1982) swinging towards something much more like Dumont's position. Between formalism and substantivism, then, there still does not seem to be much middle ground.

II: Strathern's neo-Maussian approach

There is one major theoretical alternative, if one so far largely limited to Melanesia. I'll call it "Neo-Maussian," since its genealogy can be traced from Mauss through the work of Christopher Gregory (1980, 1982) to that of Marilyn Strathern (1981, 1984a, 1984b, 1987, 1988, 1992). Strathern's work is also considered the theoretical culmination of what is often referred to as the "New Melanesian Ethnography."[15] No one could possibly deny its brilliance. Some of her key notions, like that of the "partible person," have already had a great deal of influence even outside Melanesia, in fact, even outside anthropology. Perhaps the main thing that has limited her work's appeal is that most of it is written in an incredibly difficult language, largely of her own invention—one which seems to have an endless capacity to slip away almost as soon as a reader thinks she's grasped it. It can be very frustrating to read.

I'll begin with Mauss. The main question asked in his "Essay on the Gift" is: what is it about giving a gift that makes the recipient feel compelled to return a countergift of roughly equal value? His answer—which actually harks back to Emerson (1844)—is that a gift is always seen to contain something of the giver. Hence, Mauss notes, objects given as gifts often take on human qualities. Actually, his descriptions of "gift economies" like those of the Northwest Coast emphasize the way in which everything—not only as gifts but houses, canoes, masks and serving dishes—was treated as if it had its own personality, likes and dislikes, intentions and desires. In a book called

Gifts and Commodities (1982), Christopher Gregory—an economic anthropologist working in Papua New Guinea—suggests this is a general tendency. Gift economies tend to personify objects. Commodity economies, like our own, do the opposite: they tend to treat human beings, or at least, aspects of human beings, like objects. The most obvious example is human labor: in modern economics we talk of "goods and services" as if human activity itself were something analogous to an object, which can be bought or sold in the same way as cheese, or tire-irons.

Gregory lays out a tidy set of oppositions. Gifts are transactions that are meant to create or effect "qualitative" relations between persons; they take place within a preexisting web of personal relations; therefore, even the objects involved have a tendency to take on the qualities of people. Commodity exchange, on the other hand, is meant to establish a "quantitative" equivalence of value between objects; it should ideally be done quite impersonally; therefore, there is a tendency to treat even the human beings involved like things. Giving someone a gift usually puts that person in your debt; hence, success in gift exchange becomes a matter of giving away as much wealth as possible, so as to gain a social advantage. In a commodity system, it's the things that are important; therefore, people try to accumulate as much wealth as they can.

Obviously, a system as tidy as this has got to be a bit of an abstraction. No pure gift, or pure commodity, economy actually exists. Actually, Gregory himself was suggesting nothing of the sort: as he has noted recently (1998) he created the distinction in order to understand how contemporary Papuans move back and forth between one and the other. Nonetheless, such abstractions can be useful. Most of all, they can be used as the basis of making further generalizations. If the logic of a 'gift economy' really is so different from our own, for instance, might it not also imply a different conception of the very nature of human beings or social relations? This is the direction Strathern takes Gregory's ideas, combining them with observations culled from her own experience among the Melpa-speaking inhabitants of Mount Hagen, in Papua New Guinea. The result is a kind of grand comparison of "Melanesian" and "Western" social theories.

Strathern has come into a great deal of criticism for "essentializing" difference. I don't think such criticisms are entirely fair, because Strathern never claims that all Melanesians think one way, or all Westerners another. Rather, it seems to me her work is meant as a kind of thought experiment. Western social theory is founded on certain everyday common sense, one that assumes that the most important thing about people is that they are all unique individuals. Theory therefore also tends to start with individuals and tries to understand how they form relations with one another (thus producing something we call "society"). People in Mount Hagen did not share these assumptions. With no concept of either "society" or unique individuals, they assumed the relationships came first. What, then, would a social theory be like that was founded on Melpa common sense? It's at this point she brings in Gregory's distinction between gift economies and commodity economies, and the other ethnographers elsewhere in Melanesia who might be said to have contributed to the groundwork of such a theory.[16]

Marxian critique, Maussian rejoinder

What Strathern is probably most famous for, however, is her ongoing dialogue with critical—and especially feminist—theory. Her best known book, *The Gender of the Gift* (1988), consists largely of a series of rejoinders to feminist, or feminist-inspired, analyses of one or another aspect of Melanesian society. Now, considering this is a part of the world notorious for extreme inequality of the sexes, this makes reading the book a rather surrealistic experience: Strathern is an avowed feminist, but she spends the book systematically knocking down almost every argument ever made that might justify the notion that Melanesian women are oppressed. It is not, actually, that Strathern means to deny that Melanesian men dominate women (she does in fact, acknowledge they do).[17] Rather, she wants to expose the cultural assumptions underlying the ways most such arguments are framed. Consider, for example, her reply to Lizette Josephides' analysis of Melanesian exchange systems (Strathern 1988:144–59).

Josephides provides what has actually become the classic Marxist critique of the Maussian tradition (1982, see also 1983, 1985, Bloch 1991:172). It runs like this: by focusing on "the gift," the moment when objects change hands, one is looking only at the moment the society itself places under its spotlight: the moment when two important men (it almost always seems to be men) confront one another in dramatic public acts of generosity or display. But spotlights do not only draw attention to some things, by doing so, they also draw attention away from others. Should one not also ask what is being left in the shadows here? Most obviously, someone must have made these things; there is a whole cycle of production and assembly of goods that has to go on before the exchange takes place (and usually another cycle afterwards.) Rather than be seduced by the spotlight, we should investigate its operation.

Josephides (1985) takes the example of Melpa pigs. Melpa political and ceremonial life centers on dramatic rituals, called *moka,* in which clans assemble to give gifts to one another. There are lavish feasts, dances, speeches, and gorgeous costumes. Huge heaps of food are piled up and presented to repay previous gifts of food. Important men give each other pigs, which are the most important gift of all. Hageners raise pigs especially to be exchanged; at any moment, a family will probably have a number in their yard, most of them considered as the product of one or another of these exchanges. But who does the gardening, and who actually raises these pigs? Mainly women. Married couples cooperate to raise pigs; the wife contributes the largest share of labor; nonetheless, only the husbands can exchange them in public, thus acquiring a "name." Only men can translate pigs into fame and political reputation. The whole process, Josephides suggests, can be thought of as a kind of fetishization, because it ends up making it seem as if the pigs are produced by acts of exchange rather than by the human labor that went into tending them, fattening them, and growing crops with which to do so—just as someone like Simmel would say that the value of commodities comes from the fact that someone is willing to buy them rather than from the thought and energy that went into producing something a buyer *would* desire to buy.

Strathern objects. To make such an argument one is already assuming that a person has some kind of rights in whatever they produce. We assume that, but does everyone? If you examine talk of "rights" in our own society, she observes, you quickly discover a whole series of assumptions about private property. We assume that society is made up of individuals, and most of our conceptions of human rights are based on the idea that individuals own themselves. Hence, they have the right to prevent others from intruding on their bodies, their houses, or their minds (cf. MacPherson 1962). Marxists simply go further by arguing that this includes their powers of creativity, and therefore, that individuals have a right to the products of "their" labor. Now, this argument might be useful, Strathern admits, as an outside perspective, as grounds to declare Hagen society fundamentally unjust: but certainly we cannot go on to say that exchange serves as a way of disguising this reality unless we have some reason to believe Hageners would have reason to see it in the first place.

Thus far the argument is straightforward enough. Strathern continues:

> A vocabulary, which turns on the deprivation of 'rights', must entail premises about a specific form of property. To assert rights against others implies a type of legal ownership. Does the right to determine the *value* of one's product belong naturally to the producer? (1988:142, emphasis mine)

The first two sentences are remarkable enough—apparently, there are *no* rights that do not go back to property. But the third is crucial. We're not just talking about the right of ownership—the right to determine who has access to one's product. We are also talking about the right to determine its meaning or importance. And of course, the moment an anthropologist uses a term like "natural," we all know where the argument is heading. It is we who assume the producer should always have this right. We are wrong to believe that this is universal.

The Marxist notion of alienation, she writes, assumes that work

> has a value in the first instance for the self . . . It is the person's own appropriation of his or her activity that gives it value, in so far as the person is a microcosm of the 'social' process by which exogenous appropriation by others, by 'the system,' also gives it value (1988:142–43).

This is a difficult passage, and it turns on a rather particular use of the term "appropriation." But it is decipherable. Ordinary Western common sense takes it for granted that objects—like individuals—already exist in nature (that the ultimate constituents of the world, as Gilbert Ryle used to put it, are "blokes and things.") Human action is therefore thought to consist mainly of taking those objects and "appropriating" them socially—that is, ascribing meaning to them by placing them within some larger system of categories. By "the system," Strathern seems to have in mind some sort of Saussurean code, or alternately, a system of private property, which similarly divides things up. It is this meaning that Strathern seems to be referring to when she speaks of value. "Value," then, is the meaning or importance society ascribes to an object. Marxists imply that individuals who produce objects should have the right to determine their meaning. In Mount Hagen, she objects, people do not see things in this way, since they do not see objects as having been produced by individuals. They see them as the outcome of relationships.

Here we come to the core of Strathern's argument. Like Dumont, she views Western ideology as defined above all by its individualism. We assume every individual has a kind of central, unique core that makes them who they are. Call it a self, a soul, a personality—whatever you call it, the assumption is always that no two are exactly the same, and this is what is really important about a person. It's thus we can talk about creativity as "self-expression," of "finding oneself," or of contexts in which one is more "oneself" than others. It follows that other people's perceptions of us are likely to be superficial and limited. Most people do not know who we really are. But what if one did not make this set of assumptions? Melanesians, according to Strathern, either do not recognize such a unique core, or if they do, do not attach much importance to it.[18] Therefore they assume that we are, before we are anything else, what we are perceived to be by others. One might object that this would mean we are many different things, since different people are likely to have very different impressions of us, or see us differently in different contexts. But that is precisely what Strathern *is* arguing. Her most famous concept, in fact, is the "partible" or "multiple" person. People have all sorts of potential identities, which most of the time exist only as a set of hidden possibilities. What happens in any given social situation is that another person fixes on one of these and thus "makes it visible." One looks at a man, say, as a representative of his clan, or as one's sister's husband, or as the owner of a pig. Other possibilities, for the moment, remain invisible.

It is at this point that a theory of value comes in: because Strathern uses the phrase "making visible" and "giving value" more or less interchangeably.[19]

So here too, value is simply meaning: giving value to something is a matter of defining it by placing in some broader set of conceptual categories. The difference is that it would never occur to a Melanesian that anyone would have the right to define herself, or the products of her own labor—value always exists in the eyes of someone else. But there's slightly more to it than that. Value actually has two components. Because when someone fixes on one of those "hidden possibilities" in someone else, thus making them visible, what they are bringing out is always itself seen as the product of some social relationship that existed in the past. Given the starting assumption (that persons are brought into being only through social relations) it only makes sense that this should be so. Hence a man might be seen as the product of the sexual relationship between his father and mother, or, perhaps, the exchange relation (i.e., bridewealth payments) between their mother and father's clan. Or, if he is identified as the owner of a pig, that pig is seen as being derived from the marriage relation between the man and his wife, who raised it, or else the exchange relation between that man and some other man, who gave it to him. Thus people and objects are all seen to have "multiple authors," or, in the Melpa idiom, "sources" or "origins."

At this point one can finally understand Melpa concepts of exchange. Mauss of course had insisted that in giving a gift one is giving a portion of one's self. Quite so here: the pig can indeed embody one aspect of its owner's identity. However, we are also used to thinking of the giver as the active party. Hageners—and indeed, Melanesians in general, Strathern argues—do not see it that way. Instead, they see exchange largely as a matter of extraction. Actually this is perfectly consistent with what already been set out: that one's possessions take on value (i.e., meaning) only in another person's eyes. In exchange, that other person defines the object not only as the product of past social relations, but also as something "detachable" from them. Again, take the example of a pig. If I convince the pig's owner to give that pig to me, its value is (a) that of its "origin," the social relations that brought it into being, and (b) the fact that I can "detach" it from that person, which means that pig will now embody a new social relation, between that owner and myself.[20] If I manage to convince the owner to give me his pig, I thus displace the value of one relationship onto the other. And the object now comes to embody my own ability to do this, my power to create new relationships.

If all this is true, we are in a very different world than that assumed by Marxist ideas of alienation. For a Marxist, labor is, or should be, a matter of self-expression: the ideal is that of a fine craftsman, or even more, an artist, whose work is both an expression of her inner being, and a contribution to society as a whole. Melanesians see work as an expression of one's commitment to a specific relationship. Wives, like husbands, help raise pigs to show their commitment to their marriage.[21] The pig is an embodiment of that relation until it leaves the domestic sphere and enters the public sphere of male ceremonial exchange, where its value shifts, and it comes to embody the importance of relations between men. Actually, since the ultimate effect is so similar (and since Strathern admits that the notion of the exploitation of female labor might be legitimate as an outside perspective) one might well wonder what all the fuss was supposed to be about. The Marxist could simply say, "All right, so the mystification runs even deeper than I thought," and the Maussian would then have to either concede the point, or argue that no Melanesian could ever, under any circumstances, imagine a world in which they would be able to choose freely who or what they worked for.

toward a synthesis?

Our main interest here, however, is clearly with Strathern's notion of value. I've already said that it seems, in essence, Saussurean: the value of an object, or a person, is the meaning they take on by being assigned a place in some larger system of categories.

It's interesting that this is one of the few points where Strathern decisively breaks with Gregory. Gregory (1982:47–51) preferred to limit the term "value" to "exchange value," in the sense used by economists. Therefore, he concluded, in a gift economy one cannot talk about value at all. Objects of gift exchange are, instead, ranked. Among the Mae-Enga for example (Meggit 1971), there are six different ranks of objects. The most exalted category includes only two sorts of things: live pigs and cassowary birds. One can exchange a pig for a cassowary, or two pigs, or two cassowaries for each other; but one cannot exchange a pig or cassowary for objects of any other category. The next category includes pearl-shell pendants, plume headdresses, and stone axes, which again can only be exchanged for each other, and not for anything higher or lower—and so on, down to the lowest sphere, which consists of ordinary foodstuffs. Thus, while one could perhaps say in the abstract that pigs are worth more than axes, this is all one can say. To speak of value, one would have to be able to say how *much* more: to establish just how many axes it would take to reach the value of one pig; and in the absence of exchange, such comparisons simply do not take place.

Now, this clearly has a bearing on some of the issues discussed earlier in the chapter: particularly the way that objects can be arranged along a continuum from relatively durable, particular items to relative perishable and generic ones, and therefore, by their capacity to retain a history. The kind of rank order Gregory is talking about is clearly a similar principle: indeed, one can normally expect that at the very least, whatever unique heirlooms a society has will be exchanged (if at all) in the most exalted sphere and that the most ephemeral products like staple foods will be at the bottom. And this is almost always what does seem to happen. But there is an intrinsic problem here. There is a difference between the capacity to convey history (which can at least be roughly assessed), and the actual history being conveyed. The latter does indeed tend to be unique, and therefore cannot be the basis for creating a system of value. Actually, this is why Gregory avoids using the term "value" at all when speaking of gift economies: "strictly speaking, like for like exchanges are impossible because, for example, a particular pig will be one day older and hence a different pig" (1982:50). Marilyn Strathern's notion of value seems intended to bring just such historical particulars back on board—she specifically points out that even when women in a New Guinea market are bartering lumps of fish for taro, two apparently identical batches of fish will not be considered the same because of their different origins (Strathern 1992a; Gewertz 1983). But in order to do so she has to redefine radically what she means by "value."

Where Gregory takes the most restricted definition of the term possible, Strathern does the opposite:

> An initial definition is in order. As Gregory (1982) notes, the economic concept of value implies a comparison of entities, either as a ratio (the one expressed as a proportion of the other) or in terms of rank equivalence.[22] Both like and unlike terms may be so compared. In addition, however, this part of the world (the Southwestern Pacific) is dominated by a third relation of comparison: between an entity and its source of origin. Value is thus constructed in the identity of a thing or person with various sets of social relations in which it is embedded, and its simultaneous detachability from them. Here lies much of the significance of gift exchange (1987:286).

Let me take the argument step by step. Value implies comparison. One can compare the value of two commodities in terms of their worth in money; here, one can establish proportions: i.e., five loaves of bread are worth the same as one steak-frites. Or, one can compare two valuables in Gregory's gift economies in terms of their rank. But Gregory's formula does not really explain the workings of gift economies. At least in Melanesia, she says, the critical comparison is "between an entity and its source of origin." Now, I do believe one should be as generous as possible in reading another scholar's work, but the closer one examines this passage, the less sense it makes. The first two sorts of "comparison" are not just meant to establish that two entities are "like or unlike" in *some* way. They involve evaluation. That is, they are meant to establish whether one entity is better, or more important, or more desirable, than the other. Clearly, comparing "an entity and its source of origin" does not do this. One is not saying an entity is better than or preferable to its source of origin. One is simply observing that the two are similar in some ways and different in others.[23]

As I have already observed, Strathern's definition of value is Saussurean: value is simply meaningful difference, a matter of placing something in a set of categories. In fact, the passage above bears a remarkable resemblance to Sahlins' invocation of Saussure cited in chapter 1. It also suffers from all the same problems: if one defines value simply as "difference," then the concept loses most of the explanatory power that has made it attractive to begin with. It is one thing to say that women at a market in Papua New Guinea are likely to see two lumps of apparently identical fish as different. It's quite another to say why, as a result, a given woman will want one and not the other. In order to understand *that,* one would have to realize that actors are not just "comparing" entities with their origins but comparing the origins of different entities *to each other.* And it is this process of comparing unique histories on which, as I have said, it is extremely difficult to get a theoretical handle.[24]

All of this is not meant to discount Strathern's contribution. Mainly it is meant to illustrate why it can be so frustrating to try to apply it outside the rather specific (usually polemical) contexts for which it was developed. When reading her description of gift relations, for example, it's hard to resist looking for parallels in our own society. But hers is explicitly not meant to be the basis of a general theory of gifts. It's not even meant to be a general theory of gift economies, since Strathern never makes clear how we would disentangle one from the specifically Melanesian—or even specifically Melpa—elements in her account. An obvious example: her insistence that gift-exchange be seen as a process of extraction would hardly make sense in the Mediterranean tradition of "agonistic exchange" which Tom Beidelman (1988) examined in ancient Greece, or Pierre Bourdieu in contemporary Algeria.[25] There the point of giving gifts is often to crush and humiliate a political adversary with an act of generosity so lavish and so magnificent that it could never be reciprocated. Does this mean one would need a completely different theory for Mediterranean "gift economies"? What would it be like? It is precisely this sort of question which Strathern seems to resist, leaving it to others to determine her work's broader implications.

Munn: the value of actions

So far, then, it's hard to say whether exchange theory has advanced much or not since the 1960s. Or to be more precise, there have clearly been advances in many areas; but it's specifically around the question of value that the same conundrums show up again and again. It is still, basically, a choice between the kind of value proposed by economists and a Saussurean notion of meaningful difference. Other approaches, however, have been proposed. It might be useful to compare Strathern's perspective with that of another anthropologist of Melanesia: Nancy Munn (1977, 1983, 1986). Munn's work concerns the island of Gawa, in the Massim region off the southeastern coast of New Guinea, which, like the Trobriands (to which it is closely culturally related) is part of the famous kula chain. The chain itself is defined by the exchange of immensely valuable armshells and necklaces, forms of adornment that are rarely worn, but rather, exchanged as gifts between kula partners. Much of the drama of Trobriand life revolve around kula expeditions; important men and their followers descend on distant villages in other islands to woo choice heirlooms from their kula partners. Since an armshell can be exchanged only for a necklace, and vice versa, these heirlooms are constantly moving against each other, the armshells circling the islands in a clockwise direction, the necklaces counterclockwise.

In Gawa or the Trobriands, there is very clearly a rank hierarchy of types of goods, and it does indeed correspond to an item's capacity to retain history: perishable and generic substances like food are at the bottom, and unique imperishable valuables at the top. Even among kula shells, there is an elaborate ranking system, with everyone trying to get their hands, at least temporarily, on the very most famous heirlooms, whose names are recognized by everyone in the kula ring. Previous analysts have tended to look at such phenomena in terms of "spheres of exchange," in which different sorts of valuable can circulate only among others of the same sort. This, however, implies one is looking for value primarily in objects. Munn instead refers to what others might label "spheres" as "levels of value," since for those who attain them, they mean ever greater degrees of control over, and ability to extend their influence in time and space, or, as she puts it, "intersubjective spacetime."

The basic Gawan value template is the act of giving food (1986:11–12, 49–73). If you eat too much, Gawans say, all you do is lie down and sleep; it means inaction and hence the contraction of one's control over space and time. Giving the same food to someone else, on the other hand, creates alliances and obligations. It thus implies extension of one's control over space and time. If that someone else hails from overseas, giving food creates alliances that one can then activate so as to act on increasingly higher levels of exchange, enabling one to exchange more durable valuables like shell ornaments or canoes, and by doing so exercising even greater control of intersubjective spacetime. The ultimate achievement is to attach one's name to a famous heirloom kula shell (the most famous, remember, have their own unique names and histories) by passing it along the inter-island kula circle; the continual passing of which thus creates the most exalted level of all. Note that all this is not a matter of "entering into" higher spheres or even levels of exchange that already exist. It is these actions—of hospitality, travel, and exchange—that create the levels in the first place. And at their most basic this is all "levels"—indeed, all such abstract "structures"—are. They consist of human actions.

Where Strathern starts her analysis from a web of social relationships, then, Munn starts from a notion of activity. Value[26] emerges in action; it is the process by which a person's invisible "potency"—their capacity to act—is transformed into concrete, perceptible forms. If one gives another person food and receives a shell in return, it is not the value of the food that returns to one in the form of the shell, but rather the value of the act of giving it. The food is simply the medium. Value, then, is the way people represent the importance of their own actions to themselves—though Munn also notes that it we are not talking about something that could occur in isolation: in kula exchange, at least (and by extension, in any social form of value), it can only happen through that importance being recognized by someone else. The highest level of control over space and time is concretized simply as "fame," that is, the fact that others, even others one has never met, consider one's name important, one's actions significant.

Munn's approach knits together a lot of the themes that have cropped up in this chapter, but it also introduces something radically new. Certainly, it breaks the gift/commodity dichotomy wide open. Rather than having to choose between the desirability of objects and the importance of human relations, one can now see both as refractions of the same thing. Commodities have to be produced (and yes, they also have to be moved around, exchanged, consumed . . .), social relations have to be created and maintained; all of this requires an investment of human time and energy, intelligence, concern. If one sees value as a matter of the relative distribution of *that,* then one has a common denominator. One invests one's energies in those things one considers most important, or most meaningful. One could even rework Annette Weiner's argument along the same lines: the value of objects of "transcendent value" would simply be an effect of all the efforts people have made to maintain, protect, and preserve them. Even if, from the point of view of the actors, the sequence seems as if it's precisely the other way around.

Framing things this way of course evokes the specter of Marx—the very one that most of the other authors covered in this chapter preferred to banish. We are clearly dealing with something along the lines of a labor theory of value. But only if we define "labor" much more broadly than almost anyone working in the Marxist tradition ever has. By limiting themselves to talk of "work" or "labor"—notions that are by no means cultural universals—most Marxists do lay themselves open to the sort of critique Strathern levels against them. But certainly, creative action exists everywhere, and one would be justified in being highly suspicious of anyone who claims that a given society completely fails to recognize this fact. The problem is that if you define action this broadly, there's clearly no way to make any exact count of how much of it has been invested in any given object or relation.[27] Even the outside analyst can at best make an extremely rough estimate. Within the society in question, there are of course all sorts of ways of estimating value, but the one thing one can be sure of is that most of this history—sometimes all of it—will be effaced in people's eyes.

conclusions (why so little action?)

Munn's work, and particularly her theory of value, has been little taken up by other scholars;[28] understandably, perhaps, considering it points in such a radically different direction than does most existing scholarship.

I have been arguing over the course of this chapter that theories of value have (at least since the '60s) been swinging back between two equally unsatisfactory poles: on the one hand, a warmed-over economism that makes "value" simply the measure of individual desire; on the other, some variant of Saussurean "meaningful difference." Comparing them to Munn's approach makes it easier to see one feature both approaches have in common. In either case, what's being evaluated is essentially static. Economism tends to reify everything in sight, reducing complex social relations between people—understandings about property rights, honor or social standing—into objects that individual actors can then seek to acquire. To turn something into a thing is, normally, to stop it in motion; not surprising, then, that such approaches usually have little place for creativity or even, unless forced, production. Saussurean Structuralism on the other hand ascribes value not to things but to abstract categories—these categories together make up a larger code of meaning. But Saussure himself insisted quite explicitly that this code had to be treated as if it existed outside of action, change, and time. Linguistics, he argued, draws its material from particular acts of speech, but its actual object of study is not speech but language, the rules of grammar, codes of meaning, and so on that make speech comprehensible. While speech (*parole*) exists in time and is always changing, language (*langue*)—"the code"—has to be treated as "synchronic," as if it existed in a kind of transcendent moment outside it. Both approaches, then, end up having a difficult time accounting for ongoing processes of change and transformation. Economism tends to reduce all action to exchange; Saussureans have trouble dealing with action of any sort.

Starting from hidden, generative powers of action creates an entirely different problematic. Value becomes, as I've said, the way people represent the importance of their own actions to themselves: normally, as reflected in one or another socially recognized form. But it is not the forms themselves that are the source of value.

Compare, again, Strathern. Because of her Saussurean starting point, she sees value as a matter of "making visible": social relations take on value in the process of being recognized by someone else. According to Munn's approach, the value in question is ultimately the power to *create* social relations; the "making visible" is simply an act of recognition of a value that already exists in potentia. Hence where Strathern stresses visibility, Munn's language is all about "potencies," "transformative potential," human capacities that are ultimately generic and invisible. Rather than value being the process of public recognition itself, already suspended in social relations, it is the way people who *could* do almost anything (including, in the right circumstances, creating entirely new sorts of social relation) assess the importance of what they do, in fact, do, as they are doing it. This is necessarily a social process; but it is always rooted in generic human capacities. This leads in an entirely different direction than that assumed by almost any of the theories that we've considered up to now.

Chapter 3 ▨

Value as the Importance of Actions

W hat if one did try to create a theory of value starting from the assumption that what is ultimately being evaluated are not things, but actions? What might a broader social theory that starts from this assumption look like? In this chapter, I'd like to explore this possibility in greater detail.

I ended the last chapter with the work of Nancy Munn, one of the few anthropologists who has taken this direction. Munn is not quite the only one. Another is Terence Turner, who has developed some of the same ideas, not so much in the phenomenological tradition, but with an eye to adopting Marx's labor theory of value for anthropological use. Turner's work, however, has found even less broad an audience. There are many reasons for this. Many of his most important essays (1980a, 1984, 1987, 1988) remain unpublished; others are either scattered in obscure venues (1979c, 1985a, etc.) or written in a language so highly technical it is often very difficult for the non-adept to make head or tail of them (consider, for example, 1979a:171 or 1985b:52). Hence, while a handful of anthropologists have been strongly influenced by his ideas (Jane Fajans, Fred Myers, Stephen Sangren, et al.), the vast majority has never even been exposed to them. Before outlining Turner's approach, though (or anyway my own idiosyncratic version of it) some groundwork is probably in order.

the underside of the Western tradition

At the end of the last chapter I suggested that one reason Nancy Munn's work has been so little taken up is that theories that start from action fall so far outside the main currents of the Western intellectual tradition that it's hard for most scholars to figure out exactly what to do with them. They belong, one might say, to the Heraclitean tradition, which in Western thought has always been somewhat marginal. Western philosophy, after all, really begins with the quarrel between Heraclitus and Parmenides; a quarrel that Parmenides won. As a result, from almost the very start, the Western tradition marked itself by imagining objects that exist, as it were, outside of time and transformation. So much so that the obvious reality of change has always been something of a problem.

It might be useful to review that quarrel, however quickly.

Heraclitus saw the apparent fixity of objects of ordinary perception as largely an illusion; their ultimate reality was one of constant flux and transformation. What we assume to be objects are actually patterns of change. A river (this is his most famous example) is not simply a body of water; in fact, if one steps in the same river twice, the water flowing through it is likely to be entirely different. What endures over time is simply the pattern of its flow.[1] Parmenides on the other hand took precisely the opposite view: he held that it was change that was illusion. For objects to be comprehensible, they must exist to some degree outside of time and change. There is a level of reality, perhaps one that we humans can never fully perceive, at which forms are fixed and perfect. From Parmenides, of course, one can trace a direct line both to Pythagoras (and thus to Western math and science) and to Plato (with his ideal forms), and hence to just about any subsequent school of Western philosophy.

Parmenides' position was obviously absurd; and indeed, science has since shown that Heraclitus was more right than he could possibly have known. The elements that make up solid objects are, in fact, in constant motion.[2] But a fairly strong case can be made that had Western philosophy not rejected his position for Parmenides' false one, we would never have been able to discover this. The problem with his dynamic approach is that while obviously true it makes it impossible to draw precise borders and thus to make precise measurements. If objects are really processes, we no longer know their true dimensions—at least, if they still exist—because we don't know how long they will last. If objects are in constant flux, even precise spatial measures are impossible. One can take an object's measure at a particular moment and then treat that as representative, but even this is something of an imaginary construct, because such "moments" (in the sense of points in time, of no duration, infinitely small) do not really exist—they, too, are imaginary constructs. It has been precisely such imaginary constructs ("models") that have made modern science possible. As Paul Ricoeur has noted:

> It is striking that Plato contributed to the construction of Euclidian geometry through his work of denominating such concepts as line, surface, equality, and the similarity of figures, etc., which strictly forbade all recourse and all allusion to manipulations, to physical transformation of figures. This asceticism

of mathematical language, to which we owe, in the last analysis, all our machines since the dawn of the mechanical age, would have been impossible without the logical heroism of Parmenides denying the entirety of the world of becoming and of *praxis* in the name of the self-identity of significations. It is to this denial of movement and work that we owe the achievements of Euclid, of Galileo, modern mechanism, and all our devices and apparatus (Ricoeur 1970:201–202; also in Sahlins 1976:81–82n.21)

There is obviously something very ironic about all this. What Ricoeur is suggesting is that we have been able to create a technology capable of giving us hitherto unimaginable power to transform the world, largely because we were first able to imagine a world without powers or transformations. It may well be true. The crucial thing, though, is that in doing so, we have also lost something. Because once one is accustomed to a basic apparatus for looking at the world that starts from an imaginary, static, Parmenidean world outside of it, connecting the two becomes an overwhelming problem. One might well say that the last couple thousand years of Western philosophy and social thought have been and endless series of ever more complicated attempts to deal with the consequences. Always you get same the assumption of fixed forms and the same failure to know where you actually find them. As a result, knowledge itself has become the great problem. Roy Bhaskar has been arguing for some years now that since Parmenides, Western philosophy has been suffering from what he calls an "epistemic fallacy": a tendency to confuse the question of how we can know things with the question of whether those things exist.[3]

At its most extreme, this tendency opens into Positivism: the assumption that given sufficient time and sufficiently accurate instruments, it should be possible to make models and reality correspond entirely. According to its most extreme avatars, one should not only be able to produce a complete description of any object in the physical world, but—given the predictable nature of physical "laws"—be able to predict precisely what would happen to it under equally precisely understood conditions. Since no one has ever been able to do anything of the sort, the position has a tendency to generate its opposite: a kind of aggressive nihilism (nowadays most often identified with various species of post-structuralism) which at its most extreme argues that since one cannot come up with such perfect descriptions, it is impossible to talk about "reality" at all.

All this is a fine illustration of why most of us ordinary mortals find philosophical debates so pointless. The logic is in direct contradiction with that of ordinary life experience. Most of us are accustomed to describe things as "realities" precisely because we *can't* completely understand them, can't completely control them, don't know exactly how they are going to affect us, but nonetheless can't just wish them away. It's what we don't know about them that brings home the fact that they are real.

As I say, an alternative, Heraclitean strain has always existed—one that sees objects as processes, as defined by their potentials, and society as constituted primarily by actions. Its best-known manifestation is no doubt the dialectical tradition of Hegel and Marx. But whatever form it takes, it has always been almost impossible to integrate with more conventional philosophy. It has tended to be seen as existing somewhat off to the side, as odd or somewhat mystical. Certainly, it has seemed that way in comparison with what seemed like the hard-headed realism of more positivist approaches— rather ironically, considering that if one manages to get past the often convoluted language, one usually finds perspectives a lot more in tune with common-sense perceptions of reality.[4]

Roy Bhaskar and those who have since taken up some version of his "critical realist" approach (Bhaskar 1979, 1986, 1989, 1991, 1994a, 1994b; Collier 1990, 1994; Archer, Bhaskar, Collier, Lawson and Norrie 1998) have been trying for some years now to develop a more reasonable ontology. The resulting arguments are notoriously difficult, but it might help to set out some of his conclusions, in shamelessly abbreviated form, before continuing:

1. *Realism.* Bhaskar argues for a "transcendental realism": that is, rather than limiting reality to what can be observed by the senses, one must ask instead "what would have to be the case" in order to explain what we do experience. In particular, he seeks to explain "why are scientific experiments possible?," and also, at the same time "why are scientific experiments necessary?"

2. *Potentiality.* His conclusion: while our experiences are of events in the real world, reality is not limited to what we can experience ("the empirical"), or even, to the sum total of events that can be said to have taken place ("the actual"). Rather, Bhaskar proposes a third level ("the real"). To understand it, one must also take account of "powers"— that is, define things in part in terms of their potentials or capacities. Science largely proceeds by hypothesizing what "mechanisms" must exist in order to explain such powers, and then by looking for them. The search is probably endless, because there are always deeper and more fundamental levels (i.e., from atoms to electrons, electrons to quarks, and so on), but the fact that there's no end to the pursuit does not mean reality doesn't exist; rather, it simply means one will never to be able to understand it completely.

3. *Freedom.* Reality can be divided into emergent stratum: just as chemistry presupposes but cannot be entirely reduced to physics, so biology presupposes but cannot be reduced to chemistry, or the human

sciences to biology. Different sorts of mechanisms are operating on each. Each, furthermore, achieves a certain autonomy from those below; it would be impossible even to talk about human freedom were this not the case, since our actions would simply be determined by chemical or biological processes.

4. *Open Systems.* Another element of indeterminacy comes from the fact that real-world events occur in "open systems"; that is, there are always different sorts of mechanisms, derived from different emergent strata of reality, at play in any one of them. As a result, one can never predict precisely how any real-world event will turn out. This is why scientific experiments are necessary: experiment are ways of creating temporary "closed systems" in which the effects of all other mechanisms are, as far as possible, nullified, so that one can actually examine a single mechanism in action.

5. *Tendencies.* As a result, it is better not to refer to unbreakable scientific "laws" but rather of "tendencies," which interact in unpredictable ways. Of course, the higher the emergent strata one is dealing with, the less predictable things become, the involvement of human beings of course being the most unpredictable factor of all.[5]

For our purposes, the details are not as important as the overall thrust: that the Heraclitean position, which looks at things in terms of their dynamic potentials, is not a matter of abandoning science but is, rather, the only hope of giving science a solid ontological basis. But it also means that in order to do so, those who wish to make claims to science will have to abandon some of their most ambitious—one is tempted to say, totalitarian, paranoid—dreams of absolute or total knowledge, and accept a certain degree of humility about what it is possible to know. Reality is what one can never know completely. If an object is real, any description we make of it will necessarily be partial and incomplete. That is, indeed, how we can tell it is real. The only things we can hope to know perfectly are ones that exist entirely in our imaginations.

What is true of natural science is all the more true of social science. While Bhaskar has acquired a reputation mainly as a philosopher of science, his ultimate interest is social; he is trying to come up with the philosophical ground for a theory of human emancipation, a way of squaring scientific knowledge with the idea of human freedom. Here, too, the ultimate message is one of humility: Critical Realists hold that it *is* possible to preserve the notion of a social reality and, therefore, of a science able to make true statements about it—but only if one abandons the sort of positivist number-crunching that passes for science among most current sociologists or economists, and gives up on the idea that social science will ever be able to establish predictive laws.

A last word on the Heracleitian perspective before passing on to Marx. This concerns the notion of materialism. In the Marxist tradition as elsewhere, the assumption has usually been that a materialist analysis is one that privileges certain spheres over others. There are material infrastructures and ideological superstructures; the production of food, shelter, or machine tools is considered more fundamentally material than the production of sermons or soap operas or zoning laws. This is either because they answer more fundamental, or immediate, human needs; or else, because (as with law, religion, art, even the state) they are concerned with the production of abstractions. But it has always seemed to me that to treat law, or religion, as "about" abstractions is to define them very much as they define themselves. If one were to insist on seeing all such spheres primarily as domains of human action, it quickly becomes obvious that just as much as the production of food requires thinking, art and literature are really a set of material processes. Literature, from this kind of materialist perspective, would no longer be so much about "texts" (usually thought of as abstractions that can then seem to float apart from time or space) but about the writing and reading of them. This is obviously in every way material: actual, flesh-and-blood people have to write them, they have to have the leisure and resources, they need pens or typewriters or computers, there are practical constraints of every sort entailed in the circulation of literature, and so on.

This might seem a weak, compromised version of "materialism," but if applied consistently, it would really be quite radical. Something of the power of the approach might be judged by how much it tends to annoy people. Most scholars consider acknowledgment of the material medium of their production as somehow impertinent. Even a discipline like anthropology tends to present itself as floating over material realities, except, perhaps, when describing the immediate experience of fieldwork; certainly it would be considered rude to point out, while discussing the merits of an anthropological monograph, that it was written by an author who was well aware that almost everyone who would eventually be reading it would be doing so not because they chose to but because some professor forced them to, or, that financial constraints in the academic publishing industry ensured that it could not exceed 300 pages. But obviously all this is relevant to the kind of books we write. At any rate, this is the sort of materialism I'll be adopting in this book: one that sees society as arising from creative action, but creative action as something that can never be separated from its concrete, material medium.

Marx's theory of value

The first thing one should probably say about Marx's labor theory of value is that it's not the same as David Ricardo's. People often confuse them. Ricardo argued that the value of a commodity in a market system can be calculated in terms of the "man-hours" that went into making it, and therefore it should be theoretically possible to calculate precisely how many people worked how long in the process of making it (and, presumably, making the raw materials, shipping them from place to place, and so on.) In fact, Marx felt Ricardo's approach was inadequate. What makes capitalism unique, he argued, is that it is the only system in which labor—a human being's capacity to transform the world, their powers of physical and mental creativity— can itself be bought and sold. After all, when an employer hires workers, he does not usually pay them by the task completed: he pays them by the hour, thus purchasing their ability to do whatever he tells them to do during that period of time.[6] Hence, in a wage-labor economy, in which most people have to sell their capacity to work in this way, one can make calculations that would be impossible in a non-capitalist society: that is, look at the amount of labor invested in a given object as a specific *proportion* of the total amount of labor in the system as a whole. This is its value.[7]

The concept makes much better sense if one bears in mind that Marx's theory of value was not meant to be a theory of prices. Marx was not particularly interested in coming up with a model that would predict price fluctuations, understand pricing mechanisms, and so on. Almost all other economists have been, since they are ultimately trying to write something that would be of use to those operating within a market system. Marx was writing something that would be of use for those trying to overthrow such a system. Therefore, he by no means assumed that price paid for something was an accurate reflection of its worth. It might be better, then, to think of the word "value" as meaning something more like "importance." Imagine a pie chart, representing the U.S. economy. If one were to determine that the U.S. economy devotes, say, 19 percent of its GDP to health care, 16 percent to the auto industry, 7 percent to TV and Hollywood, and .2 percent to the fine arts, one can say this is a measure of how important these areas are to us as a society. Marx is proposing we simply substitute labor as a better measure: if Americans spend 7 percent of their creative energies in a given year producing automobiles, this is the ultimate measure of how important it is to us to have cars. One can then extend the argument: if Americans have spent, say, .000000000007 percent or some similarly infinitesimal proportion of their creative energies in a given year on *this* car, then that represents its value. This is basically Marx's argument, except that he was speaking of a total market system, which would by now go beyond any particular national economy to include the world.

As a first approximation then, one might say that the value a given product—or, for that matter, institution—has is the proportion of a society's creative energy it sinks into producing and maintaining it. If an objective measure is possible, it would have to be something like this. But obviously this can never be a *precise* measure. "Creative energies," however they're defined, are not the sort of thing that can be quantified.[8] The only reason Marx felt one could make such calculations—however approximate—within a capitalist system was because of the existence of a market in labor. For labor—in effect, human capacities for action, since what you are selling to your boss is your ability to work—to be bought and sold, there had to be a system for calculating its price. This in turn meant an elaborate cultural apparatus involving such things as time cards, clock-punching, and weekly or biweekly paychecks, not to mention recognized standards about the pace and intensity of labor expected of any particular task (people are rarely, even in the most exploitative conditions, expected to work to the absolute limits of their physical and mental capacities), which enables Marx to refer to "socially necessary labor time." There are cultural standards, then, by which labor can be reduced to units of time, which can then be counted, added, and compared to one another. It is important to stress the apparatus through which this is done is at the same time material and symbolic: there have to be real, physical clocks to punch, but also, symbolic media of representation, such as money and hours.

Of course, even where most people are wage laborers, it's not as if all creativity is on the market. Even in our own market-ridden society there are all sorts of domains—ranging from housework to hobbies, political action, personal projects of any sort—where is no such homogenizing apparatus. But it is probably no coincidence that it's precisely here where one hears about "values" in the plural sense: family values, religious virtues, the aesthetic values of art, and so on. Where there is no single system of value, one is left with a whole series of heterogeneous, disparate ones.

What, then, does one do where there is no market in labor at all, or none that is especially important? Does the same thing happen? That is, is it possible to apply anything like Marx's value analysis to the vast majority of human societies—or to any one that existed prior to the eighteenth century? For anthropologists (or for that matter, those who would like to think about an alternative to capitalism) this is obviously one of the most important questions.

the "praxiological approach"

It would have been easier if Marx had given us more of a clue in his own writings. The closest Marx himself ever came to writing general social theory was in some of his earliest theoretical writings: his *Theses on Feuerbach, 1844 Manuscripts,* and especially *The German Ideology,* co-written with Engels between 1845 and 1846. This was the period when Marx was living in Paris and making a broad accounting with the radical philosophical circles in which he'd spent his intellectual youth in Germany. In doing so, these works map out a synthesis of two very different intellectual traditions: the German idealism of the Hegelian school, and the materialism of the French Enlightenment. The advantage of Hegel's dialectical approach to history, Marx felt, was that it was inherently dynamic; rather than starting from some fixed notion of what a human being, or the physical world, is like, it was the story of how humanity effectively created itself through interacting with the world around it. It was, in effect, an attempt to see what the history would look like if one assumed from the start that Heraclitus had been right. Not only was it about action: ultimately, what Hegel's philosophy was about was the history of how humanity becomes fully self-conscious through its own actions; it was its final achievement of true self-understanding (which Hegel, modestly, believed to have been achieved in himself) which laid open the possibility of human freedom. The problem was that neither the conservative Hegel nor the radical Young Hegelians (who argued the process had not been completed, and more drastic measures, such as an attack on religion, were required) started from real, flesh-and-blood human beings. Instead, their active subjects were always abstractions like "Mind," "Reason," "Spirit," "Humanity," or "the Nation." Marx proposed a materialist alternative. But neither was Marx especially happy with the materialism of his day, which was mainly a product of French Enlightenment philosophers like Helvetius. The problem with "all previous materialism," he noted in his *Theses on Feuerbach,* is that it did not see human beings as driven by self-conscious projects at all. It saw them as virtually passive: driven by a fixed set of basic, physical needs, simply "adapting" to their environment in such a way as to best satisfy them. What he proposed, instead, was a synthesis: in which human beings are seen as active, intentional, imaginative creatures, but at the same time, physical ones that exist in the real world. That (as he put it elsewhere) "men" make their own histories, but not under conditions of their own choosing.

It's certainly true that Marx's work often seems to pull in several different directions at once. Take for example his famous description of the four "moments" in *The German Ideology* in which he and Engels set out the basic material realities that have to be taken into account before one can talk about humans to be able to "make history" (1846 [1970:48–51]). What separates humans from animals is that humans *produce* their means of livelihood. He also notes that human beings, in order to exist, not only (1) need to produce basic requirements, like food and shelter; but that (2) the act of producing in order to meet such needs will always create new needs; that (3) in order to continue to exist human beings need to produce other human beings, which entails procreation, child-rearing, the family, etc., and that (4) since humans never produce any of these things in isolation, every society must also have relations of cooperation. It is only after this has been taken into account,

Marx notes, that one can begin to talk about "consciousness," which, he emphasizes, "here makes its appearance in the form of agitated layers of air, sounds, in short, of language" (1846:50–51), which in turn arises from people's needs to talk to each other rather than independently in the minds of individual human beings.

This certainly sounds like it's moving towards the sort of division between material infrastructure and ideological superstructure laid out, most explicitly, in his preface to *A Contribution to the Critique of Political Economy* (1859). But this also moves away from Marx's central inspiration: which is that consciousness is not the icing on the cake of production, but rather, fundamental to production itself. For Marx, what sets humans apart from animals was precisely that humans produce things in a *self-conscious* manner. What makes us human is not so much "reason" (at least in the modern, problem-solving sense) as imagination:

> We presuppose labour in a form that stamps it as exclusively human. A spider conducts operations that resemble those of a weaver, and a bee puts to shame many an architect in the construction of her cells. But what distinguishes the worst architect from the best of bees is this, that the architect raises his structure in imagination before he erects it in reality. (*Capital* I: 178)

Humans envision what they would like to have before they make it; as a result, we can also imagine alternatives. Human intelligence is thus inherently critical, which, in turn, is crucial to Marx's conception of history because this which for the possibility of revolution.

If one turns back to the original four moments with this in mind, however, one has the basis (with, perhaps, a tiny a bit of refinement and rearrangement) for a very powerful theory of action (Turner 1984:11; Fajans 1993:3). The result would look something like this. In any society, one might say, production entails:

1. An effort to fulfill perceived needs on the part of the producer (these, as Marx notes, must always include basic necessities like food and shelter, but are never limited to this.). It also includes the key insight that "objects" exist in two senses: not just as physical objects that actually exist in the world, but also, insofar as they are present in someone's (some subject's) consciousness, as objects of that subject's action in some sense or another—even if this is only in the minimal sense of active observation and study. (This is what he argued Feuerbach's materialism overlooked.)
2. Humans being social creatures, this also means producing a system of social relations (families, clans, guilds, secret societies, government

ministries, etc.,) within which people coordinate their productive actions with one another. In part this also means that production also entails

3. producing the producer as a specific sort of person (seamstress, harem eunuch, movie star, etc.). In cooperating with others, a person defines herself in a certain way—this can be referred to as the "reflexive" element in action. It also usually means being ascribed certain sorts of power or agency, or actually acquiring them.[9]
4. The process is always open-ended, producing new needs as a result of (1), (2) and (3) and thus bearing within it the potential for its own transformation.

So we start with a notion of intentional action, productive action aimed at a certain goal. This action produces social relations and in doing so transforms the producers themselves. Stated this way, the model seems straightforward enough. There's no element in it that's not pretty self-evident. But to apply it consistently, one would have to rethink all sorts of accepted elements of social theory. Take for example the notion of "social structure." If one starts from this broad notion of production, "social structures"—like any other sort of structure—are really just patterns of action. But they are very complicated patterns: they not only coordinate all sorts of intentional human action, they are also the means through which actors are continually redefining and even remaking themselves at the same time as they are reproducing (and also inevitably, changing) the larger context through which all this takes place. Even for an outside observer, it is not easy to keep track of all of this. There are certain points—for example, the precise boundaries between individual and collective creativity—that we can probably never fully understand. From inside the system, it is well nigh impossible.

In fact, individual actors tend to be aware of only the first of the four moments (the specific thing they are making or doing, the specific end they have in mind)[10]; it is much harder to keep track of the other three. One could well argue that all the great problems of social theory emerge from this single difficulty—whether it be Durkheim's famous observation that even though "society" is just a collection of individuals, every one of those individuals sees it as an alien force constraining them, or Marx's, about the way in which our own creations come to seem alien entities with power over us (cf. Taussig 1993).

Imagination, then, may be essential to the nature of productive action, but imagination also has its limits. Or, to put it another way, human action is self-conscious by nature, but it is never entirely so.

One might say there are two orders of critical theory. The first simply serves to demonstrate that our normal way of looking at the world—or of some phenomena within it—is flawed: incomplete or mistaken, and to explain how things really work. The second, more powerful not only explains how things actually work, but does so in such a way as to account for why people did not perceive it that way to begin with. Marxist approaches hold out the promise of doing precisely that.[11] But if one considers the overall thrust of Marx's writings, from his earlier "philosophical" works to the theory of fetishism in *Capital,* one finds that what he produced was less a theory of false consciousness than a theory of *partial* consciousness:[12] one in which actors find it almost impossible to distinguish their own particular vantage on a situation from the overall structure of the situation itself. Before setting it out, though, I must make a brief detour on the problem of structure.

dynamic structures

Anthropological ideas of structure, of course, largely came out of Saussurean linguistics. I have already described Saussure's conception of language as a system of signs that exists in a state of equilibrium, each element contributing to the definition of the others. Applying this to anthropology created notorious dilemmas. Where, exactly, was this abstract system to be found? How was one to relate *langue* and *parole,* synchrony and diachrony, the abstract system, seen as existing outside of time, and the real events—people speaking, writing, and so on, none of them fully aware of the principles that guide their own practice, even though their practice is the only way we have of getting at those principles in the first place? By now it should be apparent that this is just another variation of the same Parmenidean problem: how does one relate the models to reality?

Anthropological wisdom to the contrary, however, Saussurean structuralism was never the only one around. There is a Heraclitean alternative: the structuralism developed by French psychologist Jean Piaget (see Piaget 1970; Turner 1973)—which starts from action, and views "structure" as the coordination of activity.[13]

Anthropologists, however, have rarely found much use for Piaget's structuralism. When they mention it at all, it's usually to dismiss it as lacking in cultural depth and sensitivity.[14] Applied to Piaget's own writings, this is certainly true. Saussure was interested in the different ways different languages define reality; Piaget, in the intellectual development of children. It's not hard to see why anthropologists were drawn to one and not the other. But it also seems to me the accusation is somewhat self-fulfilling. After all, if Piagetian models lack cultural depth, it's in part because anthropologists have never seen fit to develop them.

Piaget's specific arguments about stages of child development are now considered outmoded; what's important here, though, are not the particulars, but the overall approach. Above all his premise: that "it is always and everywhere the case that elementary forms of intelligence originate from action."[15] Children interact with their environment; they develop basic schemas of action (grabbing, pulling, etc.), and ways of coordinating them. Next, children start to develop more complex and generalized modes of thought through a process Piaget calls "reflexive abstraction," in which they begin to understand the logical principles immanent in their own interaction with the world, and these same schemes of coordination—which themselves, in turn, become more refined and more effective as a result. (This allows for further processes of reflexive abstraction, and so on.) There's no need here to launch into details, but there are a few points that will be crucial to bear in mind. The first is that Piaget insists that the basis of any system of knowledge is always a set of practices: Mathematics, for example, is not derived from the "idea of number" but from the practice of counting. The abstract categories, however important, never come first. The second, that a structure can always be seen as a set of transformations, based on certain invariant principles (this can be as simple as a matter of moving pieces across a board, which stays the same): the defining feature of such transformations being that they are reversible (the pieces can be moved back again).

The crucial thing point is that what we call structure is not something that exists prior to action. Ultimately, "structure" is identical with the process of its own construction. Complex abstract systems are simply the way actors come to understand the logic of their own interactions with the world. It's also crucial to bear in mind that the process of "reflexive abstraction" is open-ended. Piaget does not believe that development is simply a matter of achieving a certain level and then stopping; there are always new and more complex levels one could generate. Here Piaget invokes the German mathematician Kurt Gödel, who managed to show that no logical system (such as, say, mathematics) could demonstrate its own internal consistency; in order to do so, one has to generate a more sophisticated, higher level that presumes it. Since that level will no be able to demonstrate its own principles either, one then has to go on to generate another level after that, and so on ad infinitum.

> Gödel showed that the construction of a demonstrably consistent . . . theory requires not simply an "analysis" of its "presuppositions," but the construction of the next "higher" theory! Previously, it was possible to view theories as layers of a pyramid, each resting on the one below, the theory at ground level being the most secure because constituted by the simplest means, and the whole firmly poised on a self-sufficient base. Now, however, "simplicity" becomes a sign of weakness and the "fastening" of any story in the edifice of human knowledge calls for the construction of the next higher story. To revert

our earlier image, the pyramid of knowledge no longer rests on foundations but hangs on its vertex, and ideal point never reached, and, more curious, constantly rising! (Piaget 1970:34)

Just as with Bhaskar's conception of scientific inquiry, perfectly content to discover ever more basic levels of reality without ever hitting bedrock, we are dealing with an open-ended system. One can always construct a more sophisticated point of view.

This might seem all very abstract, but it suggests new ways to look at any number of long-standing problems in anthropology. Take, for example, Pierre Bourdieu's work on habitus (1979, etc.). Bourdieu has long drawn attention to the fact—always a matter of frustration to anthropologists—that a truly artful social actor is almost guaranteed not to be able to offer a clear explanation of the principles underlying her own artistry. According to the Gödelian/Piagetian perspective, it's easy to see why this should be. The logical level on which one is operating is always at least one level higher than that which one can explain or understand—what the Russian psychologist Vygotsky (1978:79–91) referred to as the "proximal level" of development.[16] In fact, one could argue this must necessarily be the case, since (explanation itself being a form of action) in order to explain or understand one's actions fully, one has to generate a more sophisticated ("stronger," more encompassing) level of operations, whose principles, in turn, one would not be fully able to explain; and in order to explain that one, yet another; and so on without end.

Or consider, again, the phenomenon of rites of passage, a classic issue in anthropology since Arnold Van Gennep's essay of 1909. Van Gennep argued that all such rituals, across the world, always contain at least three stages. They begin with rites of separation, in which, say, a boy undergoing initiation is separated from his old identity, as a child, and end with rites of reintegration, in which he is reintegrated into the social order in his new identity, as a man. The liminal stage is the one that falls in between, when the boy is, as it were, suspended between identities, not quite one thing, not quite another. As Victor Turner noted (1967), this stage has a tendency to take on some very strange, "anti-structural" qualities: those who pass through it are at once sacred and polluting, creative and destructive, divine and monstrous, and ultimately beyond anything that can be explained by the order of normal life. But as Terence Turner has observed (1977; see 1993:22–26): according to the Piagetian approach, this is, again, much as should be. Because here too there is a difference of logical levels. To maintain a system of classification—i.e., one that divides males into children, adolescents, adults, and so on—requires a certain level of logical operations; it is, like any set of categories, the "other side" of a set of activities. To operate on the level where you can transform one category into the other implies entering into a higher, encompassing level; or, to put it another way, with powers of a fundamentally different nature than those which operate in ordinary life, in which people "are" one thing or another.[17] Here too, the highest level of operations is one that cannot be represented or fully accounted for—at least in social terms. Representing such powers becomes a problem. Everyday categories do not apply. Hence, the tendency to resort to mystery, paradox, unknowability, or systematic inversions of normal ways of doing things—a "world turned upside down."

It's easy to see how this perspective might have all sorts of important implications. Most Durkheimian ritual analyses turn, in one way or another, on the concept of "the sacred," usually seen a point of transformation or metamorphosis that stands apart from profane existence, and that, for a Durkheimian, is the point where the individual comes into contact with the power of society itself—society being for Durkheim an emergent reality of its own, standing beyond and constraining the individual. As I have already remarked, the notion ultimately has much in common with Marx's conception of alienation (which after all, also set off from a study of religion), the most dramatic difference between the two being one of attitude: unlike Marx, Durkheim didn't see anything particularly wrong with the fact that society seemed to impose itself on individuals as an alien force, any more than he had any problem with the existence of social hierarchies. Marx, who objected to both, saw them as two sides of the same coin. To understand fully the parallels between Marx and Piaget, however, one must look a little more closely at Piaget's notion of egocentrism.

egocentrism and partial consciousness

One of Piaget's more remarkable achievements was to take a fact that almost anyone knows—that children tend to see themselves as the center of the universe—and make it the basis for a systematic theory of intellectual and moral development. Egocentrism, according to Piaget, is a matter of assuming one's own, subjective perspective on the world is identical with the nature of the world itself. Development, in turn, becomes a matter of internalizing the fact that other ones are possible; or, to put it a bit more technically, creating structures which are really the coordination of different possible perspectives. Very young children, for example, do not understand that objects continue to exist when they are no longer looking at them. If a ball rolls out of sight, it is simply gone. To understand that it is still there is to understand first of all that there are other angles from which one might be looking at it, from which one would still be able to see it. In older children, egocentrism might mean anything from a child's inability to imagine that others might not understand what she's telling them, to the difficulty (which often endures surprisingly late in life) in realizing that if I have a brother named Robert, then Robert also has a brother, who is me.

Egocentrism, then, involves first and foremost an inability to see things from other points of view. Even if it's a matter of understanding the continual existence of objects, one is aware of them through potential perspectives: when one looks at a car, or a duck, or a mountain, the fact that there are other sides to it (other perspectives from which one could be looking at it) becomes internalized into the very nature of what one is perceiving. It would simply not look the same otherwise. Hence, for Piaget, achieving maturity is a matter of "decentering" oneself: of being able to see one's own interests or perspective as simply one part of a much larger totality not intrinsically more important than any other.

In matters social, however, one clearly cannot do this all the time. It is one thing bearing in mind, when one looks at a house, that it has more than one side to it; quite another to be continually aware of how a family must seem to every member of it, or how each member of a group of people working on some common project would see what was going on. In fact, human beings are notoriously incapable of doing so on a consistent basis. Here again, there appears to be a very concrete limit to the human imagination.

Of course, the more complex the social situation, the more difficult such imaginative feats become. Which brings us back to the original point derived from Marx: that it is almost impossible for someone engaged in a project of action, in shaping the world in some way, to understand fully how their actions simultaneously contribute to (a) re-creating the social system in which they are doing so (even if this is something so simple as a family or office), and thus (b) reflexively reshaping and redefining their own selves. In fact, according to Turner, it's really the same point: because in order to understand this fully, one would have to be able to coordinate the subjective points of view of everyone involved—to see how they all fit together (or, in the case of conflict, don't), and so on. That aspect which falls outside our comprehension, even though it is a product of our own actions, tends to seem something which stands alien, apart from us, something that constrains and controls us rather than the other way around. In early works like *The German Ideology*, Marx emphasized the paradoxical nature of the division of labor in modern society: that while it created a genuine common interest on the level of society as it a whole, since people need one another in order to survive, it does so by confining everyone to such limited interests and perspectives within it that none were really able to perceive it. It was precisely the fact that people are confined to these partial perspectives that, Marx argued, gave rise to alienation: the "consolidation of what we ourselves produce into an objective power above us," the fact that our powers appear to us in strange, external forms (Ollman 1971). Commodity fetishism is really just another version of the same thing. It is the result, above all, of the fact that the market creates a vast rupture between the factories in which commodities are produced, and the private homes in which most are finally consumed. If a commodity—a futon, a video cassette, a box of talcum powder—fulfills a human need, it is because human beings have intentionally designed it in order to do so; they have taken raw materials and, by adding their strength and intelligence, shaped it to fulfill those needs. The object, then, embodies human intentions. This is why consumers want to buy it. But because of the peculiar, anonymous nature of a market system, that whole history becomes invisible from the consumer's point of view. From her perspective, then, it looks as if the value of the object—embodied in its ability to satisfy her wants—is an aspect of the product itself. All those intentions seem to be absorbed into the physical form of the object itself, this being all that she can see. In other words, she too is confusing her own (partial, subjective) perspective with the (total, objective) nature of the situation itself, and as a result, seeing objects as having human powers and properties. This is precisely the sort of thing—the attribution of subjective qualities to objects—that Piaget argues is typical of childhood egocentrism as well (cf. Turner and Fajans 1988).[18]

The same logic is reproduced on every level of commercial life, where everyone tends to speak of products and money as propelling themselves along, selling themselves, flooding markets or fleeing from adverse investment climates; because, from their own particular, partial, interested perspective, all this might as well be true.

Which allows me to make a final observation about some of the most common objections to a Piagetian approach.

Anthropologists tend to be extremely suspicious of any general theory that even holds out the potential of arguing that certain people are more sane, more intelligent, or more rational than others. They are very right to be suspicious. It does seem that the moment such models are given any intellectual legitimacy, they are immediately snatched up by racists and chauvinists of one kind or another and used to support the most obnoxious political positions. The Piagetian case was no exception: one team of researchers, for example, administered Piagetian tests to Arunda-speakers in Australia, as a result of which they concluded that Arunda adults had not achieved "operational levels" of intelligence (see Piaget 1970:117–19). The result was another attempt to revive the notion, largely abandoned since the days Levy-Bruhl, of "primitive mentality" on Piagetian grounds (e.g., Hallpike 1979). Of course, for the anthropologist, the idea of the Arunda being simple-minded is pretty startling: after all, these are the same people otherwise famous for maintaining one of the most complicated kinship systems known to anthropological science—including an eight-section prescriptive marriage system so intricate it took Western scholars decades to unravel it. To argue that such people are incapable of sophisticated thought seems obviously ridiculous: even if, like people everywhere, they are unlikely to fully grasp the principles underlying their own most sophisticated forms of action.

Even when things are not this blatantly ethnocentric, the normal model for a mature, fully evolved individual is usually pretty culturally specific. It's much the same as the model "Westerner." One is, at least implicitly, thinking of some fortyish white guy in a suit, perhaps a banker or a stockbroker. The advantage of a Marxist take on Piaget of course is that said banker or stockbroker is no longer the model of someone who gets it right but of someone who gets it wrong: as he flips through the business section reading how gold is doing this and pork bellies doing that, he is engaging in the very paradigm of adult egocentrism. An Arunda speaker, one suspects, would be much less likely to be quite so naive.

Das Kapital as symbolic analysis

The key to a broader Marxian theory of value, though, lies most of all in Marx's analysis of money.

Economists of Marx's day, like economists now, tended to speak of money as a "measure" and a "medium" of value. It is a measure because one can use it to compare the value of different things: e.g., to say that one steak-frites is worth the same as five loaves of bread. In this capacity, the money can be a complete abstraction, there's no need for physical coins or bills to play a part at all. When money acts as a medium of exchange—that is, to actually buy bread or pay for an order of steak—this is of course no longer true. In either case, money is simply a tool. Marx's innovation was to draw attention to a third aspect of money, what might be called its reflexive moment: money as a value in itself. A tool facilitates action; it is a means to an end. From the perspective of people actually engaged in many financial transactions, Marx observes, money *is* the end. It becomes the very embodiment of value, the ultimate object of desire.

One might think of this as the flip-side of commodity fetishism. When workers agree to work for wages, they place themselves in a position in which for them, money is the end of the whole process. They perform their creative, productive actions in order to get paid. But for Marx this is of special significance, because the value that the money represents is, in the last analysis, that of labor itself.[19]

What's happening here actually goes well beyond the fetishization of commodities. And it is even more fundamental to the nature of capitalism. What money measures and mediates, according to Marx, is ultimately the importance of certain forms of human action. In money, workers see the meaning or importance of their own creative energies, their own capacity to act, and by acting to transform the world, reflected back at them. Money represents the ultimate social significance of their actions, the means by which it is integrated in a total (market) system. But it can do so because it is also the *object* of their actions; that's why they are working: in order to receive a paycheck at the end of the week. Hence, it is a representation that plays a necessary role in bringing into being the very thing it represents.

Readers coming to *Capital* expecting to read the work of a "material determinist" are often rather surprised to discover that the book starts out with what can only be called a series of detailed symbolic analyses: of commodities, money, and fetishism. But what sort of theory of symbolism, exactly, is Marx working with? The best way to think about it, perhaps, is to say that, like his theory of productive action, it combines elements of two traditions: one that we would now see as essentially German, the other French. One might call them theories of meaning, and theories of signification. The first, which had its roots in Hegel but also gave rise to hermeneutics, sees meaning as essentially identical with intentionality. The meaning of a statement is what the speaker meant to say. One reads a text in order to understand the author's intent; it is this intentionality that unifies the parts of the text into a coherent whole. Hermeneutics first developed in biblical scholarship, where this would have to be true if one assumes (as biblical scholars did) that what the Bible ultimately conveys is the will of God. "Signification"—which later found its exponent in Ferdinand de Saussure—is based on a notion of contrast, the signification of a term being the way it is different from the other terms in a set (slicing the pie of reality again). What Marx is talking about combines elements of both. Money has meaning for the actors, then, because it sums up their intentions (or, the importance of their intentional actions, which comes down to pretty much the same thing). However, it can do so only by integrating them into a contrastive totality, the market, since it is only by means of money that my individual actions and capacities become integrated as a proportion of the totality of everyone's (see Turner 1979c:20–21).

As a first approximation:

> Money is a concrete token of value. Value is the way in which an individual actor's actions take on meaning, for the actor herself, by being incorporated into a larger social whole.

Obviously, Marx was no more drawing on the hermeneutic tradition itself than he was the Saussurean; his approach goes back, instead, to Hegel, who also insists on examining actions in terms of how they are integrated into larger "concrete totalities." Any particular action, or process, becomes mean-ingful (in Hegelian language, takes on "concrete, specific form") only by being integrated into some larger system of action; just as the parts of a watch, say, are coordinated in their motion by the overall structure of the whole (thus making the parts mere "abstract content," and the watch, "concrete form"). Of course, there is no end to how long one can continue this sort of analysis: the watch itself might well be integrated into some larger process, say, a race, whereby it too becomes merely the abstract content to a larger concrete form, and so on. So here too, the system is ultimately open-ended.

marketless societies

At this point, armed with this Marxian view of structure, we can once again return to our original question: how to apply a Marxian theory of value to societies without a market.

What Turner suggests (1984) is that most Marxist anthropologists have ended up creating a slightly different version of Substantivism. That is, they too have simply examined the "way in which a society materially provisions itself," except that where Polanyi's followers mainly examined different modes of exchange, Marxists shifted the focus to production. Starting from value on the other hand would mean asking: is material production of this sort really what is most important to this social system? If we limit ourselves to stateless societies—the ones that have up until now proved the least amenable to Marxist styles of analysis—it quickly becomes obvious that the sort of activities *we* would define as economic, particularly subsistence ac-tivity, are by no means that on which they spend the greater part of their time, or "creative energies" however defined (Turner 1979c; 1984). Most dedicate far more to what, broadly speaking, could be called socialization, at least if one defines the latter to include not only primary child care but all those other actions that go into shaping human beings. This would make so-cialization a continual process that does not simply stop with adolescence, or whatever arbitrary cut off point most people implicitly impose: over the course of one's life, people are almost always engaged in a constant process of changing their social position, roles and statuses, and doing so having to learn how to behave in them. Life is thus a constant educational process.

Myself, I suspect one of the main reason for this neglect is simple sexism. Primary child care is almost everywhere seen as quintessential woman's work; analysts tend to see socialization on the whole as being too close to nurture and too distant from the kind of strenuous and dramatic muscular activity—burly men hammering away at glowing iron, sparks flying every-where—the term "production" brings most readily to mind. The model one would start from would have to be essentially feminine. But then, this only goes to underline that the most fundamental inequality in such societies is indeed that based on gender—something that in theory we already knew.

How does one then go on to analyze this kind of production? Well, in fact, the materials already exist. There is a huge, voluminous anthropological literature on the study of kinship. True, it does not start off from the same premises but it certainly provides plenty material from which to work. And even a more traditional Marxist anthropologist like Eric Wolf (1983) has used the term "kinship mode of production" to describe such societies. While it is also true that Marxist anthropologists have usually insisted that kinship systems are ultimately determined by the production of material things, there's no reason one can't simply jettison this bit and keep as much as seems useful of the rest. The real point is how one would go about analyzing a kinship system, or some similar anthropological object, in the same way that Marx analyzed the market system in capitalism.

So in what way do the actions of shaping people become embodied in value-forms, that is, forms that reflect the meaning of my actions to myself in some tangible form as some object or action that I desire? And in what way does this process allow for fetishism—to people failing to recognize the degree to which they themselves are producing value—and for exploitation—a means by which some people appropriate the surplus value generated by others?

the Baining;
production and realization

A good place to start with might be Jane Fajans' work on the Baining of Papua New Guinea (1993b, 1997; Turner and Fajans 1987). The Baining, a population of taro farmers who live in scattered hamlets in the mountainous interior of East New Britain, are somewhat notorious in the anthropological literature for their almost complete lack of any elaborate social structure. Fajans describes their society as a kind of "egalitarian anarchism" because of their lack of political structures; in fact, they lack enduring social structures of almost any kind whatever. Not only are there no chiefs or "big men," but no clans, lineages, age grades, no initiation societies, ritual or exchange associations, or anything, really, that can be called a "ritual system."[20] There was a time when anthropologists used the term "simple society" as a euphemism for "primitive"; normally, the term was an obvious misnomer, but the Baining appear as close as one is likely to find to a genuinely simple society. There are domestic groups and individual kindreds, and that's about it. Perhaps as a result, Baining society also appears to be singularly lacking in mystification.

According to Fajans, Baining society is based on something very much like a labor theory of value. What distinguishes humans from animals is the fact that humans work; work, or "sweat," is considered the quintessential human activity. It is conceived largely in terms of the generation of heat: fire or "sweat" in gardening, which is in turn seen as the quintessential form of work. Hence the basic schema of action, or what Munn would call value template, is one of the application of human labor to transform nature into culture, "socialization" in the broadest sense. It's a template of *value* because the ability to do so is the main thing that brings one prestige in Baining life. While gardening work is the paradigm, raising children (literally, "feeding" them) is seen in the same terms. It is a matter of transforming infants, who are seen as relatively wild creatures when they are born, into fully formed social beings, humans whose humanity, in turn, is defined largely as a capacity for productive action. So even here, there is a sort of minimal hierarchy of spheres. Producing food is not simply a value in itself. The most prestigious act in Baining society is *giving* food, or other consumables. To be a parent, for example, is not considered so much a matter of procreation but of providing children with food (Fajans 1993b, 1997:75–78, 88–100) an attitude reinforced by the very widespread habit of fostering, which ensures that almost every household where food is cooked has at least one child to feed in it.

Food-giving takes a more communal form as well. While the Baining lack elaborate, ceremonial forms of exchange like moka, people are in the constant habit of exchanging food, betel nut, and the like on a less formal basis. If two men meet each other on the road, for example, they will almost invariably both offer each other betel nut to chew, each then taking some of the others'. Families often exchange food, here too almost always in egalitarian same-for-same transactions; for example, two neighbors will exchange equal amounts of taro with which to prepare their dinner. Hence, while giving food to children is seen as 'reproductive,' in the sense of producing production, the apparently pointless habit of continually exchanging food is a matter of the continual production of society. In the absence of enduring institutional structures which can be seen as existing apart from individual human action, "society" itself has be re-created by individuals on a day to day basis. Yet that society has to be re-created, as it is the basis for the existence of any sorts of values at all.

Even in this remarkably minimal, stripped-down version, then, one finds one key distinction that always seems to recur; what in dialectical terms is usually referred to as the distinction between "production" and "realization." Productive labor creates value mainly in potentia. This is because value is inherently contrastive; thus it can only be made into a reality ("realized") in a relatively public context, as part of some larger social whole. Among the Baining, producing food through the labor of gardening is seen as the origin of value, but that value is only "realized" when one gives some of that food to someone else. Hence the most truly prestigious act is being a good provider to children, thereby turning them into social beings; but this in turn requires the existence of society. After all, without society, the socialization of children would not be prestigious; just as without the continual socialization of children as new producers, society itself would not continue to exist.

the Kayapo:
the domestic cycle and village structure

The Baining were, as I said, a useful place to start because they lack most of the institutions we normally associated with "social structure." This is not so of the Kayapo of Brazil, the object of Turner's own researches for the last thirty years. The Kayapo are one of the Ge/Bororo societies of Central Brazil, who, when they first became known to outsiders in mid-century, were considered remarkable for combining what seemed like an extremely simple technology with an almost bewilderingly complicated social system. Their great circular villages often consisted of several hundred houses, all arranged around a central plaza, normally replete with collective men's houses and other communal buildings. While the communal structures took different forms in different Central Brazilian societies, there was invariably some form of dual organization: the village was divided into two sides of the village (most often exogamous), there were two men's houses, identical in all respects, except that one was always for some reason considered superior. The life-cycle was divided into elaborate systems of initiation grades carried out in the village center.

In any structural analysis—and this includes any analysis of social structure—the key question is how to identify one's units of analysis. Here Turner again hearkens back to the dialectical tradition,[21] in which the basic principle is that the most elementary unit of any system is the smallest one that still contains within it all the basic relations which constitute the whole. Let me explain what I mean by this. Take the example of a kinship system, of the sort normally studied by anthropologists. The minimal unit would clearly have to be a domestic unit of some sort—a family or household.[22] Families of course can take a wide variety of forms in different societies, but whether one is talking about a suburban family in Cleveland, an Iroquois longhouse, or a Nayar matrilineal stirp, there are certain things one can always expect. One can always count on there being a recognized model of what a properly constituted household should look like. And that properly constituted household will always contain within itself all of those relationships (mother-daughter, husband-wife, brother-brother, mother's brother-daughter's husband, whatever these may be) that are reworked to create the larger system of which it forms a part. The larger systems are just based on extrapolating certain of these relations and principles on a grander scale. A system of patrilineal clans, for example, is based on taking just one of those critical relations (between fathers and sons) and making it a universal principle that can then become the basis for organizations that not only regulate relations between families, but above all (by control of bridewealth, establishment of rules of exogamy, and so forth) regulate the continual process through which new families form and old ones dissolve.

This is really the same sort of relation of mutual dependence between levels that one finds in the Piagetian notion of structure: the higher, encompassing level is entirely presupposed by the lower; yet at the same time, the lower one is not viable without it—since real households are in constant flux, endlessly growing, declining, and dividing up to create new families, and it is the broader system that regulates the process. And here again one can, in principle at least, continually generate higher levels.

In the case of the Kayapo (Turner 1979b, 1980, 1984, 1985a, 1987), the domestic unit is an uxorilocal extended family, usually three generations in depth. In a properly constituted village, there could be hundreds of these, in houses arranged in a vast circle, all opening on a central village plaza that is considered the quintessential social space. The men's and women's societies that dominate the life of the plaza are divided into moieties, though in the Kayapo case these are not exogamous. Rather, a boy needs members of the opposite moiety to provide the unrelated "substitute parents" (*krabdjuo*) who will initiate him into public life by sponsoring his entry into the men's society. Boys are removed from their natal families to live in the Men's House dormitory at about the age of eight, initiated to the next grade at about fourteen, and then, on the birth of their first child, move into their wives' households. They do so as very much junior partners: a husband is at first expected to be highly subservient to his wife's parents (there are all sorts of ritualized gestures of deference and near-avoidance), during the period when he and his wife are raising their own children. At the same time they gradually move upward in the collective organizations of the village center according to the point they have reached in their own domestic cycle (age grades include "fathers of one child," "fathers of many children," etc.). There is a parallel structure for girls: girls too are initiated into a series of age grades by "substitute parents"; however, they are never detached from their natal families in nearly so radical a way, are never dormed in the village center, and, while as elders they can achieve a dominant position alongside their husbands within their own extended families, never take on a dominant role in the plaza's political life.

In what way, then, are these communal institutions constructed out of relations that exist within the domestic unit? Turner argues that relations within the family fall into two broad groups. The first, and most important, are the very hierarchical sorts of relation that exist between parents and children, and in-marrying husbands and their wives' parents in particular. All these relations are marked by similar forms of deference: the subordinate party is "ashamed" in the presence of the dominant one, is obliged to refrain from any expression or often even reference to appetites for food or sex, the dominant party can express such appetites freely as well as generally telling the other what do to. The second set are the more solidary, comfortable relations of alliance that exist between, for example, grandparents and grandchildren, boys with their mothers' brothers, or girls with their fathers' sisters.

Each of these "complementary axes of the structure of the family" is the basis of recruitment for one of the two sets of communal organizations that dominate the village center. The first are the sets of men's and women's societies I have already partly described: societies which are themselves extremely hierarchical, as well being in principle divided into two ranked moieties. One might call this the political system. The second is the framework of Kayapo ceremonial organization (1987:25–28), which temporarily merges all such divisions together in collective dances and initiations, which culminate in the giving of "beautiful names" to certain privileged children, usually accompanied by certain pieces of heirloom jewelry called *nekretch,* the only real physical tokens of wealth that exist in traditional Kayapo society. Hence the two "complementary axes of the structure of the family" become the "complementary axes of the structure of society" as well. What's more, it is indeed through these larger, encompassing institutions that the minimal units are reproduced: regulating the dispersal of the children of old families and the creation of new ones in marriage. The communal institutions, in Turner's terms, "embody" certain aspects of the minimal units at the same time as they also serve as the necessary means for those units' continual reproduction.

The crucial thing here is that these two "axes" also correspond to the two key values of Kayapo society. Turner refers to them as "dominance" and "beauty" The first is not actually named in Kayapo, but it's exemplified in the sort of authority exerted by a father-in-law over his deferential sons-in-law, as well as that same sort of authority writ large within the age-graded institutions of the village center. The Kayapo notion of "beauty," on the other hand, implies "perfection, completion, and finesse";[23] it is evinced most of all in the harmony of grand ceremonial that unites an entire Kayapo community, of which the giving of "beautiful names" is perhaps the exemplary form. In the communal sphere, these two are combined in certain forms of public performance. These are, in ascending order of prestige, a kind of mournful keening performed by elder women at public events, the formal oratory with which senior men harangue the community on matters of collective import, and most all, a form of oratorical chanting, called *ben,*

whose use is limited to chiefs.[24] These represent the pinnacles of social value
in Kayapo society because they are seen as combining completely uninhib-
ited self-expression (i.e., a complete lack of deference, hence, untrammeled
dominance) with the consummate mastery and fullness of style that is the
epitome of "beauty."

Now, all this might seem a far cry from the analysis of factory production
in Marx's *Capital.* But Turner argues (1984) that one can, in fact, carry out
a similar value analysis because there is, indeed, a cultural system by which
productive labor is divided up according to standardized units of time. This
is the domestic cycle. One such cycle suffices to turn children into mar-
riageable adults (i.e., to produce labor power, the capacity to reproduce the
family), a second, to turn the former subordinated couple into the dominant
heads of their own extended family. The critical thing, however, is that in
that second cycle, the actual labor of socialization is no longer carried out by
the couple themselves. Instead, it is their daughters' and daughters' husbands' work that effectively propels them forward into their new status.[25]
Hence, their labor produces, in effect, a surplus. The surplus, however, is not
appropriated on the domestic level—or, better to say, not primarily so—but
on the level of the society as a whole. A male elder, for instance, can behave
in a dominant fashion in his own household; but even if he has no daughters of his own and hence can never become the head of an extended family
household, the collective labors of the younger generation nonetheless pro-
pel him through the age grades to the point where he can take on the role
of an elder in public life, and accede to the most eminent tokens of value in
Kayapo society.

Value, then, is realized mainly in the public, communal sphere, in the
forms of concrete circulating media of value—in part, the ceremonial valuables and roles mentioned above but mainly in the forms of access to the
most prestigious forms of verbal performance in public (ritual and especially
political) life: keening, formal oratory, chiefly chanting. These latter forms
are refractions of the most basic forms of value created in the domestic
sphere, at the same time as they are realized largely within institutions that
are modeled on the key relations through which those forms of value are created. They are also realized in a distinctly unequal fashion; and that inequality is a direct result of the effective appropriation by some of the
products of others' labor.

The overall picture here is not all that entirely different than the sort of
thing proposed by Dumont and his disciples. We have the same hierarchical
arrangement of spheres, the same paired set of key values, one primarily concerned with individual assertion, the other, more encompassingly social (so
power and purity in Dumont's Hinduism, honor and *baraka* among Jamous'
Berbers, and so forth.) The same can be said of Fred Myers' analysis of the

values of "relatedness" and "differentiation" among the Pintupi (1986), which is inspired mainly by Turner, but draws on certain Dumontian themes as well. The most obvious differences between Turner and Dumont though are the infinitely more sophisticated theoretical apparatus Turner provides, and the fact that, coming out of the Marxian rather than Durkheimian tradition, Turner does not assume that alienation and hierarchy are simply natural and inevitable features of human life.

tokens of value

Now, treating a form of chiefly chanting as a "medium of value" might seem to be stretching the analogy with Marx beyond all reason. What does a genre of public performance really have in common with a dollar bill? If one examines the matter more closely, one finds they have quite a number of things in common. Here is a list of the most important qualities shared by all such "concrete media of circulation" in Turner's terms:

1. they are *measures of value,* as they serve to mark a contrast between greater or lesser degrees of dominance, beauty, honor, prestige, or whatever the particular valued quality may be. This measurement can take any of three possible forms:
   a. *presence/absence.* Even if one is dealing with unique and incommensurable values, there is still the difference between having them (or otherwise being identified with them) and not. Kayapo "beautiful names" and their associated regalia, for example, are not ranked—each is a value only unto itself—but every name-giving ceremony is organized around the distinction between "those with wealth," who have them, "those with nothing," who do not—even if all other social distinctions are effectively dissolved (Turner 1987:28).[26]
   b. *ranking,* as with Gregory's hierarchy of types of gift. Kayapo performance genres are ranked as well: men's oratory is ordinarily seen as superior to women's keening; chiefly chanting, as superior to both.
   c. *proportionality,* as with money.
   In any of these what is ultimately being measured is the importance of the creative energies (in the Kayapo case, above all those spent in the creation of fully socialized human beings) required to produce them
2. they are *media of value,* as they are the concrete, material means by which that value is realized. In other words, it is not enough for tokens of value to provide a way of contrasting levels of value; there have to be material objects, or material performances, which either

bring those values into being in a way that they are—at least potentially—perceptible to a larger audience (this audience, from the
actor's point of view, more or less constitutes "society"), or are trans-
latable into things that do.

3. finally, these tokens almost inevitably come to seen as *ends in themselves*. Actual people tend to see these material tokens not as "tools"
through which value can be measured or mediated, but as embodiments of value in themselves; even, in classic fetishistic fashion, as the
origins of those very values (Turner 1979c:31–34).

The last point is crucial, because this is what finally points the way towards
reconciling social structure and individual desire, which is precisely what a
value theory was *supposed* to do.

Most Kayapo, do, undoubtedly, feel that it is right their own society
should continue to exist; in this they are like most people. But in the absence
of great catastrophes, the question of the continued existence of one's society is not something to which many give a lot of thought. Reproducing society is not, normally, seen as an end in itself.[27] Rather, most people pursue
social values in more or less concrete form: if they are Kayapo, they work
their way towards socially dominant positions in the central, communal institutions (if only so that they will be in a position to express themselves
freely and not to have to live in constant constraint and embarrassment),
they hope to be able to play an important part in the performance a truly
beautiful collective ritual, to give a "beautiful name" to their brother's
daughter, to be the sort of person others listen to as a voice of moral authority, to ensure one's children might someday be. One is tempted to say
that "society" is created as a side effect of such pursuits of value. But even
this would not be quite right, because that would reify society. Really, society is not a thing at all: it is the total process through which all this activity
is coordinated,[28] and value, in turn, the way that actors see their own activity as meaningful as part of it. Doing so always, necessarily, involves some
sort of public recognition and comparison. This is why economic models,
which see those actions as aimed primarily at individual gratification, fall so
obviously short: they fail to see that in any society—even within a market
system—solitary pleasures are relatively few. The most important ends are
ones that can only be realized in the eyes of some collective audience. In fact,
one might go so far as to say that while from an analytical perspective "society" is a notoriously fluid, open-ended set of processes, from the perspective
of the actors, it is much more easily defined: "society" simply consists of that
potential audience, of everyone whose opinion of you matters in some way,
as opposed to those (say, a Chinese merchant, to a nineteenth century German peasant farmer, or vice versa, or most anthropologists to the janitors

who clean their buildings, or vice versa) whose opinion of you, you would never think about at all. But (and this is what I think Strathern, for example, does not take fully into account) value is not *created* in that public recognition. Rather, what is being recognized is something that was, in a sense, already there.

All this I think has a definite bearing on the question of exploitation. Let me return for a moment to Mount Hagen and the argument about Melpa pig exchange. The reader will recall Josephides argued that behind the dramatic, public gestures of gift-giving between men lie hidden a whole history of less dramatic, more repetitive daily actions, largely carried out by women, by which the pigs are produced. Moka ceremonies make it seem as if the pigs' value is produced by exchange. In doing so, it disguises its real origins in women's labor. Strathern objects that such a notion presumes a certain attitude towards property, and the idea that carrying out productive labor should give one certain rights to the object produced, that Hageners just don't have. Hence it would never occur to them they are being exploited. But in fact, when Melpa women feed their pigs, they are not simply fattening animals. They are not even simply, as Strathern would have it, reproducing the relationship they have with their husbands. They are also contributing to reproducing a certain kind of social order: one organized, for example, around a distinction between the domestic sphere, in which pigs are raised, and the public one, in which they are exchanged; one that carries with it definitions of what a man is, what a woman is, what a family is, what a male reputation is, and why it is that the gift of a pig should be the most effective means by which the latter can be created. This social order is not some abstract set of categories that exists prior to action. Actions are what it is, what it primarily consists of. It is a process of constant creation. In this sense, it is not just the pigs but the male public sphere itself which is constructed in large part by female labor, even if it is also one from which women are largely excluded.[29]

From this perspective one can indeed talk about exploitation. Strathern for example points out that if one claims that Melpa women are being exploited because men control the pigs they have helped produce, you would have to conclude that men are being exploited too, because women control the crops that men have contributed to producing. This sort of logic is inevitable, really, if one thinks of value only in terms of particular objects and particular transactions, refusing to consider any sort of larger social whole in which the production of both pigs and crops take on value in relation to one another. Now, there are good reasons why Strathern wants to avoid talking about "society." First of all, like most current theorists she wants to emphasize the degree to which what we are used to calling "societies" are not bounded wholes, but open-ended networks. Second, the concept is alien to the Melpa themselves. But by doing so ends up paradoxically depriving her Hageners of almost all social creativity. A constructivist approach—such as I have been trying to develop—might help overcome some of these dilemmas. Such an approach assumes there does have to be some kind of whole;[30] but it is almost always going to be a shifting, provisional one, because it is always in the process of construction by actors pursuing forms of value—if only because those forms of value can only be realized on some sort of larger stage. If for the actor, "society" is simply the audience one would like to impress, for the analyst, it is all those actions that have gone into making it possible for that actor to make that impression that have thus, in effect, produced the value realized in this way.

value and values, fetishism

At this point on can return to the question of value versus values; that is, economic price-mechanisms versus the kind of "conceptions of the desirable" described by Kluckhohn: honor, purity, beauty, and the like. I've already noted that the latter tend to take on importance either in societies without a commercial market (e.g., the Kayapo) or, as in ours, in those contexts (church, home, museum, etc.) relatively insulated from it. According to Turner (1984:56–58), both really are refractions of the same thing; to understand the differences, one has first of all to consider what they are being refracted through. That is, one has to consider the nature of the media through which social value is realized. The key question is the degree to which value can, as it were, be "stored." Here money represents one logical extreme. Money is a durable physical object that can be stored, moved about, kept on reserve, taken from one context to another.[31] At the other extreme, one has performances like chiefly chanting, the deferential behavior of subordinates, and so on. A performance is obviously not something that can be stored and "consumed" later on. Hence, as he puts it, there can be no distinction here between the spheres of circulation, and realization. Both have to happen in the same place.

Here it might help to go back to Marx, who invented these particular terms. In a capitalist system, the typical product is made in a factory and passes from wholesaler to retailer, before finally being bought by a consumer and taken home to be consumed. In Marx's terms it passes from the sphere of production, to that of circulation, to that of realization: the latter by providing the consumer some pleasure, fulfilling some purpose, or adding to his or her prestige. In a society like the Kayapo, however, the spheres of circulation and realization coincide. Social value may be mainly produced in the domestic sphere, but it is realized by becoming absorbed into personal identities in the public, communal sphere, accessible to everyone.

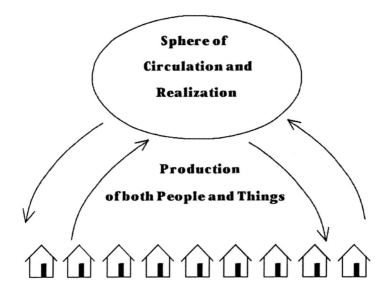

Figure 3.1

Marx, of course, was writing mainly about political economy and was not especially concerned with what went on in the domestic sphere. But I think if one expands his ideas just a little, to include the issue of social production (the production of people, and of social relations outside the workplace), one might come up with the formulation seen in Figure 3.2.

In a capitalist system, then, there are two sets of minimal units—factories (or more realistically, workplaces), and households—with the market mediating relations between the two.[32] One primarily concerns itself with the creation of commodities; the other, with the creation (care and feeding, socialization, personal development, etc.) of human beings. Neither could exist without the other. But the market that connects them also acts as a vast force of social amnesia: the anonymity of economic transactions ensures that with regard to specific products, each sphere remains effectively invisible to the other. The result is a double process of fetishization. From the perspective of those going about their business in the domestic sphere, using commodities, the history of how these commodities were produced is effectively invisible. Therefore, objects—as Marx so famously observed—appear to take on subjective qualities. Perhaps in part, too, because they are also turned there to the fashioning of people. Most commodities—as critics of

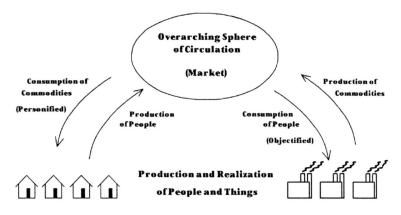

Figure 3.2

Marx so often point out end up marking different sorts of identity, and this is the ultimate social "realization" of their value in the terms outlined above. All of this could simply be considered part of the overall process of "social production": forming people both in their capacities, and, more publicly, in terms of their identities, of what sorts of person they are taken to be. But I would add: from the perspective of the workplace, everything is reversed. Here, it is the creative energies that went into producing labor power (actual human beings capable of doing whatever it is the boss wants them to do) that becomes invisible. Hence, instead of things taking on human qualities, real human beings end up taking on the qualities of things. Thus we have the "reification" that Gregory talks about, human beings or human powers reduced to commodities that can be bought and sold, and hence put to use in creating new commodities.

In a traditional society, of course, there is only one set of minimal units because the production of both people and things is centered on the household. Still, even in an extremely simple case like the Baining, there is still some kind of larger sphere in which values can be said to circulate and be realized. Still, in the Baining case, probably owing to the very minimal nature of the hierarchy, there is little that could justifiably be called fetishism or exploitation.

The Baining, however, are unusual. In most societies:

> The values which the members of society struggle to attain and accumulate in their everyday lives are ultimately a symbolic expression of the concrete realization, in their own social system, of their capacity to produce the material

and social wherewithal of their own lives, to coordinate these productive activities in such a way that they form interdependent systems and thus acquire
determinate values and meanings, and finally to reproduce the forms of this
coordination. Although people created values and meanings through the
forms of organized interdependence they assume to facilitate their own productive activity, they remain unaware that they do so. (Turner 1979c:34–35)

Just as higher-level processes, operating on that "proximal level" that
tends to elude individual consciousness, tend to be seen as existing outside
of human creativity, as something transcendent and immutable, so these tokens of value also tend to become fetishized. People tend to see them as the
origin of the values they embody and convey. Just as value seems to come
from money, so fame and glory seems to emerge from the armshells and
necklaces exchanged between kula partners, honor and nobility from possession of coats of arms and family heirlooms, kingship from the possession
of a stool, ancestral wisdom from the forms of ancestral rhetoric, chiefly authority from a chief's authoritative speech.

Or, of course, "a name" from a Melpa pig—or, to be more precise, from
the act of giving one. Because in fact, actions can be fetishized too. In an
essay called "Exchanging Products, Producing Exchange" (1993), Jane Fajans argues that this is precisely what happens in dramatic acts of exchange
like moka. Like Bloch and Josephides, she suggests that anthropologists—
particularly those working in the Maussian tradition—often fall into the
same trap. The way out, she suggests, is to make a consistent distinction between exchange and circulation. Exchange occurs when property of some
sort passes from one person to another; circulation occurs when values or
valued qualities are transferred. Within a commercial market, of course,
these usually come down to pretty much the same thing. In other contexts
they do not. In some, as we've seen, values circulate largely through modes
of performance. Knowledge, rumors, and reputations circulate as well;
hence, as Fajans notes, one might in some places be able to realize the value
of an heirloom shell only by giving it away; in others, by displaying it in a
public ritual; in yet others, by hiding it somewhere (but making sure others
know that you have done this). In either case, values circulate. Exchange,
then, is just one of many possible forms circulation might take.

There are a number of reasons why such actions, or objects, are so often
fetishized, and treated as the sources of value rather than simply the media
through which value circulates. One is because it is often not entirely untrue. Exchange, or chiefly performance, *is* a form of creative action and does,
indeed, play a certain role in producing these values—it's just not nearly so
great a one as is normally attributed to them.[33] Another even more important reason, Fajans argues, is because both (actions and objects) often have a

tendency to become models, representations in miniature, of the broader forms of creative action whose value they ultimately represent. If one examines the symbolic organization of a moka ceremony, or even, that of royal regalia or kula valuables or Hindu temples, one usually finds that they are in their own way microcosms of the total system of production of which they are a part, and that they encode a theory of creativity that is implicit on the everyday level as well, but is rarely quite brought into the open (cf. Turner 1977:59–60).

It's not hard to see how this might be. A great deal of anthropological analysis consists of unearthing just these sort of connections: for instance, finding the same symbolic patterns in the everyday habits of domestic life and the design of Gothic cathedrals (Bourdieu 1979). This is really just another way of reformulating the same observation, but here emphasizing the importance of creativity. I've already underlined that even the most workaday, least dramatic forms of social action (tending pigs and whatnot) are also forms of symbolic production: they play the main role in reproducing people's most basic definitions of what humans are, the difference between men and women, and so on. I have also emphasized that this overall process is always something that tends somewhat to escape the actors. Insofar as these fetishized objects really do embody total systems of meaning, they represent ones that are in fact produced largely offstage.

It might be useful here to return to Nancy Munn's notion of value templates. In Gawa, the most elementary cultural definitions of value are reproduced every time one gives a guest, or a child, food. Implicit in even such a simple gesture lies a whole cosmology, a whole set of distinctions between the heaviness of gardening and garden products (owned by women), and the lightness and beauty of shells and other circulating valuables (which reproduce the fame of men), one that is, in practice, reproduced precisely through such gestures, which are the most basic means for converting the one into the other. This same structure of meaning is reproduced on ever-higher levels of what Munn calls "intersubjective space-time"; that is, new levels that are created by more dramatic and more broadly recognized forms of action. It is especially in the most spectacular of these: in the creation of elaborately decorated canoes for kula expeditions, the presentation of famous heirloom necklaces, or, for that matter, in the very design of the canoes and necklaces themselves—that something like a model of the whole process is presented to the actors in something like schematic form.

The same could be said for the Kayapo. The values of dominance and beauty are created, in their simplest forms, in the pettiest details of everyday life, particularly in the family: for instance, in the deferential attitudes children should take towards their parents, or the familiar ease they can adopt with certain other relatives. But also in more obviously creative forms:

Kayapo women, for example, spend a great of their time painting the bodies of their children, as well as each other. As they do so, according to Turner's essay "The Social Skin" (1980), they are endlessly re-encoding an implicit model of the human body and society, of the transformation of inner "libidinal" powers into visible social forms. As in the Gawan case, one can say this is itself a kind of theory of social creativity, but only so long as one always bears in mind that there is no way to separate such a "theory" from practice; we are not dealing with preexisting codes or principles to which people then feel they must conform, but rather a property of the structure of the actions themselves. In the Kayapo case too, of course, these elementary schemas are endlessly reproduced on the more encompassing levels of social action (men's house politics, the ritual clowning of name-giving ceremonies, or for that matter in the structure of Kayapo myths, etc.); this is the reason why the passing of the heirloom ornaments that accompany "beautiful names" can seem so significant, or chiefly chanting so powerfully expressive, to begin with.

I have earlier suggested that a materialist analysis need not be founded on some notion of determination, but rather, on never allowing oneself to forget that human action, or even human thought, can only take place through some kind of material medium and therefore can't be understood without taking the qualities of that medium into account. Hence the importance in Turner's analysis of the notion of material media of circulation. The media have qualities in and of themselves. For all the (often quite legitimate) criticisms of Jack Goody's dichotomies between orality and literacy, for example, it is simply obvious that technologies of writing allow for possibilities that do not exist in speech (and equally, vice versa). If one memorializes the past by the performance of ritual dramas, that past will never look quite the same as one memorialized by the preservation of ancient buildings, which will not be the same as one memorialized by, say, the periodic reconstruction of ancient buildings, let alone one kept alive largely through the performances of spirit mediums. It is a fairly simple point. It should be obvious, perhaps. But it's a point that those whose theory sets out with some Parmenidean notion of code (that is, most theoretically inclined anthropologists) often tend to forget.

note one: negative value

Before discussing some of political implications of this kind of value theory, allow me two quasidigressions.

The last two chapters of Nancy Munn's *The Fame of Gawa* are dedicated to a detailed analysis of Gawan conceptions of "negative value," as exemplified in the way senior men talk about the threat posed to their communities by witchcraft. Gawans' conceptions of witchcraft form an almost exact photo-negative version of the creation of positive value through exchange: where one involves growing and then giving away food so as to create links that will eventually make it possible to spread one's fame in all directions, witches are creatures driven by an insatiable appetite, sucking the life-force from all those around them, but all in utter secrecy.

Combating the threat of such evil in turn requires a communal consensus: at public events, senior men are always inveighing against witchcraft and using their rhetorical powers to convince potential witches to desist from their evil plans. Gawa is, as Munn emphasizes, both a highly egalitarian and a highly individualistic society, and the two principles are necessarily somewhat in contradiction. The pursuit of fame itself tends to subvert equality. As a result, one of the principle ways in which a notion of communal value emerges, in Gawa, is through the negation of a negation. Witches, motivated by envy, attack those who have been too successful in rising above their fellows; in one sense, they represent the egalitarian ethos of the community, in another, absolute selfish individualism and hence, absolute evil. Communal value, what Gawans call the "fame of Gawa," is seen as directly tied to the ability of its senior men to suppress this destructive hyperindividualism and thus create a situation where everyone is free to enter into exchange relations, engage in kula, and thus, spread their own individual names in all directions.

Turner himself never takes up the notion of negative value; neither does Fajans; but this probably has something to do with the nature of the Kayapo and Baining societies. Certainly, the broader process Munn describes can be documented in many other places. Maurice Bloch (1982) has noted that in ritual, probably the most common way of representing a social value is by the very dramatic and tangible representation of its opposite: images of moral evil, of loss or decay, chaos and disorder and so on. Witchcraft is, at least in most times and places, another way of doing the same thing. It affirms certain moral values through a representation of utter immorality. And as authors such as Monica Wilson have shown (1970), these images vary a great deal between societies, in ways that have much to do with differences in their overall social structure.

The overall process Munn describes is quite similar to what I encountered in Madagascar (Graeber 1995): here too, the sense of communal solidarity was largely conceived in efforts to repress witchcraft, a witchcraft that was, however, seen as a perverse version of the very egalitarian ideals that were the basis of that same community. It could be that this will always be one of the most salient ways in which value manifests itself where one has a similar combination of egalitarianism and individualism.[34] Such questions could well bear future research.

note two:
direct versus indirect appropriation

The reader might well be wondering whether there's any way to square all of this with more conventional Marxist anthropology, what I've called the "mode of production" approach (e.g., Meillaissoux 1981; Godelier 1977). There might not seem to be a lot of common ground. For the MoP approach, as developed by Althusser, everything turns on the appropriation of some kind of a material surplus. Any mode of production is based on the relation of two classes: one of primary producers, the other, which supports itself at least in part by appropriating some portion the product of the first. What makes MoPs different is *how* this extraction takes place: This is what makes the relation between master and slave different from that between feudal lord and manorial serf, or that between capitalist employer and proletarian laborer.

Since such extraction must always, in the end, be backed up by the threat of force, this is essentially a theory of the state. Hence, as I've noted, anthropologists have had a very difficult time trying to apply this model to societies without one. Here Turner's approach might seem the perfect compliment. It was created in order to understand the workings of exploitation within stateless societies; and, indeed, it's not entirely clear what a Turnerian theory of the state would be like.

Could the two then be integrated in some way? Quite possibly. After all, one can hardly deny that where one finds a state, one does also tend to find a material surplus, and a class of people who somehow contrive to get their hands on most of it, and that this is indeed ultimately backed up by the threat of force. Hence, one might suggest that there are two different ways in which a surplus can be appropriated: either directly, in material form, or indirectly, in the form of value. In this sense, the forms of exploitation that exist within societies like the Kayapo, organized around kinship, resemble capitalist ones much more than they do the kinds of direct, tangible, immediate forms of exploitation—driving chained slaves into the fields, collecting quit-rent, having one's flunkeys show up around harvest time to appropriate half a peasant's wheat crop—typical of precapitalist states.

This, in turn, has ramifications for any theory of ideology. In this chapter of course I've been emphasizing the notion of partial perspectives, of mistaking one's particular point of view within a complex social reality for the nature of reality itself, which typically gives rise to all sorts of fetishistic distortions. Conventional Marxist analysis has tended to favor a much simpler notion of material base and ideological superstructure, the latter consisting of institutions such as church and law, which mainly serve to validate the interests of the ruling class: priests to explain to slaves why they should endure their lot, jurists to tell peasants that their relations with their landlords are based on justice. The problem with these methods of ideological control, however, as authors like James Scott have extensively documented (1990) is that they don't usually work very well. The justifications are rarely taken very seriously by the people whose goods are being expropriated, or, for that matter, the ruling classes themselves. Such regimes really are based primarily on force. This does not appear to be nearly so much the case either for the forms of hierarchy that exist in stateless societies,[35] domestic inequalities that exist within state societies, or even for capitalism itself, which (at least when it does not entirely impoverish or brutalize its proletariat) tends to be far more effective at the ideological game than almost any previously known form of exploitation. In fact, insofar as state structures do succeed in legitimizing themselves, it's almost always by successfully appealing to the values which exist in the domestic sphere, which are, of course, rooted in those much more fundamental forms of inequality, and much more effective forms of ideological distortion—most obviously, gender.

conclusion: a thousand totalities

The reader might find all this talk of totalities a bit odd. The chapter began by endorsing a general movement away from claims to absolute or total truth, an acceptance that human knowledge is always going to be incomplete. It winds up by saying that one cannot have any meaningful approach to value without some notion of totality. The constant reference to totality in Turner's works will certainly seem a bit unsettling to the modern reader; it flies in the face of most contemporary theory, which has been directed at deconstructing anything resembling a closed system. I must admit I'm not entirely comfortable with it myself. But it is an issue that opens up on all the most important questions about freedom, politics, and meaning, and therefore it seems to me that the best way to end this rather long and complicated chapter would be to take it up.

First of all, there is a difference between totalities the analyst is claiming exist in some kind of empirical sense—i.e., a pristine text, a clearly bounded "society," a mythological "system"—and totalities that exist in the actors' imaginations. Social science has long since realized that the former do not really exist, at least not in any pristine form; any closed system is just a construct, and not necessarily a very useful one; nothing in real life is really so cut and dried. Social processes are complex and overlapping in an endless variety of ways. On the other hand, if there's one thing that almost all the classic traditions of the study of meaning agree on—dialectical, hermeneutic, and structuralist alike—it is that for human beings, meaning is a matter of comparison. Parts take on meaning in relation to each other, and that process always involves reference to some sort of whole: whether it be a matter of words in a language, episodes in a story, or "goods and services" on the market. So too for value. The realization of value is always, necessarily, a process of comparison; for this reason it always, necessarily, implies an at least imagined audience. As I've already suggested, for the actor, that's all that "society" usually is.

Turner's point, however, is that while such a totality does need to exist in actors' imaginations, this doesn't mean that anything that could be described as a totality necessarily exists on the ground. It might. But it might not. This is a matter for empirical observation (as is the question of the level on which the totality exists: a society, a community, a single ritual event, etc.) Here the inspiration seems to be in part in the work of Mikhail Bakhtin, who made a distinction between the ideal closure of "chronotopes"—little universes of time and space constructed in the imagination—and an infinitely complex reality in which meaning is in fact established through open-ended dialogue.

The ideal picture a society has of itself, then, almost never corresponds with how that society actually works. The Kayapo villages discussed above actually provide a dramatic case in point. Turner generally describes Kayapo villages as if they were organized into two opposed moieties; this is because that's how Kayapo always describe them. In reality, however, no Kayapo village has contained two moieties since 1936. In every case, internal rivalries and dissension have long since caused such villages to split in two. Turner concludes this is due to an imbalance of values: while ideally, dominance and beauty should form a complementary set, in reality, dominance is by far the more powerful of the two. The moiety structure is in fact supposed to represent the highest synthesis of these two complementary principles: while one moiety is considered "higher" than the other, they are in every other sense completely identical, and the ultimate harmony of a Kayapo village is seen to lie in its inhabitants' ability to cooperate in "beautiful naming" ceremonies and other collective rites that transcend people's particular allegiances to create a transcendent sense of unity. In reality, however, the lure of beauty is never quite enough. Personal rivalries between important political actors always generate rifts, tensions rise, and finally, one half ends up breaking off to found its own, rival community, normally with no love lost between the two (Turner 1987).

Still, the important thing is not just to ask why Kayapo villages lack moieties, but also why, sixty years later, when Kayapo describe how a community is organized, they invariably describe one that does not lack them. Dual-moiety communities do continue to exist, but only in imagination. As a result, they represent a permanent possibility: a vision of what Kayapo society really should be like, and possibly still might be like. Political projects of reuniting separated moieties are occasionally discussed, though until now they always seem to end up being overruled by the dangers of having too many people with historical grudges living in the same community (Turner 1979b:210). Still, there's no reason to assume they will always be.

For Marx, of course, it is our imaginations that make us human. Hence production and revolution are for him the two quintessentially human acts. Imagination implies the possibility of doing things differently; hence when one looks at the existing world imaginatively, one is necessarily looking at it critically; when one tries to bring an imagined society into being, one is engaging in revolution. Of course, most historical change is not nearly so self-conscious: it is the fact that people are not, for the most part, self-consciously trying to reproduce their own societies but simply pursuing value that makes it so easy for them to end up transforming those same societies as a result. In times of crisis, though, this can change: a social order can be seen primarily as an arena in which certain types of value can be produced and realized; they can be defended on that basis (imagine any of the societies discussed in this chapter being forcibly incorporated into a modern state), or, alternately, they can be challenged by those who think these are not the sorts of value they would most like to pursue. In any real social situation, there are likely to be any number of such imaginary totalities at play, organized around different conceptions of value. They may be fragmentary, ephemeral, or they can just exist as dreamy projects or half-realized ones defiantly proclaimed by cultists or revolutionaries. How they knit together—or don't—simply cannot be predicted in advance. The one thing one can be sure is that they will never knit together perfectly.

We are back, then, to a "politics of value"; but one very different from Appadurai's neoliberal version. The ultimate stakes of politics, according to Turner, is not even the struggle to appropriate value; it is the struggle to establish what value *is* (Turner 1978; 1979c; see Myers and Brenneis 1991:4–5). Similarly, the ultimate freedom is not the freedom to create or accumulate value, but the freedom to decide (collectively or individually) what it is that makes life worth living. In the end, then, politics is about the meaning of life. Any such project of constructing meanings necessarily involves imagining totalities (since this is the stuff of meaning), even if no such project can ever be completely translated into reality—reality being, by definition, that which is always more complicated than any construction we can put on it.

Theories do have political implications. This is as much true of those theorists who shun any notion of totalities as those who embrace them: if there is any difference, it's that the latter feel obliged to make their political positions explicit. So we have, on the one hand, Louis Dumont's "holism," with its self-consciously conservative politics,[36] and on the other, Terry Turner's equally self-conscious libertarian Marxism. Not that the work of those who reject totalities on principle lack such political implications, it seems to me; it's just that they rarely work them out to their logical conclusions. These political implications become most painfully obvious when one comes to those who argue not simply that totalizing theories are dangerous (which is of course true enough) but that we have already entered into some giddy new "postmodern" age in which no universal standards of evaluation any longer exist: that everything is endless transformation, fragmentation of previous solidarities, and incommensurable acts of creative self-fashioning. This was a very popular position among radical academics in the 1980s and '90s; in certain circles it still remains so. But as I remarked in the introduction, by now, at least, it is apparent to most people that when the 1980s and '90s are remembered, it will not be as the dawning of a new Postmodern Age (indeed, many are already beginning to find the term a bit embarrassing, not to mention their previous apocalyptic declarations about its significance), but rather as the era of the triumph of the World Market—one in which the most gigantic, totalizing, and all-encompassingly universal system of evaluation known to human history came to be imposed on almost everything. If nothing else it makes it easier to understand why economics was one of the few things about which most postmodern theorists had almost nothing to say. Which is in turn what makes authors like Appadurai, who do address economics, so important: the neoliberal assumptions are all there, plain to see. Behind the imagery of most postmodernism is really nothing but the ideology of the market: not even the reality of the market, since actually existing markets are always regulated in the interests of the powerful, but the way market ideologists would like us to imagine the marketplace should work.

All this is not merely meant to poke fun at some self-proclaimed academic radicals but to make a broader point. Any notion of freedom, whether it's the more individualistic vision of creative consumption, or the notion of free cultural creativity and decentering (Turner 1996) I have been trying to develop here, demands *both* resistance against the imposition of any totalizing view of what society or value must be like, but also recognition that *some* kind of regulating mechanism will have to exist, and therefore, calls for serious thought about what sort will best ensure people are, in fact, free to conceive of value in whatever form they wish. If one does not, at least in the present day and age, one is simply going to end up reproducing the logic of the market without acknowledging it. And if we are going to try to think seriously about alternatives to the version of "freedom" currently being presented to us—one in which nation-states serve primarily as protectors of corporate property, unelected international institutions regulate an otherwise unbridled "free market" mainly to protect the interests of financiers, and personal freedom becomes limited to personal consumption choices—we had best stop thinking that these matters are going to take care of themselves and start thinking of what a more viable and hopefully, less coercive regulating mechanism might actually be like.

Chapter 4 ▨

Action and Reflection, or Notes toward a Theory of Wealth and Power

> Moby Duck and Donald, captured by the Aridians (Arabs), start blowing soap bubbles, with which the natives are enchanted. "Ha ha. They break when you catch them. Hee, hee." Ali-Ben-Goli, the chief, says "it's real magic. My people are laughing like children. They cannot imagine how it works." "It's only a secret passed from generation to generation," says Moby, "I will reveal it if you give us our freedom" . . . The chief, in amazement, exclaims "Freedom? That's not all I'll give you. Gold, jewels. My treasure is yours, if you reveal the secret." The Arabs consent to their own despoliation. "We have jewels, but they are of no use to us. They don't make us laugh like magic bubbles."
>
> —Dorfman and Mattelart, *How to Read Donald Duck* (1975:51)

Dutch settlers, as any American schoolchild can tell you, bought Manhattan Island from the local Indians for twenty-four dollars worth of beads and trinkets. The story could be considered one of the founding myths of the United States; in a nation based on commerce, the very paradigm of a really good deal. The story itself is probably untrue (the Indians probably thought they were receiving a gift of colorful exotica as a token of peaceful intentions and were in exchange granting the Dutch the right to make use of the land, not to "own" it permanently), but the fact that so many of the people European merchants and settlers did encounter around the globe were willing to accept European beads, in exchange for land or anything else, has come to stand, in our popular imagination, as one of the defining features of their "primitiveness"—a childish inability to distinguish worthless baubles from things of genuine value.

In reality, European merchants began carrying beads on their journeys to Africa and the Indian Ocean because beads had already been used there as a trade currency for centuries. Elsewhere, they found beads were the one of the few European products they could count on the inhabitants being willing to accept, so that in many places where beads had not been a trade currency before their arrival, they quickly became one afterward.

But why was that? What was it about beads, of all things, that make them so well suited to serve as a medium of exchange—or at least, as a medium of trade between people unfamiliar with each other's tastes and habits?

True, beads do fit most of the standard criteria economists usually attribute to money. They may not be divisible, but they are roughly commensurable, highly portable, and they do not decay. But the same could be said of any number of other objects that have never been used as a means of exchange. What sets beads apart from them seems to be nothing more than the fact that they are, indeed, pleasant to look at; or to be more precise, perhaps, that they suited for use as personal adornment. In this at least they are in much larger company. It is remarkable how many of the things adopted as currency in different parts of the world have been things otherwise used primarily, if not exclusively, as objects of adornment. Gold and silver are only the most obvious examples: one could equally well cite the cowries and spondylus shells of Africa, New Guinea, and the Americas, the feather money of the New Hebrides, or any number of similar "primitive currencies." For the most part, money consists of things that otherwise exist only to be seen. Tiny copper axes have been known to become the stuff of currency, or very thin ones, but never axes that could actually cut down a tree.

What I would like to do in this chapter—and to a certain degree, over the course of the rest of this book—is to explore why this should be, and consider some of the implications. Whenever one examines the processes by which the value of objects is established (and this is true whether one is dealing with objects of exchange or wealth more generally), issues of visibility and invisibility almost invariably seem to crop up. For instance, while it is often difficult to come by systematic information about what people actually did with trade beads after they had been traded, what evidence does exist indicates that when they were not worn as personal adornment, they were quite self-consciously cached away and hidden—often, as we will see, in elaborately ritualized contexts. To understand why, however, one has to return to the ethnographic literature and reexamine a whole series of familiar notions about value, power, exchange and the human person. Let me begin, then, by considering the display of wealth.

the display of wealth

"Kachins," wrote Edmund Leach (1954:142), "do not look upon moveable property as capital to be invested, they regard it rather as an adornment to the person." They would hardly be the only ones. Insofar as wealth is an object of display, it is always in some sense adornment to the person. In any number of societies the most treasured forms of wealth consist of objects of adornment in the literal sense: heirloom jewelry, one might say, of one sort or another. Often, as with Marcel Mauss' famous examples from *The Gift*— Kwakiutl coppers, Maori cloaks and axes, kula armshells and necklaces—they are not only the most valuable objects recognized by members of the societies that produce them, but their most important objects of exchange as well.

From this perspective, what I have just said about money might not seem particularly surprising. If objects of adornment are already so highly valued, what would be more natural than to use them to represent value in the abstract? Perhaps there really isn't much of a mystery after all. But in fact I think there is. Because the kind of value ascribed to heirloom jewelry in most societies has little if anything in common with the value we usually attribute to money. In fact it often stands diametrically opposed to it.

In using the phrase "adornment to the person" Leach was probably making an oblique reference to Marcel Mauss' famous essay on "the category of the person" (1938). In that essay, Mauss argues that in societies lacking an ideology of individualism ("archaic societies," as he called them), the person, or public self of its members is often built up out of a collection of symbolic properties: names and titles, ritual paraphernalia, or other sorts of insignia and badges of office. Often the very possession of such badges of office can be said to convey title to the office in question. However, such insignia cannot become objects of exchange in any conventional sense; giving one away would be tantamount to abandoning one's social identity entirely. A king who gives away his crown is a king no longer.

There is, however, an obvious continuity between Mauss' arguments on the person and his argument in *The Gift* (1925): that gift-giving can be a powerful a way of creating social bonds because gifts always carry with them something of the giver's self. It is in this essay that Mauss deals with the sort of "heirloom jewelry" mentioned above. Heirlooms of this sort are, typically, unique objects. Each has its own name and history—and it is the latter that is in larger measure responsible for the value it is seen to have. Since that history is almost always (at least in part) a history of ownership, the social identities of giver and receiver tend to become entangled in that of the object—and therefore always to be, to a certain extent, part of the stakes of any transaction in which it is involved.

I have already discussed the way that in many systems of exchange, and particularly in what Mauss called "gift economies," different sorts of valuable are ranked according to their relative abilities to convey history, as in kula exchange (Munn 1986:55–73, 111–18), in which there is a hierarchy of types of goods, with perishable and generic substances like food at the bottom and unique imperishable valuables at the top. Armshells and necklaces themselves are divided into nameless, generic shells, ranked at the bottom, a more valuable class of rare shells for which there is only a handful examples of any given variety, and finally, at the top, absolutely unique heirlooms with their own names and histories that everyone is supposed to have heard of. But all this serves only to underline how little the value of kula shells and other "heirloom jewelry" resembles that of money. Money does not consist of unique objects at all. At least in principle, it is absolutely generic, any one dollar bill precisely the same as any other. As a result money presents a frictionless surface to history. There is no way to know where a given dollar bill has been. Nor is there any reason one should care, since neither the identity of its former owners nor the nature of transactions in which it has previously been involved in any way affects its value. This is why transactions involving money can be said to be "anonymous": the social identities of those transacting need not become part of the stakes of any transaction—in fact, they do not have to play any part in the transaction at all.

It is an anthropological commonplace that clothing and adornment serve as markers of social identity. Insofar as they are objects of display, they act to define differences between kinds of people. The display of heirloom jewelry, too, could be said to assert the distinctiveness of its owner. And so with wealth in general: in our own society, anyone who has managed to accumulate a very large amount of money will inevitably begin to translate some of it into objects of unique historical value: old mansions, Van Goghs, pedigreed thoroughbreds—all of which may be considered adornment to the owner's person. (In fact, they would be considered rather odd if they did not.)

Clearly, money itself can never become an adornment to the person in the same way. It can mark distinction only in the quantitative sense: some people have more of it, some less. But I would argue—in fact I will be dedicating most of the next two sections to arguing—that money is quite often identified with its owner's person, if in a somewhat different sense. Rather than serving as a mark of distinctiveness, it tends to be identified with the holder's generic, hidden capacities for action.

action and reflection

If one turns to the literature on power rather than that on value, there is no lack of material on issues of visibility and invisibility. Phrases like "panoptics" and "the gaze of power" have been bandied about quite widely in social theory for some time now. Most of these usages of course go back to the work of Michel Foucault, particularly *Discipline and Punish* (1977:170–94), in which he argues that there was a major shift in the way power was exercised in Europe at the beginning of the eighteenth century. In the feudal system that had existed until then, he writes, "power was what was seen" (1977:187). It found its place in cathedrals, in palaces, and especially in the "material body of the king," which was on constant display in royal pageants and spectacles. Under feudalism, only the powerful were individualized, made "material" and "particular." Their faces were displayed on paintings and coins, their genealogies and deeds became the official history of the state, their private lives the stuff of public policy (1977:191–92). The powerless remained faceless spectators. With the end of the feudal state, however, the terms of power reverse themselves. In the "disciplinary systems" that began to emerge at this time, power is exercised by faceless, invisible bureaucracies that inspect, examine, and evaluate their objects. The logic is one of surveillance, and it is enshrined in such newfound institutions as the factory, the hospital inspection, the school examination, and the military review. Within such institutions, not only do those who wield power become depersonalized abstractions, but it is the objects of surveillance who now become individualized—at least insofar as they each can be inspected, judged, and ranked according to specific formal criteria (1977:189–92).

Now, Foucault represents this change as a clean break between two entirely different types of regime, but I think it would be better to treat these as two different modalities of power, ones that coexist in any society. After all, it's not as if pageantry, spectacle, and the display of power disappeared with the end of feudalism, any more than the display of wealth.[1] But this is not to say that there was not a certain shift of emphasis in European culture around that time. There are plenty of indications that there was—not least of them changes that took place in standards of personal adornment among Europe's elite in the period in question.

J. C. Flugel, an historian of dress, has referred to it as "the great masculine renunciation" (in Silverman 1985). By the eighteenth century, wealthy men had largely abandoned the colorful costumes of the Renaissance—bright ornamental clothing, makeup, jewelry, etc.—all of this came to be regarded as appropriate only for women. By around 1750, one already had a formal male costume much along the lines of what would soon develop into the modern business suit. As Terence Turner has pointed out (1980a:50–56), the new male garb actually developed out of "sporting clothes"—that is, hunting costumes favored by the rural gentry—and the change in attire was part and parcel of a broader ideological shift among the ruling classes; away, that is, from

the old aristocratic ethos of consumption and toward an emphasis on bourgeois sobriety and the moral value of productive work. Male costume now
implied a capacity for action; since the sphere of consumption came to be
seen as an essentially female domain, women's costume changed less.

I might add that differences in dress also came to encode an implicit theory of gender: one in which, as John Berger (1972:45–46) has aptly put it,
"a man's presence is dependent on the promise of power which he embodies," on his capacity for action—"a power which he exercises on others. A
woman's presence," by contrast, "expresses her own attitude to herself, and
defines what can and cannot be done to her." Berger's insight, I think, has
particularly interesting implications for any analysis of the politics of vision.
Forced, he says (1972:46), to live her life within the terms set by a male
power that holds that what she is what she is seen to be by others, "a woman
must continually watch herself. She is almost always accompanied by her
own image of herself. Whilst she is walking across a room or whilst she is
weeping at the death of her father, she can scarcely avoid envisioning herself
walking or weeping." A woman in this situation cannot act simply for the
sake of acting, and her self is constantly doubled into an implicitly male sur-
veyor and female surveyed.[2]

It is easy to see how dress codes reinforce this. Formal male dress is designed to hide the body. Its sobriety seems intended to efface not only a
man's physical form but his very individuality, rendering him abstract and,
in a certain sense, invisible. Clothing for women, on the other hand, not
only reveals more of the body (or at least hints at revealing it): it transforms
what is revealed into one of a collection of objects of adornment—body
parts becoming equivalent, as such, to clothing, makeup, and jewelry—that
together define the wearer as a sight, and by extension, as relatively concrete
and material.

Now, as a critique of gender relations, this analysis applies only to Western society—and relatively recent Western society at that. But the basic division between a relatively invisible self acting on the outside world and a
concrete and visible one relating primarily to itself is, I think, of much wider
significance. It may very well be intrinsic to the dynamics of human thought
and action themselves.

The same dichotomy is implicit, for instance, in Pierre Bourdieu's emphasis (1977) on how the grace and artistry of the truly competent social
actor is largely dependent on that actor's not being aware of precisely what
the principles that inform her actions are. These principles become conscious only when actors are jolted out of their accustomed ways of doing
things by suddenly having to confront some clear alternative to it—a process
Bourdieu refers to as "objectification." One becomes self-conscious, in other
words, when one does not know precisely what to do.

A similar distinction between action and self-consciousness is played out in Jacques Lacan's notion of the "mirror phase" in children's development (1977). Infants, he writes, are unaware of the precise boundaries between themselves and the world around them. Little more than disorganized bundles of drives and motivations, they have no coherent sense of self. In part this is because they lack any single object on which to fix one. Hence Lacan's "mirror phase," which begins when the child first comes face to face with some external image of her own self, which serves as the imaginary totality around which a sense of that self can be constructed. Nor is this a one-time event. The ego is, for Lacan, always an imaginary construct: in everyday life and everyday experience, one remains a conflicting multiplicity of thoughts, libidinal drives, and unconscious impulses. Acting self and imaginary unity never cease to stand opposed.

Both theorists (and I could cite many others) pose action and reflection as different aspects or moments of the self, so that experience becomes a continual swinging back and forth between them. Not only is this, I think, a compelling way to look at the structure of human experience: there is a good deal of evidence that cross-culturally, it is a very common one. It is also one that almost always finds expression in metaphors of vision. Here let me turn from contemporary French theorists to a thoroughly antiquated English one and refer the reader to Edward Tylor's discussion of the origins of the idea of the soul in *Primitive Culture* (1874:430–63).

Tylor surveys the terminology used to describe the soul in dozens of different languages across the world. Almost all of them, he finds, fall into one of two groups. On the one hand, there is what might be called the "life-soul," or vital principle in humans, often figuratively identified with the heart or breath. The connotation is of a hidden force responsible for the animation of the body, and usually for such abstract powers as thought and intentionality as well. The life-soul represents, in short, a person's inner capacity for action, their inner powers. On the other hand, there is a very different kind of "soul," typically referred to by some word whose primary meaning is either "shadow" or "reflection." In either case, the term conjures up a person's physical appearance, detached from their actual physical being. In almost all of Tylor's examples, this "image-soul" (if I may call it that) is said to be able to wander free of the body. Almost always, too, it is believed to endure after the body's death—which the "life-soul" most often is not.

Though Tylor claimed these two were ultimately identified, his own evidence makes it clear that most cultures do not identify them at all. They tend to see them as separate, if complementary, aspects of the self. The distinction may not be a universal one (certainly it isn't universal in the relatively formal terms Tylor used); but it is so remarkably common that it seems reasonable to ask why. Why should mirror images should be so obvious a metaphor for the public self? What is it about powers of action that make them seem invisible?

Perhaps the best answer to the second question comes from Thomas Hobbes (1968:659; cf. Pye 1984:93–94), who suggested, in discussing idolatry, that whatever is invisible is "unknown, that is, of an unlimited power." Total lack of specificity, in other words, implies an infinite potential. What is entirely unknown could be anything—hence, it could *do* anything as well.

What this would imply is that the hiding of the body and effacement of individuality encountered, for instance, in formal male clothing is itself a way of stating that a man is to be defined by his capacity for action—or, as Berger puts it, "the promise of power he embodies." It would also help to explain why human capacities for action in general—what Tylor called the "life soul"—should so often be defined as something impossible to see.

To be visible on the other hand is to be concrete and "specific" (a word derived from the Latin *specere,* which means "to look at"). It is also to be the object of action rather than one who acts on others: Berger notes that even when gazing into a mirror, a woman's self can be said to be split between alien, male observer and passive, female observed. In a similar way, the power exercised through the display of wealth or royal splendor is not a power that acts directly on others. It is always, in its essence, a persuasive power, meant to inspire in others acts of compliance, homage or recognition directed towards the person engaging in display.[3]

This anyway is one implication of Berger's analysis of "female presence" (1972:46–48), one of great significance for the study of power in general:

> Men survey women before treating them. Consequently how a woman appears to a man can determine how she will be treated. To acquire some control over this process, a woman must contain it and interiorize it. That part of a woman's self which is the surveyor treats the part which is the surveyed so as to demonstrate to others how her whole self would like to be treated. And this exemplary treatment of herself by herself constitutes her presence. Every woman's presence regulates what is and is not "permissible" within her presence. Every one of her actions—whatever its direct purpose or motivation— is also read as an indication of how she would like to be treated.

What Berger describes is clearly a kind of power born of subordination. Perhaps it is better treated as a mere residual of power, all that's left to those who have no access to the more direct variety. But in purely formal terms, there is little to distinguish it from the kind of power exercised through the display of aristocratic wealth or royal splendor. Kings and nobles too could be said to have decorated themselves with wealth in order to "demonstrate to others how their whole selves would like to be treated." After all, in the final analysis, a king's status is based on his ability to persuade others to recognize him as such—and to pay him tribute for that reason. By making a show of magnificence, a king is able to define himself in such a way that others are moved to transfer some of their wealth to him. They do so not as part of any implicit exchange, not by virtue of anything they expect the king to *do*, but simply by virtue of the sort of person they believe him to *be*.[4] By covering themselves with gold, then, kings persuade others to cover them with gold as well.

Max Weber (1978:490–91) once observed that feudal aristocrats tended to justify their status through their way of *being*, their mode of life in the present, while the lower orders—including the mercantile classes—tended to define themselves by what they did, created, or aspired to. Here, too, the dichotomy lives on, now largely displaced onto ideas about gender. Just as men of high status tend to be defined in bourgeois terms, as active producers, elite women have inherited the old aristocratic role of passive consumers. As the poet has it, "Man Does, Woman Is" (Graves 1964).

Weber's way of framing the issue is particularly useful in bringing out its relationship to time. In a sense, the distinction between my "action" and "reflection" is really only one between actions to be carried out in the future and ones already carried out in the past. "The promise of power" a man embodies is his potential for acting in the future; at the same time, a "woman's exemplary treatment of herself" consists of actions she has already undertaken, or at least ones she is still in the process of carrying out. The person could be said to vanish in its orientation to action because action expresses a completion that only can exist in the future. At the same time, one's visible persona, one's "being," is simply the cumulative effects of actions that have been directed towards one in the past—of all those actions that have made one what one is. Being—if it is socially significant—is congealed action, and just as every category is the other side of a set of practices (Turner and Fajans 1988), every unique being is the result of an equally singular history. By engaging in persuasive display, then, all one is really doing is calling on others to imitate actions that are implicitly being said to have already been carried out in the past.

money versus coin

So far, I've been arguing that Mauss' gifts are caught up in the specific social identity of their givers and receivers (their exterior "image," one might say); money, identified with a person's generic and invisible inner powers. I am not the first person to have made this point. In fact, something very similar can be found in the opening chapters of Marx's *Capital*, in which he talks about the dynamics of commodity exchange.

In Marx's conception of the capitalist marketplace, money and commodities are continually being redefined in the perceptions of their buyers and sellers, shifting back and forth between what he calls abstract "content" and concrete "form." The dialectical terminology may seem a bit obscure to modern readers, but the meaning of these terms is not really all that different from my own "action" and "reflection."

Let me begin with one of Marx's own examples (1967:18–62). Say one man has twenty yards of linen; another has a coat. The two agree to exchange one for the other. By doing so, they are agreeing that the value of the two objects is equivalent. However, each has a very different way of perceiving that equivalence. The first aims to acquire the coat; obviously, then, it is the particular, material qualities of the coat that are important to him. This is not at all true of his attitude toward the linen. The linen is just a means to his end: anything else would have done just as well, provided its value was considered equivalent to that of the coat. As Marx puts it, from his point of view the linen is a mere abstraction; the coat a concrete, specific "form." Of course, from the other man's point of view, exactly the opposite is true.

Marx held this is true of all transactions, including those involving money. Everything depends on the point of view—and the intentions—of the actors. If I sell a commodity, my object is to acquire money—therefore, it is money that seems a concrete "form" to me; the goods I have to sell seem a formless abstraction. From the point of view of the purchaser, of course, it is the other way around.

In other words, it is always the object of action—the object of desire—that is concrete and particular in the eyes of the person who is acting or desiring. The means have no particular features of their own. Instead, they tend to be identified with the user's own powers of action.

In his discussion of hoarding in *A Contribution to the Critique of Political Economy* (1970:125–37) and the *Grundrisse* (1971:228–34), Marx phrases the distinction between money in its abstract and concrete aspects as a distinction between "money" and "coin." "Coin," he says, is the physical object offered in exchange. It only becomes "money" in the strict sense of the term when it is temporarily withdrawn from circulation—that is, when it is not the immediate object of anyone's action but instead represents a kind of universal potential *for* action. By holding on to the stuff, the hoarder preserves his power, which is the power to buy anything at all. For the hoarder, money becomes a kind of ascetic religion—Marx likens it to Puritanism—in which the owner tends to develop an intensely personal, even secretive relationship with the source of his powers. The impulse, once one has accumulated a substantial hoard, is always to hide it in the ground where no one else can see it:

An outward expression of the desire to withdraw money from the stream of circulation and to save it from the social metabolism is the *burying* of it, so that social wealth is turned into an imperishable subterranean hoard with an entirely furtive private relationship to the commodity-owner. Doctor Bernier, who spent some time at Aurangzeb's court at Delhi, relates that merchants, especially the non-Moslem heathens, in whose hands nearly the entire commerce and all money are concentrated—secretly bury their money deep in the ground, "being held in thrall to the belief that the money they hide during their lifetime will serve them in the next world after their death." (Marx 1970:130; original emphasis)

As his example implies, Marx did not see such behavior as deriving from capitalism per se but from the nature of money itself, from its abstract and almost mystical powers. In a similar vein, Engels (in Shell 1978:41) suggested that coined money, when first introduced into the Greek world in the seventh century BC, was not seen as an economic instrument so much as a magical charm: as he puts it, "a talisman that could at will transform itself into any desirable or desired object."

Engels was no doubt getting a bit carried away with himself. But as Marc Shell (1978:62) points out in a brilliant essay called "The Ring of Gyges," the stories told in ancient Greece about the man who first coined money did focus on a magical charm of sorts. They were about a ring that could make its wearer invisible (1978:62).

Gyges, a sixth-century ruler of Lydia, was widely credited in antiquity—as he is today—with having been the first king to coin money. According to Herodotus, Gyges was not a legitimate king at all but a usurper. Originally a mere courtier and friend of King Candaules, his rise to power began when his friend, given to much lavish praise of his wife's beautiful body, finally convinced him to conceal himself in the queen's chambers in order to prove that he was not exaggerating. The queen, having discovered what happened, and outraged at this assault on her modesty, demanded that Gyges either kill the king and take his place, or forfeit his own life. Gyges therefore concealed himself once again in the same spot, waited for the king to pay his nightly visit to his wife, and did away with him.

In Herodotus, the story is, as Shell emphasizes, intended to parallel another story of usurpation, the story of Deioces the Mede. This is also Herodotus' myth of the origins of tyranny.

Deioces was a Median nobleman who developed a reputation as a judge—so great was his reputation, in fact, that when he tried to step down from his office, the people offered him the kingship in order to retain him. As soon as he had the power, Deioces hid himself behind a golden wall in his capital and established a rule that no one should be allowed to see him; at the same time, he filled his kingdom full of spies.

The two stories parallel each other in a number of ways. Gyges was the founder of the ruling dynasty of Lydia, Deioces that of Media; the meeting of their two descendants, Croesus and Cyrus, when Lydia was conquered by the Persian empire, was the culmination of the first half of Herodotus' history. In certain ways the two are also inversions of one another. Gyges used his invisibility to gain power, but it was a power that he apparently wielded in the traditional, public fashion. Deioces on the other hand managed to convert his fame, his public visibility, into power—but in doing so he transformed the terms in which that power was exercised, making it invisible and private. Gyges became a king, even if he did so through illegitimate means; Deioces became a tyrant.

Taken this way the two stories move in opposite directions, and it seems to me that it makes a great deal of sense that they should. Gyges after all was not considered the inventor of money; he was considered the inventor of coinage— and these are not at all the same thing.

Shell goes on to present a great deal of evidence that Greeks of Herodotus' time did tend to talk about money as having a certain kind of invisible power, one politically dangerous for the very reason of its invisibility. Plato first introduces the story of Gyges when one of the participants in his dialogue claims that wealth is a good thing because it can make the owner invisible to the avenging eyes of Hades when he dies (a curious echo of the Hindu merchants cited by Marx); Hades itself means "unseen," and Plato elsewhere claims that Plutus, the god of Hades, is so named because the word for "wealth" is *ploutos,* and because gold and silver "come up from below out of the earth" (Shell 1978:21n25). Since it represented private interests rather than those of the state, money was seen to have much in common with tyranny—defined as the exercise of state power in the private interest.

Public and private, visible and invisible: these were no mere casual metaphors. The distinction between public and private was central to the way the Greek *polis* defined itself. Jean-Pierre Vernant (1983) has described the emergence of the polis, over the sixth and seventh centuries BC, as a process of disclosure and unveiling, even desacralization, in which every power that had once been secret or confined to the interiors of aristocratic families was brought into the public domain of the agora where it was visible to all. Debates began to be carried out in public, laws published. "The old sacra, badges of investiture, religious symbols, emblems, wooden images, jealously preserved as talismans of power in the privacy of palaces or the crannies of priestly houses" were gradually "moved to the temple, an open and public place" (1983:54).

The furtive power of money was no exception: private hoarding was discouraged by the state. To the extent that money remained hidden, it was seen as something dangerous, subterranean, a threat to the cohesiveness of the political community. The state of course kept its own hoard, its public treasury, but it made a point of keeping it in a form that was visible to all: the Athenian gold reserves, for instance, were used to plate the monumental statue of Athena in the Parthenon. What it did release for private use, the state released stamped with its own impression.

Hence I return once again to the distinction between money and coin.

I should emphasize that Gyges was not credited with the invention of money. He was credited with the invention of coinage. They are hardly the same thing. If one simply defines money as economists do—as a measure and medium of exchange—then one can certainly say that gold and silver had already existed in the Middle East for several thousand years. It has been used in Lydia and Greece as well. It is just that before Gyges, this money was not stamped out in uniform denominations by the state. People carried it around in nuggets, lumps, and bits, and merchants kept scales with which to weigh the stuff out at each transaction. It might seem an unwieldy way to go about buying and selling, but any system maintained unchanged for thousands of years must have worked well enough from the point of view of the people using it. Why, then, did governments in Lydia and, soon after, Greece begin to change things?

What evidence there is suggests the invention of coinage did little to make trade easier. Ancient Greece was divided into hundreds of tiny city-states; every one began issuing their own coinage, each with its own system of denominations; these denominations might be based on any of a variety of entirely different systems of weights and measures. Since the coins circulated widely, the average marketgoer was likely to arrive with a pouch full of completely heterogeneous currencies, which, for all intents and purposes, might as well have a random assortment of lumps of gold and silver. For most important transactions, Greek merchants were still obliged to weigh coins out on scales. As Moses Finley (1974:166–69; Vidal-Naquet and Austin 1978) notes, coinage was not created to improve economic efficiency. It was not so much an economic measure as a political one. To be able to issue one's own currency was a mark of political independence: every city-state, however small, felt obliged to do so. But I don't think this is a full explanation: one could still ask why the issuing of coinage became a mark of independence to begin with.

What I am suggesting is that if the *polis* felt the need to stamp money with its own image, it did so because it saw money as a dangerous, furtive power that had to be tamed and domesticated *by rendering it visible.* The emblem of public authority was to be impressed on it through violence, literally hammered in. The resulting coins were often things of great beauty. Some were renowned as works of art even in their own day. But in the end, the very fact that the state was willing to seek out the finest artists of the day to cast its dies could be considered evidence of how desperate it had become to substitute some other definition of value for one that had a continual capacity to elude it. It was an attempt to transform money into an object of adornment, something visible in the most exemplary of fashions.[5]

The legend of Gyges contains no explicit reference to the invention of coinage. Still, one might say that it is itself a model for the process: the transformation of private and invisible powers into legitimate, political ones— ones made limited and particular by the public gaze.

various kinds of fetishism

Earlier I made a distinction between two sorts of social power: the power to act directly on others, and the power to define oneself in such a way as to convince others how they should act toward you. One tends to be attributed to the hidden capacities of the actor, the other to visible forms of display. By now, it should be easy to see how this same analysis can also be applied to value. If money tends to become an extension of its holder's capacities to act on the world (thus inspiring, according to Marx, the impulse to hide it), objects whose value is seen to lie in their particular histories or identities have an equally strong tendency to be assimilated to the social identity or persona of their owners, thus generating the impulse to show them off.

It is important to emphasize that these terms are never fixed. Few objects are simply one thing or another. In a market system, as Marx reminds us, money and commodities are always two things at once, since buyer and seller conceive them from opposite points of view. And in any system of value there are, at the very least, constant diversions and slippages back and forth, continual struggles over definition. Often—as in the case of the Greek polis—these struggles are quite openly political ones. And insofar as they involve attempts to reconcile such contrasting values as artistic beauty, wealth, and civic authority, one might say that in essence, they are *always* political.

The constant transformation of the visible into the invisible and back again might provide an answer to the question with which I began this chapter: Why beads? Why, in so many societies, should money consist of objects of adornment?

Recall that at the time, I contrasted money to the sort of objects of adornment that played so central a role in Mauss' writings on the gift—as in anthropological exchange theory in general. These, I said, were unique treasures, and as such entirely different from money. But Mauss himself remarks that the rarest and most valuable of them—Maori axes and cloaks, Kwakiutl coppers, and kula armshells and necklaces—were all seen as having a personality, will, and intelligence of their own. It is almost as if the very fact of an object's having an individual identity—a unique form, a name, a history—implied the presence some sort of hidden life-force or agency behind it, just as, in Tylor, the inner life-soul always lies hidden behind a person's unique exterior "image."[6]

But why should heirlooms tend to have a capacity for action attributed to them? In part, it is probably an effect of their value. Value, after all, is something that mobilizes the desires of those who recognize it, and moves them to action. Just as royal splendor calls on its audience to do as others have done, so does the perception of value in objects of exchange. "Others have sought to acquire these things," is the implicit message, "and therefore so should you."

In a broader sense, the value of heirlooms is always, as I have said, an historical value, derived from acts of production, use, or appropriation that have involved the object in the past. The value of an heirloom is really that of actions: actions whose significance has been, as it were, absorbed into the object's current identity—whether the emphasis is placed on the inspired labors of the artist who created it, the lengths to which some people have been known to go to acquire it, or the fact that it was once used to cut off a mythical giant's head. Since the value of the actions has already been fixed in the physical being of the object, it is perhaps a short leap to begin attributing the agency behind such actions to the object as well, and speak, as Mauss does, of valuables that transfer themselves from owner to owner or actively influence their owners' fates.

The obvious comparison here is with Marx's analysis of commodity fetishism and of money. According to Marx, the only thing really lying behind the specific, material form of the object one desires to buy is the human energy that went into producing it; even so, the desirer tends to see those powers as intrinsic to the object itself. They seem to give it a will and power of its own. If nothing else, commodities certainly exert a power over anyone who desires them. Marx's commodities differ from heirlooms largely because in their case, the illusion of agency emerges from the fact that their true history has been forgotten; in the case of heirlooms, the value that makes the illusion of agency possible derives from that very history, real or imagined. In either case, energies that went into creating the particular form of the object and made it desirable are displaced; they come to seem a ghostly agency that guides its present movements. The object of desire becomes an illusory mirror of the desirer's own manipulated intentions.

All this, in turn, would make the various mirror metaphors that have cropped up over the course of this chapter[7] much easier to understand. A person looking into a mirror is split into active and passive, observer and observed. The very perception of one's own image implies the existence of an unseen agent who is seeing it. Walter Ong (1977:121–44) has even suggested that it is in the nature of vision always to suggest a beyond, something unseen. Eyes take in only the surfaces of things. To tell if a coin is gold or merely gilded, you don't stare at it: you bite it, weigh it on your palm, or rap it to hear the sound. Looking at a thing, according to Ong, is always look-ing at a mere fraction of a thing, and the viewer is always at least vaguely aware that there is something further underneath.

At any rate, the continuities between action and reflection, the constant movements between visible and invisible forms of value, the fact that valued objects are so often seen as embodying a hidden power all make it easier to see how money might emerge from objects of adornment. These things are always slipping into their opposites.

At this point I can finally return to beads.

I am not sure if beads have ever, anywhere, been used as money in a fully monetarized economy. Almost always, they have played the role of trade cur-rency—as an anonymous means of exchange between people of different cultural worlds, most often between members of societies in which there is a full-blown commercial economy and others in which there is not. No doubt one reason beads lend themselves so well to this role is that they can be so easily transformed back and forth from unique forms to generic ones: they can be bought in bulk, sewn together into elaborate beadwork or onto other forms of adornment, and then—whenever the need is felt—broken up into individual, mutually indistinguishable items once again. It makes them ideally suited to pass back and forth between radically different domains (or, if you really must, "regimes") of value. Let me take up one example of how trade beads could be taken up.

Madagascar and the slave trade

Indian Ocean trade beads were in wide use in Madagascar at least from the twelfth century A.D. (Verin 1986), and probably well before. Red coral, and later red glass beads, seem to have functioned as a trade currency. In the sev-enteenth century, European merchants stopping for provisions on their way to the East Indies found that these were the only kind the inhabitants would readily accept in exchange for their cattle. During the eighteenth century, however, the importance of beads declined with the rise of the slave trade,[8] which was conducted largely in silver. Spanish dollars gradually took the place red beads once had.

Imerina, the part of Madagascar whose later history is best known, is lo-cated on the central plateau of the island, far from the major ports of trade. Imerina was, for much of this time, something of a backwater. Politically fragmented, it was a regular target for slave-raiders from the coasts; and its rulers were almost constantly at war with one another, partly to secure cap-tives they could sell to the foreign merchants—most of them apparently Indian Muslims but including the occasional European—who periodically passed through the country.

Maurice Bloch (1990:182–85) has described the economic situation that prevailed around 1777, when the first European account of Merina society was written. There were weekly markets throughout Imerina, in which all sorts of goods were available for sale. For money, silver dollars were cut up into a series of smaller denominations—the smallest being 1/720th of a dollar—and weighed out at each transaction.[9] However, as Bloch points out, the supply of silver was unreliable and if too much time went by without slave traders passing through, it would often dry up and the money economy cease to function. As soon as one appeared again, markets revived and rulers were once again able to collect taxes.

One reason the money supply could dry up so quickly was the habit of melting down imported coins to produce silver chains and other ornaments. Along with beads, silver ornaments were the most important forms of personal adornment in Imerina at this time. Chains in particular—the largest containing as much as four hundred dollars' worth of silver—often became important family heirlooms (Edmunds 1897:474–76). It was not every family, however, that was allowed to own them. The sources are frustratingly vague, but apparently there was a fairly elaborate set of sumptuary laws regarding clothes and personal ornaments. Red beads, for example, could be worn only by men or women of noble status; the bulk of the population seem, in theory, not to have been allowed to wear expensive adornment of any kind at all.

That at least is the implication of an account of the royal assembly held in 1834, at which the sumptuary laws were abolished. By this time, Imerina was a unified kingdom and its king, Radama I, signatory to a treaty with England abolishing the slave trade; the account is based on that of Radama's British advisor, James Hastie, as published in William Ellis' *History of Madagascar* (1837, 2:302–303).

The British government had sent Radama seeds and cuttings for potential cash crops that might substitute for the export of slaves, and at this assembly he distributed them to representatives of his people, urging on them advantages of commercial agriculture. Several representatives, however, objected that most of Radama's subjects had little motivation to compete over wealth, since sumptuary laws did not allow them to acquire any of the good things one could buy with it. After some discussion, the king agreed to abolish the laws. The result, according to Ellis, was an outpouring of public celebration unmatched since the abolition of the trade itself.

Around the same time—perhaps it was at the same assembly—Radama also announced that any debt incurred for the purpose of buying ornaments for the dead would no longer be considered recoverable (Ellis 1837, 2:304). It was necessary to do so, he said, because

> ... many persons, endeavouring to make a display of respect for deceased rel-
> atives, often contracted debts in purchasing valuable clothes and ornaments to
> throw into the graves of the departed, agreeably to ancient usage; and several
> instances occurred, where individuals had been reduced to slavery on account
> of their inability to discharge the debts so created. Thus the dead had been en-
> veloped in rich clothing, covered with ornaments, and surrounded with silver,
> whilst the nearest living relatives were by these means reduced to the lowest
> state of degradation.

Sumptuary laws presumably did not apply to the dead. Even if they had,
there would have been little way of enforce them, since no one would have
dared to enter an unrelated person's tomb.

It is hard to avoid the impression that taken together, these measures
amounted to an attempt to shift the competition over adornment from the
dead to the living—to bring it out into the open, so to speak. If so, it was
not a particularly successful one. Although burying expensive ornaments in
tombs probably did become less common as time went on, the habit of
wearing them never took hold among the common people. Quite the opposite: over the following decades even the rich appear to have abandoned
them. By mid-century, descriptions of wealthy people decked out in beads
and silver, so common in Radama's time, disappear from travelers' accounts
(cf. Edmunds). Many of the huge silver chains and other elaborate forms of
jewelry must have been melted down or buried. Others were retained as
family heirlooms but rarely if ever worn or displayed. The one area in which
both beads and silver ornaments did continue to be used after Radama's time
was the one way their current (mostly plastic and tin) descendants are still
used today: in the making of *ody,* or magic charms.

ody and sampy

The term *ody* was typically applied to objects that served a single purpose. The
purposes could vary enormously—to prevent attacks by crocodiles, to guarantee the success of a journey, to inspire love or to make an opponent's tongue trip
over his words in court—but they were always limited. *Ody* were also owned by
individuals; charms called *sampy* provided a more general protection for larger
social groups. Most descent groups, for instance, seem to have had their own
sampy, and there were royal *sampy* that guarded the kingdom as a whole. The
latter would periodically be brought before the king's subjects, and water in
which the *sampy* had been washed would be sprinkled on the assembled people
to protect them from sorcery, disease, and other dangers (Berg 1979).

Ody and *sampy* were not, however, objects of display. The various magical substances that made them up were almost always hidden inside a

horn, box, or small satchel, and the containers were usually kept out of sight as well. Even when one carried or wore them, it was usually underneath one's clothes. Most *ody* were kept inside, wrapped in silk cloth, on the domestic altar that was always set up in the northeast corner of the owner's house. *Sampy* were even more elaborately preserved in iron pots or chests: even when they were periodically brought out before the public, placed atop long poles in public ceremonies, they were always swathed in silk and thus effectively invisible (cf. Callet 1908:179,190–91).

As for the hidden ingredients themselves, they mainly consisted of pieces of the wood, leaves, bark, or roots of rare trees. All of it was "medicine" or *fanafody*, no formal distinction being drawn between what we would consider herbal remedies (e.g., an infusion of crushed leaves for an upset stomach) and ceremonial magic (e.g., praying to a piece of wood to direct lightning on one's enemies). Perhaps in early times, and certainly by that of Radama, beads and silver ornaments were incorporated into this pharmacological system; in many cases, popular varieties of bead were named after some kind of magical wood, whose powers that bead was then assumed to share (cf. Bernard-Thierry 1946:84). I should emphasize, however, that these powers were not seen to derive from the nature of the materials themselves. The latter were little more than a conduit.

The efficacy of a charm was referred to as its *hasina*. In nineteenth-century Imerina, almost all ritual action involved the creation or manipulation of *hasina*—a term Alain Delivre (1974:144–45) defines as the capacity to affect the world through imperceptible means. Most often, he adds, *hasina* turned on the relation between an invisible spirit and a material object through which that spirit could come into contact with human beings: ancestors were spirits one encountered mainly though their tombs or relics; Vazimba, spirits one encountered through certain trees, rocks, or springs; and so on. All these objects became conduits of the spirit's agency, and could thus be referred to as *masina*—that is, "having *hasina*." The same was true of *ody*, whose power was derived from the relation between the ingredients and a class of spirits called Ranakandriana.

To use an *ody*, one had to first remove it from its wrappings, then call on it to "wake" and address it in prayer. Often one would have to explain in some detail what the charm was being asked to do, and why. *Ody*, in other words, were treated like conscious beings; they were objects vested with a sort of disembodied intelligence. In prayers they were often invoked in such terms as "you who have no eyes but can still see, no ears but can still hear," or "you whose name is known but whose face is never seen" (Vig 1969:59–60; Callet 1908:84; cf. Ruud 1969:218). Malagasy sources are always careful to distinguish between this consciousness (and capacity for action), identified with the spirit, and the "wood" or physical ingredients of a charm (Callet 1908:82–85).

However, and this is where things get complicated, while a charm's personality and capacity for action was identified with a disembodied spirit, that spirit had nothing to do with its individual *identity*. In invocations, one called out to *ody* by their names; but the name was not that of a spirit. It was simply the name of the most important piece of wood that made them up. What made *ody* different from one another, then, were their ingredients.

All this is part of a much broader Malagasy ritual logic, one already suggested by Delivre. All spiritual forces in the Malagasy cosmos tend to be generic beings. They only take on individual identity through the objects by means of which people come into contact with them. In themselves they are all, for all intents and purposes, indistinguishable. In some myths, they are said to be quite literally identical in appearance (Ottino 1978:36); they are always identical in the uniform ambiguity that surrounds them, their complete lack of defining features—which in the case of the Ranakandriana is brought home by the continual emphasis all sources place on how difficult it is to see them. Ranakandriana were said to live in caves or lightless places where their voices were heard but their forms could not be made out. They were said to fly away as soon as one tried to set eyes on them; likewise, in prayers such as those cited above, they were regularly described as invisible or bodiless.

The uniform ambiguity of Malagasy spiritual forces has led to endless debates among foreign observers. There have been long discussions, for instance, over whether terms like *Zanahary* ("creator" or "god") should be translated in the singular or the plural. From a Christian standpoint this is obviously a very important question. But it does not seem to have been a question anyone else in Madagascar has ever found particularly important. I would suggest that the ambiguity is itself really half the point: in the absence of any sort of defining feature, "spirits" become sheer formless potential. The term *zanahary*, for example, could apply to any being capable of creation through imperceptible means; rather than ask what such beings were like, or how many of them there were, it makes more sense to see this power of creation as emerging from their very lack of definition. Their generic nature is itself a way of representing power or unlimited possibility.

By this logic, it was the fact that the ingredients of charms were hidden from sight that gave them their generic capacity for action. However, *ody* were not simply generic potential. The ingredients that made them up were specific objects, and it was those ingredients that determined the specific ways in which that capacity could make itself known. Each ingredient, in other words, corresponded to one of an *ody*'s powers.

Lars Vig (1969), a Norwegian missionary, provides some very detailed descriptions of how *ody* were supposed to work. Consider, for example, his account of a popular *ody basy*, or "rifle charm," meant to protect soldiers from enemy bullets (Vig 1969:70–72). The charm contains fifteen elements in all, most of them bits of wood. In the invocation, the name of each is called out and the element called on to act. In each case, the words used to describe the action are derived from that element's name. The first, a piece of the *arify* plant (the word *arify* is from a root meaning "to turn aside"), is called on to turn aside the bullets fired by the enemy. Another sliver of wood called *betambana* ("many obstacles") is asked to "stop the enemy from attacking, make some disaster occur that will be an obstacle to their attack" (71), and so on. In almost every case, the action of the charm is directed outward, toward someone other than the person using it—and this too is typical of Malagasy *ody*. Rifle charms never make their owners impervious to bullets. They make people shooting at them miss. Love magic does not make the user beautiful. It invokes desire directly in someone else. Rather than change the qualities of the bearer, *ody* always confer on her a certain capacity for action. Like Marx's hoards of hidden gold, or Engel's talisman, the hidden elements of charms were, in effect, identified with their owners' ability to act upon the world.

sacrifice and the creation of charms

This play of the particular and the generic, the seen and the unseen, recurred on every level of Merina ritual practice. So too did the link between words and objects implied in the prayers cited above.

Take rituals of sacrifice. *Sorona,* the word used for what we would call "sacrifice," actually had a much broader meaning. It could be applied to any "religious ceremony to obtain a desired benefit from that to which one prays" (Richardson 1885:591). Even more often, the word *sorona* was used not for the ritual itself, but for objects meant to represent that "desired benefit" and that were intentionally preserved as offerings for that reason. In this sense, *sorona* were the opposite of *faditra*—objects representing evils to be avoided—that were intentionally cast away.

Most rituals involved such acts of consecration and casting away. Each time the king dispatched a military expedition, we are told (Callet 1908:51–52), the royal astrologers would offer an unbroken silver coin[10] as *sorona,* praying that the army would remain similarly whole and not be broken into pieces by the enemy. Then they would cast a pinch of ashes from the king's hearth to the winds as a *faditra,* praying as they did so that the army should not be destroyed as had the wood now rendered ash.

Most often, the dedication of *sorona* would be accompanied by a vow. One might, say, place a bead or bulrush on the ritual shelf in the northeast corner of one's house, promising as one did so to sacrifice a sheep or a bullock to the invisible powers if the "desired benefit" was obtained. If it was, sacrificing the animal would itself be called a *sorona,* and the head and feet of the sacrificed animal would also be preserved (cf. Sibree 1880:302–303). Now, *sorona* often consisted of exactly the same kind of objects that were used as ingredients of *ody.* Like them, they did not usually represent objects so much as actions (in the example above: being destroyed, holding together). Finally, at least in some cases, *sorona* could become *ody.* Here is what Ellis (1837, I:435) has to say about the latter:

> The sorona operates as a charm to bring the desired favor, and is sometimes an animal sacrifice, of which, when killed, the principal fat is eaten. In some cases it consists in wearing some article specified by the sikidy [divination]; and in such instances it becomes, in course of time, an ody—that is, a charm or amulet—which, though adopted at first for a particular object, is ultimately regarded as possessing some intrinsic virtue, and therefore is still worn after the imagined case for its immediate use has ceased.
>
> These sorona sometimes consist of pieces of silver, or of silver chains; and sometimes of beads, more or less valuable. Occasionally strings of beads, of different colours, are made, and worn around the neck and wrists of the offerer.

Beads and silver, in other words, would be worn as a *sorona* to represent the "desired benefit" (in this case wealth) and, as such, displayed on the person of the sacrificer. And while Ellis does not explicitly say this, on becoming *ody* the ingredients were presumably hidden, as the ingredients of *ody* always tended to be. That, at any rate, seems to be what happened to *sorona* dedicated on the ritual shelf of one's house—the same place that a family's *ody* or *sampy* were normally kept. Once one's prayers were answered, they could simply be wrapped in silk to join the other *ody* (Callet 1908:56; Chapus and Ratsimba 1953:91n134).

To sum up, then:

Sorona were material tokens of request. They represented the desires or intentions of those who offered them, the action they wished the formless and invisible powers to take. They could almost be seen as physical hieroglyphs, reproducing in visible form the words with which one prayed. Once those prayers had been answered, however, the status of the objects changed. They came to be seen as the embodiments or conduits of those same invisible powers, as objects through which human beings could enter into relations with them. As a result they were no longer displayed but hidden as the elements of *ody*—placed in horns or boxes or sacks, wrapped in red silk, or otherwise put out of sight. *Ody* could almost be seen as examples of the Maussian gift in reverse: rather than being part of the giver's person, the gift comes to constitute the person of the receiver.

No doubt this was only one way among many of creating *ody.* But it appears to have been one particularly relevant to beads and money—providing a hint, perhaps, of the mechanisms by which objects of adornment could so suddenly and so generally vanish from sight and become hidden talismans. As *sorona,* beads and silver chains expressed the wearer's desire to gain wealth. Wearing them operated in the same way as any display of wealth: it was a persuasive act—even if, in this case, the object of persuasion was an abstract and invisible power. And here, too, the actions one carried out toward oneself were meant to serve as models for the action one wished to inspire others to take. By covering oneself with wealth, one hoped to move others to do the same.

Once proven effective, however, it followed from the logic of Malagasy ritual that these same objects—these *sorona*—should become identified with the powers that had answered the appeal, and so be hidden away. They became *ody,* with the power to draw wealth to the bearer on a regular basis. And even today, this is precisely the function of beads and silver ornaments. When they appear as ingredients in magic charms, they almost always act, directly or indirectly, to draw wealth to the owner.

the political dimension, or taxes as ritual sacrifice

I have not yet even touched on the political aspects of the use of money in Imerina, a topic dealt with in some detail by Bloch (1990)—or on the politics of visibility and invisibility in general. While there is no room here to enter into these subjects in any detail, it might be useful to end with an illustration of some of the directions such an analysis might take.

I have been describing Merina ritual as a series of techniques for creating and channeling *hasina.* While there is no word in Malagasy that really corresponds to our "ritual," one of the words used most often to describe rituals was (and is) *manasina:* literally, "to endow with *hasina*" or "to make something *masina*" (*masina* being the adjectival form).

Under the Merina kingdom, the verb *manasina* was most commonly used for the act of presenting gifts of money to the sovereign. This was partly because unbroken silver coins, the kind that were given in such ceremonies, were themselves called *hasina. Hasina* had to be given every time the king made an official appearance, and during public assemblies or the annual Royal Bath ceremony it developed into an elaborate ritual in which representatives of each of the various ranks, orders, and geographical divisions of the kingdom offered tribute in turn. But if one imagines the coins as a kind of *sorona,* it is easy to see how, in presenting these coins to the king, subjects gave him *hasina* in the other sense as well.

When whole silver coins were used as *sorona* or elements in charms— which they occasionally were—it is usually said that the coin, being round and unbroken, stood for wholeness and perfection. I have already mentioned one instance in which a silver coin represented the integrity of the national army. More often coins used in royal ritual were said to represent the integrity of the kingdom, the hope that its unity remain intact. The act of giving a coin as a token of loyalty, then, can be seen as itself creating the king—or, at least, creating the power by which he unifies the kingdom: in a word, his *hasina*.

This is stated almost explicitly when, at the high point of the Merina ritual year, the climax of the Royal Bath ceremony, the sovereign displayed himself before representatives of the people, who presented him with *hasina*. Immediately afterward, he hid behind a screen to bathe, crying out as he did so, "may I be *masina*." After this he emerged to sprinkle his subjects with the water in which he had just bathed, in exactly the same way as *sampy* keepers, on other occasions, sprinkled the people with water that had been used to bathe the national *sampy* (cf. Berg 1979; Bloch 1987). Here, compressed into a brief succession of ritual gestures, is the whole pattern of *sorona* and *ody:* an object, displayed to represent the desires of the kingdom, becomes an invisible charm regularly capable of bringing those desires to fruition.

prospects and conclusions

A central claim of this chapter is the existence of a very widespread distinction between the power to act directly on others (a potential that can only be realized in the future) and the power to move others to action by displaying evidence of how one's self has been treated in the past. Both, I have argued, tend to be expressed through metaphors of vision: the first represented as something hidden, the second realized through forms of visual display.

So, too, the distinction between the power of money and the power (or, if you like, value) of what I have been calling "heirloom jewelry." Money tends to be represented as an invisible potency because of its capacity to turn into many other things. Money is the potential for future specificity even if it is a potential that can be realized only through a future act of exchange. In this it stands opposed to objects whose value is rooted in past actions (whatever these may be). The latter are not only often objects of display in their own right: they have a power to inspire actions in others, a power that clearly has much in common with that of aristocratic display or royal splendor. But if, at its simplest, aristocratic display calls on the viewer to deliver wealth or render homage to the displayer because others have already done so, the most elementary form of exchange value is just the opposite: it inspires one to try to acquire an object simply because others have tried to do so in the past.

If this is so, to understand the value attributed to any particular object means that one must understand the meaning of the various acts of creation, consecration, use and appropriation, and so on, that make up its history.[11] One must ask: Which of these actions determine which aspect of its value?

Which among them are those that recognize the value being called on to repeat? And then there is the problem of fetishism, a notoriously tricky one. Perhaps the best way to describe the view of fetishism I have been developing here is to say that when one recognizes value in an object, one becomes a sort of bridge across time. That is, one recognizes not only the existence of a history of past desires and intentions that have given shape to the present form of the object, but that history extends itself through one's own desires, wishes, and intentions, newly mobilized in that very act of recognition. In fetishizing an object, then, one is mistaking the power of a history internalized in one's own desires, for a power intrinsic to the object itself. Fetish objects become mirrors of the beholder's own manipulated intentions. And in a way, the very notion of desire—at least, as I have been developing it in this chapter—demands such fetishization.

Consider Gyges, making himself invisible so as to gaze on the body of the Lydian queen—or, for that matter, any of those generically dressed bourgeois males gazing at any of those ornamental, particular bourgeois women. Invisibility and abstraction here offer a way of indicating the power to act (and looking is certainly a form of action), but can they not equally well be seen as implying that the man is a creature of desire, to be characterized (at that moment anyway) not by what he is or has but by what he is not, by an absence or a lack? After all, it is just this sense of absence, or incompletion, that moves us to action to begin with. Next, consider Marx's analysis of exchange, in which the desired object is always concrete and particular. Could one not say that the abstraction, the lack of definition attributed to the desirer and his possessions, is also a way of figuring desire? It is an absence, if one that necessarily implies the recognition of some imaginary totality that would be its resolution. In such situations, I am suggesting, the object of desire plays much the same role as Lacan's mirror-objects: it represents an imagined wholeness on which desirers can fix their own inchoate sense of self. Or—to return for the moment to Marx's own dialectical terminology—it makes the desirer seem an abstract content that can be realized only through that particular concrete form.[12]

Even at this most individual level, then, action and reflection endlessly imply each other in an infinite variety of conversions and transformations. On grander levels of historical change, similar dynamics are always in the process of transforming—or at least contesting—the very categories by which value is perceived. And if the Malagasy example—with its royal attempts to turn money-stuffs into icons of national unity, and its popular attempts to divert them into hidden sources of power—demonstrates anything, it is that these struggles over value are always, in the end, political—if only because the most important political struggles in any society (and here I return to Turner 1996b) will always be over how value itself is to be defined.

Chapter 5 ▨

Wampum and Social Creativity among The Iroquois

In this chapter, I'd like to say a little bit about wampum, the white and purple shell beads which became a currency of trade in early colonial Northeast North America. Among "primitive valuables"—a category that includes such things as kula necklaces, Kwakiutl coppers, or the iron bars used in bridewealth exchange by the West African Tiv—wampum holds a rather curious place. Simply as an object, it's by far the most familiar. The average reader is much more likely to know what wampum looks like, or to have actually seen some in a museum, than any of the others. Nonetheless, unlike the others, wampum has never been treated as a classic case in anthropological exchange theory.

There are probably several reasons for this. For one thing, the contexts in which wampum circulated is closer to what a Western observer would be inclined to see as political than economic. The heyday of wampum was also a very long time ago: in the seventeenth and eighteenth centuries, long before the birth of modern ethnography. But it's also hard to escape the impression that the case of wampum is in most other ways just a little bit too close to home. Wampum was, after all, material manufactured from clams found primarily off the coast of Long Island, whose shells are still to be found scattered on the beaches of Fire Island, the Hamptons, and other places where New York's stockbrokers and literati like to spend their summer weekends; it was used mainly for trade with the Iroquois towns that then dotted what is now upstate New York. Wampum was first manufactured in bulk by the Pequods of Connecticut, a group later to be wiped out by English settlers in a notorious massacre in 1637. This is not the sort of history most New Yorkers like to dwell on—or Americans in general, for that matter.

Finally, anthropologists' own role has not always been entirely innocent. In the late 1960s, when many of the Six Nations of the Iroquois were trying to win back control of their heirloom wampum collection from New York State museums, William Fenton, who was then and remains to this day one of the most respected Anglo authorities on the subject, took it upon himself to write a major treatise entitled "The New York State Wampum Collection: the Case for Integrity of Cultural Treasures" (1971) which made an elaborate case for refusing to accede to their requests. The essay, as one might imagine, served only to reinforce the widespread (and to a large extent historically justified) Native American impression that anthropologists were at best agents of cultural imperialism, and at worst, of even worse sorts. Resulting bitterness has made the whole issue of anthropological views of wampum somewhat sensitive.

All this is quite a shame because it seems to me that the study of wampum is of potentially enormous interest to any theory of value. For one thing, it is probably the best documented case of beads being used as a medium of exchange between European traders and a very differently organized society in which we have a fairly clear picture of what the non-European parties to the transaction did with the beads once they got them. The focus in this chapter will be on the Iroquoian peoples of what came to be known as the Five (later, Six) Nations. What I'm going to do first of all is tell the history of wampum, up to around the end of the eighteenth century, which took on an extraordinary importance in the creation of the Iroquois Federation itself. The first effect of the arrival of European traders in search of fur, and soon after, settlers, on the coast of Northeast North America was, predictably, to plunge the peoples of the interior into an almost constant state of violent upheaval: a world of endless feuding, massacres, forced migrations, whole peoples scattered and displaced, of two hundred years of almost continual war. Wampum had a peculiar role in all this. It was the principle medium of the fur trade, which had sparked so much of the trouble to begin with—wampum was one of the lures held out by the newcomers to inspire people to attack each other; but at the same time, within the Iroquois confederacy—and the Iroquois were considered by their Indian neighbors a particularly ferocious and terrifying population of warriors—it was valued primarily for its ability to create peace.

the origins of wampum

So much changed so quickly once Europeans began to arrive on the coasts of Northeastern North America that it becomes difficult to say anything for certain about the years before. There's no consensus about whether something that could be called "wampum" even existed before 1500; nonetheless, this is something of a technical question, since polished beads of one kind or another—rare stones, mica, beads of shell or quill—and similar bright and mirrored objects certainly did, and they were an important indigenous category of wealth across the northeast woodlands (Hammel 1984).

During the sixteenth century, European interest in North America focused mainly on fur—particularly beaver pelts, then in great demand for the manufacture of hats. Dutch and English traders began arriving on the coast armed with liberal supplies of glass trade beads—these were already being mass-produced in Venice and the Netherlands for use in the markets of Africa and the Indian Ocean—and usually found the inhabitants willing to accept them in exchange for pelts. For a time, they became a regular currency of trade. There was even an attempt to manufacture them in Massachusetts. But as time went on and European settler enclaves grew, their place was gradually supplanted by wampum: the small, tubular white and purple beads that the Algonkian-speaking peoples of Massachusetts and Long Island had long been in the habit of manufacturing from whelks and quahog clams. English and Dutch colonists apparently found it a relatively simple matter to force them to mass-produce them, stringing the beads together in belts of pure white or pure purple (the latter, because of their relative rarity, were worth twice as much) and setting fixed rates of exchange with the Indians of the interior: so many fathoms of wampum for such and such a pelt. Later, after the coastal Indians had been largely exterminated, colonists began to manufacture the beads themselves (Ceci 1977, 1982; Beauchamp 1901).

Wampum was not just a currency of trade. Settlers used it in dealing with each other. The early colonies were also notoriously cash-poor; silver money was almost unheard of, and most transactions between settlers were conducted through barter, credit, and wampum. Colonial governments recognized wampum as legal tender until the middle of the eighteenth century, many settlers preferring wampum to coins, even when the latter had become easily available—if only, perhaps, because Indians were more likely to accept them (Weeden 1884; Martien 1996). On the other hand there's no evidence that even the Indians living in the closest proximity to Europeans used wampum to buy and sell things to one another. We really are talking, then, about two profoundly different regimes of value.

When the first European settlers arrived, most of the coast was occupied by speakers of Algonkian languages; the woodlands west of the Hudson were inhabited mainly by speakers of Iroquoian ones. These latter were people who lived mainly in large fortified towns and who were grouped into a patchwork of political confederacies, of whom the most prominent were the Huron along the Saint Lawrence and the Iroquois, scattered across the north of what is now upstate New York. Since most of the beaver along the coast were quickly hunted out, the Huron (allied with the French traders then established in Quebec) were best positioned to control the rotes to hunting grounds out further west. In the early seventeenth century, then, we have much more detailed information on the Huron than any other Iroquoian peoples, particularly because of the fact that French Jesuits had settled in most Huron communities and kept detailed records of their work. The Five Nations of the Iroquois Confederacy to the south—the Onondaga, Oneida, Seneca, Mohawk, and Cayuga—were less well known. Most of the Algonkian peoples of the coast seem to have considered them as terrifying cannibals[1]—but the Iroquois had the advantage of alliance with the Dutch, and therefore, access to a much more dependable source of firearms. During the so called "Beaver Wars" from 1641 to 1649, they managed to destroy most of the major Huron towns, carry off a large number of Huron as captives, and scatter most of the remaining population. By 1656 the Iroquois had broken the power of the Petun and Neutral Confederations to the west as well, thus establishing a monopoly over the trade that they were to maintain for at least a century.

During the next hundred and fifty years or so, the Iroquois were involved in an endless series of wars: between the British and French, the British and American colonists, and any number of other Indian nations. It was especially during this period that wampum—which the Iroquois acquired both as payment for furs and as tribute from subjugated peoples—came to play a central role in their political life, even, one might argue, in the constitution of Iroquois society itself.[2] This is the period which I especially want to look at; but in order to understand what happened, it will first be necessary to try to at least attempt to reconstruct something of early Iroquoian social structure.

the resurrection of names

Like the Algonkian peoples to the east, Iroquoian nations were matrilineal and matrilocal. Unlike them, the Iroquoians (Five Nations and Huron alike) shared a very particular constitution: they saw their societies not as a collection of living individuals but as a collection of eternal names, which over the course of time passed from one individual holder to another.

Most of the peoples of northeast North America had a custom of the occasional "resurrection" of names. If a famous warrior, for example, were to die, another man might be given his name, and then be considered in a certain sense an incarnation of the same person; if he were a chief, he might also inherit his office. According to a Jesuit relation written in 1642 about the Huron:

> It has often been said that the dead were brought back to life by making the living bear their names. This is done for several reasons,—to revive the mem-

ory of a brave man, and to incite him who shall bear his name to imitate his courage; to take revenge upon the enemies, for he who takes the name of a man killed in battle binds himself to avenge his death; to assist the family of a dead man, because he who brings him back to life, and who represents him, assumes all the duties of the deceased . . . (JR 22: 287–89)

It was accomplished, significantly, by hanging a collar of wampum around the man's neck; if the latter accepted it, and did not shake it off, he would then become the dead man's former self.

The Iroquois, however, took this principle much further: all names should eventually be resurrected by being passed on to someone else. An Iroquois nation (or "tribe") was normally composed of a series of matrilineal clans, which were in turn grouped into two moieties. Each clan had its own collection of names and a matron who was its keeper. The most important, chiefly, names could equally well be thought of as titles—since each corresponded to a position in the political structure of the tribe or confederation. When one such office-holder died, the name was, as the Huron put it, "resurrected" by being conveyed to some person of similar qualities, would thereby also be invested in the title's associated regalia and thus in the office itself (Goldenweiser 1914; Parker 1926:61–65; Shimony 1961; Heidenreich 1978:371–72; for the Huron, see Tooker 1964:44–45). One might say then that the number of "persons"—using the term in the Maussian sense, as particular social identities fixed by socially recognized insignia of one sort or another—in the Iroquois cosmos was fixed, since, like Tylor's "images," they survived the death of the holder.[3] At any point in history, one would encounter the same basic collection of personae, the only difference being that while all the chiefly roles would be filled, some of the less exalted ones would be likely to be without occupants at any given moment.

Iroquois sources often spoke of this as "hanging the name around the neck." Evidence is sketchy, but at least among certain Iroquois nations—and perhaps all of them—each clan did have a collection of "name-necklaces" corresponding to its stock of names, and kept by the same matron responsible for keeping track of them (Fenton 1926:65). The major chiefly titles came with their own belts of wampum, which functioned as insignia of office, and which were indeed placed around the neck of the man who succeeded to it, along with other insignia of office (Hewitt 1944:65–66; Beauchamp 1901:347–49; Fenton 1946:118; cf. Druke 1981:109–110).

It is a little difficult to generalize because we are dealing with a variety of peoples whose habits were probably not entirely consistent even within any one time and place. Probably even different clans or longhouses had different practices. But it's clear that among the Five Nations in particular, the resurrection of names became crucial to the constitution of society itself. It is possible this was simply a cultural quirk, but it's hard to escape the suspicion that this had something to do with the unusually predatory nature of Iroquois society.

war and social structure

The League of the Hodenosaunee (or "Iroquois") consisted, at first, of Five Nations, the Onondaga, Mohawk, Seneca, Cayuga, and Oneida, all of whom occupied a swath of territory to the direct south of Lake Erie in what is now upstate New York.[4] The population was concentrated in a series of large, fortified towns—Dutch and English sources usually call them "castles"—perched on hilltops and surrounded by elaborate palisades.

Inside the palisades was female territory. Each longhouse was organized around a core of related women. The male domain was "the forest," with the usual emphasis on war and hunting. Villages and nations were of course connected by an overarching network of political institutions—the organization of the Iroquois League, which seems to have emerged in the years before 1500, just before Europeans appeared on the scene, was one of the inspirations for the federal system adopted in the United States. There were thus a set of different councils operating on different levels: from longhouse to village, village to nation, nation to the federation itself. There are two points here that I think deserve special emphasis. The first is that this system involved an extremely important role for women. Longhouses were governed by councils made up entirely of women, who, since they controlled its food supplies, could evict any in-married male at will. Villages were governed by both male and female councils. Councils on the national and league level were also made up of both male and female office-holders. It's true that the higher one went in the structure, the less relative importance the female councils had—on the longhouse level, there wasn't any male organization at all, while on the league level, the female council merely had veto power over male decisions—but it's also true that decisions on the lower level were of much more immediate relevance to daily life. In terms of everyday affairs, Iroquois society often seems to have been about as close as there is to a documented case of a matriarchy. The second is that for all the complex federative structure, society was in most respects highly egalitarian. Office-holders, male and female, were elected from among a pool of possible heirs; the offices themselves, at least the male political ones, were considered as much a responsibility as a reward as they involved no real material rewards and certainly granted the holder no coercive power.

Of course, most of our evidence comes from a time of constant war. It's hard to tell precisely how all this affected the relative roles of men and women. On the one hand, it could only have increased the relative importance of the male councils, which were largely concerned with matters of war and peace. On the other, it eventually created a situation in which a large proportion of the men in any given community were not really Iroquois at all, which could only have increased the authority of women on the local level.

Iroquois warfare conformed to a pattern common to much of aboriginal North America. Daniel Richter (1983, 1992:32–38) calls it the "mourning war" complex. The logic is similar to, but not quite the same as, that of the feud. The death of almost any important person might lead to the organization of a military expedition, whether or not that person had been killed by enemies. Among the Five Nations, the logic might be considered an extension of the principle of replacing the dead. Whenever a man or woman holding an important office died, his or her name would be transferred immediately to someone new: the ceremony has come to be known in the literature as a "Requickening" ceremony, because it restored the life and vitality that had been lost to the entire community through death. More humble members of society would eventually be replaced as well. But in the meantime, the effects of loss could be disastrous, especially for those closest to the deceased. The grief and pain of mourning was seen as capable of driving survivors entirely insane. Often, then, the women of the bereaved household could demand a raiding party be got together (usually from among their male affines) to capture a replacement. Normally this raid would be directed against some neighboring people who were considered traditional enemies. At times, they could escalate into major wars, replete with stand-up battles in which large parties of warriors would meet each other in "largely ceremonial confrontations between massed forced protected by wooden body armor and bedecked in elaborate headdresses" (Richter 1992:35). Death in battle was quite unusual; in part, because the main purpose of war was taking of prisoners.

As for the prisoners, their fate, once brought back to the Iroquois homeland, could be either surprisingly benign or utterly horrendous. All prisoners were formally adopted into the local family that had suffered a recent loss. It was up to family members whether they would then be tortured to death or kept on as a replacement for the deceased. European observers saw the choice as a matter of whim, almost entirely unpredictable. Those to be killed were first feasted, then tied to a stake where they were systematically cut, gouged, and most of all, burned with firebrands and red-hot metal, often over the course of an entire night before dying—ceremonies that, apparently sometimes did end with a communal feast on parts of the body of the dead (in other words, what their neighbors said was not entirely untrue). The vast majority of women and children captured on raids, and a very good proportion—probably the majority—of the men were not, however, killed but permanently adopted. They would be given the name of the deceased and, ideally, almost instantly find themselves treated like a member of the family, having all rights and relations of the deceased (i.e., a man would normally take his place as husband of the dead man's wife), and treated with the utmost tenderness by his female relatives. After a trial period during which they were carefully watched for any sign of disaffection, such prisoners could eventually become fully accepted members of society, even in some cases leading war parties or receiving higher names and offices with political responsibilities.

This anyway was how the situation appears to have worked in indigenous times. Warfare became much more severe and destructive during the seventeenth century, during which the Iroquois managed to break, one after the other, a series of rival federations, including the Mohicans, Hurons, Petuns, Neutrals, Erie, and Susquahannock—wars that often involved both unprecedented massacres (one Iroquois chief ordered eighty Huron prisoners slaughtered in one day, in order to assuage his grief and anger at the death of his brother) and the massive incorporation of alien prisoners into Iroquoian society. It was around this period one reads accounts of a society effectively divided into classes, with adopted prisoners doing the bulk of the menial labor and with members of their adopted families having the right to kill them for the slightest infractions or impertinence (Starna and Watkins 1991), and missionaries complained that in many communities most men were not particularly fluent speakers of their own nation's languages (Quain 1937). It may be that the unusually systematic nature of the Iroquoian naming practices only emerged in this period (alternately, it may be that it had existed for a very long time, and this was one of the reasons the Five Nations were able to expand and incorporate others more effectively than their neighbors). Anyway, this exceptionally brutal period did not last long: the children of these captives were considered full members of their adoptive clans.

the making of peace

At this point, let me return to the role of wampum. Wampum in fact played an essential role in the mechanics of both making war and ending it.

For example, if a man's death inspired members of his family to commission a war party, the clan matron was said to "put his name on the mat" by sending a belt of wampum to a related war chief; he would then gather together a group of men to try to bring back a captive to replace him (Lafitau in Fenton 1978:315). If the man in question had been killed, however—at least, if the killer was not from a completely alien group—the usual practice was to appoint an avenger.[5] The only way to prevent this, in fact, was for the killer's people to pay a gift of wampum immediately to the victim's family. The usual fee was five fathoms for the life of a man, ten for that of a woman (T. Smith 1983:236; Morgan 1854:331–34; Parker 1926). Within the league, elaborate mechanisms existed to ensure any such matters would be quickly resolved; councils would be convoked, large amounts of wampum raised by canvassing the important members of the killer's clan. Even then, it was still the bereaved family who had the last word. If stubborn, they could still insist on sending the avenger on his way.

The mechanics of peacemaking are especially important because this is what the League was essentially about. The Iroquois term translated "league," in fact, really just means "peace": the entire political apparatus was seen by its creators primarily as a way of resolving murderous disputes. The League was less a government, or even alliance,[6] than a series of treaties establishing amity and providing the institutional means for preventing feuds and maintaining harmony among the five nations that made it up. For all their reputation as predatory warriors, the Iroquois themselves saw the essence of political action to lie in making peace.

Wampum was the essential medium of all peacemaking. Every act of diplomacy, both within the League and outside it, had to be carried out through the giving and receiving of wampum. If a message had to be sent, it would be "spoken into" belts or strings of wampum, which the messenger would present to the recipient. Such belts or strings were referred to as "words"; they were often woven into mnemonic patterns bearing on the import of the message. Without them, no message stood a chance of being taken seriously by its recipient. In council, too, speakers would accompany their arguments with belts of wampum—also called "words"—laying them down one after the other as the material embodiments of their arguments (Beauchamp 1901; Smith 1983:231–32).[7]

When envoys were sent to propose a treaty to another nation, not only would the conditions of the treaty itself be "spoken into" belts of wampum, but the envoys would be given belts and strings to convey as gifts for the nation to whom the treaty was proposed. These might also be woven into "words"; at any rate, they would be presented one by one to the accompaniment of words of conciliation. Since Iroquois diplomacy is well documented, we have a good record of what these conciliatory speeches were like:

> They run somewhat as follows, each sentence being pronounced with great solemnity, and confirmed by the delivery of a wampum belt: "Brothers, with this belt I open your ears that you may hear; I draw from your feet the thorns that pierced them as you journeyed thither; I clean the seats of the council-house, that you may sit at ease; I wash your head and body, that your spirits may be refreshed; I condole you on the loss of your friends who have died since we last met; I wipe out any blood which may have been spilt between us." . . .

126   *Toward an Anthropological Theory of Value*

And his memory was refreshed by belts of wampum, which he delivered after every clause in his harangue, as a pledge of the sincerity and the truth of his words (Brice in Holmes 1883:242).

Afterward, an envoy might place the treaty belts themselves over the shoulders of the chief, who could either accept the treaty or reject it by shaking them off (Heckewelder in Holmes 1883:246–47). If accepted, copies of the treaty belts would be sent back with the envoy, and both sides would keep their belts as a permanent record of their mutual obligations.

Michael Foster (1985) has suggested that the exchange of wampum in such negotiations was seen first and foremost as a way of opening up channels of communication. Hence the rhetorical emphasis on "opening the ears" and "unstopping the throats" of those who received it, and of otherwise putting them at ease with one another. This was particularly important if (as was usually the case) there had previously been hostilities between the two parties. It seems to me this is true as far as it goes; but the notion of "communication" plays into much larger cosmological ideas. Iroquois religion, as Elisabeth Tooker (1970:7; Chafe 1961) has aptly put it, was in its essence "a religion of thanksgiving." Ritual was seen above all as a way to give thanks to the Creator by showing one's joy at the existence of the cosmos he had created. Even today just about every ritual event or even meeting involves thanksgiving speeches, in which the speaker lists the main elements of the cosmos—earth, trees, wind, sun, moon, sky—and celebrates the existence of each in turn.[8] This celebration or joy could also be imagined as feeling of expansiveness, an opening of oneself to the totality of creation and to the social world. In a similar way acts of condolence, such as the giving of wampum, were meant to clear all the grief and anger that obstructed the minds and bodies of those bereaved by death and to restore them to full communication with the world and other people. This is why the givers spoke not only of opening the eyes and ears and throats of their recipients but also of "revealing the sun" and "revealing the sky" to them once more. "Opening up channels of communication," then, is not simply a matter of creating an environment in which people can talk to one another; it is a matter of opening them up to the universe as a whole.

But why should gifts of wampum be an appropriate medium for this?

George Hammel (1984) provides the most plausible explanation. Throughout the eastern woodlands of North America, he suggests, there was a broad category of objects that were seen as embodying what he calls "life and light"—illumination, in Hammel's analysis, being roughly equivalent to my "expansiveness." These included a wide range of bright or mirrored objects, ranging from quartz crystals to obsidian to certain sorts of shell, as well as, later, wampum and glass beads. Even before the advent of Europeans, these constituted a category of wealth that was traded over long distances, and in special demand by those engaged in shamanistic pursuits. Wampum was thus seen as carrying an intrinsic capacity to lift away grief. A Seneca myth about Hiawatha—who was said to be the inventor of wampum, as well as one of the founders of the League—has him gathering together the first string and vowing:

> If I should see anyone in deep grief I would remove these strings from the pole and console them. The strings would become words and lift away the darkness with which they are covered. (Hammel 1984:19)

Just in these few references one can already see a fairly clear set of terms of opposition. The difference between pleasure and pain, joy and grief is conceived as one between expansion and contraction; and by extension between light (which allows extend one's vision into the world, to see the sun and sky) and darkness (in which one's vision contracts to the immediate environs of the self). Even more importantly, perhaps, it is an opposition between articulate speech and silence or inarticulate rage; strings of wampum are themselves things of light, but they are also "words," that unstop the ears and throats of those who receive them, allowing them to pass into that domain of "self-extension" which is made possible only through language (Scarry 1985). The two possible fates of Iroquois prisoners are a perfect expression of this: one the one hand, to have a name hung around the neck, in the form of a string of wampum; on the other, to have red-hot axes hung around the neck, which burn into the flesh and send the prisoner into a spiral of agony that will ultimately lead to the ultimate contraction, that of death.

the origins of the Great Peace

In 1946, the Seneca anthropologist Arthur Parker suggested that if one wished to understand his people's history, one had to begin by taking a cosmological perspective: that is, to see how Iroquoians themselves place themselves in the overall history of the universe. Those of his time saw the latter as structured around three great creative moments: the first, that of the creation of the universe; the second, that of the creation of the League, or "Great Peace," and the third, the reforms of the Seneca prophet Handsome Lake in the beginning of the nineteenth century. Around each there is an extensive oral tradition. During the period we are dealing with, there would appear to have been only two.

Iroquois legends concerning the origins of the League (Converse 1962; Hale 1883; Hewitt 1892; Parker 1916)[9] always begin by describing a time when incessant feuds and warfare had laid the country to waste. The Iroquois' ancestors had reverted to a state of savagery, fleeing to the forests and giving themselves over entirely to murder, cannibalism, and rapine. In these stories, the effects of their grief and rage are often figured as physical deformities: the people had literally become monstrous. The action begins when, in the midst of all this chaos, war, and degradation, a man named Deganawideh emerges to reform the people by magic and persuasion, and to have them agree to a Great Peace. The story follows him as he does so, meeting and joining forces with Hiawatha, and creating present day Iroquois society in the process by giving names to its constituent clans and nations. Its climax comes when the heroes are faced with most monstrous being of all, the evil sorcerer Thadodaho of the Onondaga—described (in Hewitt's version: 1882:138–40) as having the hands of a turtle, the feet of a bear, snakes for hair, and a penis of many fathoms wrapped several times around his body. Rather than do battle, they offer him thirteen strings of wampum, one after the other, accompanying each with a song. With each presentation, one of his deformities disappears, until by the end he is once again a normal human being. The reformed Thadodaho agrees to become the fire keeper of the central Onondaga council lodge and guardian of the League's wampum (including those very thirteen strings). Deganawideh goes on to speak the rules of the League into wampum strings that Thadodaho will preserve, and then disappears from the earth.

All the other protagonists of the story, including Hiawatha, remained just as the clans and nations to which Deganawideh gave names. Thadodaho himself became the keeper of the League's treasury of wampum belts; and ever since, whoever becomes the keeper of the treasury thereby becomes Thadodaho.

Note once again the parallel between the removal of grief, and the bestowal of names. Deganawideh and Hiawatha consistently do both. One might say that in doing so they create society in two senses: first, by creating peace, the potential for sociality that makes it possible; second, by establishing differentiations within this newly created peace, and thereby giving society its structure. All these primordial gestures continue to be reenacted in the present through acts of giving wampum. As in so many mythological systems, most present-day acts are not seen as fundamentally creative in the same sense; they are simply a matter of re-creating the same structure of names and offices over and over again. Nonetheless, without that continual re-creation, the Great Peace would cease to exist and humanity would presumably revert again to savagery and rage.

The climax of the myth—the reform of Thadodaho—was recapitulated in the most important League ritual: the Condolence ceremony, held yearly to "raise up" new chiefs to replace those who had died. Like the smaller clan rituals on which it was modeled, it consisted of a confrontation between two moieties, one "clear-minded," the other bereaved. At the end, the clear-minded moiety would lift the others' bereavement by presenting thirteen "words," or messages, each accompanied by a string of wampum whose pattern reproduced the message in visual form (Hale 1883, Hewitt 1944, Parker 1926, Tooker 1978:437–40). Here, too, each string was intended to remove some hurt or obstruction that had been the consequence of grief: to wipe away the tears from their eyes, remove the obstruction from their ears, unstop the throat, straighten the body, wipe the bloody stains from their beds, lift their surrounding darkness, and so on. It was only after this that new chiefs could be raised up by giving them the strings or belts corresponding to the dead ones' names.

If the ritual was performed in full, there would also be a recitation of the League's chiefly names and of its constitutive regulations (Hale 1883:54–55). The belts into which Deganawideh originally spoke the latter were kept together with the League's collection of treaty belts (treaties that were in a sense their extensions) in the central Onondaga lodge under the care of Thadodaho. They too were laid out one by one as elders explained their significance.

> At certain seasons they meet to study their meaning, and to renew the ideas of which they were an emblem or confirmation. On such occasions they sit down around the chest, take out one string or belt after the other, handing it about to every person present, and that they all may comprehend its meaning, repeat the words pronounced on its delivery in their whole convention. By these means they are able to remember the promises reciprocally made by the different parties; and it is their custom to admit even the young boys, who are related to the chiefs, to . . . become early acquainted with all the affairs of state. (Loskiel in Holmes 1883:245–46; cf. Parker 1916:48)

Such belts were almost always woven in complex pictures, which could be interpreted as visual statements of the words once spoken into them, but these pictures were in no sense hieroglyphics. They were essentially mnemonics, and would have meant nothing unless interpreted by elders who used them, as Morgan says, to "draw forth the secret records locked up in their remembrance" (Morgan 1851:120–21; Druke 1985).

circulation and history

The Iroquois of the seventeenth and eighteenth centuries, then, appear to have conceived themselves as endlessly reproducing a social order that was essentially founded on the principle of peace, even as they themselves were engaged in constant, often predatory warfare. The unusually static conception of history—especially the conception of society as a collection of permanent, named positions—seems only to have facilitated this, because it meant that the often sordid or gruesome details of actual history could, as it were, be made to melt away at ritual moments when beautiful words and beautiful objects re-created the essential foundations of society, its ultimate truth. Wampum became the necessary medium for this process. Now, on the face of it, this might seem somewhat paradoxical, since wampum was, after all, not something that Iroquois society itself produced. It came in from outside. But in a way this is only appropriate for a material that was itself seen as carrying the power of social creativity. It turns on a common cosmological dilemma: how can that which has the power to constitute a certain order itself partake of that same order? (This is of course another version of the Goedelian problems discussed in chapter 3.) The origins of Deganawideh himself were, as so often with such heroes, somewhat extra-social: he was born to a virgin mother in a Huron village. After having constituted the social order, he then vanished; alone among the characters of the story, he did not remain part of it.

Wampum entered Iroquois society in two principal ways. One was the fur trade. The Iroquois became more and more central players in the trade over the course of the seventeenth century; Dutch, French and English merchants supplied large amounts in exchange for furs. The other was through tribute. In the wars by which the Iroquois fought against other groups to take control of the fur trade, they also imposed very unequal treaties, obliging defeated groups to pay what amounted to hundreds of fathoms of wampum in tribute every year. In both cases, wampum tended to arrive already woven into belts uniform both in color and in size.[10]

Once it arrived, wampum appears to have been divided among important office-holders, a class who some early sources even refer to as 'nobles'" "It is they who furnish them," wrote Lafitau, "and it is among them that they are redivided when presents are made to the village, and when replies to the belts of their ambassadors are sent" (Holmes 1883:244); though there are some hints of ceremonial dances or other events in which office-holders would "cast wampum to the spectators" or otherwise redistribute the stuff (Michelson 1974; Fenton 1998:128; Beauchamp 1898:11). But it does not really seem to have *circulated* in the sense of being transacted, passed from hand to hand. Neither for that matter was it much used as a casual form of adornment (Morgan 1851:387–88), by notables or anyone else. Instead, it was kept hidden away in chests or pouches in its owner's longhouse until needed for some ritual or diplomatic act, whereupon the women of the longhouse would weave it into the required patterns. Beauchamp remarks that "to some councils they were taken almost by the bushel, over a hundred being sometimes used, but nearly all these were afterwards taken apart or made to do duty on some other occasion." For such league-wide events, office-holders could seem to have had the right draw on the reserves of those they represented; afterwards, they would presumably redistribute part of what they themselves received to the contributors. (At any rate, that was the case in diplomacy, which could involve even more grandiose expenditures.)

Hidden wampum, then, represented a kind of potential for political action: for making peace but also for making war. It remained invisible until something important needed to be said or done: a speech made at council, a war-party commissioned, an agreement negotiated, a mourner consoled. On such occasions one might make gifts of generic wampum, belts of pure white or "black" (purple). More often, though, one gave belts made of both white and black beads woven into concrete, particular patterns that could be displayed, one by one, as the visual complement to a speaker's arguments. If the words were truly important, the belts could be preserved in that form, placed in a chest but periodically brought out to be displayed and their words remembered; otherwise, they would be cut up into their component beads and distributed again.

One can, I think, distinguish two different forms of value here, which can also be thought of as two different ways in which wampum was similar to speech. On the one hand, the designs of wampum used to resolve disputes or to "open up channels of communication" were as ephemeral as ordinary conversation, but as in much ordinary conversation, what was said was not so important as the mere fact that people were speaking to one another. Beads, as Hammel emphasized, embodied what might be considered the ultimate value in Iroquois culture: the sense of brightness, clarity, expansiveness, of unhindered communication with the cosmos, whose social manifestation was peace and the unobstructed solidarity of human beings. But wampum was not simply a representation of value. By assembling, distributing, and presenting it as soothing words to unblock the obstructions of grief and anger in others, one actually created that peace and solidarity. Like Marx's money, wampum was a representation of a value that could only be realized through its exchange.

On the other hand, certain "words"—certain figured belts and strings— could become significant and memorable in themselves. Like the unique heirlooms discussed in chapter 4, their value was either (in the form of name-belts) tied to unique personal identities, or else (in the form of law-and treaty-belts) derived from a unique history of human action. This is presumably why, according to Lafitau, the latter could be referred to equally as "words" or as "transactions": they were the embodied memory of previous acts of diplomacy and peacemaking. If hidden, generic, or ephemeral wampum was the potential to create peace, heirloom belts were peace in its crystalline form.

creation and intentionality

Let us imagine the history of piece of wampum, circa 1675. It was manufactured from a whelk shell by an Algonkian somewhere on Long Island and became part of a solid white belt, which was then passed by its manufacturer as tribute to some Dutch official. For a while the belt circulated as money back and forth between colonists in New England and New Amsterdam, the memory of each transaction disappearing with the next. Finally, an English trader used it to purchase the pelt of a beaver that had been killed somewhere around Lake Michigan, from a member of the Seneca nation who had got it from an Ojibwa trade partner. From there the belt might have passed west to the Great Lakes, where the pelts were being extracted by tributaries of the Iroquois, and from there, passed back to the Iroquois as tribute once again; or it might have remained in the longhouse of the man who had sold the English trader the pelts. In any event, memory of each specific transaction would continue to be effaced with each new one. The value of the wampum, then, derived not from the importance of past actions but, like money, from its capacity to mediate future ones, and also, one should add, the fact that it was the medium of a larger circuit of exchange, spanning most of North America, a totality of interactions that continued to be reproduced through its medium. Again like money, it was a tiny portion of a greater, undifferentiated totality. Only if the belt were broken up and reworked into "words" would the bead's value shift from that of a potential for future actions to that of actions already taken in the past.

Note that outside of the colonies, wampum functioned only in an anonymous fashion in dealings between people who did not consider themselves part of the same society: a English trader and a Seneca, and Seneca and an Ojibwa, etc. In transactions between members of the same society, or even transactions between members of different nations intended to create peace, all this changed. Sometimes, the "words" could simply be reenactments of actions taken in the mythic past, whether of naming or condolence. Others, however, were not simply repetitions but creative acts that, if successful, could themselves end up memorialized. Here is the twenty-third clause of the League's Constitution, as translated by Arthur Parker in 1916:

> 23. Any Lord of the Five Nations Confederacy may construct shell strings (or wampum belts) of any size or length as pledges or records of matters of national or international importance.
>
> When it is necessary to dispatch a shell string by a War Chief or other messenger as the token of summons, the messenger shall recite the contents of the string to the party to whom it is sent. That party shall repeat the message and return the shell string and if there has been a summons he shall make ready for the journey.

Any of the people of the Five Nations may use shells (or wampum) as a record of a pledge, contract or an agreement. (1916:37)

The contractual language may seem a bit ex post facto, but "pledge" seems far closer to the Iroquoian conception than "gift." True, the recipient would usually keep what was given him, but even payments of white wampum in bloodwealth were considered "not in the nature of compensation for the life of the deceased, but of a regretful confession of the crime, with a petition for forgiveness" (Morgan 1851:333). A gift of wampum then revealed the intentions of the giver (when they were not called "word," they could be described as bearing the "thought" or "mind" of the giver: Hewitt 1892:146–48). But they did so in a form that was potentially permanent. It was the fact that it could be kept as a memorial that made the giving of wampum a pledge of sincerity, so that no important proposal or argument would be taken seriously without it.

The crucial moment of the act or "transaction" that was memorialized was not even so much the giving of wampum as the mere revealing of it: it came when the speaker pulled the strings or beads out of the pouch or basket in which they had been hidden, and placed them on the ground before the assembly. It was an act of revelation, of bringing the invisible, intangible contents of mind or soul into visible, physical reality. This was in a sense the quintessential creative act, by which new political realities could be brought into being.

The connection of mind specifically with words deserves further consideration, since it appears to have a particular relevance to the cultures of the Northeast woodlands in general, and particularly with notions of the person. The key text here is Irving Hallowell's ([1954] 1967) essay on conceptions of the soul among the Ojibwa, an Algonkian people of Canada. By "soul," Ojibwa refer to any being with a capacity for perception and intentionality. While Ojibwa assume that souls can take many different appearances or shift from one appearance to another, the uniform kernel behind them is never itself visible to the eye (177). On the other hand, one thing all souls do have in common is an ability to speak, and "the only sensory mode under which it is possible for a human being to directly perceive the presence of souls of *any* category, is the auditory one" (180, his emphasis). In other words, even if souls are invisible, they always make some sort of sound.

If this sort of analysis applies to Iroquois conceptions as well (and both Hallowell and Tooker suggest that it does)[11] then words themselves can be seen as mediating between the invisible and the visible in much the same way wampum does. They provide the necessary medium between hidden desires and concrete, visible realities. This is very important because, I think, it opens up the question of an underlying theory of creativity.

I have already mentioned that Iroquoian ritual is constantly marked out by thanksgiving speeches in which the officiant proceeds to draw attention to each aspect of the cosmos that gives humans happiness and pleasure and thanks the Creator for its existence. In these speeches, creation itself is always treated as an act of speech. After each aspect of the cosmos listed, the speaker comments, "this is what the Creator decided (or 'intended')"—then cites his words and confirms that these words were indeed true and continue to be true, and that for this reason we should all be grateful. Here's a brief sample of the rhetoric:

> And this is what the Creator did. He decided, "There will be plants growing on the earth. Indeed, all of them will have names, as many plants as will be growing on the earth. At a certain time they will emerge from the earth and mature of their own accord. They will be available in abundance as medicines to the people moving about on the earth." That is what he intended. And it is true: we have been using them up to the present time . . . And this too the Creator did. With regard to the plants growing on the earth he decided, "There will be a certain plant on which berries will always hang at a certain time. I shall then cause them to remember me, the people moving about on the earth. They will always express their gratitude when they see the berries hanging above the earth." And it is true: we see them when the wind becomes warm again on the earth; the strawberries are indeed hanging there. And it is also true that we use them, that we drink the berry water. That is what he did. And it is true: it comes to pass. (Chafe 1961:17–24)

And so on with springs, forests, and animals. The image of creation is always a series of deliberate, intentional acts.

It is important to stress that such thanksgiving speeches were (and are still) given at virtually every important ritual occasion, so ordinary people were likely to have heard them dozens, probably hundreds of times. This is why it is a bit surprising when one looks in collections of Iroquois myths, and discovers that in stories about the creation of the world, the origins of the universe look quite different.

The myths in question were mostly gathered in the mid- to late-nineteenth century among elderly members of several Iroquois nations and translated somewhat later (E. Smith 1883; Hewitt 1903:167, 1928:479, Converse 1908; cf. Levi-Strauss 1988:130–34.). In these stories, the original creator/protagonist, sometimes referred to as the "Holder of the Earth," is represented simply as the chief of a people who lived in the sky. At this time there was no sun or moon but a great tree in the very center of the sky that provided illumination during the day and grew dim at night. This chief, it was said, had just married a certain young woman, a young virgin. While conversing with her outside his longhouse, their breath mingled together as they talked and she became pregnant as a result. This certainly would suggest the chief's words had creative efficacy of a sort. However, he does not appear to have been aware of the fertilizing properties of his own speech, because when she later told him she was pregnant (they had not yet had sexual relations) he became profoundly upset.

Here is the original text, in the rather annoying, stilted English that translators then felt appropriate for myths:

> It is certain, it is said, that it formed itself there where they two conversed, where they two breathed together; that, verily, his breath is what the maiden caught, and it is that which was the cause of the change in the life of the maiden [that is, her pregnancy] . . .
>
> Thus it was that, without interruption, it became more and more evident that the maiden would give birth to a child. At that time the chief became convinced of it, and he said: "What is the matter that thy life has changed? Verily, thou art about to have a child. Never, moreover, have thou and I shared the same mat. I believe that it is not I who is the cause that thy life has changed. Dost thou thyself know who it is?" She did not understand the meaning of what he said. (1908:167–68)

While the chief did not understand the power of his speech, his wife was apparently ignorant even of what we would consider the normal mode of procreation. Eventually, she gave birth to a daughter. By that time the chief had begun to fall ill.

> His suffering became more and more severe. All the persons dwelling in the village came to visit him . . . They questioned him repeatedly, seeking to divine his Word, what thing, seemingly, was needful for him, what kind of thing, seemingly, he expected through his dream. Thus, day after day, it continued that they sought to find his Word . . . what manner of thing his soul craved. (1908:171)

Illnesses, as we shall see, were normally understood to arise from frustrated desires: desires that were often as not unknown to their victims, or revealed only indirectly in their dreams.

The creator, we are told, called his people to assembly, announced that he had had a dream, and asked them to "find his word"—to guess what his dream had been. Many tried and failed. Finally, someone suggested the dream was that the great tree standing next to the chief's longhouse had been uprooted, so that all were able to stare through the hole into the abyss below. This, he said, was the right answer, and so the people promptly carried it out. The tree was uprooted. The chief looked down, then invited his wife to follow suit. When she did so, he kicked her down the hole.

The myth goes on to describe how, below, she ultimately gave birth to twins. At this point, the original creator, not fully conscious of either his own creative abilities or destructive impulses, seems to split in two: into one Good Twin (who seems to correspond to the creator of the thanksgiving speeches) who does indeed create the various features of the universe and names them, trying to construct a world amenable to mankind, and an Evil Twin trying to undo everything his brother does. Still, the rather odd reference to guessing dreams deserves further explanation, as it corresponds to a very important dimension of Iroquoian ritual practice.

the dictatorship of dreams

There are a series of elements that appear to me to be crucial to the story and to the underlying theory of creativity it entails:

1. What sets off the whole sequence of events is the protagonists' fundamental ignorance of the nature of his own powers of creation
2. This ignorance then leads to anger and aggression—though, it would seem, the protagonist is not fully aware of this either. It appears in somewhat symbolic form: the desire to uproot the great tree. In the symbolism of Iroquois diplomacy, at any rate, "the tree of peace" was a symbol of the League that sat at its center, and "uprooting the tree" meant war (Jennings, Fenton, Druke and Miller 1985:122).
3. In every case, creation cannot take place alone but only through the mediation of others. The chief's "words" can bring things into being only through the medium of his wife (by making her pregnant), and then through others "guessing his word" and then translating his desire into reality.

The custom of dream-guessing appears to have been an important one among all Iroquoian peoples, and early missionary sources invariably have a great deal to say about the matter. So does Anthony Wallace, who in 1958 wrote a famous piece on the subject, called "Dreams and Wishes of the Soul." In 1649, for instance, a Jesuit named Ragueneau wrote of the Huron:

> In addition to the desires which we generally have that are free, or at least voluntary in us, which arise from a previous knowledge of some goodness that we imagine to exist in the thing desired, the Hurons believe that our souls have other desires, which are, as it were, inborn and concealed. . . .
>
> Now they believe that our soul makes these natural desires known by means of dreams, which are its language. Accordingly, when these desires are accomplished, it is satisfied; but, on the contrary, if it be not granted what it

desires, it becomes angry, and not only does not give its body the good and happiness that it wished to procure for it, but often it also revolts against the body, causing various diseases, and even death. (quoted in Wallace 1958:236)

Wallace goes over a large number of accounts of such Iroquois theories, which for obvious reasons he compares with Freud's. To realize such dreams, though, one usually needed the help of others; and Jesuit reports make it clear that neighbors or kin felt it was incumbent on them to comply with all such "wishes of the soul," insofar as they were able to do so. If it was the dream of an important person, a council might be immediately invoked to discuss its possible significance and how to realize it. Obviously unacceptable dreams might be acted out in symbolic form: a woman who dreamed of acquiring someone else's fields might have to make do with a gift of a few symbolic furrows; a man who had dreamed of being tortured to death, might receive a mere token burn (cf. Wallace op cit., Tooker 1970, Blau 1963); but sometimes they could lead to quite elaborate and, to the missionaries, quite shocking dramatizations, as in the example of an old sick Huron woman who dreamed all the young men and women of the village paired off in a great orgy inside her longhouse, and whose dream was quite literally reenacted.[12]

Quite frequently, these dreams seem to have focused on physical objects. This was certainly the case during the annual dream-guessing festivals. In these, part of the midwinter rites, people would present their dreams to one another in the form of riddles or charades—it was important at any rate that even if understood by the dreamer, they never be stated in clear, straightforward terms. Friends and neighbors would then offer objects, one by one, trying to determine if these were their "soul's desire." The same could sometimes happen when a person fell sick, and realized their illness was the result of an unfulfilled dream. The ill person—in Jesuit accounts, it most often seems to have been a woman—might not even present a riddle, but simply move throughout the village with her entourage, demanding that everyone guess her dream. In 1636 Le Jeune described a Huron ritual held

when some one says that they must go through the Cabins to tell what they have dreamed. Then, as soon as it is evening, a band of maniacs goes about among the Cabins and upsets everything; on the morrow they return, crying in a loud voice, "We have dreamed," without saying what. Those of the Cabin guess what it is, and present it to the band, who refuse nothing until the right thing is guessed. You see them come out with Hatchets, Kettles, Porcelain, and like presents hung around their necks, after their fashion. When they have found what they sought, they thank him who has given it to them; and after having received further additions to this mysterious present—as some leather or a shoemaker's awl, if it were a shoe—they go away in a body to the woods, and there, outside the Village, cast out, they say, their madness; and the sick man begins to get better. (JR 10:175–177)

Note the element of initial disruption: in other accounts, the violence is much more in the foreground. Take Father Dablon's description of an Onondaga dream guessing festival of February 1656: as soon as the elders announced it had begun, "nothing was seen but men, women, and children running like maniacs through the streets and cabins," most barely dressed despite the bitter cold:

> Some carry water, or something worse, and throw it at those whom they meet; others take the firebrands, coals, and ashes from the fire, and scatter them in all directions, without heeding on whom they fall; others break the kettles, dishes, and all the little domestic outfit that they find in their path. Some go about armed with javelins, bayonets, knives, hatchets, and sticks, threatening to strike the first one they meet; and all this continues until each has attained his object and fulfilled his dream (JR 42:155–56)

Similarly, Le Jeune elsewhere writes of "bacchantes" in outlandish costumes who during each night of the festival have "liberty to do anything, and no one dares say a word for them."

> If they find kettles over the fire, they upset them; they break the earthen pots, knock down the dogs, throw fire and ashes everywhere, so thoroughly that often the cabins and entire villages burn down. But the point being that, the more noise and uproar one makes, the more relief the sick person will experience. (JR 17:170)

The violent chaos, and indulgent patience on the part of the community, are followed by the actual guessing of dreams, whether by riddles, charades, or simply a laborious process of elimination. In most cases objects that did not turn out to be right were eventually handed back, but it would seem that large amounts of property could sometimes change hands. "It would be cruelty, nay, murder," Dablon notes, "not to give a man the subject of his dream; for such a refusal might cause his death. Hence, some see themselves stripped of their all, without any hope of retribution; for, whatever they thus give away will never be restored to them, unless they themselves dream, or pretend to dream, of the same thing" (JR 42:165). Dablon adds that he does not imagine this often happens, since faking a dream was believed to lead to all sorts of terrible misfortunes. Finally, the objects given were often seen as carrying an ongoing protective power for the dreamer; a bearskin or deerskin given in dream-guessing ritual, for instance, would thence be regarded as a "remedy," and used to cover the body or kept close by whenever the owner was threatened, as a kind of protective talisman (Carheil in JR 54:65–67).

The sequence, then, is much the same as in the myth: ignorance (the dream indicates something the dreamer had not even been aware that he or she desired), aggression (the wild threats and destruction of the evening), and the need for others to transform one's desires into reality.

Not all dreams expressed mere desires of the soul. In some it was not entirely clear whether the inspiration was from the dreamer's own soul or from a deity called the "Holder of the Skies," and also "Master of our Lives"—apparently the Creator in a particular aggressive aspect (Tooker 1970:86–88): this seems to be the reason why the dreams of important people were often considered matters of national concern. Or even of decisive import in political debates: Brebeuf claims that "if a Captain speaks one way and a dream another, the Captain might shout his head off in vain,—the dream is first obeyed" (JR 10:169). One rather doubts, though, that the same dream would weigh so heavily no matter who it was who had it.

Finally, there were also what Wallace calls "visitation dreams" (1967:61) in which gods or spirits would appear to announce news, predict the course of future events, create new rituals, or even establish new guidelines for the storage of crops. Two oft-cited examples are that of a Huron woman who had been, contrary to custom, married away to another village, and who encountered the Moon in the form of a beautiful woman: she revealed herself to be the lord of all the Hurons, declared her love the dreamer, and announced that she wished her to be dressed entirely in red and to receive tribute from all the Huron allies in a great feast that, she ordered, was also to be repeated henceforth by other villages and nations; and the sick, "disfigured" Onondaga warrior who on his return from an unsuccessful expedition against the Erie announced he had encountered the Creator in the form of a dwarf, who demanded he be given two women and that dogs, wampum, and food from each longhouse be offered in sacrifice to ensure future victories (the first LeJeune in JR 17:165–87; the latter in Dablon, JR 42:195–97). Iroquoian societies at the time appear to have been open to constant ritual innovation, and great new cosmological truths seem to have been revealed in dreams on a regular basis, usually only to fade away almost as soon as they appeared.

Midwinter ceremonial and the white dog sacrifice

It's not always easy to square the sketchy and often sensationalistic accounts of Iroquois ritual to be found in early missionary sources with the meticulous descriptions compiled since the nineteenth century. For example, the wintertime "Feast of Dreams" mentioned by several early authors was clearly part of what is now called the Midwinter Ceremonial (Tooker 1970), the Iroquois New Year and the most important event of the present-day ritual calendar. In most Iroquois communities, the midwinter rites continue to involve dream-guessing, but the general tenor of the ritual has obviously changed a great deal in the intervening centuries. Spontaneous dream-guessing seems to have vanished entirely.

The most striking of these changes is the degree to which what was obviously an extremely free-form and improvisational process has since become tamed and formalized. The "language" of dreams has now become codified, and dramatic reenactments no longer occur; instead, there is an established code of what dreams are significant and an elaborate series of correspondences with certain foods and miniature talismans that are considered appropriate gifts for each. The best account is Harold Blau's description (1963; cf. Beauchamp 1888,) of the Midwinter dream-guessing rituals among the New York Onondaga in the early 1960s. The Onondaga nation is divided, like most Iroquoians, into two moieties; at the height of the ceremony, each moiety takes its turn presenting its dreams to the other in the form of riddles and guessing those of the other side by offering the equivalent sorts of food; once a dream is guessed correctly, the dreamer moves back to his own moiety's assembly house, where a member of his own moiety has to guess correctly too; both will later provide appropriate gifts. For instance, a man who dreamed of playing lacrosse might end up with a pound of sugar and a tiny model lacrosse stick. Similarly there are all sorts of other symbolic tokens, miniature versions of the real object of desire: animals, canoes, sleds, false-face masks and any number of other things, which the dreamer will normally keep afterward as her personal amulet or protector.[13]

The climax of this ritual involves a fascinating set of inversions. After about a hundred dreams have been guessed, a man impersonating the Creator himself enters and offers his own riddles to the people of both moieties. The answer though is always the same. In the nineteenth century, the Creator's desire was for the sacrifice of two dogs, which were first strangled, then immolated, painted white, and festooned in belts of white wampum. These appear to have been substitutes for the death of war prisoners, who were, in a certain sense, seen as offerings to the Creator. Since 1885, even the dog sacrifice has been abandoned, and the Creator is offered tobacco and white ribbons instead (Hale 1885; Hewitt 1910b, 1910c; Speck 1946:145–46; Blau 1964; Tooker 1965, 1970:41–47, 102–103, 128–41). The sacrifice is marked by any number of inversions on the usual relation between Creator and humanity. Where normally people perform thanksgiving speeches and songs to celebrate creation, here the Creator himself sings a song of thanksgiving (it isn't clear to whom); where normally the thanksgiving speech emphasizes the truth of the Creator's words, here the sacrificers declare they are making the offer "to prove *their* words are true." Finally, according to Fenton's informants, "the white dog which is sacrificed to the Creator . . . is a dream token from all the people to the Creator and it becomes his guardian" (1942:17).

So we are back where we started: with a dreaming god who once again seems slightly confused about his own role in the process of creation, and who (therefore?) ends up mixing urges for destruction in his creativity.

This is not what I mainly want to emphasize, though. What really interests me is the underlying theory of creativity and its relation to conceptions of the person. We have already encountered two aspects of the latter: on the one hand, the formal, Maussian *persona*, which among the Five Nations was embodied in the eternal name; the second, the inner "soul," or seat of desires. One was embodied in visible tokens such as wampum, while the other was fundamentally invisible and perceptible mainly through dreams and voices. Both were to a certain degree exterior to consciousness, but exterior, one might say, in opposite directions: one a social imposition, the other, desires so intimate even the desirer was not entirely aware of them.

Dreams were the desires of this inner soul, or "the language" in which those hidden, invisible desires could begin to take visual form. What Wallace stresses, though, is that this process, by which hidden desires could become visible, manifest, and specific, finally taking on permanent material form—could happen only through the participation of others. "Dreams are not to brood over, to analyze, and to prompt lonely and independent action; they are to be told, or at least hinted at, and it is for other people to be active" (247). In other words, the hidden can become visible (or the generic specific) only by the individual becoming social (or the specific, generic). This social action reaches its highest form in the midwinter dream-guessing, in which the entire community is mobilized to bring material being to each other's dreams. If gifts people give on such occasions are kept and treasured as talismans and guardians, it must be because they are not only material tokens of the hidden content of a person's mind but also embodiments of the protective action of others.

Wallace places a psychological spin on all this; understandably enough, considering the nature of the material and the direction of American anthropology at the time. Iroquoian societies combined a very indulgent attitude toward children, with extreme psychological pressures on adults. Children were never to be punished; to frustrate a powerful desire in a child might endanger their health. Adults, on the other hand, especially men, were held to high standards of generosity, bravery, and above all stoic impassivity in the face of hardship. Even those tortured to death were expected to, and generally did, face their fate with a show of utter equanimity. Iroquois dream-therapy gave one a chance to be indulged in a similar way by society as a whole; the closest contemporary equivalent to the great dream feasts are the antics of the false face societies, whose members are also privileged at certain times to wreak havoc among people's houses, playing practical jokes, begging, tossing things around, and who are indulged like whimsical children. They represent the same psychological complex: "a longing to be passive, to beg, to be an irresponsible, demanding, rowdy infant, and to compete with the Creator himself; and to express it all in the name of the public good" (Wallace 1967:93).

It's also possible to look at the same phenomena from the perspectives sketched out in the first half of this book: how forms of value emerge to regulate a process which is ultimately about the creation of people. The Midwinter Ceremonial was also a time for the naming of children and consolation of mourners; and condolence, like dream-guessing, was something for which one needed the services of the opposite moiety.[14]

Generally speaking, moiety structures are ways of creating imaginary totalities: if both "sides" are present at a ritual, then in a sense society as a whole is present. Such totalities are both constructed out of, and serve as the means to reproduce, relations within whatever domestic units make up that society's basic building blocks. In the Iroquois case these were of course matrilineal longhouses, each organized around a core of women, and in which women appear to have made all the most important decisions. Dream-guessing does not seem to have been particularly marked for gender one way or the other in early times, but now it seems to have passed largely into the hands of men; condolence was always very much a male concern, one in which women played little part. Still, it was in the longhouses that the most important forms of labor took place, and therefore it is all the more frustrating that we don't have all that much detail about how they were organized. Wallace's observations on socialization are useful here, particularly his emphasis on the combination of indulgence of whims and the gradual process of "hardening" children (for instance by intentionally leaving them underdressed in winter, and occasionally dunking them in cold streams.) The two modes seem to represent opposite poles of the same process, meant to produce highly autonomous adults, as one might expect in a society that seemed to place a roughly equal stress on egalitarianism and individualism.

Both dream-guessing and condolence are clearly modeled on this labor of socialization. In each case, members of one moiety provide nurturant care for the other. They are similar in other ways as well. In each case, the focus is on the psychological condition of individuals, which are full of dire possibilities: frustrated desires can kill, and the grief of mourning can drive the mourner entirely insane. In fact, one could go further: in each case, nurturant care was set against a strong undercurrent of (at least potential) violence. The violence is most explicit in the Jesuit accounts of dream-guessing, in which the dreamers go about at night attacking people, scattering fires, and destroying furniture;[15] but even if it's not dramatized in the same way in condolence rituals, this is because it doesn't really have to be: the whole point of the proceedings is to lift away emotions that can lead to the desire for revenge and terrifying projects of war and cruelty. In each case, finally, objects change hand between the two sides that are, or become, probably the most treasured tokens of value known to Iroquoian society.

From another perspective, dream-guessing and condolence might be said to represent two opposite movements in the construction of the person. The first is about the realization of the most intimate fantasies and desires of individuals, though this can only be achieved through the help of others—in fact, insofar as dreams have to be guessed by the opposite moiety, achieved only by society as a whole. Condolence, of course, is set off not by individual desires but by the dissolution of the individual in death: in all Iroquoian societies, one of the main tasks of moieties is to bury one another's dead. It is also about the creation of sociality and what endures despite the death of the individual. Wampum is the prime medium through which that enduring life of society is re-created: both through condolence itself and the giving of names. If dream-guessing is about how the individual can only be realized through the mediation of society, then one might say the resurrection of names is about how society itself cannot continue to exist except through the mediation of individuals. Hence the objects that pass back and forth between moieties in each case: in the former, the very most particular, in the latter, the very most generic.

Hence the difference between the essential models of creativity involved in each. In one, the object reveals the mind, or "word" of the giver; in the other, it reveals the mind, or "word" of the recipient.

Not everything moves across moiety lines, however. In each case there was a complementary gift from within one's own moiety. In the Onondaga Midwinter Ceremonial, once someone of the opposite moiety guesses one's dreams, the guess has to be confirmed by someone from one's own. Both parties end up giving gifts, though it is the one from the other side who provides the actual talisman; one's own matrilineal relatives merely provide an equivalent variety of food: a bag of corn, a sack of sugar, and so on. In other words, a relatively generic gift complements a relatively specific one. In the matter of condolence it was even more extreme, since while condolence itself is something that one "clear-minded" moiety must carry out for its opposite ("the mourners"), the subsequent transfer of names occurs not only within one's own moiety but within one's matriclan. And while one is an affair of men, the other is conducted exclusively by women: even in the case of the most important federal chiefs, it is a female council that chooses the successor. In this case, in other words, one's matrilineal kin provide a relatively specific gift (a unique name) to complement a relatively generic one (the standardized gifts of even more standardized wampum) provided by others.

If these complementary gifts have anything in common, it is that they are comparatively straightforward; gifts of food or names seem to lack the overtones of peril and violence that always seem to lurk behind relations between moieties. It seems to me this is the key to the nature of the moieties themselves. Tradition has it that Iroquois moieties were once exogamous (Morgan 1851:83, Fenton 1951:46, Tooker 1970:23). If so, this doesn't seem to have been the case for some time—one is now forbidden only to marry members of one's own clan—but even if Iroquois moieties were never actually exogamous, it seems important that people believe they were. Lynn Ceci (1982:102–103) points to an Iroquois myth of the origins of wampum that is also a myth of the origins of exogamy: a young warrior from an enemy tribe is the only one able to kill a magical bird covered with wampum. He marries the local chief's daughter, and distributes the beads between his own and his wife's people as a way of establishing peace (E. Smith 1883:78–79). But as Ceci notes, normally it was exogamy itself that created peace, "since in this way young hunter-warriors are dispersed among their in-laws" (103). Iroquois marriage really could be considered an exchange of potentially dangerous young men between largely self-sufficient groups of women.[16] Hence it would only make sense that in the larger, "political" relations between moieties, these same men—and especially older men—adopted forms of ritual action modeled on the work of primary socialization, as a way of overcoming the potential for violence and disruption that ultimately originated in themselves.[17]

All of this might help to explain one otherwise curious feature of wampum. Parker (1916:46) claims that in League Belts, white beads represent the League's women, the purple or "black" ones, its men. This is not surprising in itself: by all accounts it was the white beads that embodied the values of "light and life" that made wampum suited for its political role—black ones, by contrast, represented its opposite, the negative values of grief, mourning, anger, and war, the last at least considered a male domain (Holmes 1883:241; cf. Hammel 1992). The curious thing is that despite embodying an essentially feminine virtue, wampum was one of the few important forms of property in Iroquoian society that women did *not* control.[18] Houses, fields, food, most tools, and household implements—even such items as the brass kettles that were one of the earliest and most important trade item acquired from Europeans (Turgeon 1997)—were either owned by individual women, or owned by collective groups like longhouses or clans, in which women played the most important roles. While women actually wove the beads together, outside of certain limited forms such as name belts, belts and strings circulated almost exclusively among men.

This might be considered a final way in which actions taken on the political sphere of peacemaking inverted those typical of that below: Iroquois kinship, after all, was largely a matter of groups of women exchanging men; politics, of men exchanging an essentially feminine substance. But one can also see it as the result of a necessary and inevitable tension in any philosophy of society that sees "peace" as the ultimate human value. Granted, the Iroquois defined peace about as broadly as one possibly could: as Paul Wallace put it, peace was "the Good expressed in action" (1946:7), an expression of "wisdom and graciousness" as well as a joyous unity with the cosmos. It was, as a Dumontian might say, the ultimate, encompassing value, since it was about the relation of humans to the cosmos as a whole, the ultimate "imaginary totality." Yet logically, it was entirely premised on the prior existence of its opposite. Without war, "peace" is meaningless. In a sense, then, the wampum belts themselves—or, perhaps more accurately, the process of weaving them together—was itself a model of the process it was meant to mediate, one constantly reproduced in ritual: of converting the potential for destruction into harmony by integrating it into a larger social whole.

dream economies

Let me finish with a few words of historical context.

The basic structure described in the last section appears to be very old. This is probably true both of the fundamental forms of producing people and their ritual refractions: something like dream-guessing, and something like condolence, were probably being practiced among the speakers of Iroquoian languages long before the first foreign ships began appearing offshore. The same no doubt goes for the concrete tokens of value that emerged from them: People were no doubt treasuring dream-tokens and using bright objects derived from faraway places in peacemaking for quite some time as well.

On the other hand, it was only in the late seventeenth or even early eighteenth century that wampum became the universal medium of diplomacy, and probably in the nineteenth century that the language of dreams was largely reduced to a matter of symbolic tokens. In fact, the one thing that really jumps out at one reading the Jesuit relations and other sources from the same period is just how open-ended such things were, especially in comparison with the careful ceremonial etiquette of later times. Of course, this has something to do with the nature of the sources. But it also seems to reflect a genuine change.

European merchant and fishing vessels—French, Spanish, Dutch, Swedish, English, and Basque—began appearing off the northeast coast of

North America in the 1500s, and with them came trade goods: glass beads, but also brass kettles and steel axes, which seem to have spread quite quickly. It was only in the next century, however, when European settlements began to be established and Amerindian societies drawn into the global fur trade, that one can speak of the beginnings of a dependant economy in the familiar sense of the term. The Huron Confederacy and then the Five Nations were soon dependent on Europeans for their tools, domestic equipment, clothing, weapons, even foodstuffs, all of which was obtained in exchange for a single product: fur. They were dependent on goods got through commercial transactions with outsiders in order to maintain their society, but within that society, regimes of property and distribution remained largely unchanged.

> Within the Huron community, there were no commercial transactions, properly speaking. Goods acquired were spontaneously shared within lineages (or segments of clans). This generalized practice of giving insured equality and accounted for the disdain with which the accumulation of goods was viewed; it governed the rules of courtesy at all times as well as the Huron penchant for games of chance, contributions to feasts, rituals, and carnivals, and the obligation to satisfy any desire expressed by a member of the community. As a result, there were no sellers nor buyers among the Hurons, neither commanders nor commanded, neither rich nor poor . . ."On returning from their fishing, their hunting, and their trading, they exchange many gifts; if they have thus obtained something unusually good, even if they have bought it, or if its has been given to them, they make a feast to the whole village with it. Their hospitality towards all sorts of strangers is remarkable." (Delâge 1993:52–53)

Delâge argues that among the Huron, new regimes of property and the possibility of personal accumulation, really emerged only among converts to Christianity; among the Five Nations, they do not seem to have emerged at all. However, it's hard to avoid the temptation to interpret the dramatic intensity of some of the Jesuit accounts—games in which people would bet all their personal possessions, down to their very clothes; rituals in which domestic property was smashed, and houses often burned down, in which huge amounts of wealth could change hands in order to indulge someone's dream—as arising to some degree in reaction to this situation. It is probably not entirely coincidental that the "Hatchets, Kettles, and Porcelain" hung around dreamers' necks in Lejeune's account were probably the three most important items of import during the first century of trade.

One might argue, as Delâge seems to, that this was the morality of a hunting economy, or at least one in which people's main experience of a sudden windfall is of large quantities of meat. Trade goods, which were themselves acquired in exchange for animals, were treated in much the same way. Still, factors like dream-guessing and the apparently constant appearance of new revelations and prophets leave one with the impression of a society of enormous instability, in which almost everything, in a sense, was potentially up for grabs. No doubt if one were living there at the time, one would discover an endless game of political maneuvering between women and men, young warriors and elders, young women and old matrons, those with access to foreign wealth and more traditional authorities, and so on. Of course, such struggles always exist in any society, but here the usual comparatively gentle tugging back and forth seems to have turned into a situation burst wide open, a poker game in which half the cards had suddenly been made wild.

I don't think the phrase "dream economy" is entirely inappropriate here: at least, it captures something of its combination of absolute unpredictability and ephemerality. Radical moments seem to have flickered away almost as quickly as they appeared.

There is a more common pattern here, one that has tended to be obscured a bit by the way anthropologists have approached the question of culture change. A key concept has been the "revitalization movement," a term that, in fact, was coined by Anthony Wallace (1956) with Iroquois history very much in mind. At times of extreme cultural disruption, the argument goes, one often finds the emergence of prophets with self-conscious projects of cultural reformation, the paradigm being the Seneca prophet Handsome Lake who, in the years of the Six Nations' defeat and demoralization following the American Revolution, came forward with what might be considered the final, definitive dream-revelation: a new moral code mixing Quaker and Iroquoian elements, which among other things placed Iroquois males back firmly in control of their nations' economic and political life. The kind of tumultuous world described in the Jesuit accounts, then, tends to be seen simply as the years leading up to revitalization movements—which, if the situation becomes truly desperate, can take the extreme form of millenarian cults and expectations of the imminent destruction of the world.

There are other ways to look at this. Many anthropologists and historians have noted the remarkable bursts of cultural creativity that so often occur during the first generation or two after many traditional societies are suddenly integrated into a larger world economy. If the conditions are right—if the group maintains some degree of political autonomy and happens to be in a relatively advantageous position in relation to the market—the result can be a spectacular expansion and enrichment of existing cultural forms: of art, architecture, drama, ritual, exchange. Often such a result is referred to as a cultural renaissance. It's not the best possible term, perhaps, since the notion of "rebirth" implies that something was previously moribund, or dead. Still, an analogy to, say, the Italian Renaissance is not entirely inappropriate: that too was made possible at least partially by the newfound wealth of cities in the process of being integrated into a larger world economy, much of which was invested in fairly self-conscious projects of cultural renewal, both inventing and elaborating traditions as they did. For anthropological parallels: the Kwakiutl renaissance of roughly 1875 to 1920 is probably the most famous, along with the efflorescence of Highland New Guinea exchange systems like *te* and *moka* during the 1950s and '60s; or, to take a less familiar example, of Malagasy mortuary art and ritual around the same time. Examples are legion. What they all seem to have in common is that despite the intense social struggles that so often give them force, new means are mainly being put to very old ends; more specifically, a vast flow of new resources is put to the task of pursuing traditional forms of value.

Such situations rarely last more than fifty years or so; the boot comes down eventually, in one form or another.

The kind of "dream economy" one encounters in the American Northeast in the 1600s, then, might be considered a darker possibility. In some ways it seems the sociocultural equivalent of a bubble economy, in which vast fortunes are made and lost overnight, but especially, in the at least implicit awareness that bubbles always burst. Or even more, perhaps, one might imagine the wartime economy of a probably doomed city, in which vast amounts of wealth can be scammed or stolen one day, then gambled away the next. The seventeenth century was, after all, a period that combined newfound sources of wealth, and a newfound dependency, with absolutely unprecedented epidemics, famines, and genocidal wars. Most of the population between Pennsylvania and Quebec died; during the beaver wars alone, the Petun, Neutrals, Susquahannock, Mohicans, and Hurons, among others, were destroyed as political entities, their populations massacred, scattered, or incorporated into rival societies. It would be surprising if some of this insecurity was not internalized in the life of the societies themselves.

It did so, one might say, in rather the way a theorist of commoditization might predict: through an emphasis on individual self-realization. But it was individual self-realization in profoundly different cultural terms.

Wampum took on its overwhelming importance only toward the end of this period, and primarily among the Five Nations, as they were in the process of either destroying or incorporating all the others. At this point, wampum, as the currency of the fur trade, could be seen as the very symbol of their growing dependency and of what had caused the region to collapse into a state that must have seemed increasingly reminiscent of the chaos described in the Deganawideh epic. The number of wampum beads in circulation by 1650 has been estimated as high as three million (Richter 1992:85), and they became one of the great media for the Iroquois' great political project of the times, what Matthew Dennis (1993) has described as "cultivating a landscape of peace" by gathering all the region's people together in the structure of the League. Doing so of course involved the endless repetition of the very precise etiquette of condolence, a spirit obviously very different from that of dream-guessing. But by converting the money of the trade, the very stuff of violence, into the potential to create peace, League office-holders were following an ancient ritual logic. And the beads themselves, as they moved back and forth between abstract potential and concrete forms, also created a bridge between a commercial system dedicated to the accumulation of material objects, and a social system whose great imperative had increasingly become the accumulation of people: effected, most often, by throwing a belt of wampum around a captives shoulders and thus giving them a name.

Chapter 6 🕸

Marcel Mauss Revisited

We have here an admirable example of how capitalist property is created. The appropriation of gold, in particular, is by necessity a bloody business. In the 16th and 17th centuries, the Spaniards massacred the Peruvians and Mexicans; in the 19th century the Indians of California were coldly exterminated; the Australian Aborigines, methodically destroyed. And now this same genre of collective assassination which is war is directed against the Boers. The bourgeoisie no more recoils before blood than it recoils before human exploitation. Thus we see how "private property is founded upon labor"!

> —Marcel Mauss, from "La guerre du Transvaal"
> (Le Mouvement Socialiste, June 1, 1900)

Citizens, in proposing to set off forthrightly on this path, we must never in any way forget our role as socialists and revolutionaries . . . We believe, comrades, that organizers and militants can indeed encourage the worker to foresight, and seek to create for him a little security in this unnatural and cruel society in which he lives. But we will not be satisfied with that. We will educate him for his revolutionary task by giving him a sort of foretaste of all the advantages that the future society will be able to offer him . . . We will create a veritable arsenal of socialist capital in the midst of bourgeois capital.

> —Marcel Mauss, speaking before the First National and
> International Congress of Socialist Cooperatives, July 2–5, 1900.

In earlier chapters, I have given Marcel Mauss' work somewhat short shrift, particularly in comparison with that of Marx. In fact, I believe Mauss' theoretical corpus is the single most important in the history of anthropology. He was a man with a remarkable knack for asking all the most interesting questions, even if he was also keenly aware in those early days of anthropological research, that he didn't have the means to fully answer them. In the Anglophone world, his work is now known mainly through a mere four or five theoretical essays, but almost every one of them has inspired a vast secondary literature of its own. The universally recognized masterpiece is his *"Essai sur le don"* (1925), which has generated more debate, discussion, and ideas than any other work of anthropology—and that has obvious relevance to the intellectual project I have been developing over the course of this book. In this chapter, then, I would like to test some of these ideas against Mauss' material from the *"The Gift"* itself. In doing so, however, I intend to make a larger theoretical point. In many way I think his work and Marx's form a perfect complement. Marx was a socialist with an ongoing interest in anthropology; Mauss, an anthropologist who, throughout his life, remained an active participant in socialist politics. And just as for many years few seemed to be aware of Marx's subtlety as a social thinker, almost no one nowadays seems aware of Mauss' importance as a political one. Political passions form the framework, in fact, for much of his work, and probably nowhere more so than in the case of the gift. Let me begin, then, by describing some of the background to this work.

the gift as social contract

Mauss was during his own lifetime thought of most of all as the intellectual successor to his uncle, Emile Durkheim, the founder of French sociology. The most common way to look at Mauss' work is as the pursuit of the same intellectual problems—if, as Louis Dumont emphasizes (1952), in much more pragmatic and empirical terms.

Durkheim's problems, in turn, largely emerged from a dialogue that had been going on between French and British thinkers about the direction of social change in the nineteenth century: about the rise of individualism, the decline of religious solidarity and traditional forms of authority, the rise of the market as the main medium of human relations. Most of Mauss' essays can be related to one or another of these themes: just as his essay on the "category of the person" can be read as an archeology of modern individualism; *"The Gift"* can be read as an exploration of the notion of the social contract.

Marshall Sahlins (1972) once suggested that the problem Mauss is ultimately tackling goes back to Thomas Hobbes: how do you create peace between people who have no immediate reason not to kill each other? Hobbes, of course, argued that given human beings' endlessly acquisitive propensities, a state of nature could only have been a "war of all against all"; society proper could only begin when everyone agreed to create some overarching political power. The original "social contract," then, was a matter of people agreeing to abandon their right to use force, and invest it in a state that was, in turn, capable of enforcing any contracts they might agree to with each other. By the nineteenth century, a line of argument that started with Saint-Simon and reached its apotheosis with Herbert Spencer proposed that the role of state coercion was not eternal, and that human history was seeing a gradual shift from societies based on military, to economic competition, and free economic contracts between individuals. Durkheim framed much of his sociological theory as a response to Spencer: pointing out, for example, that the growth in private contracts, far from causing the state to wither away, was causing it to intervene in citizens' lives as never before.

In an intellectual climate like this, it's easy to see how "the origin of the contract" would seem an important question—and one about which the newly emerging field of anthropology should have something to say. In the first pages of his essay, Mauss emphasizes twice that his work on the gift is part of a much wider program of research "on archaic forms of contract" that he had been pursuing for some time, along with his colleague Georges Davy.[1] He also notes that, contrary to the speculations of the likes of Hobbes, or Adam Smith, or modern economists, the first voluntary, contractual relations were not between individuals but between social groups: "clans, tribes, and families" (3). Neither were they essentially political, or for that matter economic, in nature; rather, they were, as he puts it, "total," bringing together domains we would differentiate as "religious, legal, moral and economic." Gift-giving is a perfect example of this sort of thing: because it is a purely voluntary act (or, anyway, can be) that nonetheless creates a sense of obligation. Hence his explanation of the central question he intends to answer:

> In primitive or archaic societies what is the principle whereby the gift received has to be repaid? What force is there in the thing given which compels the recipient to make a return? (page 3)

By framing his question so, one might say Mauss was posing a very ingenious reply to the free-market theorists of his day. Rather than history moving from a social contract with the state, with its monopoly of force, to free contracts among individuals, we discover that the origin of the contract long predates the state—that these contracts had much more to do with what we would now consider economic than political concerns, but that, at the same time, they looked absolutely nothing like what free-market theorists would have imagined primitive economics to be like. The working assumption of economists had been—in fact, still is—that the original form of exchange was barter, motivated by material self-interest: two people meet and agree to exchange something one needs for something needed by the other; once the deal is struck, it's over; the two need have nothing further to do with one another. What Mauss is arguing, however, is that the first agreements that could be described as economic contracts were agreements *not* to act in accord with one's economic self-interest, since if one is simply speaking of material gain, then obviously it is in the interest of the giver to demand an immediate return, and even more obviously, in the interest of the recipient to simply take the goods and keep them, rather than waiting for a discrete interval and making a dramatic counter-gift.

At the same time, though, Sahlins was surely right: the ghost of Hobbes does linger over his account. Mauss repeatedly emphasizes that on the most primitive level (one that seems to exist entirely in his imagination), there is no alternative between giving everything, and all-out war. No explanation of why members of different "clans, tribes, and families" should feel inclined to kill each other in the first place is ever offered. True, the emphasis on hostility does make the antieconomism even richer. It has often been noted that when something resembling barter *does* occur in stateless societies it is almost always between strangers, people who would otherwise be enemies. Rather than there being some fundamental contradiction between relations of violence and economic self-interest (as Spencer argued, and just about any modern neoliberal would automatically assume) the two are really just variations of the same thing: both reflect the way one acts with people towards whose fate one is indifferent. The moment one makes peace with others, one has to maintain at least the pretense that one is taking some consideration of their interests as well as one's own. Hence, as Mauss notes, within gift economies, even in cases where one really is simply interested in obtaining material goods, one has to pretend otherwise. There is no doubt a profound wisdom here. But in this case, the wisdom comes at a terrible price, because the underlying assumption that order and amicable relations are things that need to be explained, while the potential for violence and conflict does not (an assumption which came to be the basic starting point of structural-functionalism) ends up reinforcing the cynical premises which lie beneath economism if anything even more than Mauss' conclusion undercuts them.

Mauss' solution to the problem he set for himself, on the other hand, leads in an entirely different direction. Why do people feel obliged to return gifts? His answer is famous: objects are seen to partake of something of the personality of the giver.[2] It was to this effect that he introduced the testimony of a Maori sage named Tamati Ranapiri, the famous passage about the *hau* or "spirit" of the gift—according to Mauss' interpretation, that part of the donor's soul that becomes, as it were, entangled in the gift, and that, through its wish to return home, compels the recipient to make a return.

I'll be looking at this passage in a more detail later on. For now, suffice it to say that Mauss' interpretation has come under a great deal of criticism—not only from Maori scholars, but also from ambitious theoreticians like Claude

Levi-Strauss (1950) who, in the introduction to what became the popular French edition of Mauss' work, argued that Mauss had made a fundamental logical mistake in trying to explain a phenomenon like reciprocity, which he felt was rooted in the unconscious structure of the human mind, through one particular cultural exegesis. It seems to me though that all this debate rather misses the point. One could probably say that in his interpretation of the *hau*, Mauss had, himself, produced a kind of myth: but like all good myths, Mauss' did capture something essential, something that would have been difficult to express otherwise. If it had not, it would have been long since forgotten.

At any rate, the *hau* was supposed to be just one example of a constant theme, one that also appears in Mauss' analysis of kula, in which "the mechanisms of obligation . . . are resident in the gifts themselves" (1925 [1965:21]), in Northwest Coast treasures that contain spiritual personalities that possess the owner (1925 [1965:44]), in his reconstruction of early Roman law in which "the person [is] possessed by the thing" (1925 [1965:51]), and elsewhere. All of this turns on a much broader point about the relation of persons and things. Modern law makes strict distinctions between the two; it is only for this reason that modern theory can imagine that persons are motivated by something called "self-interest," which basically comes down to the desire to accumulate things. One of the main points of the essay, as Mauss repeatedly emphasizes, is to call the whole set of assumptions underlying this notion of "self-interest" into question.

In doing so, he was not simply challenging modern common sense about economic relations. He was saying that the assumptions of economics and social science do not adequately represent the common sense even of people in our own society. This is a point that, it seems to me, is lost on many—probably most—modern commentators on Mauss. True, Mauss did wish to argue that it is only with the market that it is even possible to imagine a pure self-interest—a concept that, he remarked, could not even be translated into Greek, or Latin, or Sanskrit, or classical Arabic—and that the modern ideal of the pure selfless gift is simply an impossible mirror image of this notion. But he was also trying to understand the popular appeal of socialism. To explain that, he ended up producing something surprisingly similar to Marx's notion of alienation—though Mauss himself was probably not aware how similar it was.

Let me try to place "The Gift" in its political context.

the "essai sur le don" as a
contribution to socialist theory

Most of Mauss' essays were works in progress, preliminary reports on ongoing projects of research. He spent the last half of his life surrounded by uncompleted projects: a thesis on the nature of prayer, a book about the origins of money, yet another on socialism and nationalism . . . When he did issue a progress report, it was usually because he was asked to, or felt there was some pressing reason. In the case of the *"essai sur le don,"* it's quite clear that reason was ultimately political.

Few anthropologists nowadays seem to be aware of the fact that Mauss was, throughout his life, a committed socialist. In his student years he was a close associate of Jean Jaurès, leader of the SFIO (or "French Section of the Workers International"), nowadays famous for his defense of Dreyfus and tireless anti-war campaigns, for which he was finally assassinated by a right-wing fanatic in 1914. Mauss considered Jaurès as much a mentor as he did Durkheim, though he was in many ways more radical. After the war, Mauss continued to work within the party, serve on the editorial board of socialist periodicals, and write for the left-wing press. Above all he was active in the French cooperative movement: he and a friend founded and managed a consumer co-op in Paris, he held various posts in the national organization, and made periodic journeys to other parts of Europe, returning to publish reports on the cooperative movement in Germany, in England, in Hungary, in Russia, and so on (Fournier 1994).

The early 1920s, and particularly the period around 1923 and 1924 when Mauss was actually writing "The Gift," was also one of his most intense periods of political engagement. These were also the years immediately following the Russian revolution, which had caused the SFIO to split apart into communist and socialist parties. Mauss himself had always favored a vision of socialism created from the bottom up, through cooperativization and union action aimed at the ultimate abolition of the wage system. He argued that both communists and social democrats were equally guilty of "fetishizing politics" and the role of the state; rather, he saw the role of the state as being largely limited to providing a legal framework within which workers could more easily take control over their industries and in a broader sense, perhaps, bring law into accord with popular morality. Events in Russia left him profoundly ambivalent. He was, from the start, an enthusiastic supporter of the revolution, but highly suspicious of the Bolsheviks.[3] Mauss felt the whole project of imposing socialism by force was oxymoronic;[4] he was repelled by the notion of a party line, and while he made due allowances for the difficult wartime situation in which the Soviet regime was forced to operate, decried its use of terror, its contempt for democratic institutions and above all for the rule of law. If there was one common theme to his objections, it was his disgust at the Bolsheviks' cold-blooded utilitarianism ("their cynical notion that 'the end justifies the means,'" he later wrote, "made them seem mediocre even amongst politicians.")

It is important to stress, however, that his denunciations were always set against the background of an unbreakable sense of kinship and, most of all, a sense that the revolution represented a magnificent experiment:

Since Marx the socialists have cautiously refrained from constructing utopias and drawing up the plans for future societies. On the contrary, hardly advocating anything but the general apocalyptic thesis of the 'taking over of the administration of things,' they have left vague, because unpredictable, the collective procedures of this administration. How would this revolution suppress 'the administration of men by men'?' What would emerge from all this moral effervescence, this political and economic chaos?

However irreligious my socialism, however little respect was aroused in me by the first acts of the Bolsheviks—the dissolution of the Constituent Assembly, the Treaty of Brest-Litovsk—I could not disassociate myself from them. Moscow seemed to many among us what it remains for very many enlightened people, even here, a kind of sanctuary incubating the very destiny of our ideas. (Mauss 1925a [1992:173])

Much of Mauss' published work in the years leading up to "The Gift" concerned the significance of Lenin's New Economic Policy, announced in 1921, which abandoned earlier attempts at forced collectivitization, legalized commerce, and opened the country to foreign investment. While Mauss could only celebrate the fact that the Soviet state was no longer employing terror to suppress independent cooperatives, he strongly opposed the NEP's opening of the country's resources to foreign capital—the "sale of Russia," as he called it in an article in *La Vie Socialiste*[5]—which he saw as likely to mark the beginning of the end of the revolution. Already in 1921, he was predicting its imminent collapse; at other times he allowed himself a guarded optimism, even suggesting the Soviet regime might finally be evolving toward a more genuine socialism. But clearly, the whole business not only preoccupied his mind, it left him torn and profoundly disheartened.

It was no coincidence then that Mauss' two most important published works of that decade were, on the one hand, his *Sociological Assessment of Bolshevism,* and on the other, "The Gift," both published in the same year of 1925. They were clearly meant as two legs of the same intellectual project. With the first great attempt to create a modern alternative to capitalism foundering, Mauss apparently decided it was time to bring the results of comparative ethnography—crude and undeveloped though he well knew them to be—to bear, in order to sketch out at least the outlines of what a more viable alternative might be like. He was particularly concerned with the historical significance of the market. One thing the Russian experiment had proved was that it was not going to be possible to simply abolish buying and selling by writ. Lenin had tried. And even though Russia was the least monetarized society in Europe, he had failed. For the foreseeable future, Mauss concluded, we were stuck with a market of some sort or another (1925a [1992:188–90]). Still, there had to be a difference between "the market" as a mere technique for the allocation of

certain types of economic good (for instance, between democratically organized cooperatives or professional organizations), and "the market" as it
had come to exist in the industrial West, as the basic organizing principle
of social life, the ultimate determinant of value. What Mauss set out to do,
then, was to try to get at the heart of precisely what it was about the logic
of the market that did such violence to ordinary people's sense of justice
and humanity. To understand the popular appeal of socialist parties and
social welfare programs, and by examining the ethnographic record, imagine what a society in accord with such popular standards of justice might
look like: one in which the market could be relegated to its proper function, as a technique for decentralized decision-making, a kind of popular
polling device on the relative appeal of different sorts of consumer goods,
and in which an entirely different set of institutions preside over areas of
really significant social value—for example, ones centered on "the joy of
giving in public, the delight in generous artistic expenditure, the pleasure
of hospitality in the public or private feast" (1925 [1965:67]).

What Mauss was doing, in effect, was trying to understand the appeal of
Marxist ideas with minimal reference to the works of Marx. Here is another
point that is often overlooked. Marx's work was not, in fact, all that well
known in France in the early part of the century. Most of it had not been
translated; there were no French Marxist theorists in this period; even socialist militants were more likely to be familiar with the ideas of Saint
Simon, Fourier, Proudhon, or even Robert Owen (Mauss 1920, 1924).
When "Marxist theory" was invoked, it was usually assumed to consist of
some kind of simplistic, mechanical determinism. Mauss knew better than
that; he was familiar with the subtlety of *Capital;* but he was probably not
aware that he was addressing many of the same questions as Marx did in his
early writings.[6] Where a German, Hungarian, or Russian author of the period would probably have accused the Bolsheviks of betraying their own best
inspiration, Mauss instead turned to a very different intellectual tradition.

The critical thrust of Mauss' essay is somewhat obscured by the fact its
author spent so much of it discussing the most competitive, and most aristocratic, forms of gift exchange. Jonathan Parry (1986) and Maurice Godelier (1996) have done a useful service here by reminding us of Mauss' overall
scheme. Mauss began with what he called the "total prestation." Two groups
that would otherwise come to blows end up instead creating a relation of
complete mutual interdependence by offering one another everything: as an
example, Mauss points to the relations between moieties in many Australian
and American societies, which can be seen as total contracts in which two
sides of a village are bound to rely on one another for food, military and ritual services, sexual partners, "dances, festivals and fairs," gestures of respect
and recognition, and practically everything else (1925 [1965:3–4]).

All this is rather vague. Fortunately, Mauss did later enlarge on the notion of "total prestation," in a much less speculative, and more empirical light. In lectures delivered at the Institut d'Ethnologie at the University of Paris between 1935 and 1938, he speaks of "total prestations" (or "total reciprocity") as open-ended rights that in most societies exist mainly between particular families and particular individuals:

> In the beginning was a system which I will call the system of total prestations. When an Australian Kurnai finds himself in the same camp as his wife's parents, he does not have the right to eat any of the pieces of game which he brings with him; his parents-in-law take all, their right is absolute. The reciprocity is total, it is what we call "communism," but it is practiced between individuals. In its origin, *commercium* goes together with *connubium*, marriage follows commerce and commerce follows marriage. The obligatory present, the fictive gift, what is referred to as 'legal theft,' is in reality a kind of communism with an individual, social, and familial base. The fundamental error consists in opposing communism and individualism. (Mauss 1947:104–105)

What drew Mauss' attention here was the open-ended nature of the obligations that so often accompanied marriage. A Melanesian who needed a new canoe could call on his sister's husband and his people: since he had given them a wife, they in effect owed him everything and had to provide him not in accord with any principle of repayment, but simply in response to his needs. Hence, his use of the term "communism." Mauss argued that it was a key mistake to assume that "primitive communism"—or any other sort—was a matter of collective ownership. First, because personal possessions of some sort always exist; Mauss thought modern-day revolutionaries were being absurd when they imagined they could abolish them (e.g., 1920:264; 1924a:637). Second, even where property is owned by a group, it is rarely democratically administered: the difference between a private owner and a chiefly manager is often little more than legal formality. One has to look not at titles, then, but principles of access and distribution. When someone has the right to take what she feels she needs without any direct payment or reciprocation, then this is communism. But this means that it is perfectly possible to have a system of individualistic communism: in which specific individuals are bound together by such open-ended obligations, whether (as in the case of relations between affines) one-sided, or whether (as nowadays, he remarked, between husband and wife), both parties have equal rights to call on the other.[7] These could then knit together across the society, creating "a collection of individual positions which constitute a system of total reciprocities." The result would "correspond exactly

to what we call communism, but it will still be a strictly individual thing"
(1947:105, cf. Godelier 1999:36–49).

But to return to "The Gift." Over time, Mauss argued, reciprocity can
also take on a more competitive cast as assertive individuals—first acting as
representatives of clans or other social groups, later, in their own capacity
(Parry 1986)—end up vying to see which can outgive the other. Such systems of "agonistic exchange" Mauss proposed to label "the potlatch," after
the particularly dramatic competitive exchanges that had been recently documented on the Northwest Coast of North America. Usually, such competition took mild forms, but in rare cases it could, much like the competitive
games of capitalism, tend to suck everything else into a frantic struggle to
outdo one's rivals: even if they are based on opposite premises, since of
course, the whole point here is not to accumulate possessions but rather to
express one's utter contempt for material possessions by giving as much as
possible away.

In other words, what Chris Gregory (1982) described in his famous re-
analysis is not a gift economy per se, but what Mauss would call a potlatch
system, which is a particular agonistic variation—even, in some ways, a
slightly pathological one. The gift as contest continued to dominate in aristocratic societies like the ancient Celts or Germans, or in Vedic India, but
gradually, unevenly, the rise of money and market exchange (involving definitive sale and, therefore, alienation of goods that were no longer seen as
entangled in the giver) allowed it to be eclipsed by an ethos of accumulation
for its own sake. Most of the societies of the ancient world lingered somewhere in between; it was possible to accumulate fortunes, but the rich were
considered, as Mauss put it, "the treasurers of their communities," expected—or, in the Greek liturgy system, compelled—to disburse their
wealth again in civic projects.

The obvious question: how did one get from there to here? What were
the origins of this conception of "self-interest" to begin with, and how did it
come to efface almost everything else? Alain Caillé (1994:10–12), one of the
founders of an interdisciplinary group that calls itself the *Mouvement Anti-
Utilitariste dans les Sciences Sociales,* or MAUSS, points to the role of Christianity. Roman aristocrats and grandees still kept much of the ethos of
magnificent generosity: dedicating public buildings and gardens, vying to
host the most spectacular public games. But much Roman largesse was quite
obviously meant to wound: a favorite aristocratic habit, for example, was
scattering gold and jewels into the crowd so as to be able to revel in the en-
suing animalistic melee. Understandably, early Christian theories of the gift
developed in reaction to such obnoxious practices. True charity, in Christian
doctrine, could not be based on any desire to establish superiority, or gain
anyone's favor, or indeed, from any egoistic motive whatever. To the degree

that the giver could be said to have gotten anything out of the deal, it wasn't a real gift. But this in turn led to endless problems, since it was very difficult to conceive of a gift that did not benefit the giver in any way. At the very least, doing a good deed put one in better standing in the eyes of God and thus aided one's chance of eternal salvation. In the end, some actually ended up arguing that the only person who can make a purely benevolent act was one who had convinced himself that he was already condemned to hell. From here it's hardly much of a step to the sort of cynicism discussed in earlier chapters of this book, where any apparent act of generosity is assumed to mask some form of hidden selfishness, and to take pleasure in having done a good deed is seen to somehow undercut it—really two different versions of the same idea.[8]

The modern ideal of the gift, then, becomes an impossible mirror of market behavior: an act of pure generosity untrammeled by any thought of personal gain. But as the members of the MAUSS group endlessly insist, this does not mean people no longer give gifts: even in modern, capitalist societies things are constantly changing hands without any immediate return or explicit agreement about a future one. It does not even mean that gifts are no longer important. In fact, they argue, modern society could not function without them. The gift has become the "hidden face of modernity" (Nicolas 1991): "hidden" because one can always produce some reason to say any particular gift (money given to children, wedding presents, donations of blood, dinners for business associates, offering advice to friends or spending hours listening to their tedious problems) are not really gifts at all. So too in social theory. The result, as Godbout puts it, is a science that has "come to speak of social ties without using the words that are associated with them in daily life: surrender, forgiveness, renunciation, love, respect, dignity, redemption, salvation, redress, compassion, everything that is at the heart of relationships between people and that is nourished by the gift" (1998:220–21).

In the Anglophone world, the MAUSS group has been almost entirely ignored. Those who like to think of themselves as engaged in cutting-edge critical theory have instead come to read Mauss through Jacques Derrida (1991; cf. Gasché 1972, Schrift 1997), who in *Donner le Temps* examined Mauss concept of the gift to discover—surprise!—that gifts, being acts of pure disinterested generosity, are logically impossible.

I suppose this is what one would have to conclude, if one believed that there is something that can be called "Western discourse," and that it is incapable of referring to anything other than itself. But even those of us who believe that anthropology is, in fact, possible often seem to miss the point that Mauss was not dealing primarily with discourses but with moral principles that he felt were to some extent embodied in the practice, if not the high theory, of *all* societies.

True, Mauss emphasizes that in most of the societies he was examining, there's no point in trying to distinguish between generosity and self-interest. It is we who assume the two should normally be in conflict. (This was one reason why he tended to avoid the term "gift" at all when speaking of other societies, preferring to speak of "prestations.") But—and this is where I think it's crucial to understand the political context—Mauss was not trying to describe how the logic of the marketplace, with its strict distinctions between persons and things, interest and altruism, freedom and obligation, had become the common sense of modern societies. Above all, he was trying to explain the degree to which it had *failed* to do so; to explain why so many people—and particularly, so many of the less powerful and privileged members of society—found its logic morally repugnant. Why, for example, institutions that insisted on the strict separability of producers and their products offended against common intuitions of justice, the moral "bedrock," as he puts it, of our own—as of any—society. "It appears," he wrote in his conclusions,

> that the whole field of industrial and commercial law is in conflict with morality. The economic prejudices of the people and producers derive from their strong desire to pursue the thing they have produced once they realize that they have given their labor without sharing in the profits . . . (1925 [1965:64])

Here there is undoubtedly an echo of Marx. But Mauss' theory of alienation derived from very different origins; not from the Hegelian, dialectical tradition Marx employed in his early writings on the subject (which Mauss almost certainly hadn't read), but rather from that of legal history—in which property is "alienated" when all rights in it are detached from one owner and vested in another. Particularly for the French working classes, which were not far removed from peasant and artisanal backgrounds, there still seemed something profoundly wrong in this. Mauss was trying to understand what that was—just as he was trying to understand why it was that social insurance legislation, "inspired by the principle that the worker gives his life and labor partly to the community, and partly to his bosses" (1925 [1965:65]), and therefore deserved more than a weekly wage, seemed right. His answer, quite different from Marx's, was that a relation of wage labor was a miserable and impoverished form of contract. Because, as we've seen, the elementary form of social contract is, for Mauss, precisely, communism: that is, an open-ended agreement in which each party commits itself to maintaining the life of the other. In wage labor the worker does give of the totality of himself, he "gives his life and labor," but the cash he receives in return has nothing of the same total quality about it. If one gives one's life, one's life should at least be guaranteed.

It is commonplace to dismiss Mauss' political conclusions at the end of "The Gift" as weak, inconsistent, not of the same power or brilliance of the rest of the essay.[9] It's true that it does at times seem tentative. I suspect this is partly because Mauss is writing about politics, not for his accustomed proletarian audience, but for a broader educated public. I also suspect this may be the reason for some of the essay's most idiosyncratic suggestions: for instance, Mauss' call for the return to an ethos in which the only excuse for accumulating wealth is to give it away again, in which the rich would again consider themselves as the "treasurers of the community"—a suggestion that interestingly, does not appear elsewhere in his political work. It would be easy to write off the whole thing as a stumblingly inadequate attempt to do Marx. Most of the usual complaints leveled by Marxist scholars about the weaknesses of the essay are true enough: Mauss doesn't even talk about production in preindustrial societies, he has no sense of the reproduction of social systems as wholes, he lacks a theory of value. But one could also treat Mauss' approach to alienation as providing a useful corrective to some of the more common blind spots of Marxian anthropology. By seeing alienation as something that can happen every time an object changes hands, for example, Mauss reminds us that just as socialization does not end at age twelve or eighteen, the creation of objects does not end on the factory floor—things are continually being maintained, altered, and above all, vested in new meanings, even as they are often repeatedly detached and alienated again. More daringly, Mauss appears to be suggesting that a certain degree of subject/object reversal—in certain contexts, at certain levels—might act not as a mystification and tool of exploitation, but as a normal aspect of creative processes that may not be nearly so dangerous as its opposite, the reduction of all social relations to any sort of objective calculus. This at any rate was what Mauss saw as the downfall of the Soviet Marxists: their extreme utilitarianism, in which he perceived—quite rightly, I think—the logic of the market, slightly transposed.

All in all, Mauss' work complements Marx because it represents the other side of socialism. Marx's work consists of a brilliant and sustained critique of capitalism; but as Mauss himself observed, he carefully avoided speculating about what a more just society would be like. Mauss' instincts were quite the opposite: he was much less interested in understanding the dynamics of capitalism than in trying to understand—and create—something that might stand outside it.

objects and persons

Mauss was always tentative about his conclusions, because he knew he was working with inadequate material. Ethnography was then in its infancy. This is no longer the case. If anything, the problem is the opposite: the literature on the Massim, or New Zealand, or the American Northwest Coast has become so vast it would be almost impossible for a non-specialist to do it justice. There have been some recent attempts to return to these examples and see how well Mauss' conclusions bear up: notably by Annette Weiner (1985, 1992) and Maurice Godelier (1996), both of whom use roughly the same theoretical approach. To my mind, though, the results have been uneven. Both are scholars whose expertise is mainly in Melanesian anthropology, and their accounts become more sketchy and attenuated the further from Melanesia they go. Of course, I'm not an expert in *any* of these areas (technically, my expertise is on Madagascar), but I will take the plunge. At any rate, in trying to bring Mauss' material into relation with the theoretical issues that have cropped up over the course of this book—issues of value, history, potential, visibility, and so on—I will be asking slightly different questions than they. As should be clear by now, just saying that gifts incorporate a part of the giver's self leaves many of the most interesting questions unanswered. For example: what part? Mauss' own formulation seems to span both Tylor's concrete, visible "image" soul, and his "life-soul," the invisible source of human powers or intentionality. In his work on the person, as I've pointed out, he seems interested in the degree to which persons are constituted by a set of emblems or properties (by which logic giving away one would necessarily be giving away a fragment of one's self); on the other, in the "The Gift" itself, he sticks with a Maori notion that seems to be all about intentions and inner powers. Another confusing question: to what degree are these objects really personified?

And afterward, we will see whether the results can tell us anything new about the overall aims of Mauss' analysis: understanding the relations between interest and generosity, freedom and obligation, persons and things.

case 1: kula armshells and necklaces

Mauss made great use of Bronislaw Malinowski's *Argonauts of the Western Pacific* (1922). He considered kula, the famous exchange of armshells and necklaces that linked together the island societies of the northern Massim region of Papua New Guinea, an example of a potlatch system. However, he was also rather frustrated by the fact that while they had names and histories, it was almost impossible to find examples of the heirlooms being treated as if they acted of their own accord—or, the Trobrianders being, he noted, "positivists, after their own fashion," treated as objects of cult (1925 [1990:24]). Mauss was forced to rely mainly on the poetic metaphors to be found in magical incantations.

One thing that does emerge from the literature on the cultures of the kula chain is that any adequate understanding of exchange in these societies has to begin with an understanding of local theories of procreation. Now, Trobriand opinions on the subject of procreation have been the subject of endless debate, ever since Malinowski announced (1929:153–58) that the Trobrianders he knew claimed that sexual intercourse was not the cause of pregnancy: or, more precisely, that while women could not become pregnant if they had never had sex at all, as soon as the womb had so been "opened," pregnancy occurred when certain ancestral spirits called *baloma* entered a woman while she was bathing, whether or not the woman in question had recently had sex. Descent was strictly through the mother's line; the men had nothing to do with it. The most curious thing, though, was that the same informants also insisted that children, both male and female, inherited their fathers' looks and not their mothers'. Why? No explanation appeared to be forthcoming. The best Malinowski could come up with was the statement of some unnamed informant: "maternal kinsmen are the same flesh, but similar faces they have not" (Malinowski 1929 173–78). This is not really an explanation, though; it has more the air of statement of self-evident truth. If they all come from the same origins, then what other reason could there be for the fact that they look so different—except that they all have different fathers?

In fact, a child's body was thought to be derived from its mother's substance—ultimately from the immortal substance of its mother's clan. Form or external appearance, on the other hand, was conveyed through males (Malinowski op cit.; Weiner 1976:121–23). It is much the same on Gawa (Munn 1986:142–43), where the key distinction made is between undifferentiated maternal substance inside the body, and a child's face—which is the expression of their individuality—and elsewhere in the Massim.

A child's upbringing follows the same implicit pattern. The mother and her brother provide the child with nurturance and food; the father and his sister provide for its bodily adornment, perform the beauty magic crucial both to courting and kula exchange, and, if the child is a boy, will usually give him his first kula valuable as well (Weiner 1976:123–29; Malinowski 1922:334–41; 1929:103–10, etc.). The last contribution fits in perfectly well with the others—kula valuables are after all themselves articles of adornment—but it also reveals how, as a child grows older, these same relations are transposed onto ever wider domains of activity.

This, according to Nancy Munn (1986:55–73, 111–18, etc.), is in turn the key to Gawan notions of value. What Gawan men aspire to above all is fame, the extension of one's self outward in space and time. Fame is in itself a kind of adornment to the person. If the ornaments one wears are (like one's physical appearance) external, visible aspects of the self that extend the self toward others, kula armshells and necklaces can extend it even further by circulating abroad and spreading knowledge of one's name with them wherever they go. But one can expand outward into these broader domains only after having first established a stable center or base, one that is always seen as rel-atively homogenous and feminine but at the same time as the dynamic "source" of expansion. Thus inner maternal substance lies hidden behind one's outer appearance and beauty, and kula exchange is itself based on con-tinual gifts of food (homogenous substance itself intended for the inside of the body) between affines and continual hospitality between kula partners.

Gawan men, for instance, send regular gifts of food to their married sisters; their sisters' husbands reciprocate with occasional but more substantial gifts: minor kula valuables, a painted canoe. For the man who provided the food, the latter represents not mere reciprocity but an increment in value, an exchange of "nameless and perishable" things for unique and durable items which will allow him to participate in wider, interisland transactions (Munn 1977; 1986:121–62). In Munn's terms, their greater value lies in their capacity to open the way to the control of more expansive levels of space and time. One could also see it as derived from their greater capacity to convey history—though in this instance, these really come down to the same thing, since an owner can realize the potential value of such objects only by giving them away and allowing them to circulate, thus carrying his name along with them. An ob-ject's capacity to embody history simply determines how far that name can go.

The literature on kula exchange is by now quite extensive indeed, and it would be possible to go into some detail about how kula articulates with in-ternal exchange systems on each island in the chain, in each case slightly dif-ferently: the connection between male exchange and women's mortuary ritual on Kiriwina (Weiner 1976, 1978, 1988), the transformation of canoes in Gawa (Munn 1977, 1983, 1986), the gradual conversion of courtship presents, and then affinal exchange into kula on Muyuw (Damon 1978, 1980, 1995), and so on. But it's not really necessary for present purposes. All I really want to stress here is the degree to which these valuables do indeed partake of persons; or, to be more accurate, since kula shells do not, gener-ally speaking, become permanently attached to any one person's identity, that they are made of the same stuff as persons. A kula shell is like a frag-ment of individual identity that has, as it were, broken off. What's more, the actions of engaging in kula exchange are simply an extension of those that create persons; actions that can be quite neatly divided here into those orga-nized around two contrastive values, one centering on the (dark, heavy, in-terior, invisible) aspect of the self identified with the matrilineal clan, the other, on the (bright, light, exterior, visible) aspect identified with fame and beauty. And just as proposed in chapter 4, the hidden interior of the indi-vidual is identified with powers of action, and the external particularity with a seductive power capable of inspiring actions in others.

Even the Tylorian analogy tends to hold up. This becomes especially ap-parent when one moves to the southern part of the Massim archipelago. Most of the islands here do not participate in kula exchange; rather, the "creative focus of social life," as Debbora Battaglia puts it (1983:289) lies in funerary ritual. However, the cultural assumptions are otherwise much the same.

On Sabarl, according to Battaglia, people make an explicit distinction between two aspects of the self: on the one hand an internal dynamic energy or life-force hidden within the body (here too associated with food), on the other a "soul" with an external "image"—the word used bears the literal meaning of "shadow" or "reflection," in good Tylorian fashion—that has all the usual properties of being detachable from the body and surviving death. When a person dies, the life-force is no more; the soul departs from this world to the afterworld, where it loses its "image" and becomes a *baloma*—the latter being much the same here as in the Trobriands, undifferentiated spirits of the matriclan, responsible for the women's fertility (1983: 293–94, 1990:68–71).

Funeral ceremonies, which are a major occasion for exchange, reproduce this passage on the level of goods. The dead person's paternal kin first display a number of greenstone axes—these axes, rather than kula shells, are on Sabarl the most exalted form of wealth—and then give them to representatives of that person's matriclan. (Representatives of the matriclan will later reciprocate with gifts of food.) Afterwards, the maternal kin retire to an undisclosed location where they use the axes to construct an effigy of the deceased, which is called the "corpse." Then, hiding the effigy behind a screen, they invoke it as an ancestor asking it to use its powers of fertility to reproduce more axes for the community (Battaglia 1983).

This is certainly not the only form of exchange the Sabarlese engage in but it is the most important one, and it moves in the exact opposite direction as kula—not from hidden feminine powers to visible masculine form, but the other way around. The reason is obviously because in this case the process is modeled not on the creation of the person in procreation and child-rearing but on its dissolution in death. But this does not alter the larger point, which is that one cannot hope to understand the circulation of valuables in a "gift economy" of this sort without first taking into account the more fundamental processes by which the human person is created and dissolved. And that when such general principles as action and reflection, or the movement between abstract potential and concrete form do appear—which they generally do—these too are always aspects of persons before they are aspects of things.

Battaglia too makes the Maussian point that really important valuables on Sabarl are said to have the same properties as persons: they have not only an external "image" but an inner life-force of their own (1983:301), as well as being, in their external form, models of the forms of social action which they mediate. This latter point I cannot pursue here, but I refer the reader to Battaglia's exemplary discussion of the form of axes and ceremonial necklaces (1990:128–35). Similar analyses can no doubt be carried out of the form of kula valuables themselves, which, like so many other shell valuables (Wagner 1986:58–59; Clark 1991, Robbins and Atkins 1999:16–19), seem to be such perfect embodiments of value because they combine exterior brilliance with the constant reminder of a dark, mysterious, womblike interior.

Maori versus Kwakiutl

I started with the Trobriand case because it was so relatively straightforward. The two key values correspond nicely with my own categories of action and reflection. The next two cases are far more complicated, because each leans so heavily on either one or the other.

It's interesting to contrast how differently Mauss uses his Maori and Kwakiutl material. The Maori appear largely as theorists. Mauss begins his essay, as we know, by asking why it is that people who receive gifts feel obliged to give something back in return; for an answer, he refers to the reflections of a Maori sage on the *hau* or "spirit of the gift." But he has next to nothing on the sociology of Maori gift exchange. When dealing with the Northwest Coast it's quite the other way around. There is very little reference to philosophy, but endless detail on the actual conduct of potlatches and nature of the wealth exchanged.

In a way, though, this is not altogether surprising. Already in Mauss' time, the products of Maori priestly colleges had developed a reputation as the great intellectuals of the "archaic" world: as cosmologists, philosophers, even metaphysicians. The Kwakiutl reputation, on the other hand, was as masters of theater, or dramatic and artistic display. One seemed obsessed with essences, the other with surfaces. In the rest of this chapter I would like to argue (among other things) that these reputations are not entirely undeserved. This will I think become all the more apparent when we try to fill in the missing parts of the picture: that is, to examine the actual mechanics of Maori exchange (circa 1750), or the implicit philosophy behind the Kwakiutl potlatch (circa 1895). In fact, the two seem in many ways to represent two extremes of logical possibility for a system of gift exchange, a fact that I would argue actually makes the comparisons between them all the more revealing if one wishes to understand precisely what the underlying commonalities in such systems might be.

Here I want to build on a tradition of comparison between Polynesia and the Northwest Coast begun by Irving Goldman (1970, 1975) and developed by Marshall Sahlins (1988). The basic argument comes down to something like this: Polynesian societies tended to see the entire universe as structured on a vast genealogy in that everyone is descended from the gods in one way or another. The result was a tendency toward homogenization, in which nobles were constantly trying to set themselves apart by some unique or astounding act. The Kwakiutl cosmos, on the other hand, was one of radical heterogeneity. The universe was fragmented into social groups each with their own completely unique mythological origins; their current leaders were incarnations of totemic creatures from the beginnings of time that had no real connection with each other. What the system lacked was any uniform medium for comparison. Hence Sahlins notes the difference in the demand for Western goods when each society first came in contact with the world market system: Hawaiian lords immediately sought out unique treasures to set themselves apart from other lords; Kwakiutl chiefs accumulated thousands and thousands of identical Hudson Bay trade blankets, which became a kind of uniform currency of prestige.

This seems to me a useful starting place because not only does it tie in with exchange, it also makes sense of some of the differences in ideologies of the person between the two. The Maori universe is a vast genealogy; it is entirely generated by a single principle, which is ultimately that of the interior, creative powers of gods and humans (though imagined, in this case, as an almost entirely sexual, and therefore naturalized, type of creativity.) The result is a remarkably rich philosophy of interior powers, with little explicit attention to external forms. Among the Kwakiutl it is precisely the other way around. Everything is surfaces, containers, masks. Interiors, when one finds them, always turn into yet more surfaces again. Maori histories are all about reciprocity, but almost nothing about wealth. Kwakiutl histories consist of little but detailed accounts of different sorts of wealth, with next to nothing about reciprocity. And so on.

case 2: gifts in Aotearoa

Mauss was originally drawn into the study of Maori religion while editing the posthumous papers of his colleague, Robert Hertz. He ended up becoming quite fascinated with it, teaching himself the Maori language and offering a series of lectures on Maori cosmogonic epics (Schwimmer 1978:202–203). These epics always take the form of a huge genealogy, beginning with abstract entities like Day and Night, or Thought and Desire, proceeding through the gods and ultimately including everything in the entire cosmos—forests, seas, crops, humans, even clouds and stones. All living creatures, then; indeed, every aspect of reality in the "world of light" in which humans dwell, were generated according to one single principle of sexual procreation.

Historical records simply continue the same story, telling of the great canoes that carried the first immigrants from the mythical island of Hawaiki to Aotearoa, and of the wanderings of the men and women who became ancestors of the different Maori *iwi* ("tribes"), then, later of *hapu* ("lineages" or "clans"). This was the great historical armature that provided the framework for politics, because the Maori were one of those extraordinarily rare groups whose members actually remembered their genealogies: most people could trace back their ancestors for several hundred years into the past. Genealogies, in turn, were the basis of rank: since children were ranked in order of seniority, and since in theory everyone could be placed somewhere on the same genealogical structure, everyone should know precisely where they stood in relation to everyone else. In reality, things were infinitely complicated, since Maori kinship was cognatic: one could trace to famous ancestors through either male or female links, and therefore just about any free Maori could make a claim to being a rangatira, a highborn noble, through some connection or another.

Society was organized into a series of tribes and hapu, each, in principle, under the leadership of its *ariki,* descended from its founding ancestor through an unbroken line of (male or female) senior children. Here again, real politics was infinitely more complicated; the fact that a firstborn daughter rarely succeeded to political office—but still outranked her brothers—alone allowed endless possibilities for struggles over status, shifting alliances, and political intrigue. Finally, since cognatic kinship ensures that most people had any number of choices for which group they wished to join; in any cognatic system, politics largely becomes a matter of pulling people together. Ambitious leaders could use an almost infinite variety of ties to assemble followers and effectively construct new kin groups in which they or some close relative could claim to stand as the *ariki* (Schwimmer 1978, 1990). *Hapu,* at least, were being continually re-created on such lines. But all this also meant politics became an obvious zero-sum game: there are only so many people around, and everyone one draws into one's own genealogical group is lost to all the others.

mana and tapu

Of all the metaphysical concepts the Maori have contributed to anthropology, the most famous are certainly *mana* and *tapu* ("taboo"). In Maori they are often used interchangeably, since they imply two different aspects of power: the one, power in its capacity to act; the other, power in how it must be respected by others. This is of course altogether in keeping with the terms mapped out in chapter 4, but in fact things in this case are a good deal more complicated.

For one thing, while in most of Polynesia "mana" is the power of the gods, or by extension, any invisible power capable of making things happen or "appear," among the Maori it also takes on a more explicitly political meaning. Mana can mean "prestige," "authority," or "influence." Within this usage there seems to be a recognition that political power is built largely on reputation; that it is only the fact that others believe one has it that allows it to exist. As such it required constant maintenance: Maori nobles (and just about all free men considered themselves noblemen) were notoriously touchy. To leave even an implied sleight or insult unavenged would lead to the weakening of one's mana, unless set straight by some sort of *utu,* some act of recompense, reciprocity, or revenge.

As for tapu: it referred, above all, to restrictions; or even more, to a state of being surrounded by them, thus rendering one sacred, pure, "set apart" from a relatively profane (*noa*) world characterized especially by biological processes: cooking, eating, excretion, sexuality. Cooked food especially had to be kept away from tapu objects. "Every man in Maori society," writes Firth,

> had some degree of personal tapu, varying according to his rank and becoming very intensive with the more important chiefs. Cooked food and all things connected therewith were the very antithesis of tapu, and contact with them as sufficient to destroy the tapu of any object, however sacred. Hence no man possessed of any self-respect would engage in cooking, or collect firewood, nor, since the most tapu parts of his person were his head and back, would be carry burdens of cooked food. Such work was left to slaves, who had lost their tapu, and to women, who [for the most part] did not have any. (Firth 1959:181; see Graeber 1997)

These were not static categories. Life was a process of the endless imposition, and stripping away, of tapu. To define oneself as tapu, for example, was always a matter of defining others as relatively *noa:* hence, according to one early traveler's account, Maori chiefs went to war carrying a *taiaha* staff whose blade was shaped like a protruding tongue, so as to imply the desire to turn the enemy into food. In this case it was no abstract symbol—Maori warriors did indeed feast on their defeated foes—but the same chief might hold out the same weapon as a staff when making speeches to his own people, simply as a sign of higher status (Angas 1847 I: 318). The fact that the entire universe was seen as part of a vast genealogy created a sort of cosmological dilemma: humans were the offsprings of the gods, but then, so was everything else, including the animals and plants one had to eat to survive. What's more, the divine remained present in all these things; it had to be in order for them to grow—since the divine was, above all, the principle of natural generativity. For one's sweet potatoes to grow, one had to maintain tapus to ensure the gods' presence. To be able to harvest one's sweet potatoes, one had to break them, to drive the gods away, and, effectively, make war on the crops, so as to be free to kill and eat them (Williamson 1913, Johansen 1958; Sahlins 1985b:200–206). The whole universe was an arena of endless consumption but at the same time, all driven by a principle of *utu* or recompense where everything ultimately leads to its comeuppance; i.e., eventually the gods eat us in return, which is why we ultimately must die (Smith 1972).

This ability to appropriate what rightfully belongs to the gods was the paradigm for a general possibility of reversing existing hierarchies, which in Maori myths and histories, usually plays itself out in stories of younger brothers or daring young warriors who, unencumbered by the endless taboos and protocol that hedges about senior figures, can make a name for themselves by breaking all the rules (Gudgeon 1905a:62–65; Smith 1972:62–63). By doing so, they in effect proved their mana and could eventually become highly *tapu* figures in their own right. It was a very dangerous strategy. Maori history is full of transgressive warriors who finally went too far, transgressed one rule they shouldn't have, and ended up being destroyed by it. Still, it allowed for a broad division between sorts of leaders: on the level of the tribe, sacred *ariki*, who had little immediate political power; on that of the *hapu*, figures who had largely achieved important roles through their own efforts. These were in fact the effective political actors, since it was the *hapu* (or "clan") that was the really significant economic and political unit.

Maori values

From this, one begins to get a very rough idea of the structure of value in traditional Maori societies. As an initial approximation, one can distinguish two broad terms: call them "generation," and "appropriation." The first is identified with powers of creativity and growth, which is ultimately the generative power of the gods. In human society it is embodied most of all in the figure of the *ariki*, particularly the really grand *ariki* (often women) who are the firstborn of a whole tribe: the living embodiments of ancient ancestors and ultimately of gods. Such figures were considered ultimately responsible for the fertility and spiritual state of their group's territories, but they were so hedged about by *tapu* that they did not do much, or in some cases, anything; their main role was simply to exist. The second is all about human achievement, the transgression and appropriation, and the mythic figures of younger brothers who usurped the *ariki*'s authority. One is severely fetishized, since all human powers of creation are seen as refractions of the powers of the gods; the other, while all about human assertiveness, is not seen as fundamentally creative at all, but more about destruction[10]—Tu, who is the god who represents the human side of the cosmos, is also the god of war. The two might be said to come together in a broad notion of honor, which is both one's ability to defend one's *tapu* and the ability to encompass ever more of the universe within it.

All this does recall the terms I was developing in chapter 4: the passive aristocrat, oriented toward the past, whose role is just to be; the active warrior oriented toward the future. But the particularly metaphysical quality of Maori philosophy also means that it is difficult to make a clear distinction between, say, visible forms of power identified with the display of property and hidden powers of action. First of all, the persuasive display of wealth simply was not much of a factor. Instead, one has a constant movement back and forth between visible and invisible forms, with the usual idea being that the former are simply particular, probably ephemeral, emanations of the latter; and all of this takes place in a context of danger and overall cosmic strife.

This becomes especially clear when one looks at property. The "personal *tapu*" of an important person very much extended to their possessions. This was particularly the case since anything that came into contact with one's person could thereby be considered an extension of the person himself or herself. A lord's cloak, or in fact any garment, was part of that lord and often seemed to represent that very capacity for encompassment: to throw one's garment over a prisoner meant that person was spared from death; an important unmarried woman who threw her cloak over a man thereby married him (Weiner 1992:61). If an *ariki* used a house, no one else could, for fear of violating their *tapu* (this would usually entail dire consequences). But by extension, any act of identifying another person's land or other property with the *tapu* parts of one's body or personal effects could, if unchallenged, be taken as a claim of ownership:

> Thus, a chief named Raukataura, passing through a forest owned by a friendly tribe, had one of the feathers of his head-dress torn out by a shrub. Sitting down, the chief made a little fence of broken sticks round his sacred feather. He was accompanied on this occasion by some of the men of the tribe owning the place, but they said and did nothing. Their silence and inaction were construed as an assent to ownership, and the sons of Raukataura held possession of this title until the present day . . . Sometimes if a chief should wash or comb his sacred head when journeying across a piece of land his people would claim the land, or if he slept in a temporary hut for a night, title would be asserted. These claims were not, however, made lightly, there were to be other circumstances, such as the death of a near relative at the time; something to mark the event as of importance before such claim was established, and it always had to be upheld by the law of the strongest. (Tregear 1904:132–33)[11]

The same principle however was also applied in a far more aggressive mode of appropriation called *tapatapa* ("challenge"). A chief—that is, a recognized local leader whose *tapu* was particularly great—could, in effect, appropriate an object simply by identifying it with his name or a part of his body. Maning (1863:137–39; Firth 1959:345) gives the example of a group of chiefs who, observing a fleet of canoes that their armies were about to seize as plunder, began laying claim to the best ones: "that swift canoe is my backbone," said one, "my skull shall be the baler to bale that one out," "those two are my two thighs," and so on. Each thereby effectively brought it within the circle of his *tapu*, which would then have been violated had the man who actually captured the canoe in question not immediately handed it over to him.

In all these cases we are dealing with some version of "the law of the strongest." Since simply enshrining a feather from one's headdress in a forest, or laying claim to a canoe by identifying it with one's backbone, did not in itself give anyone a right to it, such an action was a test of power: one still had to persuade others to agree (even if from fear), or defend one's claim by force. But successful persuasion, intimidation, or the application of force was, it seems clear, itself the proof of one's mana. This was perhaps the most dramatically the case with *tapatapa*, because in performing it what one was actually doing was cursing oneself. The most powerful curses (or "witchcraft," in Aotearoa it was the same thing) consisted of identifying one's victim with cooked food—an act that, especially if one has some object taken from the victim to use as a medium, is efficacious in itself in destroying the *tapu* of the victim and setting them to waste away (White 1885:150–51; cf. Dunne 1927:88–89). *Tapatapa* was slightly milder: it might consist of, say, naming one's dog after a rival chief—though, if discovered, such an act would require an act of vengeance as its *utu* (payback, reciprocity). In other words, in calling a canoe his backbone, the chief in question was creating a situation in which anyone who did not pass the canoe over to the chief would have been offering him a terrible challenge.[12]

Tapatapa, being a form of appropriation outright, does not seem to have been much used against those of equal status: White notes it was most often used to seize the property of slaves. If a chief employed it against a free person, someone with *tapu* of their own, he would be expected to eventually reciprocate—presumably in appropriately lavish aristocratic style. But as one might expect in a society in which most free men claimed noble status, such behavior was not limited to the mighty. In fact, much of what would normally be called gift exchange seems to have taken the form of mutual appropriation: one party requests some object (tacitly or otherwise); the owner immediately supplies it, then later appears to request something of roughly equivalent worth.

> Thus to admire something belonging to another person usually meant that it was immediately presented to the person who praised it. The effectiveness of

this in procuring the article desired is illustrated by a story given by John White of a noted gourmand of traditional days, Te Reinga of Kaitaia. He was of such greedy disposition that when anyone was passing up or down the valley with fish or other products he always hailed him, saying, "I am very fond of that food." This was equivalent to a direct request for it, so of course the food was handed over to him. So tiresome became this practice that at length the people of the district, to end his begging, sent a war party against him and slew him. (Firth 1959:411–412)

Te Reinga apparently had little worth requesting in return. Early European visitors to New Zealand soon had to teach themselves never to praise or admire an object of Maori manufacture, lest its owner immediately press it on them and then later expect to be able to demand something of roughly equal worth. While as Firth notes, barter itself was absent in traditional New Zealand, this is about as close to barter as gift exchange can get. Haggling might have been absent, but each party chose what it wanted from the other on the basis of a presumed equivalence. Of course as one might imagine, it is not as if anyone were free to claim anything at all. First of all, there seems to have been a broad distinction between types of valuables. Food, and objects of everyday use, was a sphere of lavish generosity; to refuse a request for food seems to have been well nigh impossible.[13] But requests for an heirloom could be refused: Johansen (1954:119) notes a proverb about a certain Tuahu Mahina who was refused an heirloom cloak: "he is a stingy man; this is evident as the dogskin cloak was not given to him." As in the Trobriands, such heirlooms were seen especially something one party extracts from another—but here, this is not seen as a result of the seductive beauty of the recipient, but their potential for action: in this case the capacity (or disposition) to reciprocate.

There seems to have been a complex set of principles governing who could demand, or give, what to whom under what circumstances—one whose finer points it is by now impossible to reconstruct. For example: sometimes people did offer important heirlooms as gifts. The recipient was under no obligation to accept (Mauss' "obligation to receive" was apparently not in effect in Aotearoa), but if he or she did, acceptance was seen as placing the donor in a situation in which he would later be able to demand almost anything in return.

An instance of this occurred when a chief called Papaka . . . while on a visit to the Ngatihape tribe, by whom he was entertained as a guest, made a present of his ear ornament to the Ngatihape chief. Now anything worn on the person of a chief is sacred, and the presentation by a chief of an ear or head ornament, is a mark of the greatest respect that can be shown by one Maori to another. Papaka was accustomed to wear attached to his ear the tail of a Maori dog called "waro," which he gave to the Ngatihape chief, and it was accepted. Soon afterwards Papaka returned and assumed the leadership of the Ngatihape tribe, and consequently a right to all their lands, which claim has continued good to his descendants to the present time . . . (White 1885:196)

"The Ngatihape tribe," he explains, "in receiving the present from Papaka virtually bound themselves to give whatever he might demand in return . . ." This is obviously an extreme case, but the same logic recurs throughout the early literature: whether it be the case of the Maori chief who, before departing on his first visit to Auckland, pressed numerous unwanted pigs on his host, so as to be able to demand some of things he expected to see there (Shortland 1856:215–17), or the conduct of important intertribal marriages, in which, according to Dunne (1927:189) the suitors would offer the woman's family a gift of heirloom weapons and ornaments; if accepted, it was "tantamount to the acceptance of the young warrior as a son-in-law."

There was yet another form of traditional appropriation. Within kinship groups, goods were constantly changing hands through a kind of ritualized pillaging called *muru* (Maning 1863:83–91; Johansen 1954:140–46). Anyone who was considered to have damaged the honor or safety of a group by violating an important *tapu*, by sexual indiscretions, by accidentally injuring another or even accidentally injuring themselves, would be subject to a raiding party of their own kin—its size varying with the gravity of the offense—that would descend on the culprit's homestead, heavily armed, and strip it entirely bare of movable possessions. To be the object of such a raid was considered no little honor. Neither were they by any means a rare occurrence—Maning remarks that anyone who accumulated an unusual store of wealth would tend to be observed constantly for possible infractions, and that he had himself observed, during the time he was living in a Maori settlement, the same European coat change ownership six times by means of *muru*, ultimately ending up in the hands of its original possessor.

mauri and hau

So far then, we have established that a person's property is seen as a continuation of their person, or at least what Firth calls their "personal *tapu.*" We have also established that this does not stand in the way of a remarkably fluid situation in which most objects are subject to potential appropriation by others—indeed, it could even serve as a means to facilitate it. Not only were relations between humans and gods conceived in terms of ritual appropriation, but so, to a surprising degree, were relations between humans.

Most authors who have considered the relation of property and the person in Aotearoa—Mauss included—have not looked so much at *mana* and *tapu* as the terms *mauri* and *hau*. This will require a brief excursus. At first glance, Maori theories about the constitution of the human person (Best 1900, 1901a) do seem to fit the classic Tylorian mold. There is indeed one aspect known as the *wairua*, or "double," particularly immanent in reflections and shadows, which is also the aspect that survives death; alongside it, a set of terms concerning hidden, invisible powers identified with life, mind, strength, productivity, and so on. But the first term is used in only a very limited fashion: mainly, for ghosts, and for that aspect of the self that wanders abroad in dreams. It is the invisible principles that are really developed; and, critically, they that became caught up in one's possessions. All the emphasis is on the terms *hau* and *mauri;* both of which refer to an active life-force that exists both in human beings, and—appropriately enough for a philosophical system which sees the entire universe as emerging from the same generative powers—is immanent in animals, plants, and features of the landscape as well.

When one speaks of the *hau* or *mauri* of a forest or coastal inlet used as a fishery, one is speaking first of all of productivity: that which makes it live and grow, and produce fish and birds and eels. When one speaks of the *hau* or *mauri* of a person, however, one is not talking about "productivity" in anything like the same sense: the term does not appear to have anything to do either with human fertility, or to material production of any sort. Rather, it appears to be rooted in a certain notion of essence. Firth (1959:255) calls it "vital essence": the assumption being that behind any material form is an invisible, dynamic power that makes it what it is. It is at once the source of appearance *and* potential for action, which, as various authors (Johansen 1954, Schwimmer 1978) note, was for Maori philosophers seen as merely an expression of an inner nature. If interfered with, contaminated, or "lost," the object or being that is its emanation—in this case, a human being—will therefore begin to lose its integrity, decay, or simply die.

When speaking in such broad terms, *mauri* and *hau* could be used almost interchangeably. Insofar as they were distinguished, it was largely by the ways they became invested in material objects. As a rough formulation, I might offer the following: insofar as this essential power became caught up in objects that mediated relations between people, especially in ways which open some of them to peril, then those objects were called *hau;* when it was instead invested in an object that was then hidden away to preserve and protect that power, that was a *mauri* (cf. Gudgeon 1905b:127–28).

For example, if a magician wishing to curse someone managed to get hold of the clippings of their hair or nails, leftovers from one of their meals, or even the impression of their footprint, this would be called a *hau*. Having thus attained access to the source of that person's powers, as embodied in the object, he would have much opportunity to harm her. But one could also employ a similar process to invest the generative powers of, say, a forest in a "talisman": say, the branch of a tree from the forest, or some similar metonymic token, or more often some unusually shaped stone or other object. One could convey the powers to this object by the chanting of spells, then hide it as a *mauri*. It would then normally be buried in a secret place in the forest, so as to both protect the fertility of the forest by embodying it in a form that enemies could not find to harm. Usually, it was also placed in a lizard, which thus became immortal and wandered unseen in the forest. Only by capturing this lizard or finding the hidden talisman would enemies (who seem to have been legion in most such matters) be able to destroy the forest's or fishing-place's fertility. Similar *mauri* were placed near fisheries (e.g., Mitchell 1944:42–43).

There is something to me quite fascinating about such hidden talismans. Descriptions of them (see Best 1909, 1929, 1942) almost invariably emphasize that their power was twofold: not only did they increase the fertility of birds or fish, but they also drew them in from other forests, or other parts of the sea. Clearly, there seems to be an echo here of the zero-sum game of cognatic kinship; the hidden powers of the *mauri* of a forest or fishery were models for the sorts of power that could create descent groups—both natural fertility, which is the basis for kinship itself, and the more political power of gathering and assembling, drawing in individuals from other localities, since, in a cognatic system, one has a fixed number of individuals all of whom could be members of any number of different groups.

There are two points to be made here. First of all, the generative power was not seen as human, but divine. One might recall that Maori agricultural ritual was seen as a way of bringing in the gods (who gave the field its powers of growth and fertility), during which time the field was laden with *tapu*, and then, before harvest, banishing them to free the place for human beings. Normally, such fields also contained a *mauri* either buried in the soil, or displayed in the form of "kumara gods" (Best 1925:199–203); it was usually removed after the harvest. Also, the very first sweet potato from each field was left as an offering for the gods—this offering was called a *hau*, and it was this that lifted the *tapu* state of the field and crops so it could eaten by ordinary humans.

Second, this idiom of generation and gathering—modeled on the creation of human, political groups—was not so clearly set out when those terms were applied to the human groups themselves. Hence there is in effect a double displacement.

the hau *of the gift (one more time)*

Mauss' "*hau* of the gift" argument has sparked an apparently endless discussion and debate (Firth 1959:279–81, 417–21; Johansen 1954:116–118;

Levi-Strauss 1950; Panoff 1970; Sahlins 1972; 1992; Gathercole 1978; MacCall 1982; MacCormick 1982; Cassajus 1984; Guideri 1984; Taïeb 1984; Weiner 1985, 1992:49; Thompson 1987; Racine 1991; Babdazan 1993; Godelier 1996:49–56; Salmond 1997:176–177; Gell 1998:106–109; Godbout and Caillé 1998:131–134). In a way it's rather odd that it should, since just about none of these authors accepts Mauss' own interpretation—that in Maori philosophy, gifts were seen as containing something of the giver's soul (his *hau*), and that it is the desire of this fragment of the soul to return to its native lands and former owner that obliges the recipient to offer something in return.

The most famous text that Mauss made the center of his analysis is actually from an essay on bird-snaring (Best 1909). It appears to be taken from a letter written by a Maori sage named Tamati Ranapiri, in response to a series of inquiries on the subject sent him by Elsdon Best. What follows is quite possibly the most quoted paragraph in all of anthropology:

> I will now speak of the hau, and the ceremony of *whangai hau*. That hau is not the wind that blows; no, not at all. I will explain it carefully to you. Suppose that you possess a certain valuable (*taonga*), and you give that valuable to me. We have no agreement about payment. Now, I give that article to a third person, who, after some time has elapsed, decides since he has the valuable, he should to make some return for it, and so he does so. Now, that valuable that he gives to me is the hau of the one I first received from you and then gave to him. I must hand it over to you. It would not be right for me to keep it for myself, whether it be desirable or otherwise. I must hand it over to you, because it is a hau of the other valuable. Were I to keep such an equivalent for myself, then some serious ill would befall me, even death. Such is the hau, the hau of personal property, the hau of the forest . . . (Ranapiri in Best 1909:439, 441)[14]

All of this is offered to explain a ceremony called *whangai hau* ("feeding the *hau*"), meant to lift the *tapu* from a forest when Maori fowlers come to collect its birds. The first they trap must be cooked on a sacred fire and a certain share offered to the forest's *mauri:* the talisman that embodies its life-force, and part also to the priests who placed it there. Since "it is the *mauri* that causes the birds to be abundant in the forest," Ranapiri notes, "these birds are the property of, or belong to, the *mauri.*" This gift, he explains, is also called a *hau*.

Now most commentators have turned this one passage over and over—and I am not going to be so entirely different—but it's important to note that this is by no means the only reference in the Maori literature to "the *hau* of the gift." Mauss himself listed quite a number in the accompanying footnotes: especially, concerning the expressions *hau whitia*, "averted *hau*" or *kai*

hau "eating the *hau*"—both of which refer to the consequences of not returning a gift. Nine years earlier, Best had written:

> Should I dispose of some article belonging to another person and not hand
> over to him any return or payment I have received for that article, that is a
> *hau whitia* and my act is a *kai hau,* and death awaits me, for the dread terrors
> of makutu (witchcraft) will be turned on me. For it seems that that article of
> yours is impregnated with a certain amount of your hau, which presumably
> passed into the article received in exchange therefor, because if I pass that sec-
> ond article on to other hands, it is a hau whitia (averted hau).
>   I was having a flax shoulder-cape made by a native woman at Rua-tahina.
> One of the troopers wished to buy it from the weaver, but she firmly refused,
> lest the horrors of the hau whitia descend upon her. (Best 1900:198)

Where Mauss sees the *hau* as a fragment of the human soul, endowed
with its own desires, Best sees it in more passive terms as a kind of spiritual
substance, one which overflows the person and can be absorbed in its possessions. Both seem alien to the Maori conception. Here Best's own final example serves as a counter-illustration. In the case of the woman at
Rua-tahina, no object had yet changed hands. Rather, what would have been
"averted" was a declared intention—an intended movement of objects between people.

In fact, if one examines other uses of the term *hau,* one finds they often
turn on some sort of notion of intentional movement. At its simplest *hau*
could mean "the wind that blows," which is very close to pure movement and
nothing else; as a verb it could mean "to strike," but also "to command," or
"to animate, inspirit, urge on" (Williams 1844:46–47; Tregear 1891:52). Here
we simply have a movement from one intentional subject to another, or better, a movement of intentional action, a project, that starts from one person
and then proceeds through another. The same seems to apply to the intended
movements of objects, such as Mr. Best's flax shoulder cape. At its broadest,
hau could refer to fame and reputation, the process by which one's name is
heard and broadcast far and wide. Here of course it overlaps with *mana.*

If so, one might say that an object becomes a *hau* when it mediates such
an movement and that this *hau* is "averted," or "eaten," when such a movement is not allowed to take its normal course. Perhaps so. But this wouldn't
tell us much: after all, any object that plays a part in human society mediates action in some way or another.

In the end, then, I think it will pay to look at Ranapiri's text again. What
Ranapiri seems to be doing, there, is drawing a parallel between two differ-
ent common uses of the word "*hau.*" On the one hand, according to
Williams' Maori dictionary (1844:47), *hau* could mean "return present by

way of acknowledgment for a present received"—any return gift, whether or not a third party was involved. The other usage refers to offerings made to gods to lift *tapu* (Williams, Tregear 1891:52). It might be best to examine this parallel in greater detail.

giving, taking, and the gods

The ritual described in Ranapiri's text, called *whangai hau* (feeding the *hau*) is, as I've already mentioned, actually just this sort of ritual of *tapu* removal. Forests were heavily *tapu'd* during most of the year, during the period when the gods were present doing their productive work, filling the trees with birds, plants, and wildlife. Cooked food, for example, must never be brought into such a place. In order to harvest what they have produced and reduce it to human food—to move from the moment of divine generation to that of human appropriation—it is necessary to remove this *tapu*. This is somewhat obscured in Ranapiri's text which makes the whole process rather magical: he emphasizes that the forest's hidden *mauri*, and hence its productive capacity, is seen as having been placed there by the priests. Nonetheless, almost all other texts (e.g., Best 1909:12, 1922:26, 1929:3) make it clear that the power of a *mauri* is ultimately that of some *atua*, some divine power of generation.

Hence, the significance of the fact that the birds offered to the priests— and *mauri*—were cooked. Jean Smith observes that this was typical of *tapu*-removal rites: a gift is offered to the gods, but in a form—say, by placing cooked food in the mouths of their images—that was polluting and destructive of the *tapu* that enforced their power. Such gifts were "an agent of control disguised as an act of propitiation" (1972:33).

The word *hau* was especially used to refer to one type of *tapu* removal ritual, called *pure*. *Pure* referred, most often, to gifts of either cooked food or human hair that had been cut off, which had a similar ability to destroy the strength of divine powers. Now, I've already observed that cut hair, nails, and similar exuviae were referred to as *hau* when used as the means to curse someone. What precisely is the connection? Babdazan (1993:61; Gell 1998:108) has suggested that both represent a capacity for growth: one's fingernails and hair are the parts of one's body that are most obviously and continually growing, and can thus be seen as tokens of the generative potential of the individual. I would add: both are tokens of the generative potential that are not capable of further generation themselves. Hair or nails in themselves are simply dead matter, incapable of growth. By cutting them off, one is rendering a part of the person that embodies growth utterly infertile. Sweet potatoes—the paradigmatic foodstuff—are still capable of generating new life, even after they've been harvested, but this is why the emphasis is on *cooked* food; in cooking a tuber, one destroys its generative potential and renders it fit only for consumption.[15] The same is of course true of the cooked birds offered in Ranapiri's text.

The parallel with cursing (which is also referred to as "witchcraft") is quite clear, then. In one case, "sorcery" is said to use the medium of the victim's hair or nails (*hau*) to destroy the victim's life-force (*hau*); in another, curses declare him to be cooked food. In fact, these are precisely the same thing (cf. Shortland 1856:114–15).

According to Smith, by placing cooked food in the mouth of an image or tossing cut hair at a sea monster, one was ostensibly making a gesture of propitiation but really attempting to destroy its strength and subordinate it to humans. One is in an attenuated way doing the same thing to the gods as one does in cursing a human being; neutralizing its generative power and reducing at least an aspect of its creation to food. The objects, then, embody processes. They form a compressed icon of the actions accomplished through their medium: growth, detachment from the source of growth, destruction of the generative power in a way that makes its products appropriable for human beings. It's a motion that renders the two key principles of value in Maori society—divine generation and human appropriation—two moments of a single frozen narrative.

Does the gift of a *hau* as return present do something similar? Well, on one level, it could certainly be said that it does. It removes the *tapu* from the original object. Hertz himself had noted that if one were to steal an object, that object is still full of "taboos" and "signs of ownership" that charge it with a kind of power (called either mana or *hau*) which will punish the thief (in Mauss 1925 [1990:90n29]). Until a counter-gift is offered, the object is still within the circle on the giver's *tapu*, not the recipient's. As such it constitutes a danger: it can be used as a medium of attack, destroying the recipient's own *tapu* (as in cursing), or perhaps, as Mauss suggests, operating all of its own accord.

But it seems to me there is a broader sense in which a "return present" operates to lift *tapu*—one that can be fully understood only when one considers the peculiarly appropriative style of Maori gift exchange. If you accept a valuable gift from another, this places you in a position in which that person can demand pretty much anything the giver deems to be equivalent: even, in some cases, one's lands or one's daughter or one's self. One can refuse only at the risk of a total collapse of honor (not to mention the threat of "witchcraft"). So in effect, all one's possessions are potentially within the donor's power. This is the very opposite of *tapu;* to be *noa*, free of *tapu*, also means to be "within another's power."[16]

Hence the logic of Ranapiri's analogy between the two sorts of gift becomes almost perfect. The donor really is in the position of the generative god. The god (or *mauri,* if you like), after all, has created the birds that have just been harvested through its generative powers; they belong to it. In order to appropriate the birds for themselves, the human hunters give back a small portion as a "first fruits offering," but in a cooked form that implies at least the temporary destruction of that power. The god should properly have rights to everything. Not only the forest but its products are under its *tapu.* Through the medium of the *hau,* humans lift the *tapu* the god has previously imposed while its generative power was in effect. It is quite the same as with sweet potatoes. Now, the power of the donor is not quite so sweeping as that of the god; except in exceptional cases, like Papaka's, he does not have the right to demand *everything.* But he does have the right to demand *anything,* and so his power hangs over all the recipient's possessions in a similarly undifferentiated, encompassing fashion. But this means that by offering a return present, a *hau,* one effectively heads this prospect off. By offering a portion, one frees the rest of one's possessions from the threat of falling under the donor's *tapu.*

What I'm suggesting then is that one reason offering a return gift could be seen as a *hau* was that a Maori of the time would not have automatically assumed this to be the normal practice. When we think of gift exchange we normally assume a scenario in which A offers something to B, and then B, after a discrete interval, offers something back again. This does not appear to have been the scenario which an eighteenth or nineteenth century Maori would necessarily have had foremost in their mind. As we've seen, when goods changed hands, it was often—probably most often—through one of various complex forms of appropriation. If so, then offering a return gift— say, by giving the *taonga* to a third party, getting something in return, and passing it back to A again—could be seen as among other things a rather clever stratagem; a way of taking the initiative and salvaging one's autonomy.

heirlooms

At this point I can return to Annette Weiner's treatment of the Maori literature in *Inalienable Possessions* (1991). Weiner is trying to salvage the core of Mauss' argument: that the obligation to return a gift is, for the Maori, due to the identity of the gift being caught up in that of its original owner. Or at least, she argues this is true of certain types of gift, heirlooms classed as *taonga.*[17] These, she claims, can for this reason never really be given away at all. They so partake of the identity of their original owners that they are always seen to belong to them, and therefore, in a certain sense they can never really be given away at all.

Of the two most important categories of heirloom, one—greenstone weapons and ornaments—were seen as fundamentally male products, and

the other—various elaborately crafted flax, feather, or dogskin cloaks—as female ones. Such objects, she argues, tend over time to be seen as the veritable embodiments of the ancestors. This is perhaps the most obviously the
case for greenstone: in fact Weiner suggests (1992:56–58) that in the earliest periods of human settlement in New Zealand, before greenstone came
into common use, the main treasures were actually made from ancestral
bones. And if greenstones were bones, cloaks were an extension of the skin.
Even in recent times, at funerals of important men or women, such valuables
would be laid at the body's side, sometimes along with the bones of other,
earlier ancestors, and usually, buried with them for a time, before being recovered and ritually freed of *tapu* to become valued heirlooms once again
(Tregear 1904; Metge 1974:263; Best 1924 II;54–55; cf. Taylor 1855:62).
Heirlooms quite literally partook of the dead and stories of the recovery of
long lost heirlooms almost always culminate in a scene in which "it was carried to the village, where it was wept over, as though it had been a long lost
and dear relative" (Gudgeon 1905a:57)—after which it was usually laid to
rest in a collective tomb.

I have already remarked that there is a certain incoherence in Mauss'
analysis of the *hau* of the gift. If the gift I give to you contains a portion of
myself, one that wishes to return home, then why should it be satisfied by
your giving me something else? Wouldn't this just compound the problem?
You would think if this ideology were used to justify anything, it would be
the return of the object itself. In fact, this is precisely what Weiner is arguing. To continue the analogy: if I give you my father's skull as a gift, it does
not thus become your father's skull, no matter what you give me in return.
Unless exchange is seen as effecting a complete alienation of rights, and
rights are all that is considered important, it will certainly be seen as still be-
longing to me. In Aotearoa at least, this meant such an object could never
really be given away. Gifts of heirlooms were really only loans. Often two
chiefs concluding an alliance would swap heirloom weapons, or two sections
of a tribe would pass an ancestral heirloom back and forth between them;
sometimes they were given as gifts during marriages or funerals; but in every
case, whether or not there was a return gift, it was understood that the object was given only for safekeeping, as a kind of trust; eventually, it would
have to be given back.

But of course, Maori heirlooms were not really made from human bodies. The question is how it was that certain objects came to be so entangled
in history that they are treated as if they might as well be. Here, Weiner
speaks broadly of objects embodying the "cosmological origins" of a group;
and one does hear occasionally of such things as adzes once used to separate
Heaven and Earth in the beginning of time (Gudgeon 1905a:55–57), or
tribes that still owned axes their ancestors had used to carve the canoes in

which they first migrated to Aotearoa, centuries before (Mitchell 1944:187; White 1887 III:301–302; IV:17–18). Heirlooms like these would be handed down in the senior, *ariki* line of the tribe.[18] Now, there is already something immediately interesting about these heirlooms. Axes or adzes are tools. Tools are, by definition, not created to be significant in themselves, but to be useful; they exist in order to become the media for human actions. Hence, if they are valued as heirlooms today, their value is that of the *actions* they facilitated in the past—actions that, in turn, contributed to the fame of the actors, whom the tools can then memorialize.

These acts can be acts of creation or also acts of destruction. Many of the most famous heirlooms were weapons.

> The meré is highly regarded as a tribal treasure, and the best of them had bad records; there are no notches on them to indicate the number of heads they have split, but these are all memorized and the circumstances in relation to each can be recounted by members of the tribe as accurately as a gramophone repeats a record. (Dunne 1927:187)

Even when what is memorialized are acts of creation, however, these do not seem to include the creation of the object itself. Many heirlooms are now considered works of art; still, the names of the artists or craftspeople who made them usually remain obscure—even if the names of subsequent holders are known in extraordinary detail.[19]

The emphasis on active powers seems appropriate considering the overall metaphysical quality of Maori thought. Of course feminine goods represent the other side of the equation: if Weiner is right, the visible exterior skin as opposed to the hidden inner bones (enablers of action). Where male treasures create or destroy, female ones are, as we've seen, tokens of the power of encompassment. But even here, the value of the object arises above all from the actions that have surrounded it, or which—somewhat paradoxically—its own desirability have given rise to.

It might be useful here to consider how such valuables appear, when they appear in Maori historical accounts.

Before I do so, though, a word on Maori history. The surprising thing when one goes through Maori oral histories, rich and detailed as they are, is that heirlooms rarely play much part. These are mainly the histories of migrations, of begettings, insults and vengeance, exploration and romance, with occasional feats of magic or even exploits of hunting or fishing. There are seductions and elopements and treacherous murders, and endless wars, but very little about property (it's especially striking if one compares them to, say, the Kwakiutl histories gathered by Boas, which seem to be entirely about property)—unless, that is, an item was drawn into the action of the

.ma itself. On the other hand, if these stories contain little about property, a..d almost nothing about gifts, they are very much about reciprocity. The notion of *utu,* of paying back debts, is the central theme of most of them: it is just that the idiom of reciprocity is overwhelmingly one of violence. Here is my abbreviated summary of one of the few accounts in which an heirloom—in this case, a dogskin cloak—does take center stage:

> In about 1675, a certain inland chief had possession of two famous treasures, a greenstone war club called Karioi-Mutu and a dogskin cloak called Pipi-te-Wai. Two rival chiefs from the coastal Kawhia region set out to ask him for them; the more prominent, Tuahu Mahina, failed;[20] but his rival Pakaue succeeded. After an ally warned Tuahu Mahina that now no one would consider him a man as long as Pakaue lived, he attacked Pakaue's fort. Pakaue fled and was eventually hunted down and killed by a relative of Tuahu Mahina named Tuatini Moko, who appropriated the heirlooms.
>
> Most of Pakaue's people fled to a nearby tribe where they found allies, raised an army, and ultimately took their revenge on Tuahu Mahina, killing him and many of his followers. Satisfied with their vengeance, they made peace with the survivors. Pakaue's son Te Wehi however was not satisfied because his father's killer remained alive and in possession of the heirlooms; eventually he found allies of his own, two brothers who were famous warriors from Waikato. Their expedition was successful; they took the fort where Tuatini Moko was living, and when the latter tried to flee with the heirlooms, Te Wehi ran him down and killed him. He quickly secreted the treasures under his cloak, but the two brothers had sent a spy who reported what had happened. So the two asked him for the heirlooms, and he was obliged to hand them over.[21]
>
> These two brothers, who conquered much of Waikato, eventually became such outrageous cannibals that they began to kill and eat even their own relatives; eventually, their neighbors raised a huge army to take revenge, and after great battles, they were killed.
>
> The history goes on to detail yet another cycle of vengeance, as one of the warrior's sons grew up and discovered the fate of his father. There was no word of the treasures, though, until many generations later, when a Waikato chief named Te Whata Karaka was making peace with the Ngati Maru tribe to the north. To seal the agreement, the Ngati Maru chief handed over the dogskin cloak. No one was quite sure how it came into their possession, but many speculated his tribe must have taken part in the battle in which the two brothers fell. At any rate since it was returned to its "original owners," it has never passed to any other tribe. First it was laid up in a secret limestone cave; later, when Europeans discovered the cave, it was moved to the family burial vault where it has remained, "along with other tribal heirlooms," ever since.[22]

One of the most striking things about this story is that we never learn anything about the heirloom's origins. Clearly, when the story begins, Karioi-

Mutu and Pipi-te-Wai must have already had some significant history—otherwise they would not have been desirable heirlooms. But about the cloak we only hear that it came originally from a different tribe, the Whanganui, to the south; about the club we don't learn even that much. But in a way this makes sense. Because if this was a token of the history of Whanganui, that's where the club should properly end up; instead, the point of the narrative is to establish how it became entangled in the history of Waikato. The value of the cloak, then, became that of the murders which Pakaue's acquisition of it inspired, and the subsequent wars of vengeance, all of which were enough in themselves to attach it to the territory and descendants of Waikato.[23]

If acts of exchange are only rarely included in the histories (Pakaue's solicitation clearly only appears because it led to violence), it's because they did not in themselves contribute to establishing or demonstrating the object's value. To the contrary, as with the medieval relics discussed by Geary (1986), which in their histories were always being stolen, the idea that someone might part with such an object voluntarily suggested that it might not be so desirable as the narrator would wish to imply. Even when the cloak did change hands voluntarily, it was always at another's request.

Maori heirlooms, Anne Salmond once suggested (1984), created fixed points in what was otherwise an endlessly shifting terrain of descent, marriage, war, and appropriation. Still, it was extremely difficult to keep these points fixed. Some heirlooms do seem to have been passed down from eldest child to eldest child in unbroken succession—but this itself was a great accomplishment. The presence of famous *taonga* inspired attack, and weak groups would often offer up their most famous heirlooms to an enemy raiding party, hoping to assuage it. Salmond herself describes Captain Cook's impressions from the 1770s, of an island in which powerful territories full of *taonga* alternated with impoverished ones full of heavily fortified settlements, victims of constant raids by their neighbors, in which there were no taonga at all. All of them had long since been carried off, or given away. While the exchange of heirlooms could seal a peace, their very existence could inspire wars, and, as the story of Pipi-te-Wai suggests, if the resulting conflict was sufficiently bloody, the object could end up entangled in the history of an entirely different descent line and hence "belong to" someone else. Indeed, one is left with the suspicion that one reason for the habit of hiding such heirlooms away in caves or tombs beneath the earth was precisely to avoid this: to ensure that, rather than making further trouble, they would be permanently bound to the group's mana, its invisible potency.

Maori systems of value, then, were based not only on a remarkably strong emphasis on invisible, creative powers, and very little on exterior display, but also on a peculiar cosmology that saw powers of creativity—even those hidden within humans—as partaking of the divine, and in which the most characteristically human forms of action instead consisted of one or another sort of appropriation, consumption, or destruction. It was through the latter—especially, through transgressive exploits of one sort or another—that one made oneself an individual and left one's mark on history. It is only once one bears this in mind that the notoriously difficult metaphysics of Maori exchange, which have fascinated anthropologists from Mauss onwards, can really make sense.

case 3: the kwakiutl potlatch

Mauss' observations on the potlatch were not limited to the Kwakiutl—he used information on many other Northwest Coast societies as well—but it would seem more manageable to hold them down to the one, best documented, case. Actually, terminologies have recently changed; "Kwakiutl" now refers to a subgroup among the nation that refers to itself by the unpronounceable name Kwakwaka'wakw, which means "those who speak the Kwakwala language." However, since most of the information we have comes from the Kwakiutl themselves (the four tribes that live around Fort Rupert, on Vancouver Island) there seems no need to drop the name entirely.

This material presents certain problems the Maori case does not. For the Maori, I thought it possible to take a single point in time—around 1750—as an ethnographic baseline. In dealing with the Kwakiutl, this isn't really possible. The most interesting material is derived from roughly the time when Franz Boas was doing his fieldwork; but this was a time of extraordinarily rapid social change. Therefore, while I will try to focus on what's called the "Fort Rupert period," which ran from roughly 1849 to 1925, I'll be drawing on a range of historical periods. Another problem is that Boas' material, while very rich, is rather difficult to deal with. Much of it consists simply of Kwakwala texts (a clan history, an account of a marriage, an exposition on traditional handicraft techniques, etc.) presented without even the most minimal ethnographic context: for instance, clan histories do not come with any indication of who the narrator is, let alone any description of the present composition of the group. More conventional ethnographic material does exist, but mainly from a much later period.

One thing almost everyone who writes about Northwest Coast cultures emphasizes is the incredible bounteousness of the physical environment. This was a place veritably bursting with food: salmon ran so thick that the rivers seemed black with fish, and there were endless supplies of berries, roots, seals and other aquatic mammals. As a result, it was capable of supporting a quite dense population on hunting, gathering, and especially fishing alone, and because so much of the food was storable, there was a physical surplus capable of supporting a class of non-producers. Even in the eighteenth century, Kwakwala speakers lived in great cedar plank houses, full of carved boxes of preserved food, in villages in which aristocrats amassed wealth for great ritual distributions and prepared the paraphernalia for dramatic ceremonies; commoners did the work of food collection and preparation; there was even a small stratum of slaves who fetched firewood and performed other menial tasks. The Kwakiutl thus lived in communities more permanent, and more stratified, than almost anything elsewhere documented for people who do not practice agriculture.

For hunter-gatherers, the Kwakiutl were doubly remarkable because they appeared to work much harder than they really had to. At least this was the conclusion of most early observers:

> In a region where subsistence demands could have been met easily by concentration on getting and storing enough of a few natural products such as salmon and berries, the Kwakiutl chose the grand manner in production as well as in the great displays, distributions and even destructions of wealth so distinctive of their culture . . . The Kwakiutl [were] among the best housed and most lavishly supplied, as well as the best fed, of the peoples of the New World. Pluralization was a conspicuous feature of much of this manufacturing. Each household made and possessed many mats, boxes, cedar-bark and fur blankets, wooden dishes, horn spoons, and canoes. It was as though in manufacturing as well as in food production there was no point at which further expenditure of effort in the production of more of the same items was felt to be superfluous. (Codere 1950:19)

These themes run through Kwakiutl life: the tendency to break tasks down into highly specialized and differentiated bits, each involving its own specialized set of tools; the tendency for endless duplication, and for making piles of wealth. It is very difficult to explain all this in terms of ecological "adaptation" (though many have tried); more reasonable to approach it as a question of value. If value is ultimately about how people portion out their creative energies, then most hunter gatherer societies known to anthropologists behave much like agricultural societies such as the Kayapo: they devote most of those energies not so much to the production of material things as that of certain sorts of people. In anthropology, the mechanisms by which they do so tend to be labeled "kinship systems." The Kwakiutl, then, are remarkable because they were a group of people who really did devote a huge proportion of their time and creative energy to the gathering of food and to related material production, not out of necessity, but because that's what they considered really important. It is not fortuitous, then, that Kwakwala texts give us endless details on food preparation and next to nothing on household structure. Indeed, though we know a good deal of the cedar-board construction of Kwakiutl houses, actual household composition, circa 1900, remains something of a mystery.

For people living in such a bounteous environment, the Kwakiutl seemed to place a peculiar emphasis on hunger. The spiritual beings that populated the Kwakwala cosmos, as Stanley Walens (1981) has emphasized, were creatures driven primarily by their ravenous appetites—spirits, animals, and humans all endlessly consuming one another. Ritual involved constant creation of the experience of hunger: as Walens notes, not only was self-control and self-denial at table considered a crucial mark of noble status, but rather than being moments of collective indulgence, feasts were almost always solemn affairs at which the portions served were unsatisfyingly small—and nobles were not even supposed to finish their portions. Everything was happening as if the system was meant to create a feeling of deprivation where none really needed to exist.

The most reasonable place to look for an explanation, it seems to me, is in the existence among the Kwakiutl of something very much like a class system. The two anthropologists who have written the most extensively on Kwakiutl cosmology, Goldman (1975) and Walens (1981), both emphasize that this was essentially a hunting cosmology, of a sort familiar in a variety of forms from Siberia to South America. Such systems are often based on the supposition of a kind of cooperative relationship between humans and their prey: when one kills game one must do it properly, and this is all the more true of the disposal of animal remains; this is a ritual responsibility that ensures the continued reincarnation of the animals. Such cosmological systems are all about food, and the circulation of souls and substance between humans and their prey. They almost never become ideologies of rule or support for the existence of an aristocracy of non-producers, because in hunter-gatherer societies such a stratum almost never exists. In other words, it would seem that the existence of rich, storable food surpluses on the Northwest Coast both eliminated much of the insecurity which tends to generate such an emphasis, and at the same time allowed the emergence of a kind of ruling class that then maintained that same cosmology as justification of its rule. Nobles did not hunt or fish. But they maintained the circulation of souls that made hunting and fishing possible.

Already one can see how different all this is from a cosmology of the Polynesian variety. In fact, in many ways Kwakwala assumptions seem exactly the opposite. Where the Maori saw humans as dependent on supernatural powers in order to reproduce themselves, here, it's if anything the other way around.

Here is one area where one simply cannot brush aside questions of history. Deep cosmological structures to the side, we'll probably never be able to know how much of this rather unusual situation was true for Kwakala speakers of, say, the seventeenth or eighteenth centuries, because the information we have begins in a period of enormous social upheaval. The authors of Boas' texts were living in a time when the overall Kwakiutl population had been declining precipitously for a hundred years, as a result of newly introduced diseases and lack of medical attention from the Canadian authorities, and in which the Kwakiutl had been incorporated not only into the Canadian state but a larger market economy in ways that exerted both enormous pressures and, especially at first, enormous opportunities for the accumulation of unprecedented new levels of wealth. The main immediate result of both was a crisis of authority—what some have dubbed the "Fort Rupert class struggle" (Kobrinsky 1975, Masco 1995, Wolf 1999), after the Canadian fort around which most of the most important Kwakiutl tribes assembled. Commoners had more and more resources with which to challenge their previous marginality; an ever-dwindling aristocracy was desperately trying to fend them off and maintain its privileged position while at the same time engaging in ever more dramatic and magnificent competition with one another. One result was the enormous inflation of potlatches—ceremonial gatherings in which nobles established their rights to important titles by the distribution of furs and other property, but that began to involve the lavishing of what even in Western terms was remarkable wealth (tens of thousands of blankets, fifty phonograph machines, a thousand silver bracelets, sixty washbasins, etc.) on people whom the giver usually claimed to consider enemies. It also resulted in a veritably dazzling spate of ritual and artistic creativity: the generation of new dramatic forms and techniques, new ritual, and an outpouring of works of material art, of masks, sculptures, and paintings, so inspired that Levi-Strauss was moved to remark (1982:4) that it was as if one small society had produced seven different Picassos all at the same time.

But it's important to bear in mind that just about all of this was part of what was in the end a losing struggle—an effort of an elite to redefine its privilege in the face of equalizing forces—and that the accounts that Franz Boas and his assistant George Hunt gathered, both clan histories and accounts of traditional practices, were very much part of it. It's not just that these accounts present an almost exclusively male, aristocratic point of view—one can never be quite sure how much the historical memory itself is somewhat reconstructed with political ends in mind. Were eighteenth century Kwakiutl aristocrats, for example, really forbidden to hunt or fish? Was this true of a whole third of the population, or just a few most exalted title holders? Were feasts always organized to create an illusion of hunger, or was that a later development? It's impossible to say.

Of course most texts are problematic in one way or another. I'm emphasizing the matter here only because it bears somewhat on what I am mainly interested in: the relation between cosmological conceptions, notions of the person, and the exchange of gifts.

kinship

One might say there are two main forms of productive action that remain largely hidden in the material assembled by Boas. The first is the normal operation of domestic units (particularly commoner ones); second, related social relations of a cooperation (cf. Codere 1956). In part this is because what we call "kinship" was, for Boas' Kwakiutl informants, largely a matter of the transfer of titles and heirloom treasures. The life-cycle of an aristocrat was marked out by potlatches and the distribution of property; the life-cycle of a commoner (a "house person") was not. Hence Boas and Hunt found it impossible to collect information about kinship relations among commoners. Aristocrats claimed commoners did not marry but "stuck together like dogs"; commoners said they would be too ashamed to even speak of such matters. It would seem most houses, for example, contained both aristocratic and commoner families, but it's impossible to know how these related to each other, because in the accounts, commoners simply disappear.

Boas did provide some fairly detailed information on the organization of the most important kinship groups. There were two of these. The smallest unit, which Boas sometimes called a "clan," sometimes a "gens," was called the *numaym*. In earlier times a typical numaym consisting of perhaps a hundred people. Several would be grouped together into a "tribe," which shared a single winter village.[24] Neither were precisely descent groups. Boas in fact ended up concluding they were best seen as collections of named offices or titles: it was of these "seats" that a numaym was really seen to consist (1966:50).

A tribe would, generally speaking, be named after the ancestor who founded it. These ancestors were almost never human. Usually the legend related how some mythical animal (a gull, a thunderbird, a whale, etc.) came down to earth and removed its animal mask, and thus became a human being. This founder was considered the ancestor not of the tribe as a whole but only of the chief aristocratic line of its highest ranking *numaym*. Usually, each of its other *numayma* was founded when an entirely different mythical figure, or sometimes a pair of them, "descended" to earth in similar fashion (Boas 1935:41–52; 1966:41–44) to become ancestors of its senior line. The founder's animal masks—and other, associated paraphernalia—were then given as a gift to his descendants, to be transferred, along with the founder's name, as heirloom treasures *(tlogwe)*, ideally from father to eldest son, along with the name of the ancestor himself. The head of the group, then, was considered the living incarnation of the founder. Each however was the result of an entirely different original event.

To make the sense of discontinuity even more extreme: other titles held by a *numaym* might derive from entirely different events (the encounter of an ancestor with a supernatural being for example). And it usually turns out that the bulk of its members of these groups were not related to the chiefly founder at all. In myths the commoner members were said to descended from guests who stayed after one of his feasts (Boas 1897:383), or from people he created out of gulls' eggs, or seashells, or who emerged from the posts of his house (Boas 1935:43). In more prosaic histories, they often turn out to be clients attached to the core line for any number of different reasons, as well as younger children of the core line who did not inherit aristocratic status.[25] Below them, slaves were not considered members of the group at all.

The key to understanding the system is to understand that one's identity thus became caught up in one's possessions. Each numaym possessed—indeed, in the Kwakwala view largely consisted of—a collection of aristocratic names or titles, each with its associated treasures. From a Western perspective these treasures were both material and immaterial. A founder's title might carry with it the right to paint a certain emblem, or "crest"—say, a bear or killer whale—on one's house or other possessions, the right to perform a certain dance or song at a potlatch or Winter Ceremonial, and so on. Others were quite corporeal, including houses, carved house-poles, masks, dance costumes and related paraphernalia, feast dishes, and so on, all of which tended to have their own names and histories. But it is probably deceptive to distinguish corporeal and incorporeal property at all.

Here an example might be useful. An important Kwakiutl house would normally contain four or five named "feast dishes," carved in the shape of some mythic creature. Ownership of such a dish carried with it the right to distribute certain sorts of food at collective feasts; it also carried with it rights of access to certain territories where that sort of food (berries, fish, etc.) could be collected. When such famous dishes changed hands, the actual physical object was usually destroyed—what was really transferred was simply the right to reproduce it and to call the new dish by its name.[26] Similarly, transfer of a dance-name would give its recipient the right to play a certain part in the dramas of the Winter Ceremonial; it would be accompanied by a great wood box containing the actual costumes and paraphernalia, though here again the physical objects might well be destroyed and replaced in the process.

The ownership of the treasures, then, was everything. Not surprising, then, that the family histories provided by Boas are overwhelmingly about property, its acquisition and transfer. Or that Claude Levi-Strauss (1981), despairing of trying to figure out the Kwakiutl descent system through more conventional means, ended up creating an entirely new concept, "the house," in order to do so, arguing that, much like Medieval aristocratic families, Kwakiutl descent was really organized around a patrimony—houses, lands, heirlooms, a sense of family honor—more than any principle of descent, a patrimony that could be conveyed in a number of ways, by inheritance, marriage, gift, and so on.

Obviously, in any such system, the rules of transfer become all-important. Here the key distinction seems to have been between two broad classes of title (each with a different sort of accompanying property). One class was attached to the *numaym* itself. Each *numaym* contained a certain number of named positions, often called "seats" because they afforded their owners a place in potlatches. The sources insist that these titles—the canonical number for the Kwakwaka'wakw as a whole is usually given as 658[27]— were all ranked in relation to each other: both within *numayma,* and overall, since numayma and tribes were all ranked in relation to each other. As with most ranking systems, however, it was impossible to get the same version from any two informants.[28] At any rate, these ranked positions were the very substance of a *numaym.* Ideally, they should pass from father to son, or at least to eldest child. But anyone who received such a title became a member of the *numaym* simply by the act of holding it.

The second variety were titles that could pass back and forth between *numayma:* these included, especially, feast names or titles that gave one a role in the Winter Ceremonial. Many of these could be passed on only by marriage.

Potlatches were, for the most part, the occasions on which names of either sort were "fastened on" to a new holder and in doing so, "given weight" by distributing more ephemeral forms of wealth to one's fellow title holders.

Ideally, titles of the first sort should have passed from father to son (or, exceptionally, to daughters).[29] But it would seem that even from early on, things were much more flexible. Often, names would be passed on from wife's father to daughter's husband in marriage, or even more, to the latter's children. As a result the system was effectively cognatic. One could also acquire such names by gift, from an entirely unrelated holder—it was considered crucial for elderly nobles to give their titles away before they died—or in fact by killing the former holder and appropriating their names and possessions. In fact, a well-connected nobleman could acquire a number of seats, and hence to be a member of several different *numayma* at the same time,[30] though this appears to have become especially common only during the "Fort Rupert period," when the total population was undergoing catastrophic decline.[31] Even when the total population had hit rock bottom, however, and the total number of adult males was well below the number of available titles, distinctions between aristocrats and commoners were maintained—through it often took the aristocrats frantic efforts to prevent titles from passing to those they considered unworthy. In fact, they managed to prevent very many titles from passing to chiefly women, even though such transferals were not, strictly speaking, forbidden but merely frowned upon. However all this could be accomplished only by developing an inheritance system of truly baroque complexity, so intricate and pliable that it is almost impossible to reconstruct how property had been transferred in simpler times.

elements of the person

It should be clear enough by now that this was a society in which property played a crucial role in the constitution of social identity. At least in the case of titles and their associated treasures, on taking possession of them, one literally became someone else. Mauss himself made note of this phenomenon in his famous essay on the "Category of the Person," written in 1938. Mauss began by noting that the Latin word "persona" is in fact originally derived from an Etruscan word, *phersu*, meaning "mask." "The person," in ancient Rome, was defined by having a certain legal standing (the father of a family was a jural person, its women, children, and slaves were not, but were absorbed into his legal personality and thus had to be represented by him), but an older usage was also reflected in the term *dramatis personae*, a cast of characters, especially because Roman theater was one of stock characters (the Sycophant, the Braggart Soldier, etc.), each with his or her own easily identifiable mask, costume, and emblematic props. Presumably, wrote Mauss, such a system is ultimately derived from something like the Kwakiutl one, in which only nobles had true *personae*, and these were embodied in certain sorts of emblematic property, passed in the ancestral line, that literally made the person who he was. Historical speculation aside, the analogy could hardly be more perfect. As we'll see, not only were the public personae of Kwakiutl aristocrats made up of just such emblematic properties, but these were entirely caught up in a kind of theater; in fact, the properties themselves could, for the most part, equally be considered theatrical props.

Here the contrast between the Maori and the Kwakiutl is especially striking. In the former case, there's an endless wealth of material on aspects of the "soul," of spiritual powers like *mana*, vital energies like the *mauri* and *hau*, and so on, but very little parallel to these material tokens of identity. In Boas' texts, the difficult thing is finding anything on the nature of the soul.[32] Such speculation just doesn't seem to have been a topic of much interest for his informants. It's especially interesting considering that both Goldman (1975) and Walens (1981) see the Kwakiutl cosmos as a vast system for the recycling of souls, which flow endlessly back and forth between human and animal realms. But even here, explicit theories of the soul are lacking; the picture these authors provide is largely reconstructed, by extrapolating what they take to be the implicit logic lying behind Kwakiutl myth and, especially, intense moments of theatrical display.

Goldman (1975:62–63), for example, had to coin the term "form souls" to describe them. Recall here the ancestral figures who came to earth and cast off their animal masks in order to become human beings. In myths, animals and humans turn into one another quite easily by slipping out of their masks or skins. In stories about the foundations of lineages, however, the mask remains: or, to be more exact, the original, physical mask eventually disappears, but its form remains. The right to reproduce that form— whether it be a killer whale, or bear, or eagle—now becomes a possession of the (now human) descendant who bears its name and is thus its current heir and incarnation, who also has the right to wear the mask at certain significant moments at potlatches or other ceremonial events. He also has the right to paint the design on the outside of his house, or carve it onto its supporting poles, or otherwise use it as an emblem of his *numaym*'s identity: this is what Boas (1897:554) referred to as a family "crest."[33]

Actually, Goldman ends up arguing that the Kwakiutl recognized three aspects of the human soul, which he labels the personal soul (which everyone has, even commoners), the name soul, and the form soul (these two belong only to nobles). The first is almost entirely unelaborated. Actually, it's arguable that the other two are really two aspects of the same thing, since there's no reason to believe that Kwakwala speakers made an explicit distinction between a title and the emblematic treasures that came with it.

They did—as noted—make a distinction between two broad classes of titles and their respective costumes, powers, and paraphernalia. There was a primary one passed down within the *numaym,* ideally from father to eldest son, and a subsidiary one that passed from wife's father to daughter's husband, or to the latter's children. A better way to phrase this, though, is that certain names were an intrinsic part of the *numaym* to which they belonged, so that if an outsider acquired the name, that person became a member by doing so. If someone obtains such a name in marriage, or as a gift, or for that matter by killing its previous holder (in which case the killer had the right to all the names and possessions of the victim), that person becomes a member in the *numaym* simply by doing so. This is not true of the host of secondary names and paraphernalia—feast names, Winter Ceremonial names, and the like—that normally passed between groups on marriage and represented, one might say, subsidiary aspects of an aristocrat's persona. Even in pre-contact times, it would seem that one of the great aims of any great noble was to accumulate as many of these subsidiary names as possible, to literally swell oneself up with more and more identities; as a Kwakwala speaker would no doubt put it, to become increasingly "weighty." This notion of weight, as we'll see, was the key to the underlying notion of value.

It would be easy to take this too far. A noble with several titles was not seen as simply the incarnation of a set of mythical figures; there was some notion of a unique individual who united them, had acquired them, and had the potential to acquire more. But again, about this "personal soul," and its powers, we learn almost nothing. It's not clear if a nineteenth-century Kwakwala speaker would have felt that there was anything that could be learned or was worth learning. This seems to be a general rule of the Kwakiutl cosmos. Strip away one layer of exteriority and one is likely to encounter yet another surface. The masks that represented founding ancestors—often magnificent works of art—tended to be masks within masks: the beak of a giant bird that opened to reveal not the wearer's own face but another mask inside; sometimes even that mask would open to reveal another one. Stanley Walens (1981:46–49) argues that among the Kwakiutl the person is conceived as a kind of a box. The Northwest Coast art is famous for its elaborately carved boxes, and these played a critical role in Kwakiutl culture. Potlatches largely consisted of taking various sorts of wealth out of one set of boxes, displaying them, and transferring them to others. Masks and costumes were generally kept locked up in huge boxes until the time came to take them out for ceremonial occasions. Of course, if one opened up such boxes, what one found inside was just another set of exterior "form souls." And inside those, another set of surfaces. Walens suggests that the Kwakiutl saw almost everything as a box: clan territories were boxes, houses the boxes inside them, human bodies the boxes inside those. Social groups like *numaym* are conceptual boxes, defined through physical ones: there are collective property and food storage boxes for the *numaym* as a whole, in addition to which, each family has their own smaller storage box. As for the individual: one's name is seen as itself a kind of box in which one's various powers, qualities, and rights are contained.

> Humans are born from boxes, swaddled in boxes, catch, store and serve their food in boxes, live in boxes, travel in boxes, and when they die are buried in boxes. Even the body itself is a type of box: humans not only live and die in boxes, but are themselves boxes . . . Names act as containers for invisible spiritual matter in the way that wooden boxes contain material items. (Walens 1981:46)[34]

Boxes become souls, then, when they acquire names and become eternal; this is for Goldman too why a "form soul" can be called a soul; it is a soul because it will always exist.

Throughout the literature there is almost no speculation about the ultimate energetic forces that move creatures, or about generative powers: inside boxes there are, generally speaking, just more containers, or if not that, sheer undifferentiated potentiality. When hidden potentiality is imagined, too, it is in remarkably dramatic, tangible form: largely as digested and regurgitated food. At "oil feasts," for example, guests were ladled oulachen (candlefish) oil to drink, challenged to consume as much as possible before regurgitating; meanwhile, the same kind of oil poured continually onto a central fire through "vomit beams," wooden faces with wide open mouths.

> For the Kwakiutl, vomit is not a substance of filth. Vomit is to a culture with oral metaphors what semen is to a culture with sexual metaphors: an important category of material existence, a symbol of undifferentiated matter with no identifying features and a total potential for becoming. All the power of vomit is potential, not realized. Vomit is the first stage of causality, the state of existence that precedes order and purpose. All things about to begin the process of becoming—fetuses, corpses, the universe before Transformer changed it—are symbolized by vomit. The act of vomiting is not an act of rejection but a positive act of creation, a necessary step in the process of transformation.
>
> Vomit is the transformed identity of the most precious of spirit gifts—food. All food, even though it may not be regurgitated, becomes vomit at one stage in the digestive process. Food and vomit are complementary aspects of single substance: the bodies of animals transformed into, respectively, cultural and spiritual forms. Vomit is thus the symbol of transformed substance: and the cycle of ingestion, digestion, and regurgitation is a metaphor for the cycle of death, metempsychosis, and rebirth. (Walens 1981:146–147)

While probably somewhat overstated, this passage gives some idea of how such matters were dealt with in Kwakiutl ritual symbolism. The hidden, undifferentiated interior was indeed considered to represent pure potentiality, but it was in an utterly tangible, material form—a kind of cosmic soup.

Walen's comparison of vomit and semen is especially intriguing because it once again implies that this was an ideology that emphasizes the production of food over the production of people. Goldman (1975:50–52, 139–40, 202–205), however, is the most explicit here: in fact, he spends a good deal of time trying to reconstruct the implicit theory of creative powers that lie behind the different sorts of heirloom treasures. He concludes that there are two basic sets, one that correspond to the ranked, *numaym* titles, the other with those that are transferred only by marriage. The ranked titles that make up a *numaym,* which go back to supernatural Founders, and also grant one rights to hunting, fishing, and berrying territories represent, he suggests, an ideal of asexual reproduction. They are passed on between men (women can, exceptionally, hold them, but if so they too are considered males) at ritual feasts and distributions. As in so many hunting societies, sexual intercourse itself is considered inimical to the hunt; bodies that have had anything to do with reproductive processes give off a scent that disturbs animals and drives them away. However, sexual powers do enter in again in the second, subsidiary set of properties, which are not ranked,[35] but which are transferred only at marriage, given from the bride's family to the groom's. Here again, the contrast with the Maori is striking. For the Maori, everything in the universe is generated through a single principle of sexual reproduction; it's only when one wishes to think about the reasons for differentiation between various features of that creation that one invokes a second principle, which has to do with competition and violence, and attempts to reduce others to the status of food. For the Kwakiutl, there is no single story of the creation of the universe as a whole; instead, there is an endless series of little creations by Founders, all in isolation from one another, which are seen as establishing an essentially asexual order that regulates relations between human beings and food; sexual reproduction enters only later, as a subordinate principle that creates links between all these heterogeneous groups.

But this is all very abstract. It might help to look in greater detail at the actual practice of Kwakiutl marriage.

marriage

As I mentioned, marriage was concerned primarily with the transfer of ancestral property; so much so that commoners, who had none, were not considered to marry at all.

Marriage was often represented as the equivalent of war. Great nobles went out "all over the world" to win over princesses and acquire new names and powers by so doing. To succeed was always framed as a feat, a contest: the suitor's party often faced a mock battle on coming ashore at the woman's father's village; these mock battles could sometimes shade into the real thing, and people could be wounded, even killed. Or the suitors might have to undergo ordeals—having to run through doorways hung with torches, to sit unmoved as the master of the house poured oil onto the fire, scorching everyone. Often, these trials would exactly reproduce events in myths in which wandering heroes encounter some terrifying supernatural monster, and, in prevailing against it, acquire great treasures, or its beautiful daughter as his wife.

Such habits underline what is without a doubt one of the most salient features of Kwakwaka'wakw culture: its remarkable sense of theater, its flair for the magnificent gesture, and particularly, for simulated horror. Hunt recounts the case of a man who raided a graveyard the night before a suitor was to appear to ask for the hand of his daughter, and gathered seven human skulls and "a large number of long bones" and placed them in the jaws of a huge bear mask. When the suitor entered the room, a man emerged costumed as a bear, the so-called "Devourer of the Tribes." The bear opened the jaws of his mask, the skulls rolled out to shatter on the ground. "Such was the fate," he warned him, "of the last six men who tried to win my daughter" (1897:363). Kwakwala performances were full of this sort of thing, shot through with a kind of carnival buncombe love of trap doors, fake blood, and cannibal monsters taking bites out of carefully simulated rotting corpses. It is in part for this reason that rituals themselves could be referred to, in the Kwakwala language, as "frauds"—though this made them no less sacred. Indeed, the presence of sacred power, *nawalak,* was seen above all in its ability to make its audience shiver with fear.

In the most important marriages, though, the suitor's party is almost always seen as drawing the woman out of her natal household—not by gifts, but by the mere display of inherited powers and paraphernalia (Goldman 1975:79). There was, in effect, a contest of the attractive powers of the suitor's wealth, which, just by being displayed, would tend to draw the princess to him. The symbolism here is important, because it recurs in potlatches as well. The princess is always represented as being infinitely heavy: unmovable, evoking mythic women who are literally rooted to the floor of their houses. In part, she is heavy with property, which is arranged around her or on her person in the ceremony (in Kwakiutl rhetoric, weight and wealth are practically synonymous); in a broader sense, one might say simply heavy with importance, or value. "Chiefs of the tribes!" says a suitor in one of Boas' texts (1925:249–69), who has assembled a host of allies to assist him. "We have come to this great wedding. Now we shall show the powers residing in us and transmitted to us by our ancestors, and with them we shall shake from the floor the princess of this chief of unblemished ancestry." He then calls on them one by one to display their treasures: one displays a bow, which his ancestor acquired in the wilderness and used to vanquish his enemies; another a harpoon given by his ancestor, the Thunderbird; the next a quartz crystal "which the wolf vomited into my ancestor Great Smoke Owner," the next, a Grizzly Bear growl. After each speech, the chief notes that the princess has thus been moved further from the center of the house, until finally she is drawn to the door.

Now, the groom did in theory pay a "brideprice" to his bride's father— usually a modest sum in skins, or, later, blankets. Kwakiutl informants always made note of this, so much so that Boas suggested that they saw marriage as a kind of purchase. But if one examines the full cycle of transactions, one invariably discovers that the amount "paid" by the bridegroom and his family was negligible in comparison to the vast flow of wealth that moved in the opposite direction. Consider one fairly typical historical account from the late eighteenth century. The groom gave a total of fifty-four animal skins of different sorts; the father-in-law gave (over the course of three payments) over three hundred skins, two major titles, a copper shield, six slaves, five different dances with accompanying dance names and paraphernalia, and a "cannibal pole" (Goldman 1975:78–79). In the nineteenth and twentieth centuries the disparity remained no less dramatic.

What's more, unlike the bride's father's payments to the groom, the groom's payment had to be repaid. Some years after the marriage, a wife's father could "repurchase" the bride, paying back, again, far more than the original amount; the woman was thereby considered free of the union (she could stay on if she desired, but it was considered a bit unseemly.) Sometimes this was done to raise the status of one's daughter—a woman who had been married and repurchased four times was considered to have obtained the highest degree of nobility—but in part, too, it seems to have been to gain control of the children. This I think helps explain the otherwise mysterious way in which so many chiefs willingly parted with such a huge share of their heirloom possessions to their sons-in-law: much of what they donated was what might be called "constitutive property." The names that they gave, sometimes directly to the husband but more typically to any offspring of the union, were names that belonged to their own *numaym;* in giving them, they were effectively reproducing their own group. On some occasions, the suitor himself would thus be turned into a member of his wife's *numaym;* at the very least, his children would have the option of becoming so if they took on those names. And of course, if the bride was repurchased and no longer living with the father of her child, this would make the latter outcome all the more likely.

potlatches

This in turn makes it easier to understand what happened at a potlatch. Potlatches were, as noted, meant to "fasten on" names. There were a whole succession of increasingly important categories of names to be fastened on over the course of a young noble's life, starting with modest titles reserved for children or youths, which only gave one the right to distribute minor objects to close kin, to more and more important ones, which carried with them the right to distribute property to members of other *numayma,* or to rival tribes.[36] These titles were also called "seats" because each corresponded to a place of honor at collective gatherings: guests would sit in rank order according to their titles, as the hosts appeared and displayed their various treasures and privileges, made the sort of boastful or vainglorious speeches for which the Kwakiutl have become so famous, and of course distributed property to all. After having held a potlatch and fastened on a name, then, one had the right to take that seat at subsequent potlatches or feasts. (If one held several seats, one would only take one place oneself but leave wooden boxes on the other to receive blankets or other property.) The objects distributed at such events, whether blankets, oil, flour, silver bracelets, or Singer sewing machines, were not in themselves constitutive wealth, and for that reason nobles would make a point of speaking of them with disdain, referring to them as trifles or literally, "bad things." Still, there was a sense that in distributing property, one established one's right to bear the name of an original Founder by reproducing, in a limited way, a Founder's defining action—that of giving things away (Goldman 1975:124).

It's interesting to think for a moment about the conception of historical action at play here. If one reads things very literally, it might seem that there is none at all. All the great deeds that created society were performed long ago, in mythic times; the key social actors are themselves reincarnations of those ancient heroes, but now reduced simply to acting out the same gestures in a much lesser key. If one looks a bit deeper, though, things are somewhat more complicated. First of all, it's not as if there were no idea of nobles as individual, conscious actors who are assembling these identities and disposing of them, but who remain essentially continuous throughout. "Doing a great thing," holding a potlatch or a feast or otherwise giving away property, not only added weight to a name but contributed to the fame of the actor behind the mask, as it were. True, there was little way for that fame to endure beyond the living memory of those who'd witnessed those deeds, because, in the long run, it was the eternal names, rather than the actors that held them, that would tend to be remembered. But even here there was a kind of play of mirrors. Because the names themselves almost invariably refer to wealth and the habit of it giving it away. A famous list of titles reads: Creating Trouble All Around, The Great One Always Alone in the World, Four Fathom Face, Making Potlatch Dances All the Time, Copper, From Whom Property Comes, Giving Wealth, Giving Food, Giving Potlatch Everywhere, To Whom People Paddle, Whose Body Is All Wealth, From Whom Presents Are Expected, Great Mountain, About Whose Property People Talk, Always Giving Potlatch, Envied, Around Whom People Assemble, Throwing Away Property, Always Giving Blankets Away While Walking, Satiating, Getting Too Great (Boas 1897:339–40; Goldman 1975:61, Codere 67).

This is perhaps the greatest paradox of all. Even the names, which hark back to the inimitable deeds of mythic ancestors, do not refer to these inimitable deeds but rather to actions in the present. Even more, they refer to the impression these actions make on a broader audience. Even the heirloom treasures themselves, which did tend to refer to mythological events, took the form of costumes and props full of tricks and stage illusions—often replete with complex apparati of pulleys and strings, all meant to wow the appreciative spectator:

> The clan Haa´nalino have the tradition that their ancestor used the fabulous double-headed snake for his belt and bow. In their potlatches the chief

of this gens appears, therefore, dancing with a belt of this description and with a bow carved in the shape of the double-headed snake. The bow is simply a long carved and pointed stick to which a string running through a number of rings and connecting with the horns and tongues of the snake is attached. When the string is pulled, the horns are erected and the tongues pulled out. When the string is slackened, the horns drop down and the tongues slide back in. (Boas 1966:100)

Ultimately everything goes back to theater, to what one can put over on a (demanding but appreciative) public. The titles and treasures would be meaningless without it; everything about them refers to the presence of an audience. And as suggested in chapter 3, the dimensions of this audience corresponds, from the actor's point of view to the dimensions of the society as a whole. And of course here "the actor" is to be taken in the most literal sense, which brings us back to my original point about history. These performances are not in themselves remembered. If potlatches did enter into historical accounts, it appears to be only when they served to "fasten on" some new names and privileges won in marriage—this because heroic marriages can be seen as an example of the basic Kwakwala myth in which the hero wanders far away to edges of the universe to win great prizes from the beings he encounters there. Otherwise "great deeds," like most great performances, tend to disappear. Kwakiutl theater is semi-improvisational; the costumes and props and performances themselves undergo constant innovation and refashioning, but almost none of the creative energies that go into them leaves a permanent trace on collective memory.

property, distribution, and cosmology

A word or two on potlatches as cosmic events.

Princesses are always represented as heavy; men use displays of wealth as one way to draw them out. Similarly, wealth and distributions of wealth are all about adding "weight" to one's name, becoming big and heavy in one's turn. If there is a single notion of value that pervades Kwakiutl culture it is this notion of "weight"—which, in the case of a formal title, was measured by the total amount of wealth given in order to fix the title on (cf. Oberg 1973:125). A title's rank often seemed a secondary matter in comparison.[37] At least, this was what really seemed to stir passions and foster rivalries. The consummate image of success is that appealed to periodically in Boas' rendition of potlatch speeches, in which the host is likened to a giant mountain, infinitely heavy, from which blankets and other wealth flow down like an avalanche of property, simultaneously enriching and imperiling everyone around. It's an image that perfectly sums up the peculiar Kwakiutl combination of aggression and generosity.

204 Toward an Anthropological Theory of Value

The image of the mountain is telling, I think, because Boas himself (1935:334) notes that in many origin myths, the first ancestor of a *numaym* is said to have descended from heaven to earth either on a "moving mountain," or along a "potlatch pole"—the latter being the pole beside which the host stands when speaking and distributing gifts at such affairs. Apparently, we are dealing with what Mircea Eliade would call a kind of *axis mundi:* the common mythological image of a central tree, pole, or mountain that is the point at the center of the universe where everything comes together—sky and earth, visible world and invisible Otherworld, life and death, mundane present and mythic past—and where it is possible to move back and forth between them. In most systems, this is reflected in ritual, where an altar, post, or tree, or statue represents that cosmic center, but just by way of a refraction or stand-in for a real center (Mount Meru, Jerusalem, Aztlan.) that's usually assumed to be very far away. The problem is of course that in a Kwakwala universe fragmented into an endless number of unconnected founding events, there is no one single cosmological center but an almost endless number of possible ones. Everyone, in effect, claims to represent the center of the universe. Part of the notorious grandiosity and hyperbole of the Kwakiutl chiefs, I think, stems from the fact that all shared an ultimately impossible ambition.

With all these particular, incommensurable centers, it should be obvious why some generic medium of comparison became so important. Hence the appeal of Hudson trade blankets. Before the Kwakiutl were in regular contact with Europeans, the closest there was to these were animal skins, which were, in effect, generic "form souls":

> The animal skin is also a form, a garment that originally converts a human inner substance into animal form. In myth, animals easily slip in and out of their skins to become momentarily nonanimal . . . From the mythical perspective, the skin is the animal's essential attribute from which, however, it is separable, in the way in which soul separates from body . . . Thus the animal skin . . . is like a mask. But it is not, of course, a crest. Crests are individual, and have epithetic names; animal skins are generalized, and are namelessly generic. (Goldman 1975:125)

Hence, since crests are passed down within precise channels of descent, "animal skins circulate ceaselessly among the tribes."

In other words, rather than a division between particular objects, identified with one's exterior persona, and generic ones (like money) identified with interior powers, one has an endless variety of exteriors: these are ranged, however, into more relatively particular and generic forms. Hence crests and associated treasures tended to accumulate the deepest and most specific histories, dating back to mythic times; treasures transferred by marriage were much harder to keep track of, and thus tended to have shorter, more fragmentary ones. The skins, being without history, could thus represent a kind of undifferentiated soul-stuff or vitality; according to both Goldman and Walens, part of the overall purpose of ritual was, as in most hunting cosmologies, to aid in an endless recycling of souls. But even the skins were not really a uniform medium of exchange: while they could be seen as representing the souls of individual animals, they were obviously of different sorts, sizes, and qualities. Hence, as Sahlins notes, the immediate and overwhelming popularity of the Hudson Trading Company's woolen blankets, which were analogous to skins but, being mass-produced, all utterly identical. They immediately became the currency of the system—or, they did until the 1910s or '20s, when they began to be replaced by actual Canadian currency.

Before going on I should enter another proviso about history. When Goldman and Walens analyze Kwakiutl ritual as centering on a circulation of souls, what they are doing is offering a reconstruction of a ritual system assumed to have existed around the middle of the eighteenth century, based on analogies with other hunting cosmologies, particularly other Native American ones. There's nothing in the actual texts that directly states that giving away skins or blankets has anything to do with recycling souls. Again, it makes one wonder whether what one is dealing with in historic times is a ritual system originally based on keeping a cosmic balance among sources of food, now transformed into something different: an endless quest to establish cosmic centrality in a world that had become rapidly unhinged.

The introduction of trade blankets allowed for a number of other innovations. The most important was the creation of what might justly be considered a system of high finance. In earlier periods, a noble wishing amass wealth for a potlatch would normally have had to appeal to the members of his *numaym*, or tribe, for contributions. Blankets allowed the introduction of the principle of the 100 percent interest loan, which Drucker and Heizer (1967:78) plausibly suggest was probably inspired by the example of some early Fort Rupert loan shark. If a chief wished, for example, to start a son on a potlatch career, he'd first contribute a hundred blankets, which the boy would then immediately loan out to allies, and call in the loans as soon as possible. Eventually he would have enough blankets to buy one of the cheaper heirloom coppers that circulated within the community: these were engraved copper plates that were the most important circulating treasures in Northwest Coast societies. It was a matter of principle that anyone buying a copper should pay more for it than its last purchaser had. Hence, before holding a potlatch, one could sell it again to a rival clan, which would then feel obliged to provide an impressive increment. Almost all major distributions seem to have been proceeded by the sale of a copper, which moved

Boas to describe them as having "the same function which bank notes of high denomination have with us" (1897:344; 1966:82)—a description that, I think, is not entirely without justice. Coppers were the ultimate repository of value and, of all forms of forms of wealth, the ones that came nearest to representing life in the raw.

the role of coppers

About the origin of these coppers there has been a good deal of debate. Local legend has it that copper was first discovered and first smelted by the Bela Coola nation to the far northeast of Vancouver Island. Even in the eighteenth century, European accounts of different Northwest Coast societies report that sheets of beaten copper, roughly shieldlike in appearance, were one of the most treasured forms of local wealth. It is not clear though how many such ancient, aboriginal coppers there were: while many hundreds of Kwakiutl coppers have been preserved, none are made from native metal. Instead, the copper invariably turns out to have come from copper sheeting bought from European merchants or salvaged off the sides of European ships in relatively recent times.

There has also been a fair amount of debate about the copper's characteristic form: usually about two feet long, wider at the top, with a cruciform frame and the top half in the form of a schematic face. Some suggest coppers are meant to represent the forehead of a sea monster named Komogwa, who bestows great wealth on those mortals lucky enough to find his palace beneath the sea (Waterman 1923). Widerspach-Thor argues (1981) it is simply a schematic representation of the human body. Whatever the case, the value of coppers seems to derive at least in part from the fact that they are considered equivalent to human lives.

In early times this seems to have been quite literally so, since coppers were seen as equivalent of slaves (war captives). Only the greatest nobles owned either, and what's more, they owned them as personal possessions—neither were they attached to any other sort of heirloom property but could be disposed of at will, to circulate between groups. Slaves were sometimes sold; the dedication of houses or totem poles, at funerals, initiations, and similar important events would often be marked by sacrifices, in which the owner would either kill a slave, or liberate her—in either case, owners were abandoning their property in such a way as to lend glory to the event. With the colonization of Vancouver Island in 1849, and the construction of Fort Rupert, war and slavery both came to an end; but it seems to be around this time that coppers began to be produced in large numbers, and they seem to have gained in importance both as instruments of finance, but also, as substitutes for slaves—they too could be sacrificed, broken or literally "killed" on momentous occasions (Kan 1989:238–41).

It is important to emphasize that these coppers were not heirlooms in the same sense of most of the "heirloom treasures" I have been discussing—crests, masks, or winter dance privileges.[38] They neither have particular historical origins, nor do they become part of their owner's social persona. In myths, coppers are won from sea monsters and ogres at the edges of the universe; but the origin of individual coppers is always a mystery; they are seen as coming from far away, outside of the community, a kind of generic Elsewhere. And while each copper was unique, with its own name and design, and therefore had the capacity to accumulate histories, insofar as it did, these histories were extremely brief (e.g., Duff 1981:153, Jonaitis 1991:40–41). Rarely would they go beyond the name of last owner or two—and of course how many blankets they had received for it.

Often coppers would flow in the same direction as brides: a father-in-law would send one or two along with his daughter and perhaps provide additional coppers later on, when his son-in-law or grandchild needed to fund a potlatch to fasten on a name he had provided. In one long account of the sale of a copper provided by Boas (1967:84–92), the copper itself is treated almost as a bride: there is a constant emphasis on its extraordinary weight, as the *numaym* that assembles its resources to purchase the copper piles up an ever heavier pile of blankets, which ultimately becomes capable of drawing the copper toward it. It appears, once again, to be a drama about the creation of cosmic centers: the mountain of blankets being again a kind of *axis mundi,* as the seller, it would seem, poses as a Dzonoqwa, one of the ogres from the edges of the world responsible for first giving coppers to mankind.

The mythological associations of coppers are extremely complicated. Goldman, for example, claims that they are identified with the sun, with salmon, with fire, and with blood, and that they were the one form of wealth that brought together all cosmic domains (sky, sea, coast, and interior; 1975:126–27). They seem to have been as close as the Kwakwaka'wakw came to abstract representation of life, or vital energy, itself. Widerspach-Thor calls coppers a "metaphor of energy," a "container and catalyst of energy held in each individual, each chief, each tribe" (1981:172); Sergei Kan argues that coppers were like slaves in that they were in a certain sense persons and in a certain sense not; also "like slaves, coppers were 'alive,'" and hence were the quintessential wealth exchangeable for all other types of property" (1989:246, cf. 345n65).

It was because they were alive that coppers could be killed. This leads us, finally, to one of the most notorious features of Kwakwaka'wakw culture: the ceremonial destruction of wealth and status competition. I have saved this element for last for two reasons. First of all, because especially since the work of Ruth Benedict (1934), the importance of status rivalry and "fighting with property" has been vastly exaggerated, to the point sometimes of making the Kwakiutl seem paranoid megalomaniacs. Once again, this seems to be a result of the Kwakiutl love for theatrical effect: in this case, one might say that their theatrical skills were a bit too effective for their own good. Second of all, because it finally brings us to the issue of reciprocity.

Now, it did sometimes happen that there were two claimants to the same title, or even that two *numayma* or tribes might challenge their relative standing, and therefore each would compete to throw the grandest potlatch to validate its claims. Sometimes, these would turn into what Drucker and Heizer (1967:102–103) call "fictitious rivalries" between two chiefs over long-dead claims no really cared about anymore, where at any notable potlatch where they were both in attendance, one might destroy a canoe, the other a minor copper, and back and forth, each trying to outdo the other. Most of this was really just another example of fun and showmanship, but at other times, such "fighting with property" could take a more serious turn.

Some twentieth-century informants claimed that in the distant past, a noble might try to embarrass or belittle a rival simply by offering him a splendid gift, so as to dare him to try to return something of roughly equal grandeur (Drucker and Heizer 1967:119). This is of course the classic gift scenario, but it does not appear to have occurred in historic times. Examples from historic times invariably involve destroying something, most often, coppers. For example, if one noble felt another had in some way insulted him or his family, he would normally take a valuable copper and break it into pieces, thus "killing" it, giving the various pieces to other chiefs, and then presenting the T-shaped cross-piece to the culprit, who would then be considered defeated unless he was able to "kill" a copper of equal value of his own.[39] Such coppers could still be patched back together again: the recipient would usually be able to sell off the cross-piece for a considerable sum to some other chief interested in assembling all the pieces, and thus be in a good position to buy a new copper; for this reason, a really determined rival might simply presenting the cross-piece briefly and then taking it offshore to "drown" it in the sea.[40] Another focus of rivalry was oil feasts, in which hosts would pour oulachen oil into the central fire of their houses until guests' clothes were scorched, daring them to flinch; a rival guest might—especially if he felt he had thrown a greater feast—rise up and try to "put out the fire" by throwing in blankets, coppers, and canoes, forcing the host to answer him in kind, which could, on occasion, turn into what seemed to outside observers like paroxysms of destruction, in which rival chiefs vied to express their contempt for wealth and their absolute dedication to the magnificent gesture.

exchange and reciprocity

Maori histories are all about reciprocity—or at least, about revenge—with next to nothing on property; Kwakiutl family histories are quite the other way around. In fact, one of the striking things about the Kwakiutl material is how little a role reciprocity plays. There has been a great deal of misunderstanding on this point in the past, particularly because of Franz Boas' mistaken impression that everything distributed at a potlatch eventually had to be paid back double. This inspired Mauss to write that "the obligation to reciprocate constitutes the essence of the potlatch" ([1925] 1990:41), which in turn has colored most discussion of the subject since. But in fact, under normal circumstances, there does not seem to have been any obligation to reciprocate involved. Frank Curtis had already pointed this out in 1915. When the host distributed blankets, or oil, or other "trifles," at a potlatch, he does not appear to have placed the recipients under any sort of obligation at all. Certainly none of the recipients would then feel obliged to hold a potlatch of his own and distribute property to hundreds of different people just because the previous donor would be among them. Drucker and Heizer (1967:37, 56–57) observed that if the host of a potlatch had recently received something from one of his guests, he might give that person a somewhat larger share than the others (say, two cans of oil instead of just one), but when they asked hosts if they expected a return, the normal response was that obviously only a fraction of the guests were likely to hold potlatches of their own at any time in the foreseeable future, and anyway, no one was keeping precise accounts. Curtis (1915:143, Testart 1998) observed that if a chief receiving goods at a potlatch so much as remarked that he had given more to the donor at one of his own, most people would consider this to his profound discredit, since a real chief shouldn't care.

In another sense, though, the fact that some of the guests were going to hold potlatches of their own was absolutely crucial. This was because one held a potlatch to establish one's right to hold a title. It was only when the former host received property under that title at someone else's potlatch that one could say that the potlatch had succeeded. Hence, at one's own potlatch, one passed judgment on others' status; at their potlatches, they passed judgment on one's own (Barnett 1938, 1968; Rosman and Rubel 1971). Insofar as anything even remotely like "repayment" was involved, it was not in the object given (a mere "trifle"), but in the act of recognition giving it entailed.

So: titles and related constitutive property were transferred, whether from parent to child, or from wife's father to daughter's husband, without any "obligation to repay." The titles were then fastened on at collective distributions, which also did not involve any principle of reciprocity. In fact there are only a few contexts in which one can talk about reciprocity:

1. In "finance": outside of potlatches, loans of blankets had to be repaid at rates of 30 to 100 per cent. This does not appear to create social ties, though it usually proceeds along existing ones.
2. In marriage: while the overall relation is entirely lopsided and unreciprocal, a wife's father can "buy her back." This not only does not create ongoing ties, it negates existing ones.
3. In rivalry: direct challenges between people lead to an attempt to give gifts the other cannot match.

Of the three, it's only in the last that there is anything like the classic dynamic of gift and counter-gift. Otherwise, Kwakiutl exchange appears to have worked on entirely different principles.

Perhaps this is not the place to try to unravel all of these principles; but there is one that I think is absolutely crucial. Insofar as gifts were identified with any party to the exchange, it was less with the giver than with the recipient. In the case of constitutive property, one literally becomes what one is given. The same principle applies to acts of rivalry: the main way of making a challenge, for example, was to "kill" a copper, which was as we've seen identified with a human life, and then hand the broken pieces to one's rival. Doing so was considered analogous to an act of violence, it was "striking" him. And finally, it was entailed in the distribution of potlatch gifts before the advent of Hudson Bay trade blankets: the skins of sea mammals like seals and otters were reserved for high nobility, forest mammals for other nobles, cedarwood bark robes for commoners (Goldman 1975:136–37; Sewid-Smith 1986:63). All of which suggests why such generic gifts, as, blankets, or silver bracelets, or Singer sewing machines were officially disdained as "bad things," the distribution of which could itself be seen as a kind of assault on the recipients. They were bad because they were all the same. A potlatch turned on a contrast between two sorts of transfer: the host received a unique title, thus defining himself as unique and particular, while at the same time defining the guests as faceless and generic in comparison. It was a way of reproducing, in material terms, the relation of the particular, "specific" actor and faceless spectators. Even if, ironically, he had to wait until he was himself a guest and was recognized under that title for the value thus produced to be completely realized.

Again, all this is almost an exact inversion of the Maori principle by which important valuables would continue to be identified with the giver. But in order to understand the differences, it will be necessary to make a more systematic comparison.

conclusions I: unraveling some things

We have obviously come a long way from Lenin's New Economic Policy. Let's see if we can't tie some of the many threads of this chapter together.

First of all, what conclusions can we come to about the relations of persons and things? Here, I think we can say that Mauss' overall conclusions have been quite clearly confirmed. In every case, the most valuable objects in gift economies are valued primarily because they embody some human quality, whether this be the creative potential of human action, or fertility, or the like, or particular histories and identities that have already been achieved.

Of course, I've already argued something similar about market economies as well; but here, one can say that the ideal of the complete detachability of persons and things (which Mauss emphasized) is part of that same overall movement that led also to the separation of the spheres of production and consumption, emphasized by Marx, which allows these essential links to be obscured. In this sense it is not gift economies but market economies that deny "the true soil of their own life," since they are constantly obscuring the fact that all "economic" activity is ultimately a means to the creation of certain sorts of person.

On the other hand, one thing that has definitely emerged is that gift economies can vary enormously in *how* they do this; and particularly, in how personal identities become entangled in things—far more, one suspects, than Mauss himself would have anticipated. Two of his key examples seem to represent the limits of possibility in either direction. To put the matter succinctly: the most important Maori heirlooms were so caught up in the identities of the owner that they couldn't really be given away at all; among the Kwakiutl, they were so identified with a particular person that if given away, the recipient became the person who the giver used to be. At either extreme, identification does not facilitate reciprocity. It makes reciprocity impossible.

pink cadillacs and autographed baseballs

Such apparently exotic practices might seem to put some strain on Mauss' assumption that we are dealing with a moral logic that, in its most elementary forms at least, exists everywhere. But it's not hard to find familiar parallels. In the case what I've been calling "constitutive property," the most obvious one is inheritance. When a Kwakiutl aristocrat passes his name, with all its attendant rights, costumes, and paraphernalia, on to his son this is clearly a combination of what we'd call "inheritance" and what we'd call "succession to office." Even when a man passes a Winter Ceremonial name to his daughter's husband, it is usually to be held in trust for his grandchildren. Even in our own society inheritance is the most common, and ambiguous, form of gift: on the one hand, to pass on one's wealth is obviously not an act of pure self-interest; on the other, it is gifts of this sort that are responsible for most of society's fundamental inequalities.

One might propose then that among Kwakwala speakers, all gifts operated a bit like we assume inheritance to operate. But this is only a first approximation.

On a deeper level, it might be useful to distinguish between two modalities of gift-giving: one of which turns primarily on the identity of the giver, the other, on the recipient. Again, let's take a familiar example. Many celebrities—rock stars, ball players, movie stars—are in the habit of giving away tokens of themselves to fans they happen to meet: bits of clothing, or jewelry, a guitar pick or the like; so, in many times and places, have kings and holy men. In cases like this one might well say the giver gives a fragment of himself, in the way Mauss proposes; one that the recipient will then keep as a way of vicariously participating in the giver's identity. But that recipient does not really become more like Elvis for having been given a rhinestone ornament, or a Cadillac, or more like Darryl Strawberry for owning a baseball he hit out of the field, or more like the President of the United States because she has the pen with which he signed an important piece of legislation. Neither, of course, is the recipient in such cases under any obligation to make a return gift; to give a piece of one's own clothes, or one's own pen, would be rather insulting (or at best comical); rather, one could say the very willingness to accept such an object is an act of recognition in the Kwakiutl sense.

At the other extreme, consider a badge of office. Such badges can at the very least be considered "emblematic property," in that only a policeman is legally allowed to possess a policeman's badge, and only the English sovereign can wear the Crown Jewels. In some cases, though, matters go even further, and such badges become constitutive: the badge *is* the office, or at least so one is told, and whoever takes possession of it thereby accedes to it. In the Ankole kingdom in what is now Uganda, an ancient drum, kept in a shrine in the royal compound, was considered the real embodiment of the unity of the kingdom and its people (Oberg 1940:150–57).[41] On the death of a king, his heirs fight a war for its possession, "and many Banyankole claim that if a foreign king were able to capture the royal drum he would automatically become King of Ankole" (ibid:156). This is clearly "constitutive property." Though one must bear in mind that in almost all such cases, we are dealing with something of a figure of speech: a daring foreign burglar who made off with the drum presumably would not be considered to have much of a claim on the kingdom. The "drum" in other words was really a metonym for a whole package of rights and properties, including the royal compound itself, much in the way Kwakiutl property appears to have been.

Even this sort of principle is not so exotic as one might think. An English dukedom includes a manorial residence, an entailed estate including manorial lands, the right to use certain heraldic emblems, and so on. In effect, whoever comes into possession of these things is the Duke. True, there are rules that ensure that this cannot be just anyone, and certainly someone who simply murdered the duke and occupied the place with a band of thugs would not thereby become nobility. So one might say these are emblematic but not constitutive. But if so, this is largely because the English nobility is preserved as a kind of museum piece: in the tenth century this approach might well have been effective. As with the Ankole king's stool, one seems to be dealing with access to a kind of productive apparatus, properties that are emblematic of rule because they play a key role in the continual creation of a mystique of office; of just the sort of evocative display described in chapter 4, so typical of aristocracies, in which a history of past acts of recognition or obeisance is seen as emerging from the nature of the objects themselves. And of course if a duke were to pass his title and attendant paraphernalia to an adopted successor, and that would be in effect giving the dukedom as a gift.

So why, then, does the identity of the modern celebrity not rub off in a similar way, if only slightly, with the transfer of guitar picks or autographed photos? The answer, I think, is that the celebrity's mystique—if one wishes to call it that—is seen as being derived not from an exterior apparatus, but from within. The great blues guitarist B. B. King, for example, never goes anywhere without his famous guitar, which is called Lucille. Almost any blues fan is likely to know this. But even if B. B. King were to give away Lucille, it wouldn't make the recipient any more like B. B. King because what makes B. B. King famous is ultimately not his guitar but his ability to play it. The celebrity's identity does not carry over to the recipient because it was seen as having been derived from *inside,* from some interior essence or capacity (which we usually label "talent") rather than from anything he or she *owns.*[42]

In a system like the Kwakiutl, these capacities are alienated onto property. Even the right to sing a certain song or tell a certain story is often owned by a specific individual. The right to play a specific role in great ritual performances is dependent on owning the paraphernalia. One might say here the key issue would be not the ability to play the blues but the right to do so, which possession of Lucille could, in such a system, give you.

The Maori/Kwakiutl comparison, in turn, allows us to add nuance to some of the distinctions mapped out in chapter 4. Money, I noted, being generic, cannot accumulate history, and hence cannot add to the holder's identity. Unless, that is, one has a *very* large amount of it. At time of writing, for example, Bill Gates, founder of Microsoft, is famous primarily for being the richest man on earth. If Bill Gates were to wake up one morning and decide to sign over his entire fortune to me (and incidentally, in the unlikely circumstance that Bill Gates is reading this: this might not be an altogether bad idea), I might not thereby become the founder of Microsoft or a brilliant salesman, but I *would* become the richest man on earth. I will have acceded to the most important part of his current identity. Now, it might seem odd that this can be true of money—the ultimate, generic, historyless stuff—and not of specific historical objects like Lucille; but herein, I think, lies a hint as to what is really going on. If Bill Gates were to give me the rights to some software he designed, it would not make me the designer. It is because of money's resistance to history that its identity does not cling to the former owner. Similarly, in fact, with a Kwakiutl dance title. Constitutive property of this sort does not change in its essence—or perhaps we should better say, in theory *should* not change in its essence—because of any actions a previous holder might have undertaken. How well, or how badly, any former owner danced the Bear Dance at past winter festivals is quite irrelevant. The internal capacities of the individuals involved are not an issue. Everything is alienated onto the object. This is equally true regarding the duke's entailed estate: it is a notorious feature of aristocracies of this sort that even if the duke turns out to be a Communist, or is convinced that he is Jesus Christ, it does not make him less a duke, any more than a Catholic priest's sexual indiscretions should make him less qualified to perform the Eucharist. Neither should the dukedom change in its nature afterward as a result.

If so, the crucial fact about Maori-style heirlooms would seem to be that they are not entirely resistant to history: as we've seen in the case of the dogskin cloak Pipi-te-Wai, entanglement in dramatic historical events can erase their former significance and give them an entirely new one. This might seem to contradict Weiner's notion of "inalienability," but I don't think it really does. After all, if Maori *taonga* could not absorb the identities of their owners, then they would still belong not to the giver but to whoever first made them—and in fact, in almost every case, the identity of that person wasn't even known. Rather, they tended to become identified with a lineage through a cumulative history of being passed on, used, lost and recovered, protected and maintained. Kwakiutl treasures, on the other hand, almost invariably received their historical significance in a single dramatic event in the distant past. Either some mythic being came to earth and became human, or some heroic human passed into the Other World and encountered one; similar events could perhaps still happen in the present day, but in that case they would add new treasures, not transform old ones; therefore, a treasure's value and significance was seen as permanently fixed. It would mainly be used to reenact the original event, in events that were thus by definition so minor in comparison they could do little to change the significance of the object.

This attitude toward history helps to explain one otherwise rather puzzling similarity in Kwakiutl and Maori attitudes toward their treasures. Both these societies are famous for their spectacular visual arts; yet in either case, the creativity of the artists who actually designed most of these objects was not ordinarily considered a significant factor in their value—even if in each case this seems to have been for completely different reasons. Kwakiutl

artists (who are mostly chiefs) are mainly seen to be simply reproducing treasures whose prototypes were given to humans in the ancient past; carving a
new mask, or crest, or feast dish is not seen as creation but re-creation, an
act on the same level as performance. The reason why the role of Maori
artists (who are also supposed to be of aristocratic rank) in creating heirlooms was so rarely mentioned seems more complicated, but I might suggest
two factors. One is that if the meaning of an object is identified with the
artistic creativity of its creator, its meaning is in effect fixed from the beginning: as in our own system, where even entanglement in quite dramatic
events will have little effect on the meaning ascribed to a Matisse or
Michelangelo. Another is that the primary *human* value in Aotearoa focused
on a logic not of creation but appropriation. Here though we get back to the
crux of the problem of the difference between Maori and Kwakiutl systems
of value.

a final comparison

For much of the chapter, I have been developing a set of systematic contrasts
between Maori and Kwakiutl cosmologies, systems of value, and patterns of
exchange. Perhaps it would be helpful to place the most salient of them
alongside one another on the following table:

Maori:	*Kwakiutl:*
• Single overarching cognatic descent system	• Groups of utterly heterogeneous origins
• Elaborate philosophy of interior/invisible/generic powers with taonga (the most important items of wealth) as important specific exceptions	• Next to no theory of soul, emphasis on surfaces, with coppers (the most important items of wealth) as important generic exceptions.
• Reciprocity as endless theme in stories	• Little reciprocity except in antagonistic relations
• Very little emphasis on property in histories	• Histories about nothing but transfers of property
• Emphasis on self-realization through appropriation	• Emphasis on self-realization through giving
• Gifts maintain the identity of the giver	• Gifts constitute the identity of recipient

One could go even further. Maori thought is dominated by a metaphysical theory of powers and dynamic essences, which takes its highest form in
the arcane lore of the priestly "House of Secrets"; it seems only appropriate

then that the Kwakiutl emphasis on forms and surfaces took its highest form instead in moments of public theatrical display. What's more difficult to account for is how all this leads to the last two terms on the table.

Here, it may be remarked, the two systems often look like precise mirror images of one another. In some cases its really quite extraordinarily. Among both Maori and Kwakiutl, for example, it was the custom that if an important man made a major social faux pas, say, by injuring himself or violating some ritual restriction, or (in the Kwakiutl case) being caught arguing with his wife in public, the only way to restore his status was to denude him entirely of his possessions. The major difference: in the Kwakiutl case, it is the chief himself who invites everyone present into his house and bids them take away all they can carry; in the Maori custom of *muru,* the man's kin organize a raiding party and pretend to appropriate his goods by force, even when they are really acting with his complete acquiescence. The custom is precisely the same, except in the one hand the idiom is of complete, open-handed generosity; in the other, aggressive appropriation.

Why? It seems to me the easiest way to resolve the conundrum is to examine the kind of dilemmas each cosmological system creates for a would-be historical actor. An ambitious Maori was the product of a gigantic genealogical system of generation that gave him the right to make certain claims over others' allegiances, but almost everyone else had analogous rights to some degree or another. To turn them into reality was a matter of assembling people about one but in the process differentiating oneself from them. To put it in another way: Maori actors were armed with generic powers, but those powers were, in essence, the power to make oneself an individual. It was the peculiar effect of Maori cosmological assumptions as Schwimmer pointed out, that since the generative power of the gods was what made people fundamentally the same, differentiation was seen as an effect of conflict and strife. Appropriation, and in particular violent or implicitly violent incorporation of land, property, or persons, was the corresponding social form. It was the means through which one established one's unique historical identity. For an ambitious Kwakiutl the fundamental historical dilemma was very different. Unique individual identities there were aplenty. The problem was not, as it was for the Maori, one of how to set oneself off from society (a society that ultimately embraced the entire cosmos), but rather of how to *create* society in the first place. Because there was no assumption of a fundamental prior unity or even necessary connection between most Kwakwala speakers—a unity that, I must hasten to point out, logically did have exist on some level, at least a cultural one, or else people would not have shared the common assumption that it did not. The dilemma then was not about self-definition but about the definition of others. In this light, the potlatch was a mechanism for the endless re-creation of society: society defined, as I have suggested it is so often defined, essentially as a potential audience, the totality of those people whose opinions matter to a social actor. Reproducing society is about assembling and having a dramatic effect on audience; this is the aim of really significant social action; gifts, and accompanying recognition, correspondingly its medium and its final realization.

conclusions II: political and moral conclusions

My habit of using examples like American celebrities or tycoons as a way to come to grips with apparently exotic practices might seem a bit forced, but really it is a quite intentional strategy. It is my way of declaring my sympathies for Mauss' own intellectual project, which was to explore the common moral basis of all human societies. Of course my comparison of the Maori and Kwakiutl might seem to tend in the opposite direction, to show just how different even gift economies can be; but in fact, even the differences between the Maori and Kwakiutl are largely differences of emphasis. For all the Maori emphasis on appropriation, for example, in the exchange of food, and particularly in the organization of collective feasts, the Maori often did try to outdo each other in generosity in ways strikingly reminiscent of the potlatch.[43]

The problem is always one of finding viable terms of comparison, and in this case I think the problem is particularly acute. Mauss' own terminology— the "potlatch," the "total prestation," "the gift," "reciprocity"—served well enough for making broad moral points about the logic of the market, but as terms of cross-cultural comparison, they are blunt instruments: extremely imprecise. In fact, I would argue that the muddiness of his terms made it impossible for him to frame his basic questions—particularly, "Why is that gifts have to be repaid?"—in a way that they could be meaningfully answered.[44] Not that Levi-Strauss (1950) did much better: in fact, the term he fixed on to solve the problem, "reciprocity," is really the bluntest instrument of all. As currently used, "reciprocity" can mean almost anything. It is very close to meaningless.

so: why do gifts have to be repaid?

As should be obvious by now, gifts do not always have to be repaid. The question should really be: When do they have to be repaid? What sort of gifts? In what circumstances? And what precisely can count as a repayment?

The conclusion would have been impossible to avoid had Mauss made a serious effort to explore his own notion of the "total prestation" (which he also referred to as "total reciprocity"), instead of moving directly to "the potlatch." Because in the former, gifts do not have to be repaid. This is because unlike competitive gift exchange, "total prestations" created permanent relationships between individuals and groups, relations that were permanent precisely because there was no way to cancel them out by a repayment. The demands one side could make on the other were open ended because they were permanent; nothing would be more absurd than for the member of an Iroquois moiety to keep count of how many of the other's side dead each had recently buried, to see which was ahead. This is why Mauss considered them "communistic": they corresponded to Louis Blanc's famous phrase "From each according to his abilities, to each according to his needs." Most of us treat our closest friends this way. No accounts need be kept because the relation is not treated as if it will ever end. Whatever one might conclude about the realities of the situation (and these can vary considerably), communism is built on an image of eternity. Since there is supposed to be no history, each moment is effectively the same as any other.

The real problem, it seems to me, came when Mauss moved from here to unilateral relations, in which only one party has an unlimited right to draw on the other's resources. It must have seemed a logical step, considering Mauss was drawing his main examples from relations created by marriage. Where sister exchange is the predominant form of marriage, both sides see themselves as standing in a relation of permanent mutual debt[45]; where women flow in only one direction, the debt is all on one side, and the wife-giver can often make unlimited demands on the wife-taker's family, while the latter can make no effective claims at all. But how exactly can this be considered an example of "reciprocity"? It seems about as far from reciprocity as one can possibly imagine. Of course with a term that vague, one can always come up with something, and this is what Mauss did, suggesting that such unequal relations generally form an overall circle in which accounts ultimately balance out (1947:105–106).

This was precisely the argument that Levi-Strauss was later to latch onto, and develop in *The Elementary Structures of Kinship* (1949). He referred to such circular marriage systems as "generalized exchange," a phrase that has always borne a confusing similarity to Marshall Sahlins' "generalized reciprocity" (1972), which, however, is not really the same thing at all but is actually back to from-each-according-to-his-abilities communism again. It's as if each author had developed a completely different aspect of Mauss' "total prestation." Levi-Strauss takes up Mauss' point about the unlimited debts of wife-takers to wife-givers to describe a system of extremely hierarchical relations, which, however, can cancel out if everyone marries in a circle. Sahlins, on the other hand, defines "generalized reciprocity" as the kind of open-ended responsibility that prevails among close kin, all of whom will do whatever they can to help the other, not because they expect repayment, but simply because they know that in a similar crisis, the other *would* do the same. He contrasts it with the "balanced reciprocity" that prevails between people who, though less close, are nonetheless close enough that they feel obliged to deal with each other on a moral basis. "Balanced reciprocity," interestingly enough, would thus include *both* classical gift exchange and the less cutthroat forms of trade or barter.

The connection is worth making. Actually, if one eliminates the confusing term "reciprocity" from the picture, it soon becomes apparent that the classic gift-countergift scenario has a lot more in common with market exchange than we normally assume: at least, in comparison with the sort of open-ended communism Mauss took as his starting point. Where the latter is all about maintaining a permanent sense of mutual obligation, the former is about the denial of obligation and a maximum assertion of individual autonomy. In fact, one could even say that gift exchange of this balanced sort is actually more concerned with asserting the absolute autonomy of the actors than most market contracts. Consider a rental contract, for example. I rent you an apartment for some months, after which you agree to pay me a certain amount of money. Parties to such a contract act as if they were bound by obligation, but they aren't really. Unless the contract is backed up by the force of law, we are both perfectly well aware that you might simply leave town and skip out on your responsibilities; or (a more likely scenario, perhaps) I might ignore my contractual obligations to provide adequate heat or repair the bathroom floor. We are pretending to be more constrained than we actually are. In the classic gift scenario, it is precisely the opposite: the giver pretends he expects and desires nothing whatever in return, the recipient, that he is not bound by any sense of obligation to make a countergift. Both parties are claiming to be far freer and more autonomous than they actually are.

The emphasis on autonomy is, I think, the key to understanding this sort of gift exchange. Insofar as it is about "creating social relations," it is really about creating relations of the most minimal, temporary kind: ones that can be completely canceled out. What's more, while they exist they are completely unequal; the initial giver is at first superior and maintains his autonomy; the recipient's autonomy is called into question until such time as he can make an appropriately magnificent return; but the moment he does so, the relationship is ended. Or, at any rate, it is if the parties wish it to be, since no outstanding obligations remain. At every point the emphasis is on minimizing any sense of obligation or dependency, even where it does exist. While it is certainly true that tit-for-tat exchange of this sort *can* help create an ongoing, mutually supportive relationship, it has only really done so when it stops being strictly tit for tat.

Marshall Sahlins suggested something similar when he noted, somewhat tentatively, that in most "primitive" societies

> balanced reciprocity is not the prevalent form of exchange. A question might
> even be raised about the stability of balanced reciprocity. Balanced exchange
> may tend towards self-liquidation. On the one hand, a series of honorably bal-
> anced dealings between comparatively distant parties builds trust and confi-
> dence, in effect reduces social distance, and so increases the chances for more
> generalized future dealings . . . On the other hand, a renege acts to sever rela-
> tions—as a failure to make returns breaks a trade-partnership. (1972:223)

Not only a renege: with gifts, simply paying back effectively cancels any
outstanding obligations between the two parties, unless, that is, the recipient was so lavish in trying to outdo the original gift that he sparked a cycle
of one-upmanship. There is a reason why the two Kwakwala transactions
that most resemble the gift-countergift form are the practice of "buying
back a daughter"—which is a way of *ending* a social relation—and gifts between rivals, which the Kwakwala themselves referred to as "fighting with
property." Among the Maori tit-for-tat giving was more common; but
even here the real meaning of the famous *hau* of the gift—if my interpretation is correct—is precisely its ability to free one from the perils of such
a relationship.

Rather than "generalized" or "balanced" reciprocity, then, it might be
better to think of reciprocity as relatively "open" and "closed": open reciprocity keeps no accounts, because it implies a relation of permanent mutual commitment; it becomes closed reciprocity when a balancing of
accounts closes the relationship off, or at least maintains the constant possibility of doing so. Phrasing it this way also makes it easier to see the relation
as a matter of degree and not of kind: closed relations can become more
open, open ones more closed.

It seems difficult to avoid the impression, then, that the closed reciprocity of gift and countergift is in fact the form of gift exchange that *least* embodies what makes a "gift economy" different from one dominated by
market exchange. It is competitive, individualistic, and can easily (as in the
Maori case) slip into something resembling barter. Why, then, did Mauss
put it at the center of his analysis—even to the point of largely ignoring
those networks of individualistic communism that, it turns out, were actually far more important in most of the societies he was dealing with? Once
again, I think, the answer lies in the essay's political purposes. For that, the
fact that even a free market economist will be likely to feel somehow reduced
if he cannot return a present is a perfect starting place: the "obligation to return" gifts, in modern society, cannot be explained *either* by the market ideology of self-interest or by its complement, selfless altruism.

At least this is part of the reason. I think there is another, deeper one as
well, which has to do with freedom. Mauss emphasized that our accustomed

sharp division between freedom and obligation is, like that between interest and generosity, largely an illusion thrown up by the market, whose anonymity makes it possible to ignore the fact that we rely on other people for just about everything. In its absence, one must necessarily be aware that, unless one wishes to live a solitary life, freedom largely means the freedom to chose what sort of obligations one wishes to enter into, and with whom. Nonetheless, one could hardly deny that the kind of open-ended, "communistic" relations Mauss highlighted can quite easily slip into hierarchy, patronage and exploitation. Even moieties are generally ranked. The real crux of the problem, it seems to me, lies in the organization of the family, which is almost everywhere *both* the main locus of such open-ended commitments and also the locus of a society's most elementary forms of hierarchy, its primordial models of authority. Of course there are exceptions to anything; families are obviously organized very differently in different societies; usually they provide a society's primordial models for equality as well; but nonetheless, everywhere, in different ways and to different degrees, communism and authority tend to overlap.[46]

In fact, I strongly suspect that the more hierarchical relations within the household, the more likely it will be that relations between male heads of household will be mediated by such balanced and potentially competitive forms of gift exchange. One thinks immediately of the highlands of Papua New Guinea, with its famous *te* and *moka* exchanges, or the gift-as-challenge of the ancient Mediterranean or modern North Africa. Are these not areas notorious for the extreme subordination of women? Or for that matter the aristocratic rivalry of the Celtic, or Vedic, world, once again premised on aristocratic households within which the principles of exchange were altogether different. In many cases, it's quite clear that this is what gives the element of rivalry its edge. As Tom Beidelman (1989) demonstrates in his analysis of Agamemnon's failed attempt to settle his quarrel with Achilles in the beginning of the *Iliad* by returning Achilles' slave along with endless additional wealth, if one offers a gift so lavish that the other party could never possibly reciprocate, the result is to reduce him to same the level as a member of one's household, a child or a dependent rather than an equal. No man of honor could accept such a gift.

Perhaps then we have an answer to our initial question: When do gifts have to be repaid? If one is speaking of strict equivalence, the answer is: Gifts have to be repaid when "communistic" relations are so identified with inequality that not doing so would place the recipient in the position of an inferior. Such forms of exchange then are about establishing a kind of fragile, competitive equality between actors who are almost always themselves hierarchical superiors to someone else.

a structuralist interlude (on value)

The reader might be wondering how all this ties in with questions of value, which have so far made only a sporadic appearance in this chapter. Actually, there are several important points to be made here.

First of all, on the subject of competitive gifts: in order to be able to create this kind of fragile, competitive equality, there has to be some kind of standard of equivalence between things. Otherwise it would be impossible to say that the return gift was indeed of "equal or greater value" to the first. Standards of equivalence between objects, then, can emerge from the need to establish social equality. Of course, it is theoretically possible to imagine a system of gift exchange that does not establish such standards. Presumably one could have a system where people give and return exactly the same things: as in Levi-Strauss' famous example of two men forced to share a table at a cheap French restaurant, each of whom pours the other a glass of wine from their collective bottle (1947 [1954:58–59]). But a system in which fish could be exchanged only for fish, or yams for yams, would be remarkably impractical, unless there was next to nothing in the way of division of labor, or economic necessities could be distributed entirely through other means.

Still, in the literature on reciprocity, such apparently senseless exchange of identical things has taken on a surprisingly important role. Consider the following analysis, offered by Edmund Leach, who takes this principle to its logical extreme by arguing that this is the *only* way to establish social equality:

> Thus the English greet one another with a verbal formula, a reciprocal 'How do you do?,' but simultaneously they shake hands. Neighbours affirm their friendship by reciprocal hospitality. More distant friends exchange letters or Christmas cards, and so on. In all these cases the reciprocity is like-for-like and the message that is encoded in the action is roughly: 'We are friends and we are of equal status.'
>
> But the majority of person-to-person exchanges are not of this like-for-like kind. Correspondingly, most of the persons in a close network of relationships are of unequal rather than equal status. The inequality of the exchange is congruent with the inequality of the status. (Leach 1982:150–151)

Surely this is too simplistic. Still, such *reductio ad absurdae* can be useful in clarifying the issues at hand. Leach's analysis actually typifies an assumption shared by a surprising number of Western social theorists: that any systematic difference in social roles must necessarily also be a form of inequality. To a degree this is probably just an effect of the intrinsic ambiguity of the word "inequality," which can mean either that things are ranked in relations of superiority and inferiority, or just that they are not the same. More broadly: all such generalizations, it seems to me, suffer from a similar fault in logic. They ignore the fact that in order to make any sort of ranking between two terms, one has to be able to establish some initial ground of similarity between them. If two terms were utterly unlike, they could not be compared at all. (This is why "black" is the opposite of "white," and not of "frog"). If they could not be compared, they could not be declared "unequal" in the first place.[47]

The same goes for the act of declaring two things equivalent. By doing so, one is not stating that they are the same in every way: one is simply stating they are the same along those dimensions one considers important in that context, and that other possible criteria are, in that context, irrelevant. "All human beings are equal because they are all equally in possession of an immortal soul; therefore, the fact that their feet may vary radically in size has no bearing on the question." The element of value, here, turns on *which* criteria are considered meaningful, or important, in any given context. Unless one is a cynic, or a Dumontian, there's no reason to assume the most important contexts will normally be the most invidious.

All this is fairly self-evident if you really think about it. Matters become more complicated when one moves from what people feel should not be compared to what they feel cannot: for example, Dumont's version of the first premise of modernity, "All human beings are equal because they are all unique individuals." Our individuality makes us incommensurable, hence effectively equivalent. Still, even in the case of incommensurability there are degrees: dogs are all unique individuals too, but few believe this makes them quite our equals. So once again it is really an initial ground of similarity ("humanity") that makes the incommensurability take on the meaning that it does.

This, in turn, brings us once again to a paradox that has cropped up repeatedly over the course of this book: how can one thing be more unique than another? You would think this would be a contradiction in terms. But by now it should be abundantly clear that many systems of value are based on making precisely this sort of distinction. To return to people and dogs: most Americans, it seems to me, apply such a system to the value of different sorts of living creature. Every individual animal—or plant, for that matter—is assumed to be unique in its own way, but certain varieties are clearly considered more unique than others: humans are thus assumed to be more individual than dogs, dogs than cattle, cattle than fish, fish than roaches, and so on.[48] The more unique each individual representative of the category, the more objectionable it is to kill it. Hence, cats should not be killed lightly; fish can be slaughtered with relative impunity; killing roaches can become a moral imperative. One might well argue that distinctions of a similar logical order are made for works of art: at any rate it's certainly true that the fact that all beautiful paintings are unique in their beauty does not mean that one cannot say some paintings are more beautiful than others.

All this is not so much a digression as it might seem. What I am trying to suggest is that in order to understand the workings of any system of value, one has to examine both what should not, and what could not, be measured or compared within it. In the case of a gift economy, then, the refusal to keep track of inputs and outputs in communistic relations could be considered an example of the former; the emphasis on unique valuables in balanced gift exchange, of the latter. As we've seen, such valuables often do end up being ranked by the degree of their incommensurability. Obviously not always: there are also valuables like wampum or coppers or Fijian whale teeth. But for simplicity's sake, let's imagine a system in which this was the exclusive principle of ranking (or a kula system along the lines described by Nancy Munn, which comes quite close). At the lowest level is cooked food. It would be a fairly simple matter to keep track of who had given who the largest meals of cooked yams; therefore, unless one is particularly stingy or ungracious, one does not try to do so. It would be impossible to measure the comparative merits of two famous kula ornaments, or one such ornament and an equally famous greenstone ax; therefore, it is appropriate to give one for the other in strictly balanced exchange. Something like this seems to occur in almost any marketless society: one can almost always make out at least a distinction between a sphere of everyday consumption, quite often marked by an ethos of open-handed hospitality (Sahlins 1972), and a "prestige sphere," characterized by all sorts of careful accounting. The Maori are one obvious example.

Looking at things this way produces some interesting results, especially if we consider such spheres as Munn insists, as spheres of human action. It then becomes clear that as one proceeds upward, the actor's role becomes increasingly obscured. In the first case, it is clearly deeds that are at issue: one is refusing to compare who has *given* more. In the last, the incommensurability shifts entirely to the object itself. Of course this is partly because the object becomes the embodiment of a history of other people's actions, stretching back, usually, into the distant ancestral past. Whatever the reason, though, one could say that as one goes further up the scale, the origins of the value become increasingly mystified and increasingly likely to be seen as an intrinsic property of the object itself. Still, what I'd really like to emphasize is that this mystification, if that's what it is, happens to a surprisingly limited degree. Mauss clearly overstated his case here: Kwakiutl coppers, kula armshells, Maori warclubs, and the like were *not* normally seen to have their own minds and purposes; in fact, the striking thing is how much more likely one is to run into blatant subject/object reversals in flipping through the pages of the *Wall Street Journal*—where money is always fleeing one market to another, bonds are doing this, pork bellies doing that—than in participants' accounts of the operations of a gift economy. Great mystifications do normally exist in such societies, but for the most part they lie elsewhere.

summary and perspectives

To give a gift is to transfer something without any immediate return, or guarantee that there will ever be one. This is the definition adopted by the MAUSS group (e.g., Godbout and Caillé 1998), and it seems about as good a general definition as we're going to get. It also makes it clear that the term can apply to an enormous variety of transactions, and that the term "gift economy" can apply to any not organized on market principles. One purpose of this chapter is to begin to explore just how different such economies can be.

I have not proposed an exhaustive typology of types of gifts, but I have tried to use Mauss' ideas to develop what might serve as a reasonable backbone for one. The notion of "total prestation" is in fact an excellent place to start, provided one is willing to break it down into its constituent elements. This means that timeless relations of open-ended, communistic reciprocity, whether they apply to groups like moieties or clans, or members of a family, or a network of individuals (as in Mauss' "individualistic communism") have to be distinguished from balanced gift-exchange. While the former can often slip into relations of patronage and exploitation (and it is often very hard to tell, from either the analyst's or actor's point of view, just when one definitively turns into the other), the latter has a tendency to degenerate into outright competition—most often the kinds of contest of generosity that Mauss labeled "the potlatch" but which should probably be best referred to just as "agonistic exchange." Alternately, as it focuses more on the objects, it can become continuous with forms of exchange that look increasingly like barter. As structures of action, one is concerned with maintaining the value of a timeless human commitment; the other, that of a more ephemeral autonomy.

These are both forms of exchange that are reciprocal—a term here defined as one in which two parties act, or are disposed to act, toward one another in equivalent ways.[49] Within relations of presumed inequality, no presumption of reciprocity exists. Alain Testart (1998:98) makes the obvious point that if you give a dollar to a beggar on the street, this will not make said beggar inclined to offer you a dollar if you run into him again; in fact, it will almost certainly make him more likely to ask you for a further contribution. In such cases, one could argue that the underlying logic is much the same as it is when the celebrity gives the fan an autograph, or a Kwakiutl chief throws a potlatch: the recipient's very willingness to accept such an object serves as an act of recognition. It is a microscopic version of the creation of persons, which almost everywhere is based on the assumption that inner qualities (talent, generosity, decency, etc.) can be realized only in another person's eyes. But to call this a kind of "reciprocity"—or even to assume that a desire for recognition is the *only* significant motive on the part

of the giver—is equally absurd. That would just be playing circular economistic games again.

Annette Weiner (1985, 1992) and Maurice Godelier (1996) argue that
Mauss' emphasis on exchange was itself somewhat misguided; the ultimate
valuables of a society or group will normally be those that are never given
away; there are always sacred treasures and these are the real origin of the
power of the objects that are actually thrown into competitive games of exchange. Actually this seems to be Weiner's particular version of a problematic that crops up in a surprising number of authors we've been looking at:
how to reconcile a lower sphere of self-aggrandizement with a higher one of
a society's eternal verities (e.g., Parry and Bloch 1989; Barraud, de Coppet,
Iteanu, and Jamous 1994, also A. Weiner 1978, 1980, 1982). I should make
my position clear here. No doubt in any human society there will be many
situations in which individual concerns will be seen to conflict with higher
authority or the general good, however conceived; but to take such an argument too far, it seems to me, is to do just what Mauss was warning us not
to: imposing our own assumptions about individual self-interest onto others
who probably do not share them. Anyway, it's perfectly clear that in neither
the Maori nor the Kwakiutl cases were the prime objects of exchange in any
sense subsidiary versions of sacred treasures held within families. Instead, we
have encountered extremely complicated systems of transfer in which the
exact dimensions of "groups" are rarely entirely clear, in which strategic
games of self-aggrandizement are, as Mauss would have predicted, so intrinsic to the nature of projects of cosmic reproduction that it would be impossible to disentangle them.

At this point, finally, we can think once again about the political and
moral implications of Mauss' work. Let me begin with a warning. There is a
great danger of oversimplification here, particularly of romanticizing "the
gift" as a humanizing counterweight to the impersonality and social isolation of modern capitalist society. There are times when things can work
quite the other way around. Let me take another familiar example: the custom of bringing a bottle of wine or somesuch if invited to a friend's for dinner. It is a common practice, for example, among American academics. In
America, though, it is also common for young people of middle-class background to move, from the time they first begin to live independently of their
parents in college, from relatively communal living arrangements to increasing social isolation. In an undergraduate dorm, people walk in and out of
each other's rooms fairly casually; often a residential hall is not unlike a village with everybody keeping track of everybody else's business. College
apartments are more private, but it is usually no big deal if friends drop by
without warning or preparation. The process of moving into conventional,
bourgeois existence is gradual, and it is above all a matter of establishing the

sacred quality of the domestic threshold, which increasingly cannot be crossed without preparations and ceremony. The gift of wine, if you really think about it, is part of the ritualization process that makes spontaneity more difficult. It is as much a bar to sociality as an expression of it.

I am saying all this not to make a plea for some kind of universal *communitas,* or even as a gripe from someone who never knows what wine to buy, but mainly to make a point about critical perspectives. To adopt a critical perspective on a practice or institution (as I have just done) is usually a matter of placing it within some larger social totality, in which it can then be seen to play an intrinsic part in the reproduction of certain forms of inequality, or alienation, or injustice. This is what Marxists usually accuse Mauss of forgetting to do, and not entirely without reason. But here the Maussian could well reply that for criticism to have any purpose, one must also be able to place *some* practices or institutions within an imaginary totality in which they might *not* contribute to the reproduction of inequality, alienation, or injustice. Such questions were clearly rarely far from Mauss' (the cooperativist's) mind, and for me, this is precisely what is most radical about his thinking. It encourages us—to put the matter in a somewhat Hegelian way—to view practices and institutions in terms of their potentialities, to force on oneself a kind of pragmatic optimism. Take for example his apparently idiosyncratic definition of "communism," as a matter of dispositions and practices rather than property rights. Where the ideologists and propagandists responsible for what passes for public discourse in this country seem never to miss an opportunity to claim that something they call "capitalism"—usually defined as broadly as possible as any form of self-interested financial calculation—is always present everywhere (newspaper headline: "Even in African Refugee Camps, Capitalism Thrives"), Mauss' definition would do the opposite. It would present us with the possibility that the specter of communism might lurk not only within families and friendships but within the very organization of corporate capitalism itself, or pretty much any situation in which people are united in a common task, and inputs and outputs therefore organized only by the actors' capacities and requirements rather than by any balancing of accounts.

Without a critical perspective as well, such a gesture is just as meaningless as the habit of seeing "capitalism" everywhere. Even if this is a kind of communism, it remains lodged within larger structures that are anything but egalitarian. But as Mauss also emphasized, it is the presence of such practices and institutions that make it possible for people within the society to see those larger structures as unjust. Mauss did not say it, since at the time he was thinking mainly of affinal relations, but it would not take much of an extension of his ideas to argue that the very experience of the organization of work within many capitalist enterprises may often directly contradict the moral basis of the wage labor contract on which that enterprise is ultimately based.

Allow me a final word about political visions.

Those interested in broadening our sense of human possibilities, in imagining different—more just, more decent—ways to organize economic or political life quite often turn to anthropology for ideas and inspiration. It would be nice if anthropologists had something to offer them. Something, that is, more than warnings, however legitimate, that gift economies too have been known to trample people underfoot. I have tried to organize my own analysis in a way that might not prove completely useless in this regard. In my discussion of contexts, levels, and imaginary totalities at the end of chapter 3, and my (related) suggestions about value, incommensurability, and equality in this chapter, such questions were never far from my mind. True, most of these observations have been on a very abstract level. There are any number of ways one could put the pieces together, if one wanted to use such ideas to help develop a concrete visions of how a more egalitarian society might work. In a way, though, I think this is quite as should be. It strikes me that what we really need now is not one but as many different visions as possible. I like to think this would be altogether in the spirit of Mauss.

Chapter 7 ▨

The False Coin of Our Own Dreams, or the Problem of the Fetish, IIIb

One man is a king only because other men stand in the relation of subjects to him. They, on the contrary, imagine that they are subjects because he is the king.

—Karl Marx, *Capital,* 63

Of the many wonderful tales Moor told me, the most wonderful, the most delightful one, was "Hans Röckle." It went on for months; it was a whole series of stories . . . Hans Röckle himself was a Hoffman-like magician, who kept a toyshop, and who was always "hard up." His shop was full of the most wonderful things—of wooden men and women, giants and dwarfs, kings and queens, workmen and masters, animals and birds as numerous as Noah got into the Ark, tables and chairs, carriages, boxes of all sorts and sizes. And though he was a magician, Hans could never meet his obligations either to the devil or to the butcher, and was therefore—much against the grain—constantly obliged to sell his toys to the devil. These then went through wonderful adventures—always ending in a return to Hans Röckle's shop.

—Eleanor Marx, on her father
Karl's bedtime stories (in Stallybrass 1998:198)

In this final chapter I want to move from an emphasis on value and exchange to the other side of the equation proposed in chapter 4 and to talk a little bit about the phenomenon of social power. Odd though it may seem, I think the easiest way to do this will be to look at the notion of fetishism—one that has cropped up periodically over the course of the book but that I have not so far fully developed.

Mauss' project of investigating "archaic forms of social contract" has a distinctly nineteenth-century ring to it, but it seems to me there is still something very important here for the twenty-first. I began this book by saying that social theory is at something at an impasse, in part, because it has boxed itself into a corner where it is now largely unable to imagine people being able to change society purposefully. I have argued that one way to overcome this problem is to look at social systems as structures of creative action, and value, as how people measure the importance of their own actions within such structures. If so, then one is necessarily seeing "society" as to some degree an intentional thing. Even if it does not embody some sort of collective project, it is at least made out of them, and acts as their regulative principle.

The problem is that in Western social thought, social contract theory is one of the only idioms in which it has been possible to talk about society this way, and it is a woefully inadequate one. To imagine society as a contract is to imagine it in distinctly market terms. Given the tremendous power of economistic ideologies in the world today, relentlessly hammered in on everyone in a thousand different ways, words like "contract" have become pretty obviously unsalvageable—there is no way to use them without assumptions about isolated individuals (usually assumed to be males about forty years old) coming to a rational agreement based on self-interested calculation. Those who think differently simply don't have the power or influence to create new definitions in peoples' minds, or at any rate, any significant number of them. Mauss tried to change the way we think about contracts in "The Gift," and even though the essay was enormously influential in other ways, his efforts had no effect whatever.

All this is very frustrating because it effectively leaves us without a language with which to discuss some very important phenomena. Since Marx, we have been used to talking about how social orders become naturalized; about how what are ultimately arbitrary conventions come to seem like inevitable constituents of the universe. But what about the degree to which social orders are not naturalized? Even among those societies Mauss would consider the most "archaic," there are always some social arrangements that were seen as created through mutual agreement, and, I strongly suspect, always a certain degree to which the social order as a whole is not seen as something inherent in the nature of the cosmos but can be seen as something which is in some sense the product of mutual consent or agreement—if only as one possible perspective among many. And when it does, it is, clearly, not in the sense imagined by Hobbes or subsequent market theorists. It is not as a collection of individuals interested only in acquiring as much as possible of the things they want who make a rational calculation that they can only do this efficiently by agreeing to respect one another's property or honor commercial agreements. It is as people who already have profound and ongoing commitments to others who see themselves as extending something of the same sort to a larger group—something which does indeed, as Mauss was perhaps the first to recognize, imply a kind of elementary communism, an agreement to treat others' perceived needs and interests as matters of significance in and of themselves. One need only look at the Iroquois case to find an example that corresponds almost exactly to what Mauss had in mind. Society was seen not as something given but as a human creation, a set of agreements, which were the only alternative to endless cycles of destructive violence. The story of the origins of the League does begin with something very like a Hobbesian "war of all against all." The difference was that the Iroquois did not see the danger of violence as arising from the fact that humans were solitary individuals competing over scarce resources, but because they assumed them to already be enmeshed in relationships with others—relations which were in fact so intense, and so intimate, that the death of a loved one could cause them to descend into paroxysms of destructive fury. The way of creating society, in turn, was through establishing long-term open-ended commitments: whether to bury one another's dead or to be willing put aside principles of property rights when faced with a sufficiently profound need, as revealed in another's dream.

Among the Five Nations, of course, there was no internal market. For this reason it's quite interesting to compare the North American case with what was happening in West Africa around the same time, in the sixteenth century. There European merchants arrived (at first, in search of gold) to discover a complex patchwork of societies, most of which had not only been tied into larger circuits of trade for centuries but had their own markets, currency, and forms of self-interested exchange. Trade with the newcomers came to be regulated by ritual objects that the Europeans referred to as "fetishes," on which they were asked to swear oaths and that were held to bind together otherwise unrelated people in contractual obligations. The power ascribed to such objects were in this case quite similar to the sort of sovereign power imagined by Hobbes: not only were they tokens of agreement, but they were themselves capable of enforcing those agreements because they were essentially forms of crystallized violence. Most of them were personifications of diseases or other afflictions, which could be called on to destroy those who betrayed their obligations.[1] Where wampum represented the exact opposite of the cataclysmic terror introduced through the fur trade, here it was as if the power and abstraction of money itself were turned back against itself as a form of imaginary violence that could prevent its own worst implications.

Looking at mechanisms for creating collective agreements, then, is a fairly dependable way to find social forms that are not completely naturalized. This is not to say that in all of these societies there are not also social forms that were indeed viewed as given in the very nature of the universe or created long ago by creatures profoundly different from human beings (or at least different from any human beings one might actually know). Most seemed to have divided up different aspects of the social universe in this respect: both the Iroquois and Kwakiutl, for example, saw aspects of personal identity as given in this way but larger social arenas as having to be endlessly created; the Maori seem to have imagined matters quite the other way around. But even this is simplifying things somewhat. The really striking thing is how often people can see certain institutions—or even society as a whole—*both* as a human product and also as given in the nature of the cosmos, both as something they have themselves created and something they could not possibly have created. One might well argue that the Iroquoian "Holder of the Earth," the creator who seems unable to fully grasp his own powers of creativity, is one way of trying to come to terms with this paradox. But I think some of the most striking examples can be found in the literature on African "fetishes," which could be extended to include my own material of Malagasy *ody* and *sampy*, covered rather perfunctorily at the end of chapter 4 and more generally in the anthropological literature on magic—ideas about magic being veritably rife with paradoxes at every turn. If one reads Merina rituals of state with all this in mind, I think it will make it easier to understand both just how little mystified by their own political institutions people in "traditional" societies can often be; how much they can, in fact, see those institutions as human creations, in what we might consider strikingly realistic terms; but at the same time, why it might sometimes not make a whole lot of difference that they do.

the king and the coin

Outside of Madagascar, Merina ritual is mainly known through the work of Maurice Bloch, who has written a series of very famous articles about mortuary ritual (1971, 1981, 1982), circumcision ceremonies (1986), and ritual language (1975). He has also written two equally famous essays on Merina royal ritual (1977, 1989), focusing particularly on the Royal Bath ceremony. Bloch's conclusions, however, are very different from the ones I outlined in chapter 4: in fact, his conclusions about what the ceremonies were effectively saying about the nature and origins of royal power are almost exactly the opposite of my own.

Let me start then with Bloch's essay "The Disconnection Between Power and Rank as a Process: An Outline of the Development of Kingdoms in Central Madagascar," written in 1977. He starts the piece by talking about Louis Dumont's famous observations on the Indian caste system (1966), particularly Dumont's insistence that one must make a strict distinction between caste, which Dumont says is basically a religious institution, and the actual organization of kingdoms, with all the often tawdry and brutal realities of political power they entailed. Bloch observes that much the same distinction can be made in Imerina. The first kingdoms in highland Madagascar were little more than bandit fiefdoms, their "royalty" basically just gangs of thugs who ensconced themselves in hilltop forts and started shaking down surrounding farmers. During the seventeenth and eighteenth centuries, Imerina was divided among a number of such petty kingdoms, while at the same time the countryside was continually ravaged by slave-raiders from the coast, who would carry villagers off to feed the rising demand for plantation labor on the European-held islands of Mauritius and Reunion. Most of the local lords soon came into collusion with the slave trade as well.

The official ideology of these kingdoms[2] stood in striking contrast to all this. It too represented society as a vast graded hierarchy, in which about a third of the population were considered "noble" (*andriana*), and in which every group was ranked according to the degree to which they possessed *hasina*—which Bloch defines as a kind of ineffable grace, or intrinsic superiority: "power, vigor, fertility, efficacy or even sainthood" (1977:61). *Hasina* was something humans had simply by virtue of their being, or at any rate because they had received it from their noble ancestors, not because of anything anyone had done. What's more, royal rituals were coordinated to the natural cycle, and people who were particularly *masina* (who had much *hasina*) were seen as being able to bless crops, so that "power [came to be] represented as an unchanging essence closely linked to nature and only transmitted to legitimate holders" (op cit.).

Hasina then was a sort of inherent grace, given by the very nature of the cosmos. Humans could not create it; in fact, it existed in a domain largely beyond the effects of human action of any sort. At most people could display *hasina* or pass it on to their descendants—and this was what royal ritual was principally about. One could hardly imagine a more extreme contrast between this ideological representation of timeless hierarchy and the sordid details of actual politics, full of constant murder, extortion, and kidnapping.

But Bloch also notes that the word *hasina could* be used another way: to refer to certain large silver coins (most often, Maria Theresa thalers, later Spanish or Mexican dollars) given as ceremonial tribute to the king. Just about any event at which the monarch appeared before his subjects would begin by their "giving *hasina*" to him. It seems reasonable to assume there was some connection between these two usages. Bloch suggests an analogy with the English term "honor." Certain people are said to "have" honor, to be intrinsically honorable. But the word can also be a verb: you can "honor" people by treating them as if they were that sort of person. In theory, by honoring them you are simply recognizing something they already have; in reality, of course, they have it only because people treat them that way. Just so with *hasina*. Having *hasina*—in the sense of intrinsic superiority (which Bloch labels "*hasina* mark 1")—is like having honor; giving the coins ("*hasina* mark 2") is like honoring people.

He then takes the argument a bit further. In most royal rituals, he says, there is a pretense of exchange. On certain occasions, when subjects give the king *hasina* in the form of coins, he responds by sprinkling them with water, a gesture of blessing that conveys fertility, prosperity, good health, and that only the king's mysterious sanctity (his *hasina* mark 1) allows him to do. The most important instance of this was the annual Royal Bath ceremony, the great national festival that stood at the head of the Merina ritual year. Here, the same logic is extended to the entire kingdom. In the first stages of the festival, children have to present *hasina* (or similar tokens of deference) to their parents, and people in general offer it to their immediate hierarchical superiors; it culminates in a ceremony in which representatives of each of the major orders and groupings of the kingdom present silver coins to the king. After receiving the coins, he hides behind a screen, bathes himself in warm water, calling out as he does so, "May I be *masina,*" and then emerges to sprinkle the bath water on the representatives. Later, parents will also bathe and sprinkle the water on their children, thus in effect conveying the blessings down through the kingdom, and of course further naturalizing the king's authority by making it seem continuous with descent.

For Bloch, the critical thing is the way all such rituals serve to mystify the real source of royal power, which is precisely the monarch's ability to make other people pay tribute and otherwise treat him like a monarch by claiming that power comes from a domain beyond human action. It is all about disguising the connection between *hasina* mark 1 and *hasina* mark 2. But from the first time I read the essay as a graduate student, I found something very odd about this argument. If the whole point is to disguise the connection between the two forms of *hasina,* well, why call them by the same name to begin with? Isn't that a bit of a giveaway?

After I had actually begun living in Madagascar and developing a first-hand knowledge of contemporary Merina ritual language, it seemed increasingly difficult to believe that the use of the term *hasina* could have been mystifying much. Granted, I did my fieldwork almost a hundred years after the abolition of the monarchy, but still, I'm not sure I ever heard *hasina* used to convey a notion of intrinsic hierarchical superiority. *Hasina* still means the power to act through invisible, or imperceptible means; the verb *manasina* ("to give *hasina,* to make something *masina*"), used in the nineteenth century for giving coins to a king, is as close as there was to a term for "to conduct a ritual." I heard the verb used all the time. Mostly it was used for what might be called acts of consecration: for instance, one might make offerings to a certain tree, or at a watery place where a forgotten ghost was thought to dwell, or the tomb of an ancient king, in order to add to the places' *hasina* and also to appeal to the very power one was thus creating or enhancing to do something: say, to cure one of sickness, cause one to conceive if one had been infertile, to become wealthy, or pass an exam.

The people I knew made it quite clear that *hasina* was *always* created by human action. It also had to be constantly maintained. Often, for example, when asking about, say, a certain stone once used as a place for carrying out ordeals, or a tree said to protect a village's crops against hail, people would remark that the tree or stone in question was once very *masina,* since it had been given *hasina* in rituals long ago, but the rituals hadn't been carried out for a long time, so there was no way to be sure whether it still had any left. On the other hand, such objects usually had taboos, and even the act of observing those taboos could be referred to as "giving them *hasina*" in the most diffuse of senses, so the mere recognition of such things as powerful was perhaps enough to keep them powerful.

It was also through *manasina* that one created *ody,* the Malagasy equivalent of "fetishes" or "charms," which I have already discussed in chapter 4. Charms also have *hasina,* but here too it is only because people put it there, by bringing together a series of specific ingredients (bits of wood, beads, silver ornaments, etc.) and a nameless, invisible spirit. I've already argued that it's this very lack of definition that makes spirits pure, abstract embodiments of power. In the end, though, it is always human actions that *make* ody powerful. In the nineteenth century, this could, as noted, be carried out through vows: dedicating some kind of small material token that represented the action one wished the invisible powers to take, then preserving and hiding it as the embodiment of the power to carry that action out on a regular basis. This might not have been the most common way of creating an ody, but was a common one, and it is significant because it exactly parallels the ritual of giving *hasina* to the king: where at the height of the Royal Bath ceremony, after everyone has presented coins to the king, he hides himself behind a screen, says "May I be *masina,*" and then emerges to sprinkle the bath water on the assembled multitude. Whenever these whole coins appear as ingredients in charms—which they occasionally did—they always represented an unbroken totality. As offerings, they represent the desire to maintain the integrity of something that could otherwise be broken up, dissolve away into a multitude of tiny little pieces; as elements in charms, they represent the power to maintain it. By this logic, presenting a whole coin represents the people's desire to unify the kingdom, to make a totality out of the various individuals and groups that made it up—it betokens the very desire of the assembled subjects to become subjects, to be unified by the power of the king. Afterwards the king hides himself and, newly charged with *hasina*, sprinkles everyone with water, which also parallels pretty precisely what one does with the most important charms, called *sampy*—one "bathes" them in water and then sprinkles it over the people they are supposed to protect. So the king in effect becomes a charm, an object with the power to maintain the unity of the kingdom.

These sampy, incidentally, were extraordinarily important ody that had their own names and personalities and provided a kind of generalized protection over whole social groups. The Merina kingdom, for instance, was protected by a kind of pantheon of royal sampy, sometimes called "royal palladia" (Domenichini 1977; Delivre 1974), each with a kind of priesthood of guardians. They too were brought out before the people on ritual occasions, received *hasina*, were bathed out of sight, whereon their keepers—or sometimes the king himself—would emerge to sprinkle people with the water. So in the Royal Bath ceremony the king really was playing the role of a magical charm in the most literal way.

At this point, there might not seem to be much left of Bloch's argument. *Hasina* does not, in fact, refer to intrinsic superiority. It is simply one form of power.[3] *Hasina* is not, in fact, inherent in the nature of the world. Human beings create it. By giving unbroken coins, representatives of the kingdom are effectively creating the power that unifies them as a kingdom, thus engaging in a form of collective action that, in effect creates them (as subjects) at the same time as it creates the king (as king). Not only was this implicit in the logic of the ritual; at least in some contexts, nineteenth century Merina seem to have been perfectly capable of stating it explicitly: there was, for example, a proverb that stated that it is really the giving of coins that makes a king a king (Méritens and de Veyrières 1967).

We are back again to social contracts. The message seems to be: kingship emerges from popular consensus. This consensus has to be constantly reaffirmed; the ceremony of creating the king has to be performed over and over again. Here too there's a suggestive parallel with charms. According to at least one missionary source, important ody—presumably he's thinking of those that protected families or larger groups—had to be consecrated by a "pledge of allegiance" before they were thought to have any power. "Until the consecration service has been held, and the pledge of allegiance given, the charm, although finished as regards its construction and general characteristics, was only a piece of wood to them" (Edmunds 1897:63). So its power to act too depended on a kind of popular consensus, at least among the people it protected. And as I already mentioned, this consensus also had to be maintained by constantly "giving *hasina*," which in the case of a charm might mean anything from rubbing it with honey and castor oil to sacrificing a sheep or cow or simply observing certain taboos. At the very least, there always seems to be some sort of notion of agreement and always too a sense that this agreement was established primarily through the power of words— two facts brought together by the fact that persuasive words themselves could themselves be referred to as *masina.*

The Malagasy term one would use in discussing such issues is *fanekena,* which can actually mean either "an agreement," as in a contract or understanding reached between two or more parties, or a more diffuse state of communal consensus; but in either case the implication is of creating or maintaining mutual responsibilities similar to those that would normally obtain between kin, among people who are not. Usually, at least implicitly, creating such an agreement also involves creating some invisible force of violence that has the power to enforce it (much as ancestors punish their descendants who do not respect their mutual obligations). The king was seen in these terms as well: much of his power was a power to mete out spectacular punishment. Neither was the connection between giving *hasina* to the king, and ordinary contracts, merely an effect of language. It was quite explicit. In fact, during the nineteenth century, every time anyone in the Merina kingdom agreed to a contract of any kind, whether it was a local community agreeing to irrigation rules or two people settling an inheritance dispute, the way of making it official was always by presenting *hasina* to the sovereign.[4] If one examines nineteenth century archival records, it quickly becomes clear that this was by far the most common way in which the monarch's power really entered into people's everyday affairs: in effect, by gestures meant to constantly re-create the king's power to enforce agreement, in both senses of the term.

second thoughts

So as I say, at this point it might seem that Bloch was simply wrong and that's all there is to say about it. Certainly that was my initial conclusion. Then I went back and examined the nineteenth century sources Bloch was using as his main source material (e.g., Callet 1908, Cousins 1968) and discovered that there are in fact statements which do represent *hasina* as a quasi-natural force, tied to fertility, passed down from royal ancestors, held by certain groups more than others, and doing pretty much everything else he claims about it. This is especially true of statements made in official histories and, above all, over the course of the royal rituals themselves.

This is where things became really puzzling. It suggests that royal rituals were saying two completely contradictory things. On an explicit level, they declared that royal power is given in the nature of the universe; but at the same time, the whole logic of the ritual seems to say kings only have power only because people want them to.

How to think about this? If the purpose of royal ritual is to naturalize power relations, why undercut the message? Even stranger: why does undercutting it not seem to make any difference? Obviously, if we want to think of the hidden message as some sort of subtle internal critique of the monarchy—as some would no doubt do—it was a remarkably ineffective one, since these rituals played a crucial role in constituting the very object they would presumably be critiquing. Alternately, if the idea that kings are embodiments of popular will does not really undercut their authority, why not just state that outright? Because it was never quite stated outright in the ceremony. Nor would one need a proverb saying, "Really it's the coin that makes the king a king" if this were entirely self-evident. Instead, we have a ritual that seems to assert one thing and then immediately take it back; as if one first declared that kings were divine creatures that had descended from the sky, and then added, "but, of course, not really—actually what makes them kings is the fact that they can get us to go along with such nonsense." (I chose this example because there's another Malagasy proverb that says, "Kings didn't really descend from the sky.").

If someone were designing such a ritual out of whole cloth, all this would be utterly bizarre. But of course, no one did. Merina royal ceremonial was, as Bloch himself emphasizes, largely a patchwork of elements borrowed from elsewhere; it was stitched together out of bits of ritual practice that already encoded their own conceptions of power. This also accounts for much of the difference between Bloch's analysis and my own. Bloch, in his ethnographic work, has focused overwhelmingly on rituals tied to kinship and descent: circumcision ceremonies, speeches paying respect to ancestors, observances surrounding tombs. In fact, these are the only rituals not referred to as *manasina*. He is specifically interested in the way such rituals produce a certain image of timeless, immutable authority; in fact, he defines kinship itself as "a way of viewing relationships between people in terms of the links established by sex and parenthood so that the social ties which are represented in this way appear as natural, inevitable, and unchangeable to those who operate them." (1986a:121). Many would no doubt add that kinship is about other things as well, but it is true that if one looks for analogies in royal ritual, this is precisely where one finds *hasina* being represented as immutable, natural, and so on. I on the other hand was looking at what might broadly be described as "magical practice," which is all about humans *creating hasina* and seems in some ways explicitly opposed to kinship. So it's hardly surprising that when royal ritual draws on this tradition, it seems to be saying something very different.

One might of course object that this doesn't really resolve anything, because the real question is why royal ritual should have drawn on two so contradictory traditions to begin with. This is true enough. But I think the distinction between these two types of ritual practice is a useful point of departure.

When I was first working out my own analysis, for instance, one of the things that really puzzled me was the fact that Bloch has almost nothing to say in any of his work about charms and medicine—what would loosely be called "magic." Perhaps this is not too shocking, since no other anthropologist who's worked in Madagascar has had very much to say about the subject either (the literature on Malagasy magic is almost entirely the work of missionaries and colonial officials). But in Bloch's case, this is just about the only aspect of Merina ritual he *doesn't* talk about. I finally came to the conclusion it was because Bloch is writing very much in the Marxist tradition. Marxist anthropologists have always found it somewhat difficult to figure out what to do with magic. Not religion: Marxist theory, starting with Marx's own work, have always had a great deal to say about religion.

It strikes me this is an interesting phenomena in itself. Why is this? And what might a Marxist theory of magic be like?

magic and Marxism

Much of Marx's early work—notably his responses to other Young Hegelians like Feuerbach and Stirner—was concerned with the analysis of religion. One might even say that his work on ideology was largely a matter of applying concepts developed for the critique of religion to the economic sphere. Fetishism itself is only one of the more famous of such concepts.

The logic behind Marx's critique of religion was fundamental to his way of thinking about the human condition in general. To repeat a familiar argument: human beings are creators. The social (even, to a large extent, the natural) world we live in is something we have made and are continually remaking. Our problem is that we never seem to see it fully that way and therefore can never take control over the process; everywhere, instead, people see their own creations as controlling them. Religion thus becomes the prototype for all forms of alienation, since it involves projecting our creative capacities outward onto creatures of pure imagination and then falling down before them asking them for favors. And so on.

All this must by now be painfully familiar; but it makes it easier to understand why magic is such a problem. Consider some of the ways early anthropology (Tylor, Frazer, etc.) defined the difference between magic and religion. Tylor defined religion as a matter of belief ("the belief in supernatural beings"), but magic as a set of techniques. It was a matter of doing something meant to have direct effects on the world, which did not necessarily involve appeals to some intermediary power. In other words, magic need not involve any fetishized projections at all. Frazer is even more explicit on this account, insisting that magic achieves effects "automatically"; even if a magician does, say, invoke a god or demon, she normally imprisons him in a pentagram and orders him around rather than begging him for favors. Magic, then, is about realizing one's intentions (whatever those may be) by acting on the world. It is not a matter of people's intentions and creative capacities being projected out into it and appearing to those people in strange, alienated forms. If anything, it's just the opposite. To phrase the matter in appropriately nineteenth century terms: if religion is the way people project (imaginary) human personalities and purposes onto (real) natural forces, then magic would have to be a matter of taking real human personalities and purposes and arming them with imaginary natural powers.

This is simply not fetishistic in the classic sense. It is about humans actively shaping the world, conscious of what they are doing as they do so. The usual Marxist critique would not apply. On the other hand, magicians also tend to make all sorts of claims that seem pretty obviously untrue and at least in some contexts do act to reinforce exploitative systems of one sort or another. So it's not as if Marxists could actually endorse this sort of thing, either. Hence perhaps the tendency to avoid the subject altogether.[5]

But the Malagasy example—and I am sure there are others like it— suggests this is the very reason magic is important. Because it is precisely this unfetishized quality, the fact that magic locates the source of social creativity in human action rather than outside it, that makes it possible to yield such an apparently realistic understanding of kingship—in fact, one remarkably close to what a social scientist might have.

Of course, this doesn't explain the apparent dual message. Here I think it might be useful to look at more recent anthropological theories of magic.

magic and anthropology

Most twentieth-century anthropologists have not seen themselves as engaging in an essentially critical project; until a few decades ago, almost none did. Since the early part of the century, mainstream anthropology has tended to be persistently relativistic. So where Marxists tend to find magic problematic because of what it doesn't misrepresent, most other anthropologists find it difficult because of what it apparently does. Magic has proved notoriously difficult to relativize. For evolutionists magic had simply been a collection of mistakes. For Edward Tylor or Sir James Frazer, that was essentially what magic was: the category "magic" included all those techniques that the observer thought couldn't possibly work. The obvious task for the relativist, then, is to demonstrate some sense in which magical statements are true. But this has proved extremely difficult; for one thing, it has led analysts to downplay endlessly what would probably otherwise seem to be one of magic's key defining features: the way it's almost always surrounded by an air of trickery, showmanship, and skepticism.

The anthropological literature on "magic" is not itself very large. It mainly consists of two substantial monographs, by Evans-Pritchard (1937) and by Malinowski (1935), both written when anthropologists still felt old evolutionist issues were at least worth engaging with; there have been very few since. Much of the debate on the subject—for instance, a large part of the so-called "rationality debate" that came out of Evans-Pritchard's *Witchcraft, Oracles and Magic among the Azande*—was conducted by philosophers and other non-anthropologists. In the 1960s there was a spurt of essays inspired by new linguistic models, of which the most important was the work of Stanley Tambiah (1968, 1973), especially his suggested analogy between magical spells and performative speech acts, which are statements (i.e., "I apologize") that accomplish something just by being uttered. Just about every anthropological work on magic since has been, in one sense or another, an elaboration on Tambiah. Not that there are very many of them. In fact, most anthropologists have long since abandoned the term "magic" entirely, preferring to organize data that might have once been labeled magic under rubrics like witchcraft and sorcery, shamanism, curing, cosmology and so on, each of which implies different questions and different problematics. Now, let me say right away that I think there is good reason for this. As a tool of ethnographic description, the term "magic" *is*, largely, useless. I didn't use it either in my own Malagasy ethnography (1995, 1996b, 1997b). I mostly used the term "medicine," since that was the simplest English translation of the word a Malagasy speaker would be most likely to use when referring to such things. Still, the theoretical debate about magic is itself illuminating.

For a relativist, then, the problem is how to show that magical statements are not simply false. Now, insofar as magicians claim their magic has social effects, one can certainly say they are in some sense right. Generally, it does. Insofar as their claims seem to go beyond that, one runs into some real problems. To take an obvious example, if someone tells you he has the power to direct lightning on the heads of his enemies, it is very difficult for the outside observer to avoid the conclusion that he is not in fact able to do this. The statement is wrong. Therefore the speaker is either mistaken, or he is lying. (Most evolutionists, including missionaries, favored a heady mix of both these possibilities.) The only way to avoid the horns of this dilemma completely would be challenge the very notion of "truth": magical statements, one could argue, are not meant to be "true," at least not in the scientific, empirically verifiable sense the word has to a Western audience. They are poetic or rhetorical, expressive rather than instrumental, illocutionary, performative, etc. Probably the main reason for Tambiah's fame is that at least in his earlier essays (1968. 1973), he takes the most extreme position in this regard.

Tambiah's most famous example is a Trobriand gardening spell called *vilamalia*, recorded by Malinowski (1935), which ostensibly purports to anchor yam storehouses by making them fat, bulging and weighty, and making both the storehouses and the yams inside them heavy and durable. Tambiah notes that when Malinowski asked magicians about how the spell worked, most were careful to explain that it doesn't *really* operate directly on the yams or storehouses. Really, they said, the spell affected human bellies—bellies being considered the seat of the intellect as well as the seat of magical power. It does so especially by convincing people to keep their hunger under control so they won't fill their bellies with yams so the storehouses will be full instead. The conclusion of course is that magic is a public performance meant to sway people or, as he puts it to "restructure and reintegrate the minds and emotions of the actors" (1985:118), not a mistaken technique for swaying things.

The problem, though, is that this is a fairly unusual spell. Trobrianders also made use of spells meant to control the wind or make canoes sail quickly, and there seems little reason to believe that their effects were seen as purely rhetorical. But note the analogy to Merina royal ritual. Here, too, we have statements of apparently extraordinary, naturalized powers in the ritual itself (that kings' power is rooted in nature, that magicians' words can affect the physical world), which then seem to be almost immediately undercut by statements, implicit in the ritual and stated more explicitly just offstage, that really this is not so, that in reality all this is just a matter of swaying people's intentions.

It's also significant that Trobriand magic is itself largely a matter of public performance. Claims that magic is never really thought to affect the material world, but only other people are much harder to take seriously when dealing with, say, Evans-Pritchard's Zande material or for that matter, ceremonial magic practiced in the ancient world (Faraone and Obbink 1991, Graf 1997), where most ritual performance took place in secret.[6] This does depend somewhat on how formally one wants to define "performance." Let me go back to the example of casting lightning. Once, while living in the small town of Arivonimamo, I was visiting the apartment of a certain mediumistic curer named René, and flipping through a notebook full of recipes for ody that he had left somewhat ostentatiously on the table. René noticed this and immediately pointed out a page that, he said, contained instructions for how to make a lightning charm. "Bear in mind, I would never use such a thing myself," he said "They're intrinsically immoral. Or, well, actually, once I did. Years ago. But that was to take revenge on the man who killed my father. Which I know I shouldn't have, but . . ." He paused, gave a slightly distressed shrug. "Well, it was my father!"

How to analyze this event? It was certainly a performance of a sort. But it was carried out in ordinary conversational speech that was indeed meant to be judged by true/false criteria. You can't say it is "inappropriate" to ask whether René had really blasted someone with lightning or not. So one is indeed stuck with the choice between mistaken and lying. But the main point I want to make is that just about every Malagasy person I mentioned the incident to had no hesitation about their conclusion. Obviously he was lying. (If you really do have such awesome powers you don't go bragging to strangers.) Of course, most probably felt there was the small possibility that he might really know how to cast lightning, just enough to make one think twice before doing anything that would really annoy him, and that was pretty obviously the real "social effect" his performance was meant to have; but this almost means that the degree to which people thought his speech was meant only to have social effects was the degree to which they didn't believe him.

Anthropologists usually acknowledge this sort of skepticism—the aura of at least potential disbelief that always seems to surround the sort of phenomena that gets labeled "magic"—but almost always, only to immediately dismiss it as unimportant. Evans-Pritchard, for instance, noted that most of Zande he knew insisted that the majority of witchdoctors were frauds and that there were only a handful of "reliable practitioners." "Hence in the case of any particular witchdoctor they are never quite certain whether reliance can be placed on his statements or not" (1937:276). Similar things have been reported about curers almost everywhere. But the conclusion is always the same: since everyone, or most everyone, agrees there are *some* legitimate practitioners, the skepticism is unimportant. Similarly with the tricks, illusions, and sleights of hand used by magical performers like shamans or mediums (pretending to suck objects out of people's bodies, throwing voices, eating glass). The classic text here being of course Levi-Strauss' "The Sorcerer and his Magic" (1967), about a young Kwakiutl man who learned shamanic techniques in order to expose their practitioners as frauds, but who ended up becoming a successful curer anyway. The point is always that while curers (for instance) can hardly help but know that much of what they are doing is stage illusion, they also think that since it does cure people, on some level it must be true. So again, the tricks are of no significance. Now there are good historical reasons why anthropologists have tended to take this attitude—the existence of missionaries being only the most obvious—but what if we were to turn things around and consider this skepticism as interesting in itself? Take attitudes toward curers. Evans-Pritchard says that at Zande seances, no one in the audience "was quite certain" whether or not the curer they were watching was a charlatan; I found this to be equally true in Madagascar. People tended to change their minds about particular curers all the time. But consider what this means. Curers, genuine or not, are clearly powerful and influential people. It means anyone watching a performance was aware that the person in front of them *might* be one whose power was based only on their ability to convince others that they had it. And that, it seems to me, opens the way for some possibly profound insights into the nature of social power.

Of course this doesn't mean such possibilities were necessarily realized in any way. But I think one can make a very good case that in many times and places, they are. Trickster stories, for example, often seem to be fairly explicit meditations on the relation between fraud, trickery, and social creativity. In Madagascar, this genre tends to focus either on wandering con men (who often pose as magicians) or political figures like usurping kings. Or on a much more mundane level: most people I knew in Madagascar considered it a matter of common sense that if a person really didn't believe in medicine, it wouldn't work on them. Very early on, for instance, I heard a story about an Italian priest sent there to take up a parish who, on his first day in the country, was invited to dinner by a wealthy Malagasy family. In the middle of the meal, everyone suddenly passed out. A few minutes later two burglars strolled in through the front door, and then, realizing someone was still awake, ran out again in fear. It turned out they had planted an *ody* in the house timed to make everyone in it fall asleep at six P.M. but since the priest was a foreigner who didn't believe in that kind of nonsense, it had no effect on him.

That much was common knowledge. Several people went even further and insisted that even if someone was using medicine to attack you, it wouldn't work unless you knew they were doing it.

Now, the first time I heard this it was from fairly well-educated people and I strongly suspected they were just telling me what they thought I wanted to hear. After all, it almost precisely describes the attitude of most people in America: that if magic does work, it is purely by power of suggestion. But as time went on, I met a number of astrologers and curers, people who had next to no formal schooling and clearly would have had no idea *what* Americans were supposed to think (one of them was actually convinced I was African), who told me exactly the same thing. And just about anybody would agree with this if you asked them in the abstract. Usually they would then immediately begin to offer all sorts of qualifications—yes, it was true, unless, of course, it was something they'd put in your food. Or unless it was one of those really powerful love charms. Or unless . . .

The bizarre thing is that this principle was utterly, completely, contradicted by practice. Everyone would agree to it, but no one ever acted as if it were true. If you got sick, you went to a curer. The curer would usually tell you that your illness was caused by someone using medicine of some kind and then, reveal who it was and how they'd done it. Obviously, if medicine can harm you only if you know someone is using it on you, the whole procedure would make no sense. In fact, the theory contradicts practice on almost every level. But if no one ever acts as if it were true, why did the theory even exist?

In a way, though, this is pretty much the same contradiction we've already seen in royal ritual and Tambiah's yam spell, except this time we're seeing it in reverse. People begin with an interpretation in which magical action has purely social effects, then immediately start qualifying and undercutting it. Nonetheless you have the same uncomfortable relation between two premises that are pretty clearly contradictory, yet in practice seem to depend on one another. After all, what would Malagasy society be like if everyone really did act as if medicine only worked if you believed in it, or if you wanted it to? Harmful magic—which is most magic—would simply cease to exist. But harmful magic obviously did exist: as one woman rather wistfully remarked to me, "I guess I must believe in it, because ever since I moved here to the countryside, I keep getting sick all the time." Perhaps one could say something similar about the nature of political power, or at the very least, of obviously coercive forms like the organization of a state. To a large extent, power *is* just the ability to convince other people that you have it (to the extent that it's not, it largely consists of the ability to convince them you *should* have it).[7] Now, even aside from the question of whether this means that the very nature of power is somewhat paradoxically circular, could there really be a society in which people acted as if they were perfectly well aware that this was the case? Would this not mean that power itself—at least in its nastier, most obviously harmful manifestations—would cease to exist, in much the same way as harmful magic would? One can almost imagine an earlier Malagasy farmer coming to the same conclusion about one of Bloch's bandit kings that my friend did about medicine: Well, I guess I must believe in them; or, in this case: they must really be emanations of my desire for a unifying power that will make us all members of the same unbroken kingdom, since after all, I do keep giving them unbroken coins.

magical and religious attitudes

One reason why anthropologists don't really like the word "magic" is that it is so closely allied to self-conscious illusions and tricks. It is no coincidence that when most people in America think of "magic" nowadays they think of men in tuxedos pulling rabbits out of hats. I am suggesting though that this is precisely what's interesting about it. It seems to me that insofar as the term "magic" is still of any use to anthropology, it would be best to define it around two features. First of all, that it is not inherently fetishistic, in that it recognizes that the power to transform the world ultimately goes back to human intentions. That is, even if alienated forces or invisible spirits of one sort or another are involved, the action always begins by some human intention and ends with some tangible result. Second of all, it always involves a certain degree of skepticism, a hesitation between stating that the power involved is something mysterious and extraordinary and that it is simply a matter of "social effects," which in some cases means simply being aware that power is sort of a scam, but that this doesn't make it any less real or significant.

One could easily reanalyze many of the examples in this chapter with this in mind. Boas' turn-of-the-century Kwakiutl informants, whose word for "ritual" was the same as that for "fraud" or "illusion," seemed to have some very magical tendencies in their way of thinking about social power. At the same time the ultimate origins of those powers were profoundly fetishized. The Maori sources on hidden *mauri* seem to hesitate between a magical and theological explanation: in some versions the power of the hidden talisman is that of the gods, in others (notably Ranapiri's), that of the priests. In either case, it's an estranged image of the human powers that are really responsible for generating social groups. And so forth.

Now the point of proposing this is not so that people can have a new excuse to enter into scholastic debates over whether a given practice is "magical" or "religious/theological." It would be much better to think of these things as attitudes, so that among those participating in a rite, different people might be thinking of it in diametrically different ways. The main point is that such an attitude at least opens the possibility for what can only be called a strikingly realistic way of thinking about the phenomena of social power. I have already shown how this takes form in Merina royal ritual, almost precisely to the degree that it draws on magical practice. Nor was this sort of attitude towards power limited to ritual. A famous example is King Radama I, who reigned in the first decades of the nineteenth century and was the first Merina ruler to have any real dealings with Europeans. According to most accounts Radama was an almost complete cynic. One of his favorite pastimes was trying to figure out and expose the tricks used by his own royal magicians. He never seems to have been especially comfortable in his dealings with missionaries, but apparently, he hit it off immediately with free-thinkers like his French portrait-painter Copalle, with whom he found himself in agreement on most issues. He told Copalle, for instance, that he felt religion was merely a political institution, and he seems to have believed it, given his subsequent decision to abandon royal ritual as soon as he was in possession of a modern, standing army.

A lot of anthropological theories would find it difficult to account for the very existence of such a person. Actually, ironically enough this is especially true of a strain of anthropological theory that comes directly out of debates about magic: that strain that develops out of Evans-Pritchard's suggestion

that the Azande were not able to question the very foundations of their own
mode of thought (1937:122), and that takes its most extreme form in some
of the arguments by Robin Horton, that people who believe in magic live in
a closed mental universe full of unfalsifiable propositions that can never be
challenged by empirical reality (unlike Westerners, of course, who are scientific and open-minded). Now it seems to me to the contrary that someone
like Radama is especially likely to come out of an environment dominated
by magic—that is, full of stories of wonders and trickery and constant speculation about different forms of personal power and manipulation, an environment in which the mechanics of power, the trap doors and mirrors, are
never completely out of sight.

One of the things I am trying to do here is to shatter some of the artificial
distance that so many anthropological theories end up often unintentionally
creating between observer and observed. I myself really doubt anyone, anywhere, is *unable* to question the foundations of their own thought; although
it's probably also true that the overwhelming majority of people in the world
also don't see any particular reason why they should. If there's any way to answer the question of why Merina royal ritual seems to be saying two such contradictory things, it would have to lie here. One might say that statements
like "Kings descended from the sky, except, not really" are about as far as one
can go in defetishizing power without creating some sort of discourse, some
way of talking and thinking about power, that is not itself entirely entangled
in the practice of power—or that at least aspires to stand apart from it. In
order to create these exterior spaces, however, one must *want* to do so. In
practice, it implies some sort of conscious program of social change. In the
absence of such a project, meditations on paradox or cynical remarks about
the pretensions of the powerful are all one is likely to get.

To say, as I have, that Merina ritual comes very close to an unfetishized
or social scientific understanding of the real nature of Merina kingship
might be a tiny bit deceptive since it does rather imply that it is *trying* to
achieve such an understanding, which of course it is not. Ritual is not trying to reach outside itself. For those involved, it's not ultimately all that important whether or not kings really did descend from the sky; what's
important is that they might as well have.

cthulhu's architect

When I speak of the limits of analysis, I don't mean to imply that people in
eighteenth- or nineteenth-century Madagascar were incapable of imagining
radically different political alternatives, and trying to bring them into being.
Revolutions did happen, ruling elites were sometimes ousted in popular up-
risings; there are groups on the West Coast, like the Vezo and Tsimihety, who

not only managed to resist being incorporated into the kingdoms of the region, but that appear to have created social orders that were in a sense egalitarian experiments designed in conscious opposition to them; even rural Merina, whom nineteenth-century observers described as utterly unquestioning in their loyalty to the queen, seem to have changed their opinions on the subject of royal power almost instantly after the monarchy was overthrown in 1896 and now tend to describe it, or any kind of power which some people the right to give arbitrary orders to others, as fundamentally immoral (Graeber 1995). Insofar as people did remain mystified, it doesn't seem to have made a great deal of practical difference. What I was referring to instead was the emergence of a fully self-conscious notion of social reality (a point I will return to shortly). But it does leave us with the rather surprising conclusion that if one is looking for unfetishized consciousness in non-Western societies, one of the most likely places to look is precisely around objects Westerners would be inclined to refer to as "fetishes." I suspect one reason has to do with the nature of revolutionary action itself—that is, if one interprets the word "revolutionary" in the broadest possible sense.

Consider some of the curious ambiguities, for instance, within Marx's thinking about revolutionary action. As I have noted in chapter 3, Marx assumes that human creativity and our critical faculties, are ultimately rooted in the same capacity for reflexive imagination. It is this that makes us human. Hence his famous example of the architect who, unlike the bee, raises her building in her own imagination before it is raised in reality. This is the ambiguity, though: while our ability to revolutionize emerges from this same critical faculty, the revolutionist, according to Marx, must never proceed in the same manner as the architect. It was not the task of the revolutionary to come up with blueprints for a future society and then try to bring them into being, or, indeed, to try to imagine details of the future society at all. That would be utopianism, and Marx has nothing but contempt for revolutionary theorists who proceeded along these lines.

Why the difference? Is it because the revolutionary break was to be so total, a leap into an entirely new stage of history? This is probably the simplest and most common explanation. One might say: that a revolutionist trying to design a new society would be like an architect trying to design a building to be constructed in a universe where the laws of physics would be entirely different. Or a medieval scholastic trying to imagine the workings of the New York Stock Exchange. Taking this approach leads to a series of familiar questions: How relativistic was Marx, really? How radical a break did he expect to come with socialism? Did he believe in the existence of any social or moral principles that transcended particular historical epochs? All this has been much debated. But there is another and, it seems to me, more interesting approach, which would be to forget the notion of a fundamental break and look at the question as one of scale. After all, any act of creativity is unprecedented and new to some degree. It's just that usually that degree is very small. So with architects: while each new design is to some degree unique and thus can be considered an expression of the architects' personal, creative vision(s)—and this is true to a limited extent even of, say, a traditional house in a traditional society built collectively—it is also obviously in another sense just a repetition of a familiar genre of activity. People design and build new buildings all the time.

What's more, such a project is always caught up in a larger series of practical categories, which are also essentially patternings of action. An architect may be given a great deal of artistic freedom in matters of design; he may even have a dramatic vision of an entirely new style; but if he were to decide that he was bored with the tedious bourgeois distinctions between residences, garages, and department stores, he would soon find that the designs raised in his imagination remained in his imagination, or at any rate got no further than blueprints, or sketches in avant-garde magazines. Creative action, one might say, is at any level encompassed within a larger system of actions in which it becomes socially meaningful—that is, in which it takes on social value. All creative action is to some degree revolutionary; but to be revolutionary to any significant degree, it must change that larger structure in which it is embedded. At which point one can no longer imagine one is simply working on objects, but must recognize that one is also working on people. And that system of action and meaning is, of course, always encompassed by another. We are dealing with a continuum. This does not mean that revolutionary social change with something of the same creative, intentional quality as the architect's is not possible; it does mean that it is a lot harder to get a handle on, because it proceeds through a far more subtle, collective media.

One could look at the same problem from the opposite perspective, too. If any act of creation is to *some* degree revolutionary (even if only to a very minor one: i.e., similar to that to which a fish is a unique individual), what does this revolutionary quality consist of? Presumably, it consists of the degree to which that act is unprecedented, and hence can be thought to belong particularly to its creator(s). But this also means that the creative or revolutionary aspect of action is also its historical aspect: at least if one accepts—as I do (Graeber 1995)—that an act can be considered historical to the degree to which it could not have been predicted before it happened. In every case we are talking about what seems, from the perspective of a system, to be "arbitrariness," but from the perspective of the individual, "freedom." Insofar as any system of actions is also historical, it is in a permanent condition of transformation, or, at the very least, potential transformation.

In chapter 3, I suggested that Marx's fetishism could be seen as a species of Piagetian egocentrism, a matter of confusing one's own particular perspective within a larger system with the nature of the system as a whole—of failing to coordinate the relevant points of view. To put it this way, however, would seem to imply, first of all, that the larger totality does in some sense exist and that it would be possible to know something about it. At the time I was careful to point out that this also need be true only to a limited extent: it is really quite impossible for anyone to be aware of all the perspectives one might have on a situation, or usually even those of everyone concerned with some particular situation (every member of a family, or a bowling club, let alone a marketplace). In most contexts, though, this doesn't matter, because in most contexts, one is dealing with things that happen over and over in pretty much the same way. Even if one cannot know how every actor in the marketplace actually sees things, if one understands the logic of the system, one can understand enough to know why, say, a given product has the value that it does. If so, it also follows that the more historical creativity is involved in a situation, the less this is the case. In a moment of profound historical change, no one involved could possibly know what the total system in question actually consists of. One is caught in what a Hegelian would call a moment of dialectical unfolding. Knowledge is necessarily fragmentary; totalities that the actors are working with are necessarily imaginary, or prospective, or numerous and contradictory.

What would all this mean for a theory of fetishism? Or value, for that matter?

When it comes to establishing value, one common response to such confusing situations is to circle off a space as a kind of minimal, defacto "society," a kind of micrototality, as it were. The potlatches I described in the last chapter might serve as one example of this sort of thing. Another would be the Homeric games analyzed by Beidelman (1989): chariot races or other contests in which warriors vied for a variety different sorts of prizes, usually looted from their enemies: fine armor, cauldrons of precious metal, comely slaves. Turner (1989:263–64) notes that in a case like this, there is simply no way to establish a common ground of value, in labor or anything else, by which to treat such objects as different proportions. The endless—and otherwise apparently somewhat pointless—games and contests between leaders of the army besieging Troy served (doubtless among other things) as circling off a field, creating a kind of imaginary miniature of Homeric society in which they could be treated as proportions of each other in the course of being ranked as first prize, second prize, and so on. As in the case of the potlatch, the presence of an audience is what makes it possible.

One could extend this sort of analysis to all sorts of other classical anthropological cases. What I want to focus on here is the peculiar role of objects in situations of historical agency—in particular those which, like money, serve as the medium for bringing into being the very thing they represent. Recall again the analysis of money in chapter 3. Money, in a wage labor system, represents the value (importance) of one's productive actions, at the same time as the desire to acquire it becomes the means by which those actions are actually brought into being. In the case of capitalism, this is only true only from the particular, subjective perspective of the wage-earner; in reality—that is, social reality—the power of money is an effect of a gigantic system of coordination of human activity. But in a situation of radical change, a revolutionary moment in which the larger system itself is being transformed, or even, as in the case of West African fetishes or so many Malagasy charms, a moment in which new social arrangements between disparate actors are first being created, this is not the case. The larger social reality does not yet exist. All that is real, in effect, is the actor's capacity to create it. In situations like this objects really do, in a sense, bring into being what they represent. They become pivots, as it were, between imagination and reality. Obviously, when a group of people takes an oath to create new rights and obligations among each other and call on an object to strike them dead if they fail to live up to those obligations, that object does not thereby acquire the power to do so. But in another sense, it—or the faith people place in it—really does have the power to bring a new social order into being. Here, perhaps Mauss was not entirely off the mark when he saw subject/object reversals as an integral part of the creation of social ties and obligation: the kind of social contracts whose subterranean history he was trying to bring to light.

conclusions

I ended my discussion of Merina royal ritual by suggesting that while magical attitudes can sometimes provide something surprisingly close to a social scientific perspective on social power, it is unreasonable to expect anything like a social science, any systematic attempt to decipher the nature of social reality—that is, to create a discourse that aims to stand outside the practices of power—actually to emerge except as part of a very particular kind of social project. One might even say, "utopian project." Historically, imagining there could be a discourse that would not partake of practices of power and inequality was closely related to imagining there could be a world that wouldn't. It is only at the point in history—roughly around the Enlightenment, the years leading up to the French and American revolutions—when one has a notion that it would be possible (or, perhaps more accurately, legitimate) to imagine what a new social order might be like, and then bring it into being, that a notion of social "reality" seems to emerge as well; as the other side, one could say, of a belief that one can (in the words of the famous slogan from May 1968) give power to the imagination.

This is a point that often tends to be overlooked by those who see anthropology as basically a product of imperialism. The emergence of what we call "social science" (at this point rather for lack of a better term) came about in an intellectual milieu that was not only marked by imperialism on a world scale but also obsessed with the possibility of revolution, its own sudden and dramatic transformation into something different. Certainly, it was the creation of vast European empires, incorporating an endless variety of social systems, that made modern anthropology possible. But this is hardly an explanation in itself. There had been plenty of multicultural empires in human history, and none, as far as we know, had ever before produced a project for the systematic comparison of cultural difference. In fact, even if we confine ourselves to the Western tradition itself, what evidence there is points if anything in the opposite direction. In the ancient world, one could make a case for example that something like anthropology was emerging in fifth century Greece, for example in the works of geographers like Hecataeus and historians like Herodotus. Certainly, such writers were developing ideas about how customs and mores might be systematically compared (Hogden 1964:21–43). This was during a period in which the Greek world was not even politically unified, let alone the center of a vast multicultural empire. When such empires did arise shortly afterward, this sort of literature disappeared: neither the Hellenistic empires nor Rome produced anything resembling anthropology. The reasonable explanation would seem to be that fifth century Greece was a period of political possibility: full of social experiments, revolutions, utopian schemes for the founding of ideal cities. Comparing social orders was one way to discuss the potential range for political (for Greeks the equivalent of saying "human") society. This clearly was not the case during the centuries of Roman rule. In fact, it would seem it was the very political fragmentation of fifth-century Greece which encouraged this kind of thought. Since the basic political unit was the city state, a relatively small community, the space for political experiments was in fact wide open: new Greek colonies, and hence political units, were in fact being founded all the time, new constitutions being mulled and created, old regimes overthrown.

This is not the way the story is usually told, of course. Most scholars, I suspect, if they were to make any notice of the first glimmerings of ethnographic inquiry at all, would probably see it as just one aspect of the rise of scientific inquiry: the same spirit of systematic comparison that Greek thinkers were applying to physics or geometry at the same time. I don't think this is necessarily wrong, but as so often, invoking the word "science" brings so many other issues to the table that it probably confuses more than it illuminates. More interesting, it seems to me, is to consider the possibility that the willingness to give power to the human imagination itself leads to a need to recognize a substratum of resistant "reality" of some sort (which must then be investigated). They are reverse sides, as it were, of the same process. It would at least make it easier to understand why so many of the most idealistic people in recent history have insisted on calling themselves "materialists," or at least how a commitment to some sort of materialism has so often accompanied the most daring utopian projects.

It might even be possible to document at least a loose connection between ethnographic curiosity and sense of political possibility, over the last five hundred years of European history. One could start in the sixteenth century, which saw both the first statements of what was to become modern relativism in authors like Montaigne, and a sudden burst of utopian speculation and revolutionary movements. During the century that followed both the curiosity and the sense of possibility fell somewhat into retreat in most places; only to be suddenly revived together in the years leading up to the French revolution. This was followed by another retreat during the reactionary years following Napoleon's defeat, and another, even stronger revival after the revolutions of 1848. It was the last period that saw the emergence of anthropology as a professional discipline. It is easy to forget how much the specter of revolution hung over European society of that time: even stodgy Victorians like Edward Tylor or Sir James Frazer were keenly aware of the possibility that their own society might be suddenly be transformed into something profoundly different. Most early anthropologists no doubt dreaded the prospect, a few might have even found it exhilarating,[8] but none could possibly have been oblivious to it. Rather than a perverse contemplation of some utterly alien and distant Other, then, early anthropology was inspired at least in part by the suspicion that someday one might wake up to discover that one had become the Other oneself.

We have, perhaps, a cluster of related elements: a sense of social possibility, a feeling that people should be able to translate imaginary schemes into some sort of reality; a concomitant interest in both understanding what the full range of human possibilities might be—as well as in the nature of "reality" itself. It hardly seems a coincidence that in the 1980s and '90s each of these three came under attack at exactly the same time. In some disciplines postmodernism came to mean abandoning dreams of mass action for revolutionary change, along with belief in any possible "foundationalism," any grounding in a resistant reality; in anthropology, it came to mean questioning that very comparative project. This was what was widely taken as radicalism at the time—and insofar as "radical" means getting to the root of something, then certainly it was radical in a sense. But one question that I have been asking over the course of this book is whether this is really the cluster of roots we should be attempting to pull out. For my own part, I think there is clearly another set that would make a far more convincing set of intellectual villains: a convergence between Parmenidean fixed forms, a certain extreme individualism that has long dogged the Western tradition, and the assumption that human nature is founded on essentially infinite, unquenchable desires, and that therefore we are all in a state of fundamental competition with one another (the latter an assumption that Marshall Sahlins has dedicated much of his career to exposing: see Sahlins 2001). Certainly these have been my main intellectual antagonists in this book: and they seem to me far more challenging ones, because they are all far more deeply embedded in ordinary common sense.

Marx versus Mauss—take two

Perhaps the most difficult challenge of all is to look at the world in what I've called Heracleitian or, if you prefer, dialectical terms. Over the course of this book I've argued that systems of categories, or knowledge, are really just one side of a system of action; that society is therefore in a sense always an active project or set of projects; that value is the way actions become meaningful to the actors by being placed in some larger social whole, real or imaginary. To adopt a dialectical approach means to define things not in terms of what one imagines them to be in a certain abstract moment, outside time, but partly by what they have the potential to become. It is extremely difficult to think this way consistently. But when one is able to, any number of seemingly impossible quandaries dissolve away. Let me take just one example before trying to tie things together more generally.

Levi-Strauss (1958) long ago pointed out one such profound quandary in the very notion of anthropological relativism: that while we reject the notion that some people are barbarians and insist that the perspectives of different groups are all equally valid, it almost invariably turns out that one of the first tenets of faith in most of those groups is that this is not the case. Hence the famous fact that most indigenous societies in North and South America referred to themselves by some term meaning "human beings" and to their neighbors by some term (cannibals, murderers, eaters of raw fish, etc.) that implied they were less than human. Levi-Strauss' own conclusion, that the only real barbarians are people who think others are barbarians, is so obviously circular that one has to assume it was meant as a kind of joke.

It was on the basis of this same kind of structuralism that Michel Foucault (1972) could then go on to argue that the very notion of "man" or humanity on which the human sciences are based is not really a universal category but a peculiar Enlightenment doctrine that will someday pass away. He attracted a lot of attention by doing so. But few have pointed out that the whole argument rests on an extremely Parmenidean, even positivistic way of thinking about conceptual categories. After all, the American societies that Levi-Strauss was originally discussing might have called themselves "human beings" and made it clear they felt other societies fell short, but most also prided themselves on their ability (like the Iroquois) to adopt children, or even adults, from other societies and turn them into proper human beings. There is no evidence that most thought they could do the same with fish or slugs. A universal category of humanity was in fact present then, but as a set of potentials, just as universalistic religions such as Christianity or Zoroastrianism or Islam—long before the Enlightenment—did indeed recognize a universal category of humanity in beings who had the potential to convert to Christianity or Zoroastrianism or Islam. One can apply the same logic to any number of other notorious problems. Universal ideas are not ideas that everyone in the world has, that's just false positivism; universal ideas are ones that everyone in the world would be capable of understanding; universal moral standards are not ones on which everyone in the world currently agrees—there is obviously nothing on which everyone agrees—but ones that, through a capacity for moral reasoning and experience of forms of moral practice that we already do share, we would be able to work out together and agree to (and probably will have to on some level if we are all to survive in the world), and so on.

It is because I think that anthropology is necessarily part of a moral project—in the past often not a very good one, but always potentially very good—that I have framed so much of this book around the dichotomy between Marx and Mauss, two men who were both fascinated by cultural difference and dedicated to the revolutionary transformation of their own societies. In most other ways they were diametrically opposed. Mauss was interested in finding a universal moral ground for a criticism of capitalism and looked to other societies for clues to the shape of institutions that might take its place; Marx dismissed any such critiques as inevitably partaking of the "petty bourgeois" morality of artisans and peasants and insisted that the role of knowledge in the revolutionary process was almost exclusively critical: a matter of understanding the internal contradictions and laws of motion of capitalism itself. His approach was in fact so relentlessly critical that he insisted it was impossible to find anything in the existing social order that could provide the basis for an alternative, except for the revolutionary practice of the proletariat itself, whose historical role, however, stemmed from the fact that as the one class that had absolutely no stake in the existing capitalist order, it could liberate itself only by that order's absolute negation.[9] Writing three quarters of a century later, Mauss had had the opportunity to observe how easily dismissals of petty bourgeois morality could degenerate into condemnations of "bourgeois sentimentality"—a phrase the Bolshevik leadership employed to dismiss anyone who objected on principle to murdering others in cold blood. He apparently ended up concluding it was precisely Marx's refusal to take popular, moral critiques of capitalism seriously that allowed so many of his followers to fall into a cold-hearted, cynical utilitarianism that was itself a slightly different version of the morals of the capitalist market. On the other hand, Mauss himself moved so far in the opposite direction that he ended up with conclusions that could be at times startlingly naive: for example, that aristocratic societies really did work the way aristocrats liked to pretend they did, or that capitalists could, given sufficient encouragement, end up being driven by their own competitive instincts to give their capital away.

The interesting thing about this dichotomy is that it never seems to go away. I have already had a bit to say, for example, about the fate of critical theory in the 1970s—what happens if one seriously tries to complete Marx's project of developing, as he put it in an early essay, a "ruthless critique of everything that exists." The likely result is a picture of the world so relentlessly bleak that in the end, criticism itself comes to seem pointless. On the other hand, as the debates over the exploitation of female labor in Melanesia, for instance, reveal, it's not clear that neo-Maussians such as Marilyn Strathern or Annette Weiner have been able to do much better on this account.[10] Where the Marxian approach would incline one to see the ultimate significance of any apparent instance of female autonomy or power to lie in the degree to which it contributes to the reproduction of a larger system in which women are subordinated, Maussians often end up denying the meaningful existence of any larger system at all. While feminist anthropologists are of course quite right to point out that male anthropologists have always tended to ignore female concerns and areas of female autonomy, if you take this approach to its logical conclusion, rather than seeing the problems as insoluble it becomes very difficult to demonstrate that a problem even exists.[11]

Obviously, the question is not whether it is necessary to come up with a compromise between these extreme positions; the question is how. Or perhaps even more, the question should be: What it is that drives otherwise sensible social theorists to take such oddly maximal positions in the first place? After all, most of us don't find it all that difficult to steer a path between cynicism and naiveté in our ordinary lives. Why should social theory, which can open our eyes to so many phenomena to which common sense is blind, also make us so blind to problems that actually do have common-sense solutions? I hope that if I have accomplished anything over the course of this book, it's to suggest where one might at least look for a solution: that much of the problem lies in the Parmenidean logic behind the very notions of "society" or "culture," which lead to irresolvable paradoxes between individual motivation and social form, and that an approach that begins instead from questions of value, creativity, and an open-ended layering of real and imaginary social totalities, might do much to help resolve them.[12]

perspectives: from meaning to desire

The appeal of market-based ideologies is not that difficult to understand. They draw on a picture of human nature and human motivation that lies deeply rooted in the religious tradition of the West, and that in our market-based society seems endlessly confirmed by everyday experience. It also has the advantage of presenting us with an extremely simple set of propositions. We are unique individuals who have unlimited desires; since there is no natural cutoff point at which anyone will have enough power, or money, or pleasure, or material possessions, and since resources are scarce, this means we will always be in at least tacit competition. What we call "society" is, if not pure obstruction, then a set of tools to facilitate the pursuit of happiness, to regulate the process, perhaps clean up after its mess.

Market principles can then be balanced, as need be, by their opposite: family values, altruistic charity, selfless devotion to a faith or cause—all principles that are, as it were, brought into being as complements to the pure psychology of "rational, self-interested calculation." These are as Mauss reminds us really just two sides of the same false coin. The key move, one might say, the most important ideological work in all this is done by extracting all the most fundamental questions of desire from society, so that it is possible to conceive of happiness largely as one's relations with objects (or at best, people one treats like objects): the moment it is necessary to have Rousseau to remind us that in fact, there would be no point in killing everyone else to attain their wealth because then there would be no one to know we had it, we have already long since lost the ideological game. And it is of course exactly this extraction that allows promoters of the market to claim to be acting in the name of human freedom, as simply opening the way for individuals to make up their own minds about what they want from life without anyone noticing that most of the individuals in question spend the vast majority of their waking hours running around at someone else's beck and call. It's a pretty neat trick if you think about it.

Much of the power of market theory stems from its very simplicity. It does contain within it a theory of human nature, a theory of desire, pleasure, freedom, and even, in its own way, a theory of society. The fact that in all these areas the argument is so simplistic as to be full of holes is, for ideological purposes, of almost no significance, particularly if no one is proposing a more coherent alternative. In fact, it often seems that all the other side has to offer (aside from all sorts of ingenious critiques) is a collection of scattered insights that, however brilliant, are drawn from such different theoretical traditions that it is impossible to make a coherent argument out of them. One problem I found myself running into fairly often while writing this book, for instance, was the lack of a theoretical language with which to talk about desire. Unless one is able to convince oneself that there really is a compelling reason to believe that language itself has a special affinity to one's father's penis, and is therefore willing to adopt the ideas of Jacques Lacan, or unless one is willing to adopt the Nietzschean approach adopted by authors like Deleuze or Foucault, which makes desire, or the desire for power, the fundamental constituent of all reality—a position that if carried at all far invariably seems to lead to truly bizarre conclusions, such as left-wing academics singing the praises of the Marquis de Sade—one is pretty much stuck. It's still possible, of course, to try to mine such theories for insights without endorsing the whole, as I did at the end of chapter 4 when I, effectively, tried to come up with a non-Freudian version of Lacan. But it must be admitted this was a pretty desperate maneuver. Surely there must be some alternatives.

That argument incidentally was distantly inspired by an early essay on fetishism by Jean Baudrillard, one which might be said to have taken Lacan's notion of "specular desire" to its logical conclusion. What is the reason, Baudrillard asked, for the profound sexual allure created by certain forms of complex personal adornment, say (as Levi-Strauss claims) by the intricate tattooing of Caduveo women, which leaves their faces covered with a complex maze of lines and symbols? Is it not because what really evokes desire, as with all fetish objects, is the existence of a kind of perfection, a self-enclosing systems of signs?

> What fascinates us is always that which radically excludes us in the name of its internal logic or perfection: a mathematical formula, a paranoiac system, a concrete jungle, a useless object, or, again, a smooth body, without orifices, doubled and redoubled by a mirror, devoted to perverse autosatisfaction. It is by caressing herself, by the autoerotic maneuver, that the striptease artist best evokes desire. (1981:96)

This is not perhaps a theory of desire so much as a theory of frustrated desire. It was largely in reaction to this sort of autoerotic model that Gilles Deleuze proposed we look instead to the polymorphous perversity of the infant; for him, desire becomes a kind of universal primordial force of production flowing in all directions between bodies and between bodies and the world (e.g., 1983:26–27). What we call "reality" is really its side effect. But even aside from the Nietzschean problems mentioned above, this isn't really a theory of desire at all—it's more a declaration of why one isn't necessary.[13]

At the beginning of this book I suggested that a theory of value might itself be able to produce an alternative. I think that such a theory at least points in some promising directions.

One of the key arguments of this book has been that what we call "structure" is not a set of static forms or principles but way in which changes—or in the case of social structure, action—is patterned; it consists, as Piaget (or Turner) would put it, of the invariable principles that regulate a system of transformations.[14] As such, it is a notoriously elusive thing. It is not elusive just because everyone tends to lose track of the way their own actions contribute to reproducing and reshaping themselves and their social context. It is also elusive because social performance is usually considered truly artful and accomplished—or even, competent—largely to the extent that it can make those structures—the templates, or schemas, or whatever you wish to call them—that lie behind it disappear. But even as they do so, those templates or schemas tend to reappear in the dislocated spectral form of imaginary totalities, and these totalities tend to end up inscribed in a series of objects that, insofar as they become media of value, also become objects of desire—largely, by representing the value of an actor's own actions to herself. The object in question might be almost anything: a ritual performance, an heirloom treasure, a game, a title with its associated regalia. The critical thing is that whatever it is, it can on some level be said to contain everything. Such objects imply within their own structure all those principles of motion that shape the field in which they take on meaning—in much the same way as, say, a household contains all the elementary forms of relation at play within a larger kinship system, even if at times in strange inverted forms. In any case, they become frozen images of those patterns of actions that in practice are called into being by the very fact that people value them; they are, as I said, mirrors of our own manipulated intentions.

Normally, these microcosmic tokens have a strange duality about them. On the one hand, they embody a closed perfection that tends to be, much as Baudrillard suggests, appealing in itself, and besides which the actor can only seem a lack, a wound, an absence, an abstract content to be completed by this concrete form. But hidden behind that glimmering image of perfection is almost always the awareness of something imperceptible, a looming absence of its own (this is, I suggested, why idioms of vision so often seem appropriate—a visual surface always implies something invisible beyond). This absence tends to be perceived not as a lack but as a kind of power. But the ultimate illusion, the ultimate trick behind this whole play of mirrors, is that this power is not, in fact, power at all, but a ghostly reflection of one's own potential for action; one's "creative energies," as I've somewhat elusively called them.

However elusive, creative potential is everything. One could even argue that it is in a sense the ultimate social reality. For me, this is what is really compelling about Bhaskar's "critical realism." Bhaskar suggests that most philosophers have been unable to come up with an adequate theory of physical reality because they see it as composed simply of objects but not what he calls "powers"—potentials, capacities, things that are of themselves fundamentally unrepresentable, and in most real-life, "open system" situations, unpredictable as well.[15] It seems to me it is quite the same with powers of social creativity. What makes creativity so confusing, to both actor and analyst, is the fact that these powers are—precisely—so fundamentally social. They are social both because they are the result of an ongoing process whereby structures of relation with others come to be internalized into the very fabric of our being, and even more, because this potential cannot realize itself—at least, not in any particularly significant way—except in coordination with others. It is only thus that powers turn into value. Many of the more striking rituals described in this book, from Iroquois dream-guessing to the mechanics of Malagasy *sorona* and *faditra,* could be seen as meditations on this notoriously difficult reality.

I would suggest that it is precisely this social aspect which that opens the way to what is missing in so much theory. It becomes even clearer if one moves from theories of desire to those of pleasure. Mauss and Marx both provide tantalizing hints (if only hints) of what a social theory of pleasure might be like: Marx, in the idea of unalienated labor, essentially a suggestion that the difference between taking pleasure in creativity rather than experiencing it as pain lies in the nature of the social relations in which it is embedded; Mauss, in his emphasis on "the delight in generous artistic expenditure, the pleasure of hospitality in the public or private feast" (1925 [1965:67]). One need only try to imagine a theory of pleasure that started from either of these in order to see how much the kind of pleasures market theorists seem to have in mind when they create their models of human behavior are fundamentally solitary ones. When market theorists think about a pleasurable, rewarding experience, the root image they have in mind seems to be eating food ("consumption")—and not in the context of a public or private feast, either, but apparently, food eaten by oneself. The idea seems to be of an almost furtive appropriation, in which objects what had been parts of the outside world are completely incorporated into the consumer's self. In fact, one doesn't even really need to start from Marx or Mauss: one need only imagine how different the theory might look like if it set off from almost any other kind of enjoyable experience: say, from making love, or from being at a concert, or even from playing a game.

It is a commonplace that pleasure involves a certain loss of self. Some (e.g., Scarry 1986) have gone so far as to argue that since pain is a phenomenon that tends to make everything but the hurting self vanish, pleasure should best be conceived as its opposite: if one's hand touches another person's skin, insofar as one feels that other skin, one is experiencing pleasure; insofar as one is feeling one's own hand, that's pain. This is perhaps an extreme formulation but in its broadest outlines, one suspects it would have made perfect sense to a seventeenth-century Iroquois, since in Iroquoian cultures, beauty and pleasure were seen above all as a matter of overcoming those obstructions that prevent the self from opening itself and expanding into the surrounding world and entering into communication with others. What strikes me as especially significant in the Iroquois formulation, though, is the presence of a principle of creation. In thanksgiving speeches, one does not merely list the features of the cosmos one by one, one describes their coming into being, the fact of their creation. I think one might even go so far as to say that in all the most sophisticated formulations, pleasure ends up involving not just the effacement of self, but the degree to which that effacement partakes of a direct experience of that most elusive aspect of reality, of pure creative potential (whether biological, social, or aesthetic—though the best sorts I suppose partake somewhat of all three)— that very phenomenon which, as the Holder of the Earth discovered, can, if one is entirely unaware of the larger social context in which it takes place, also produce unparalleled misery.

Notes

Chapter 1: pp. 1–22

1. In *Entangled Objects,* Nicholas Thomas even has a section called "value: a surplus of theories" (1991:30), though in it, he really cites only three.
2. Or at least, the more this is the case, the more chance there is that its predictions are accurate.
3. I might note in passing that this simplified presentation might seem like something of a straw man; most accomplished economists are considerably more subtle. But in fact, anyone who has taken introductory courses in, say, rational choice theory is likely to have found themselves face to face with precisely these sorts of arguments.
4. Similarly, power is often defined as the ability to influence other people's actions, which is again, not very similar to private property.
5. These have often been referred to in anthropological literature as "utilitarian approaches," a phrase made famous by Marshall Sahlins (1976). I've decided to use the term "economistic," because the meaning is more self-evident, and there's no danger of confusion with the specific nineteenth century doctrines.
6. Though it must be admitted that many of the economistically minded will try to take it as far as they can. Even the slightest reflection demonstrates that the mere fact that humans are biologically disposed to want food and sex means little in itself; after all, we can all think of forms of culinary or sexual experience that others crave, the infliction of which we would consider the direst punishment.
7. This seems to be a very crude popular version of the thought of nineteenth-century social thinker Herbert Spencer, whose work in scholarly circles is, oddly, considered utterly discredited.
8. Another way to imagine this would be to say each language begins with the complete color spectrum, and chops it up arbitrarily, assigning a word to each division. This is sometimes referred to as "slicing the pie" of reality.
9. Most subsequent authors called it "semiotics" instead.
10. A system that merely indicated that the steak-frites was worth more would, technically, be a ranking system. One that specifies precisely how much more adds an element of "proportionality."

11. Hence too politically: in France in the '60s, Structualists were famous for their political passivity, or even conservatism (since in practice being 'apolitical' usually means being moderately right wing).
12. Critiques are numerous; I have offered my own alternative model in Graeber 1997.
13. One might note that he has thus managed to add to a simple Saussurean model an element of ranking (but not one of proportionality).
14. This is not to say that Dumont is arguing all societies have these spheres exactly; it's simply an instantly recognizable illustration.
15. To take a more symbolic example from the Western tradition: while in the secular sphere, it is women who give birth to men (a clear gesture of encompassment), on the higher level of cosmic origins, it was the other way around, with Eve produced from Adam's rib.
16. In traditional societies, one cannot really speak of "individuals" at all. There is no clear distinction between subjects and objects; rather, actors themselves are made up of different aspects or elements that have different hierarchical values.
17. It served this purpose most famously in Edmund Leach's (otherwise not at all Formalist) *Political Systems of Highland Burma* (1954). In the Indian case power (*artha*) is not at all implicit, but a consciously articulated value (see Dumont 1970:152–66), though it still seems to me to stand on a quite different order than "purity."
18. In fairness, Dumont himself has argued that it is one of the advantages of his hierarchical, holistic approach that it does not make such clear either/or distinctions (1986:253–56), because hierarchies are inclusive not exclusive, and are defined by their centers and not their edges. But this seems largely a philosophical statement not much reflected in ethnographic practice.

Chapter 2: pp. 23–47

1. Another factor was the belated publication of Marx's own "Precapitalist Economic Formations," which also took a much more flexible approach than later Marxists had imagined.
2. In the French-speaking and Spanish-speaking world it has remained a much more prominent intellectual trend.
3. The debate between Marxists and Structuralists, then, was between the legitimacy of a critical perspective, the Structuralists taking up the relativist mantle and coming up with all sorts of arguments that Marxists really were ethnocentric after all. Marilyn Strathern, as we shall see, continues this tradition.
4. There has certainly been some discussion of Marx's terms "use value" and "exchange value" (e.g., Godelier 1978, Modjeska 1985, most notably, perhaps: Taussig 1980). I tend to agree with those who argue that "use value" and "exchange value" should best be used to describe the inner workings of a capitalist system, and not outside it.

5. This conclusion was already implicit in Durkheim's notion of "organic solidarity," in which social solidarity emerges from mutual dependence created by the division of labor.

6. Bourdieu even cites Polanyi on the lack of a "self-regulating market" (1977:183).

7. Bourdieu is pretty up-front about the fact that he is applying economic techniques of analysis to just about every field of human action—it is not that all fields are ultimately reducible to economics, he argues, but rather that those studying the economic field have done the best job in isolating certain processes and phenomena (competitive strategies, the formation of certain types of capital, etc.) that actually go on in every field, but are elsewhere, disguised.

8. This can of course be met with the usual objections: if one might as easily be maximizing wealth, or smiles, what's the point of describing it as "maximizing" at all?

9. Gnostic in the sense that it is assumed that the world we live in is utterly corrupt and unredeemable, and that the only salvation possible for humans lies in knowing this. It is only fair to note Bourdieu himself has more recently criticized Derrida for arguing that true gifts are by definition impossible, concluding that "the purely speculative and typically scholastic question of whether generosity and disinterestedness are possible should give way to the political question of the means that have to be implemented in order to create universes in which, as in gift economies, people have an interest in disinterestedness and generosity." (1997:240).

10. As it turned out, it was individual consumption, which is what prosperous academics were doing with their spare time anyway. Bourdieu, true to form, bucked the trend and immediately began critiquing consumption as reproducing inequality (1994).

11. As Marilyn Strathern has pointed out, 1992:171, cf. also Comaroff and Comaroff 1992:151.

12. "In a surprisingly wide range of societies . . . it is in the interests of those in power to completely freeze the flow of commodities, by creating a closed universe of commodities and a rigid set of regulations about how they are to move" (1985:57). He never mentions any cases in which powerful people try to increase the scope of exchange, or powerless ones, to limit it.

13. Though some of the essays in the collection do: notably Patrick Geary's superb discussion of the circulation of medieval relics (1986).

14. Similarly, where Levi-Strauss (1949) argued that men create society by exchanging their sisters with other men, in marriage, Weiner (1987) emphasizes "sibling intimacy," the degree to which even after marriage, men refuse to give their sisters up.

15. It traces back originally, perhaps, to the work of Roy Wagner (1975). It is hard to trace precise genealogies: in what follows, for instance, I emphasize the degree to which Strathern's theoretical models draw on Gregory's ideas; but Gregory has pointed out his own work was in large part inspired by Strathern's early ethnography (1975; see Gregory 1998:10).

16. Objecting to such a project on principle seems odd. The danger is if one mistakes the model for reality: for instance, taking exception to someone else's interpretation of a particular Melanesian exchange because "Melanesians" couldn't possibly think like that—although admittedly it's a temptation next to no one who develops this kind of model, Strathern included, seems entirely able to resist.

17. What really seems to really annoy most feminist critics, I think, is that in a work about gender that is 344 pages long, she feels this admission can be postponed until page 325.

18. It's not clear which of the two she is arguing; I tend to assume the latter, because there is some fairly strong evidence that even the Melpa-speaking people she takes as her primary example do recognize such a unique creative core (see e.g., A. Strathern 1979).

19. When reading Strathern, it helps to develop one's own glossary of Strathernian terms and the words a more conventional scholar would probably use in their place. Mine includes:

to elicit	to perceive
value	meaning (or importance)
compared to	distinguished from
enchainments	obligations
to coerce	to persuade, or make someone feel obliged to do something

20. This is inspired in part by a particularly Melpa idiom of "cause" and "origin" (though see also Errington and Gewertz 1987). The donor is the "cause" of the gift being given, while its "source" or "origin" is whatever, in that context, is seen as giving rise to it. These different sources or origins in turn are the reason why pigs that might be identical in size or other physical criteria are seen as different, and therefore of different value.

21. The Melpa according to Strathern make a distinction between work and exchange: the former is an expression of one's invisible "mind," or perhaps "will"; the latter, the manipulation of objects that are intrinsically visible— "on the skin." As a result exchange can create new relations, while work can only serve to reinforce ones that already exist.

22. Actually Gregory doesn't say this; but it's a minor point, as Strathern could just as easily argue that he should have.

23. Or even that they have a historical or productive relation.

24. People do it all the time. But there's little chance social scientists will be able to understand the precise bases of their decision, any more than one could create a model to predict which heirlooms someone is likely to salvage from a burning house.

25. Where we in the West tend to see domination as a matter of one party squelching another's subjectivity, and preventing them from acting, she argues, Melanesians see it as a matter of causing others to act. Hence the rather

odd way Strathern often speaks of acts of persuasion—notably, convincing another person to engage in exchange—as "coercion," as if they were tantamount to violence.

26. Or "transformational value," as she sometimes calls it.

27. As Strathern notes of Hagen pigs: "food fed to a pig by the wife is grown on land of the husband's clan, cleared by the husband, planted by the wife, and only an exogenous theory of labor extraction would hierarchize these mutual investments" (1988:162–63). One could expand the list of inputs endlessly: why not count the energy spent growing the food that fed the couple or of teaching them how to plant, or some tiny proportion of it?

28. Those who do tend to dwell on her use of phenomenology rather than her theory of value (e.g., Nicholas Thomas 1991; cf. Weiss 1996, Foster 1990, 1995).

Chapter 3: pp. 49–89

1. It's been a bit difficult for modern scholarship to figure out precisely what Heraclitus' position actually was; his ideas have to be pieced together through fragments or summaries preserved in the work of later authors who disagreed with them. It's not entirely clear whether Heraclitus ever actually said "you can't step into the same river twice"—Kirk (1962) suggested he didn't; Vlastos (1970) and Guthrie (1971:488–92), that he did, and that the phrase "on those who step into the same rivers, different and again different waters flow" does not reflect his original words. However, as Jonathan Barnes observes (1982:65–69, cf. Guthrie 1971:449–50) the debate rather misses the point, since this later gloss is in fact an accurate description of Heraclitus' position, as it can be reconstructed from comparison other fragments (notably his observation that the "barley drink," which was made up of wine, barley and honey, "existed only when it was stirred."). Heraclitus did not deny that objects exist continually over time; he emphasized that all such objects are ultimately patterns of change and transformation. It appears to have been Plato, in his *Cratylus,* who popularized the former interpretation, suggesting that if Heraclitus were correct, it would be impossible to give things names because the things in question would have no ongoing existence (McKirahan 1994:143).

2. Heraclitus of course was the intellectual ancestor of Democritus, founder of atomic theory, who argued that all objects can be broken down into indivisible particles that existed in constant motion. Marx, who harked back to this same tradition via Hegel, wrote his doctoral thesis on Democritus.

3. This "epistemic fallacy," he argues, underlies most Western approaches to philosophy: Decartes and Hume are two principal culprits.

4. One reason, perhaps, why Marx's dialectic, in however bowdlerized a form, proved to have such popular appeal. At any rate, Hegel's approach was to see models as always relatively "abstract," and hence "one-sided" and incomplete, compared with the "concrete totalities" of actual reality. All of the

dialectical tradition assumes that objects are always more complex than any description we could make of them.

5. This does not, incidentally, imply that such events cannot be explained ex post facto; Bhaskar also objects to the positivist assumption that explanation and prediction are ultimately, or should ultimately be, the same thing.

6. Of course, having bought the worker's capacity to work, what the capitalist actually gets is their "concrete labor"—whatever it is he actually makes his workers do—and this is how he makes his profit, because in the end workers are able to produce much more than the mere cost of reproducing their capacity to work, but for the present point this is inessential.

7. Note all of this is made possible by the existence of standards of what Marx calls the "socially necessary labor time" required to produce a certain thing: i.e., cultural understandings of what degree of exertion, organization, and so on that can determine what is considered a reasonable amount of time within which to complete a given job. All of this is spelled out very clearly on page 39 of *Capital* (1967 edition).

8. This is true even if one tries to work with some notion like "labor" (a culture-bound notion anyway); certainly it's true if one adopts a more abstract term like "creative energies," which are intrinsically unquantifiable. One cannot even say that a society has a fixed sum of these, which it then must apportion—in the familiar economic sense of "economizing" scarce resources—since the amount of creative potential floating around is never fully realized; it would be hard even to imagine a society in which everyone was always producing to the limit of their mental and physical capacities; certainly none of us would volunteer to live there.

9. Actually, either by dint of identity or simply by dint of learning, or otherwise acquiring certain powers through the process of action itself. "By thus acting on the external world and changing it, he at the same time changes his own nature" (Capital page 177).

10. Of course, in many forms of everyday action, one is hardly aware even of that. But Turner, like Marx, is concentrating on the sorts of action in which one is most self-conscious, so as to examine their limits.

11. Of course, Freudian ones as well; one reason, perhaps, they are so often paired as critical tools of unusual power.

12. Though false insofar as those who have this partial consciousness do not recognize its partiality.

13. Piaget in fact argues that structuralism in the social sciences made a profound mistake in taking Saussurean linguistics for its model, since language, practically alone among social forms, is based on an utterly arbitrary code that can therefore be seen to stand entirely apart from practice. It is this that allows Saussure's famous distinction between langue and parole. In almost every other domain of human activity it would be impossible to even talk about a "code" except in terms of practice (Piaget 1970:77–78).

14. So Sahlins 1976:121n49; Bloch (1989:115–16) is only a tad more generous.

15. " . . . first in sensory-motor action and then practical and technical intelligence, while advanced forms of thought rediscover this active nature in the constitution of operations which between them form efficacious and objective structures." (1965 [1995]:282). As with so many such authors, Piaget develops his own unique terminology, which requires no little study to master fully.

16. This is actually derived a theory of education that assumes that children are always capable of learning tasks and generally operating on a level one step more advanced than they can explain, or in fact, have fully internalized. But one could easily adopt the idea to adult operations as well.

17. As Turner notes (1979c:32): in our own society, it is common at weddings to acknowledge that individual marriages are created by real-life men and women but assert that the institution of marriage was created by God.

18. Piaget himself never much elaborated on the similarities between Marx's ideas and his own (but cf. "Egocentric and Sociocentric Thought," 1965 [1995:276–86]), but he made it clear that he was working in the same dialectical tradition. That egocentrism tends to involve an inversion of subjects and objects similar to that which Marx thought typical of fetishism is a theme that recurs throughout his work. He makes the interesting observation, for example, that children have a systematic tendency to describe almost every feature of the physical world as if it had been instituted by some benevolent intelligence for their benefit; though of course, from a Marxist perspective, this is not entirely untrue, as it is precisely the means by which everything in our environment has been designed for our convenience in one way or another that becomes disguised by the market, leading to very similar attitudes on the part of many adults.

19. Actually in this case, technically, "abstract labor" or the worker's capacity to labor—which is formed in the domestic sphere in ways that are effectively invisible from the sphere of production, just as much as the work that formed the product becomes invisible from the other side (see diagram below).

20. The one exception are certain elaborate and beautiful masquerades, about which, however, they offer no exegesis, dismissing the whole business simply as "play." I might remark in passing that as anarchist societies go, they fall about as far as one can go on the collectivist (as opposed to individualist) side of the spectrum.

21. As for example in the debate in Russian psychology about the minimal units of analysis, starting with Vygotsky, and running through later "Activity Theory" (see Turner and Fajans 1987).

22. He has been known to refer to it as a "minimal modular unit of articulation," which admittedly lacks a certain elegance. According to Turner this concern with the minimal unit of structure also helps explain Marx's approach to Capital, in which the factory fulfills a similar role.

23. "Beauty" is a quality which the Kayapo attribute to things or actions which are complete, in the sense of fully realizing their essential nature. potential, or intended goal. "Completeness" in this sense thus has the connotations of

perfection," and also, considered as action, of "finesse." Ceremonial activity, properly and fully performed, is "beautiful," but the capacity to perform certain of its most essential and specialized roles, like the distribution of its most prestigious valuables, is not evenly distributed in the society." (Turner 1987:42).

24. The term translated "chief" in fact literally means "those allowed to chant."
25. Their new status can be seen as a proportion of the totality of social labor time, as measured by those units, though in this case in an infinitely less complicated sense. This is because the young adults are the products of two consecutive cycles of social production, and the elders, of three.
26. Incidentally, this does not mean that all systems of value most be socially invidious: it just means a distinction must be made. The comparison could also be made, say, in temporal terms, between a previous state in which one did not have said value, or a future on in which one might not.
27. As in most societies, it's not even something that human beings feel they are themselves really responsible for.
28. A process that, we have seen, tends to have emergent properties not entirely comprehensible to the actors involved. This is actually quite similar to Roy Bhaskar's "transformational model of social action" (1979:32–41), though the latter is formulated much more broadly.
29. Strathern does acknowledges this in a sense when she says that the "aesthetic" rules according to which some things are recognized as valuable and others not tend to become invisible in a gift economy. In this way, she suggests, it is the opposite of a commodity economy, in which the external forms of the objects are all that are stressed and the human relationships involved disappear. This is to my mind a fascinating suggestion, quite brilliant actually, but it does rather dodge the question of how that aesthetic code is produced and reproduced to begin with. Probably this is inevitable considering the British social anthropology tradition in which she is working: it has always insisted on a clear divide between "culture," seen as a set of expressive meanings, and "society," seen as a web of interpersonal relations—which in the American cultural anthropology tradition tend to be seen as two aspects of the same thing. Strathern has little use for either "society" or "culture" as explicit concepts; but she ends up reproducing the division between in her distinction between the social relations, which people are consciously trying to reproduce, and the hidden "conventions of reification" that determine which forms (a pig, a shell, a woman's body) can embody certain types of social relations and which cannot (compare, e.g., Leach 1954).
30. Or more likely, perhaps, different ones that exist on different social levels.
31. As the example should make clear, I am talking not merely about the physical properties of the media (though these do indeed make a great deal of difference), but also the ways in which they are used. "Abstraction" is not a physical quality.
32. Obviously this is a total simplification: I am, in effect, fusing all sorts of social organizations in which people realize themselves personally into the "do-

mestic sphere," ignoring the fact that formal education is separated from the home, and so on. But such simplifications can sometimes be useful, always provided one does not confuse them with reality.

33. It does, as Strathern puts it, tend to "eclipse" all the other, less dramatic actions involved.

34. The Baining, after all, seem to be remarkably nonindividualistic egalitarians; for the Kayapo, egalitarianism does not seem to be all that important a factor.

35. Indeed, almost by definition, since states are normally defined by the systematic use of force.

36. Dumont obviously likes hierarchy and feels that modern, individualistic/egalitarian societies are in some sense abnormal or even perverse—though he also seems to feel that it is impossible to get rid of them (see Robbins 1994, especially his amusing conclusion, "what does Dumont want?").

Chapter 4: pp. 91–115

1. If one consults the anthropological literature on "relations of avoidance," and formal relations of deference more generally, one reads over and over about contexts in which one must not gaze directly, or at all, at those in authority or at least not do so until they have first gazed at you. I suspect this principle shows up, in some form, everywhere—despite the fact that there are usually other contexts in which staring at these same figures of authority is what one is expected to do (cf. Graeber 1997a).

2. Hence, he says, the artistic stereotype of the woman staring in a mirror.

3. A telling example is to be found in Nancy Munn's analysis of Gawan notions of "beauty" and its role in kula exchange (1986:101–103). For Gawans, she says, display is held to be intrinsically persuasive: "the beautified person persuades by exhibiting his or her persuasive potency as a visible property of the self" (103). In this case the effect is to make others want to give the beautified person kula valuables—objects of decoration similar to those with which one beautifies oneself. I note this analysis is entirely in keeping with that of aristocratic display developed below.

4. This at least is the aristocratic ideal. In reality, of course, no king has ever relied exclusively on display to convey his authority. Such techniques work only insofar as they are combined with more active forms of persuasion. I am perfectly well aware that the theoretical dichotomies I am mapping out here, like most theoretical dichotomies, do not anywhere exist in their pure forms—that in reality, the exercise of power will always require an ability both to act on others and to define oneself. But degrees vary. Even more, certain types of people—whether bourgeois males, feudal monarchs, or whatever—will always tend to identify themselves (and be identified) with certain characteristic ways of exercising power more than with others.

5. As Finley points out, "no money-changer gave a better rate for a four-drachma Syracusan coin because it was signed by [the famous artist] Euainetos" (1974:167).

6. Or dominance behind beauty, and so on.
7. When one looks in a mirror, of course, one is looking at an image of oneself reflected in some other object. So one could say there is an immediate affinity between mirror images and "adornment to the person," in the sense in which I have been using the term: both have to do with an extension of one's self or person into some thing outside one's body, in a form that can only be realized by being seen (on beads and mirrors, see J. and J. L. Comaroff 1992:170–97; Hammel 1983).
8. Madagascar was exploited as a source of labor for European plantations in Mauritius and Reunion.
9. Beads were apparently no longer in use as a medium of exchange by this time—that it is, if they had ever been, in Imerina itself.
10. Called *vola tsy vaky*. Remember that money was usually used cut up into smaller divisions.
11. This applies both to its actual history and to the history ascribed to it by those who consider it valuable.
12. I would not want to suggest that all desire is necessarily fetishistic. In fact, it might ultimately be possible to make a distinction between metaphoric and metonymic desire: only in the first, then, would the desired object become an imaginary representation of the wholeness of the desirer's self. Allowing for the possibility of the second would also allow for the possibility that one could wish to unite with other persons or things because of their actual differences rather than their imagined similarities. I might note that this would be in accord with Lacan's own thinking: he always treated the imaginary or "specular" as an inferior, pre-Oedipal level of desire in relation to the more indexical sort that comes with language.

Chapter 5: pp. 117–149

1. "Mohawk" in fact is from an Algonkian word meaning "cannibal." "Iroquois" seems to be derived from one for "killer."
2. This was the period in which wampum was no longer playing the role of currency among settlers: as of circa 1652–54, it was no longer recognized as legal tender in the English colonies. The Dutch kept using it, but the English then began to dump supplies for fur and Dutch goods to create a severe inflation in the New Netherlands.
3. Among the Huron, at least, there was one aspect of a person's "soul" that was said to be reborn when the name was resurrected; another that ascended to an otherworldly village of the dead (Heidenreich 1978:374–75). I have not been able to find any information exactly paralleling this from Iroquois sources.
4. Later a sixth, the Tuscarora, was added on, but only in a subordinate, non-voting capacity.
5. Whether through giving him the victim's name (as with the Huron) or through the giving of a belt, we are not told.

6. Eric Wolf makes a great point of this (1982:168–70): in no major conflict in which they were involved did all of the nations of the league even take the same side.

7. In the absence of wampum, other gifts could be substituted, such as hatchets or beaver pelts (Snyderman 1954:474; Druke 1985). The crucial thing was that some object had to change hands. But all sources agree that wampum was the proper gift; at times, parties to negotiations who did not have any wampum on hand would simply give sticks as a pledge for wampum to be provided later.

8. The formal speeches may have been inspired to some degree by missionary influence (Fenton, personal communication, 1999), but almost all Iroquois rituals can be seen as thanksgiving rituals in one way or another.

9. For two recent treatments of the epic, with full background on the various extant versions, see Dennis 1993, chapter 3; Fenton 1998, chapters 5–6.

10. One purple belt was worth two white ones, since the purple beads were more rare. In exchange with European settlers the logic of supply and demand still held, so white beads were worth less, despite the fact that they were held to convey the highest value in Iroquoian terms. Over time most of the pelts arrived as tribute as well.

11. Hallowell 1960:52; Elisabeth Tooker (1979b) agrees.

12. Some dreams implied dangers not just for the dreamer but the community as a whole, or alternately were seen as prophecies: hence, if a man dreamed of being burned to death by enemies, it was often felt necessary to carry out some kind of milder version of this fate, so as to prevent it from happening for real. I note in this case the desire appears to be not the dreamer's soul but the Creator's.

13. Wallace too notes that the "soul," the inner invisible aspect of the person is identified with intentions and desires, though the terms for this are continuous with those for the talismans given to satisfy them (Hewitt 1885:113).

14. This is most explicit among the Onondaga (Blau 1962) but appears to be a general principle even in places where dream-guessing is no longer such an important part of the ceremonies (e.g., Fenton 1936:17–18, Speck 1949:122, Shimony 1961:182–83).

15. It's much less pronounced in contemporary material; it appears primarily in the antics of the False Face society, whose members were drafted by means of dreams on a cross-moiety basis (e.g., Fenton 1936:17).

16. For example, a young man's brothers would probably be scattered across different clans and his father would belong to the opposite moiety.

17. Though of course women could also be the immediate cause of war, since when someone died, it was usually their female relatives who would demand a mourning war (cf. Dennis 1993:109–10).

18. The obvious exceptions were name belts and strings; still, the more generic forms, the closest to the raw power to create political realities, seem to have been exchanged almost entirely between men.

1. Davy had published *Foi Jurée,* an investigation of the legal basis of the Northwest Coast potlatch, a few years earlier, in 1922. Elsewhere (1921b:388) Mauss claimed that they had been working on the problem "since well before the war."

2. Some trace the notion back to Ralph Waldo Emerson's essay, "gifts" (1844), which also contains a description of the degree to which someone receiving a gift often feels to have undergone a kind of assault, which can be put right only by returning something of equal value. Mauss in effect fused these notions together.

3. Maurice Godelier (1996 [1999:63–64]) describes Mauss as a "staunch anti-Bolshevist" and social democrat. But Godelier was writing before the republication of Mauss' political writings in 1997, which show his profound ambivalence about the Russian revolution, and the fact that, in many ways his political vision was closer to that of anarchists like Proudhon than his mentor Jaurès.

4. Mauss also felt it was tactically disastrous: "Never has force been as badly used as by the Bolsheviks. What above all characterizes their Terror is its stupidity, its folly" (1923).

5. 18 November 1922, p. 1–2 (Fournier 1997:472–76).

6. The point should not, perhaps, be overstated. *Capital* had long been available in French, and members of Durkheim's circle had at one point created a reading group to discuss it. Mauss himself seems to have become more familiar with Marx's ideas later in his life, when he became interested in the question of techniques. Some of his pronouncements on the subject seem clearly inspired by Marxian notions of praxis: for instance, "Man creates and at the same time he creates himself; he creates at once a means of livelihood, purely human things, and his thoughts inscribe in these things. Here is elaborated true practical reason" (in Schlanger 1998:199). Still, I am particularly concerned here with Marx's ideas of alienation, which are developed especially in his earlier work, and with which Mauss does not appear have been very familiar. At least, I have been unable to find any reference to "alienation" in the Marxist sense in Mauss' published work (1968–69, 1997).

7. If they were unidirectional, he remarks, they would generally cancel out in the end, so that A takes from B, B from C, C from D, D from A again. The influence on Levi-Strauss' later conception of "generalized exchange" (1949) is obvious. Another of Mauss' concepts in his lectures, "alternating reciprocity," in which one repays what one's parents has given one by doing the same for one's children, has not received the same attention.

8. One might compare Jonathan Parry's observations on the gift in Hinduism (1986); he see suggests that the emergence of universalistic religions tends to lead to an ideal of unrepayable gifts. On Islam, see Dresch 1998.

9. For a typical dismissal from a knee-jerk right wing point of view see Mary Douglas (1990).

10. Schwimmer goes so far as to suggest that these are also two poles of a Maori philosophy. Since everyone descends equally from the gods, the question arises of how differences between species came about; why they have different *tikanga* or natures; the answer is the universality of strife.

11. Most of these examples are actually derived from White (1885:197–98), who also provides a long list of factors that might be invoked when a tribe or *hapu* lays claim to a particular stretch of land: among others, that members ancestors are buried there, or died there, or won or lost battles there, or committed famous deeds there. Actions too, then, could contribute to the process whereby property was assimilated to a person's unique identity.

12. Similarly, a troublemaker could curse a local chief by calling someone else's pigs by that chief's name; if the chief heard this had happened, the only way to salvage his honor would be to arrive with military force to take the pig; hence, its owner would usually feel obliged to hand the pig over as soon as the chief was cursed.

13. What's more, food rather than heirlooms constituted the principle material of exchange: see Polack 1840 II:159.

14. Best's translation, with various changes based on Bruce Biggs' (in Sahlins 1972:152), and Grant MacCall's (1982) and others'.

15. E.g., cooked food was incapable of any further growth or "unfolding of its own nature" (*tupu*), and could serve only to be incorporated within and hence aid in the growth of something else.

16. Just as to be *tapu* means, among other things, "beyond one's power, inaccessible" (Williams 1844:450).

17. Actually the word *taonga* could be used for anything one treasured, not only for heirlooms, for which the more appropriate term seems to have been *manatunga* (Johansen 1954:100, see Williams 1844:202, 445). Weiner claims Ranpiri felt only *taonga* had a *hau;* actually, even return gifts for food were called *hau* (viz. Mauss: 1965:90–91n31).

18. Firth notes (1959:93) that one of the chief of a tribal *ariki* was the guardianship of such tribal heirlooms, along with the oversight of the *mauri* of forests and fisheries (cf. Johansen 1954:106).

19. Generally it was said that only aristocrats could make such precious objects, but as we've seen this did not really exclude much of the population. For a notable exception, see Stirling 1976:162. In part, the fact that artists are not remembered follows from the nature of Maori exchange. Craftspeople, like priests who provided ritual services, or tattooers, were repaid with gifts that seem to have effected a definitive alienation (Firth 1959:299–304; 413–14; cf. Thomas 1991).

20. Since, as the proverb has it, he was a stingy man.

21. Note how after all that he felt he had no choice to refuse a direct request; though in his situation he probably already considered himself heavily in their debt.

22. My summary follows Kelly 1949:223–227, 275–77; Jones 1995:260–71, 360–61.

23. I could find no evidence in Te Whata Karaka's recorded genealogy that he was a descendant of Pakaue, so it was in a sense just given to Waikato, in the person of its chief.

24. Like so many hunter-gatherers, the Kwakwaka'wakw alternated between scattered settlements in the summer and large concentrated settlements in the winter, which was also the ceremonial season.

25. Only the first four children, of whatever sex, were said to inherit their parents' noble status; the fifth was considered a "slave"—though in practice this seems to have meant a commoner.

26. More likely only the lids would be transferred, and the rest rebuilt for the new owner. Note how similar this is to the transmission of titles: it's really the name that's passed on, and new physical entities are created to inherit it, and become in effect new embodiments of the original.

27. Since family histories and other more detailed accounts invariably provide all sorts of titles not included in those paradigmatic lists, it seems obvious the real number of titles—or at least, potential ones—was far larger.

28. Helen Codere argued that the overall ranking system emerged only in the end of the nineteenth century, when the Kwakiutl became concentrated around Fort Rupert and began using their newfound access to wealth as a way of competing over status.

29. Since these were, however, all male names, women could hold them only as a sort of honorary male, or in trust for their children; even during the period of worst demographic collapse, when the number of noble males was far below that of available titles, it was quite unusual for a woman to be allowed to succeed to such a title.

30. These were, however, still considered separate personalities for potlatch purposes, and would, for instance, receive their share of distributed property separately.

31. Wolf 1999:77 cites figures suggesting the population fell from perhaps eighty-five hundred in 1835 to roughly a thousand around the turn of the century.

32. The one notable exception for the Northwest Coast is Kan 1989:49–75.

33. Such crests were particularly prominent on chiefly houses, thus representing the house itself as a kind of external body of the *numaym,* in which all members were in a certain sense encompassed in the personality, the form-soul, of its Founder, and his living representative.

34. Hence, when mythical animals strip off their disguises and become humans, they are only showing another surface, much like the masks within masks.

35. Neither are women's titles, which do exist. Each *numaym* has a number of noble titles reserved for females, but unlike the male titles, these are considered unique and incommensurable.

36. Potlatches were also held to make up for embarrassing accidents: for example, if a noble child was injured playing, or fell out of his canoe, his parents would normally distribute property by way of compensation.

37. In part, of course, because rank could not be changed, or not so easily. The relative standing of different tribes and *numayma,* and hence the rank of their respective titles, could be altered by potlatching but this seems to have been extremely difficult to effect. Of course, as in most such systems, there was no absolute unanimity on exactly how matters stood at any time.

38. The notion that there are two sorts of copper, one more valuable, and kept within clans (Weiner 1992:164n11,180n1; Godelier 1999:59–60), appears to be based on Mauss' misreading of some material in Boas (1897:564, 579; Mauss 1991:194n245).

39. Barnett (1938) suggests this was really derived from the custom of what he calls the "face-saving potlatch," in which one gives up or destroys wealth to compensate for some slight or indignity, say, falling from a canoe. Similarly, if a guest stumbles on one's way into a host's house, he'll normally give a blanket or two.

40. Breaking coppers was a particularly effective way for nobles to squash those they considered upstart commoners trying to elbow their way into potlatching; the early twentieth century literature is full of this.

41. Margaret Weiner refers to this as the excalibur principle: "whosoever bears this sword is henceforth king" (1995:67).

42. Hence we are even obliged to pretend that hack politicians got where they are mainly because of their personal qualities. (Incidentally, it is my understanding that B. B. King has gone through quite a number of Lucilles over the course of his career. Having such a famous object in a situation like this actually creates enormous pressures to dispose of it: to auction it off for charity, for example, or give it away in a spectacular gesture. Some of this pressure I suspect comes from the need to reestablish that it is indeed inner capacities that are at the root of one's identity, and not such emblems or historical artifacts.)

43. See here the literature on Maori feasting: e.g., Firth 1954, chapter 8.

44. In fact, Mauss sometimes stressed the obligation to repay gifts; at other times, he stressed that there were three important obligations: the obligation to give, the obligation to accept, and the obligation to repay. As Alain Testart has noted (1993, 1999), "obligation" has a number of meanings in French and it's not clear if Mauss meant a feeling that one ought to, or a duty with actual sanctions. In any case, it should be clear even from the material already presented in this chapter that these three obligations are rarely equally weighted: Maori gifts, for instance, usually did not have to be accepted, but they did have to be returned; among Kwakwala speakers one had to give, but usually there was no obligation to repay.

45. Moieties usually imagine themselves as standing in such a relation, even when, as in the Iroquois, they have not actually done so for a very long time.

46. Sahlins therefore concludes that most hierarchical relations fall under the rubric of "generalized reciprocity," though to my mind this is yet another example of the dangerous ambiguities of the term "reciprocity" itself: I

would say that in any meaningful sense, most such relations are not reciprocal at all.

47. In fact, they would become in a rather paradoxical way equivalents again, at least by default.

48. One might argue that by "more individual" I really mean "differ from others of the same class among more dimensions (that are considered important)." The incommensurability, it might then be argued, comes from the very number of those dimensions, in the way that one cannot say one person is more intelligent than another if intelligence is really made up of hundreds of different sorts of incommensurable scales. But this assumes that those dimensions themselves could, at least hypothetically, be measured, which strikes me as in itself somewhat positivistic.

49. It can become a bit confusing because even the most unequal relations usually *can* be represented as somehow reciprocal by the actors involved, when they want to represent their societies as ultimately just. Usually, however, this sort of rhetoric is appealed to only in certain very specific contexts, and even then, one is never sure how seriously the actors themselves take it.

Chapter 7: pp. 229–261

1. See William Pietz' famous essays on the "problem of the fetish" (1985, 1987, 1988; MacGaffey 1994).

2. Like that of the "take-off states" that grew out of them, whenever one local lord managed to begin organizing large-scale public works, usually by having his followers drain swamps and create irrigation works, then parceling out the new land to families that became his immediate retainers.

3. *Hery* is the word for simple force, but it is applied especially to things like moving rocks or hitting people on the head; *hasina* is force that works in less tangible ways.

4. In practice, to his local representative. The actual amount afforded on such occasions was considerably less than a silver dollar; in fact it was a very modest fee, but it was called *hasina* nonetheless.

5. Marx himself did seem to rather approve of magicians, at least in the bedtime stories he told his daughters, as the epigraph to the chapter would indicate.

6. Tambiah himself eventually moderated his position somewhat in grappling with such cases (esp. 1992).

7. Even when power is purely violent and repressive, it is still a matter of convincing those who have weapons or are otherwise part of the apparatus of repression.

8. Lewis Henry Morgan dreamed of a civilization in which private property would no longer be the dominant institution; Alfred Haddon was a socialist; Radcliffe-Brown was known in his undergraduate days as "Anarchy Al."

9. Geoghegan (1987:22–34) gives a useful summary of the historical relation of Marx and Engels to utopian thought, one that turns out to be far more ambivalent than is usually represented. For Marx's reaction to moral cri-

tiques, especially that of Proudhon (an important intellectual ancestor of Mauss' socialism) see Thomas 1980:175–248.

10. Weiner also makes it clear that her approach is inspired largely by Mauss, certainly more so than Marx. It would probably be unfair to say that Weiner denies that women are in any sense subordinated, since she does not explicitly do so; on the other hand, like Strathern she devotes all her energies to attacking arguments by others that state or imply that they are.

11. This is in fact a constant dilemma in feminist anthropology—and the only reason it's so much easier to see it in this case, I suspect, is that feminist anthropology is one of the few areas of anthropology that remain politically engaged.

12. No doubt the systematic application of such an approach would throw up all sorts of irresolvable paradoxes of its own. It would be naive indeed to imagine that it wouldn't. But at least there is good reason to believe that these irresolvable paradoxes would be more fruitful ones.

13. At least a theory about why desire is different from anything else. One could say much the same of Foucault's theory of power.

14. Not even the board on which checkers can move around, but even more, the principles that tell us which marks on the board are important and why.

15. Until, of course, after they've been realized. From this perspective might one say that desire is not the fundamental constituent of reality, as in the Nietzschean version, but rather a metaphor for potential, which is.

References Cited

Ahern, Emily
    1979   "The Problem of Efficacy: Strong and Weak Illocutionary Acts." *Man* (n.s.) 14 no. 1:1–17.

Akins, David and Joel Robbins
    1999   "An Introduction to Melanesian Currencies: Agencies, Identity, and Social Reproduction." In *Money and Modernity: State and Local Currencies in Melanesia* (David Atkins and Joel Robbins, eds.), pp. 1–40. Pittsburgh: University of Pittsburgh Press.

Albert, Ethel
    1956   "The Classification of Values: A Method and Illustration." *American Anthropologist* (n.s.) 58:221–248.
    1968   "Value Systems," in *The International Encyclopedia of Social Sciences* (David Sills, ed.), vol. 16, 287–91.

Anderson, Perry
    1974a   *Passages from Antiquity to Feudalism.* New York: Verso Press.
    1974b   *Lineages of the Absolutist State.* New York: Verso Press.

Angas, George French
    1847   *Savage Life and Scenes in Australia and New Zealand.* 2 volumes. London: Smith, Elder and Co.

Appadurai, Arjun
    1986a   "Introduction: commodities and the politics of value." In Arjun Appadurai (ed.), *The Social life of Things: Commodities in Cultural Perspective,* 3–63. Cambridge: Cambridge University Press.

Archer, Margaret, Roy Bhaskar, Andrew Collier, Tony Lawson, and Alan Norrie, eds.
    1998   *Critical Reason: Essential Readings.* New York: Routledge.

Babadzan, Alain
    1993   *Les Dépoulles des dieux: Essai sur la religion tahitienne à l'époque de la découverte.* Paris: Maison des Sciences de l'Homme.

Barnes, Jonathan
1982   *The Presocratic Philosophers.* New York: Routledge.

Barnett, Homer G.
1938   "The Nature of the Potlatch." *American Anthropologist* 40:349–58.
1968   *The Nature and Function of the Potlatch.* Eugene, Oregon: Department of Anthropology, University of Oregon.

Barraud, Cecile, Daniel de Coppet, André Iteanu, and Raymond Jamous
1994   *Of Relations and the Dead: Four Societies Viewed from the Angle of Their Exchanges* (trans. Stephen J. Suffern). Oxford: Berg Press.

Barraud, Cecile
1979   *Tanebar-Evav: un societe de maisons tournée vers le large.* Atelier d'Anthropologie Sociale, Maison des Sciences de l'Homme, Paris.

Barth, Fredrik
1966   "Models of Social Organization." *RAI Occasional Paper 23,* Glasgow.

Barthes, Roland
1967   *Système de la Mode.* Paris: Seuil.

Battaglia, Debbora
1983   "Projecting Personhood in Melanesia: the Dialectics of Artefact Symbolism on Sabarl Island." *Man* n.s. 18:289–304.
1990   *On the Bones of the Serpent: Person, Memory and Mortality in Sabarl Island Society.* Chicago: University of Chicago Press.

Baudrillard, Jean
1968   *La Systeme des Objects.* Paris: Denoël.
1972   *Pour un critique de l'economie du Signe.* Paris: Gallimard.
1976   *L'échange symbolique et la mort.* Paris: Gallimard.

Beauchamp, William M.
1885   "The Iroquois White Dog Feast." *American Antiquarian* 7:235–39.
1895   "An Iroquois Condolence." *Journal of American Folklore* 8 (31):313–16.
1898   "Wampum Used in Council and as Currency." *American Antiquarian* 20 (1):1–13.
1901   "Wampum and Shell Articles Used by the New York Indians." *New York State Museum Bulletin* 41 (8): 319–480.
1907   "Civil, Religious and Mourning Councils and Ceremonies of Adoption of the New York Indians." New York State Museum Bulletin 113.
1922   *Iroquois Folk Lore.* Port Washington, NY: Ira J. Friedman (Reprinted 1965).

Beidelman, Thomas O.
1989   "Agonistic Exchange: Homeric Reciprocity and the Heritage of Simmel and Mauss." *Cultural Anthropology* 4:227–259.

Berg, Gerald
1979.   "Royal Authority and the Protector System in Nineteenth Century Imerina." In *Madagascar in History: Essays from the 1970s* (R. Kent, ed.) Albany: The Foundation for Malagasy Studies.

Berger, John
1972   *Ways of Seeing.* London: BBC and Penguin Books.

Best, Elsdon
1900   "The Spiritual Concepts of the Maori, part 1." *Journal of the Polynesian Society* 9:173–99.
1901   "The Spiritual Concepts of the Maori, part 2." *Journal of the Polynesian Society* 10:1–20.
1909   "Maori Forest Lore, Part III." *Transactions of the New Zealand Institute* 43:433–81.
1922   *Spiritual and Mental Concepts of the Maori.* Dominion Museum Monographs No. 2
1924a   *The Maori.* 2 vols. Memoirs of the Polynesian Society, volume 5. Wellington, New Zealand.
1924b   *Maori Religion and Mythology.* Dominion Museum Bulletin 10. Wellington, New Zealand.
1925a   *Maori Agriculture.* Dominion Museum Bulletin 9. Wellington, New Zealand.
1925b   *Tuhoe: Children of the Mist.* Memoirs of the Polynesian Society, vol. 6. Wellington: Polynesian Society.
1929   *Fishing Methods and Devices of the Maori.* Dominion Museum Bulletin No. 12. Wellington, New Zealand.
1942   *Forest Lore of the Maori.* Dominion Museum Bulletin No. 14. Wellington, New Zealand.

Bhaskar, Roy
1979   *The Possibility of Naturalism.* Hempstead: Harvester Wheatshaft (Second edition 1989).
1986   *Scientific Realism and Human Emancipation.* London: Verso.
1989   *Reclaiming Reality.* London: Verso.
1991   *Philosophy and the Idea of Freedom.* London: Verso.
1994   *Plato Etc.* London: Verso.

Blau, Harold
1963   "Dream Guessing: A Comparative Analysis." *Ethnohistory* 10:233–49.

1964   "The Iroquois White Dog Sacrifice: its Evolution and Symbolism." *Ethnohistory* 11:97–115.

Bloch, Maurice
1971   *Placing the Dead: Tombs, Ancestral Villages, and Kinship Organization in Madagascar.* London: Seminar Press.
1975   "Introduction" to *Political Language and Oratory in Traditional Societies.* London: Academic Press
1977   "The disconnection between power and rank as a process: an outline of the development of kingdoms in central Madagascar." *European Journal of Sociology* vol. 18:303–30.
1982   "Death, Women and Power." In *Death and the Regeneration of Life* (M. Bloch and J. Parry, eds.). Cambridge: Cambridge University Press, pp. 211–30.
1986   *From Blessing to Violence: History and Ideology in the Circumcision Ritual of the Merina of Madagascar.* Cambridge: Cambridge University Press.
1986a   "Hierarchy and Equality in Merina Kinship." In *Madagascar: Society and History* (C. P. Kottak, J.-A. Rakotoarisoa, A. Southall and P. Vérin, eds.) Durham: Carolina Academic Press, pp.215–228.
1989   "The Ritual of the Royal Bath in Madagascar: The Dissolution of Death, Birth, and Fertility into Authority." In *Ritual, History and Power: Selected Papers in Anthropology.* London: Athlone Press, pp.187–211.
1990   "The Symbolism of Money in Imerina." In *Money and the Morality of Exchange* (M. Bloch and J. Parry, eds.). Cambridge: Cambridge University Press, pp. 165–90.

Boas, Franz
1897   "The Social Organization and Secret Societies of the Kwakiutl Indians." *Report of the U.S. National Museum for 1895,* 311–738.
1921   "Ethnology of the Kwakiutl." *Bureau of American Ethnology Thirty-fifth Annual Report,* parts 1 and 2, 1913–1914. Washington, DC: Government Printing Office.
1925   "Contributions to the Ethnology of the Kwakiutl." *Columbia University Contributions to Anthropology,* volume III. New York: Columbia University Press.
1930   "The Religion of the Kwakiutl Indians." *Columbia University Contributions to Anthropology,* volume X. New York: Columbia University Press.
1935   "Kwakiutl Culture as Reflected in Mythology." *Memoirs of the American Folklore Society* 28. New York: G. E. Stechert.
1940   "The Social Organization of the Kwakiutl." In Franz Boas, *Race, Language and Culture,* 356–69. New York: Free Press.
1966   *Kwakiutl Ethnography.* (Helen Codere, ed.). Chicago: University of Chicago Press.

Bogart, John
1957   "The Currency Crisis in New Amsterdam." *De Halve Maen* 32
       (1):6–77.

Bohannan, Paul
1955   "Some Principles of Exchange and Investment among the Tiv." *American Anthropologist* 57:60–67.

Bohannan, Paul, and Laura Bohannan
1968   *Tiv Economy.* Evanston: Northwestern University Press.

Bosman, William
1744   A New and Accurate Description of the Coast of Guinea. London:
       Frank Cass & Co., 1967.

Bourdieu, Pierre
1979   *Outline of a Theory of Practice* (Translated by Richard Nice.) Cambridge:
       Cambridge University Press.
1990   *The Logic of Practice* (Translated by Richard Nice.) Cambridge: Polity Press.
1997   "Marginalia—Some Additional Notes on the Gift." In *The Logic of the
       Gift: toward an Ethic of Generosity* (Alan D. Schrift, ed.), pp. 231–41.
       New York: Routledge.

Buck, Peter
1950   *The Coming of the Maori.* 2nd ed. Wellington: Whitcombe and Tombs.

Burling, Robbins
1962   "Maximization Theories and the Study of Economic Anthropology."
       American Anthropologist 64:802–21.

Caillé, Alain
1984   "Deux mythes modernes: la rareté et la rationalité économiques." *Bulletin du MAUSS* 12:9–37.
1989   *Critique de la raison utilitaire: Manifeste du MAUSS.* Paris: Editions la
       Découverte/MAUSS.
1994   *Don, intérêt et désintéressement: Bourdieu, Mauss, Platon et quelques
       autres.* Paris: Editions la Découverte/MAUSS.

Callet, R. P.
1908. *Tantara ny Andriana eto Madagascar.* Tananarive: Académie Malgache.

Cannizzo, Jeanne
1983   "George Hunt and the Invention of Kwakiutl Culture." *Canadian Review of Sociology and Anthropology* 20:44–58.

Carrier, James G.
1990   "Gifts in a World of Commodities: The Ideology of the Perfect Gift in American Society." *Social Analysis* 29:19–37.
1991   "Gifts, Commodities, and Social Relations: A Maussian View of Exchange." *Sociological Forum* 6:119–36.
1992   "The Gift in Theory and Practice in Melanesia: A Note on the Centrality of Gift Exchange." *Ethnology* 31: 185–93.
1995   *Gifts and Commodities: Exchange and Western Capitalism since 1700.* London: Routledge.

Ceci, Lynn
1977   "The Effect of European Contact and Trade on the Settlement Pattern of the Indians in Coastal New York, 1524–1665." Ph.D. dissertation, The City University of New York.
1979   "Letters: The Cowrie Shells from the Little Neck Bay Area, Long Island." *Archaeology* 6:63.
1980   "The First Fiscal Crisis in New York." *Economic Development and Cultural Change* 28:839–47.
1982   "The Value of Wampum among the New York Iroquois: A Case Study in Artefact Analysis." *Journal of Anthropological Research* 38:97–107.

Chafe, Wallace L.
1961   "Seneca Thanksgiving Rituals." *Bureau of American Ethnology Bulletin* 183.

Chapus, G.-S., and E. Ratsimba (eds.)
1953–58   *Histoires des Rois* (4 vols. A French translation of Callet's *Tantara ny Andriana*). Tananarive: Academie Malgache.

Clark, Jeffrey
1991   "Pearl-Shell Symbolism in Highland Papua New Guinea, with Particular Reference to the Wiru People of Southern Highlands Province." *Oceania* 61:185–93.
1995   "Shit Beautiful: Tambu and Kina Revisited." *Oceania* 65:195–211.

Codere, Helen
1950   *Fighting with Property: A Study of Kwakiutl Potlaching and Warfare, 1792–1930.* American Ethnological Society Monograph 18. Reprint, Seattle: University of Washington Press.
1956   "The Amiable Side of Kwakiutl Life: The Potlatch and the Play Potlatch." *American Anthropologist* 58:334–51.

Cole, Douglas, and Ira Chaikin,
1990   An Iron Hand Upon the People: The Law against the Potlatch on the Northwest Coast. Seattle: University of Washington Press.

Colenso, William
  1868   "On the Maori Races of New Zealand." *Transactions of the New Zealand Institute* 1:339–424.

Collier, Andrew
  1994   *Critical Realism: An Introduction to Roy Bhaskar's Philosophy.* London: Verso Press.

Comaroff, John, and Jean Comaroff
  1992   *Of Revelation and Revolution: Christianity, Colonialism and Consciousness in South Africa.* Chicago: University of Chicago Press.
  1992   *Ethnography and the Historical Imagination.* Boulder: Westview Press.

Converse, Harriet M.
  1908   "Myths and Legends of the New York State Iroquois" (Arthur Parker, ed.). *New York State Museum Bulletin* 125, Albany. Reprint 1981.

Cook, Scott
  1966   "The Obsolete 'Anti-Market' Mentality: A Critique of the Substantivist Approach to Economic Anthropology." *American Anthropologist* 68:323–45.

Coppet, Daniel de
  1969   "Cycles de meurtres et cycles funéraires. Esquisse de deux structures d'échanges." In *Echanges et communications. Mélanges offerts à Claude Lévi-Strauss* (J. Pouillon, P. Maranda, eds.), pp. 759–81. The Hague: Mouton.
  1970   "1, 4, 8; 9, 7. La monnaie: présence des morts et mesure du temps." *L'Homme* 10 (1):17–39.
  1972   "Premier troc, double illusion." *L'Homme* 13 (1–2):10–22.
  1982   "The Life-giving death" In S. C. Humphreys and H. King (eds.), *Mortality and Immortality: The Anthropology and Archaeology of Death.* New York: Academic Press.
  1985   "Land Owns People." In *Contexts and Levels: Anthropological Essays on Hierarchy* (R. H. Barnes, Daniel de Coppet, and R. J Parkins, eds.) JASO Occasional Paper No.4. Oxford: JASO.
  1995   "'Are'are Society: A Melanesian Socio-Cosmic Point of View. How are Bigmen the Servants of Society and Cosmos?" In *Cosmos and Society in Oceania* (Daniel de Coppet and André Iteanu, eds.), pp. 235–74. Oxford: Berg Press.

Cousins, William E.
  1963.   *Fomba Gasy* (H. Randzavola, ed.). Tananarive: Imarivolanitra.

Curtis, E. S.
  1915   *The North American Indian, volume X. The Kwakiutl.* New York: Johnson Reprint.

Dalton, George
   1961   "Economic Theory and Primitive Society." *American Anthropologist*
           62:483–90.
   1965   "Primitive Money." *American Anthropologist* 66:44–65.

Damon, Fredrick H.
   1978.   *Modes of Production and the Circulation of Value on the Other Side of the
           Kula Ring.* Ph.D. Thesis: Princeton University.
   1980   "The Kula and Generalized Exchange: Considering Some Unconsidered
           Aspects of the Elementary Structures of Kinship." *Man* (n.s.)
           15:267–92.
   1983   "Muyuw Kinship and the Metamorphosis of Gendered Labor." Man
           (n.s.) 18:305–26.
   1989   "The Muyuw *Lo'un* and the End of Marriage." In *Death Rituals and Life
           in the Societies of the Kula Ring* (Fredrik Damon and Roy Wagner, eds.),
           pp. 73–94. DeKalb: Northern Illinois University Press.
   1993   "Representation and Experience in Kula and Western Exchange Spheres
           (Or, Billy)." *Research in Economic Anthropology* 14:235–54.
   1995   "The Problem of the Kula on Woodlark Island: Expansion, Accumula-
           tion, and Overproduction." *Ethnos* 3–4:176–201.

Davy, Georges
   1922   *La foi jurée: Étude sociologique du problème du contrat et la formation du
           lien contractuel.* Bibliothèque de philosophie contemporaine. Travaux de
           l'Année sociologique. Paris: Alcan.

Delâge, Denys
   1993   *Bitter Feast: Amerindians and Europeans in Northeastern North America,
           1600–64.* Vancouver: University of British Columbia Press.

Deleuze, Gilles, and Felix Guattari
   1983   *Anti-Oedipus: Capitalism and Schizophrenia.* Minneapolis: University of
           Minnesota Press.

Délivré, Alain
   1974.   *L'Histoire des rois d'Imerina: interprétation d'une tradition orale.* Paris:
           Klincksieck.

Dennis, Matthew
   1993   *Cultivating a Landscape of Peace: Iroquois-European Encounters in Seven-
           teenth-Century America.* Ithaca: Cornell University Press.

Derrida, Jacques
   1991   *Donner le temps*, volume 1. *La fausse monnaie.* Paris: Galilée.

Dominichini, Jean-Pierre
1977.   *Les Dieux au Service des Rois: Histoire des Palladium d'Emyrne.* Paris: Karthala.

Donne, T. E.
1927   *The Maori Past and Present.* London: Seeley Service & Co.

Dorfman, Ariel, and Armand Mattelart
1975   *How to Read Donald Duck: Imperialist Ideology in the Disney Comic.* New York: International General.

Douglas, Mary
1990   "Foreward: No Free Gifts." In *The Gift: The Form and Reason for Exchange in Archaic Societies.* (translated by W. D. Halls), pp. xii-xviii. New York: Norton.

Drucker, Philip, and Robert F. Heizer,
1967   *To Make My Name Great: A Reexamination of the Southern Kwakiutl Potlatch.* Berkeley: University of California Press.

Druke, Mary A.
1981   "The Concept of Personhood in Seventeenth and Eighteenth Century Iroquois Ethnopersonality." In: *Occasional Publications in Northeastern Anthropology.* George's Mills, N.H. no. 6, 1980. pp. 59–70.
1985   "Iroquois Treaties: Common Forms, Varying Interpretations." In *History and Culture of Iroquois Diplomacy* (Francis Jennings, William Fenton, Mary Druke, and David Miller, eds.), pp. 85–98. Syracuse: Syracuse University Press.

Duff, Wilson
1981   "The Killer Whale Copper: a Chief's Memorial to his Son." In *The World is as Sharp as a Knife: an Anthology in Honour of Wilson Duff* (Donald Abbott, ed.). Victoria, B.C.: British Columbia Provincial Museum.

Dumont, Louis
1952   "Marcel Mauss: A Science in Process of Becoming," lecture delivered at Oxford, preserved in *Essays on Individualism* (1986), pp.183–201.
1966   [1980] *Homo Hierarchicus: The Caste System and its Implications.* Chicago: University of Chicago Press (From French edition of 1966).
1971   *From Mandeville to Marx: The Genesis and Triumph of Economic Ideology.* Chicago: University of Chicago Press.
1982   "On Value." *Proceedings of the British Academy* 66:207–41. London: Oxford University Press.

1986   *Essays on Individualism*. Chicago: University of Chicago Press (from French edition of 1976).

Durkheim, Emile
1893   *De la division du travail social. Étude sur l'organisation des sociétés supérieures.* Paris: Alcan.

Durkheim, Emile, and Marcel Mauss
1903   "De quelques formes primitives de classifications. Contributions à l'étude des représentations collectives." *L'Année Sociologique* 6:1–72.

Edmonson, Munro S.
1973   "The Anthropology of Values." In *Culture and Life: Essays in Memory of Klyde Kluckhohn* (Walter Taylor, John Eischer, Evon Vogt, eds.), pp.157–197. Carbondale: Southern Illinois University Press.

Edmunds, William
1897   "Charms and Superstitions in Southeast Imerina." *Antananarivo Annual and Malagasy Magazine* 22:61–67.

Ellis, William
1838.   *History of Madagascar.* 2 vols. London: Fisher & Son.

Errington, Frederick, and Deborah Gewertz
1987   "The Remarriage of Yebiwali: A Study of Dominance and False Consciousness in a Non-Western Society." In *Dealing with Inequality: Analysing Gender Relations in Melanesia and Beyond* (Marilyn Strathern, ed.), pp.63–88. Cambridge: Cambridge University Press.

Evans-Pritchard, E. E.
1937   *Witchcraft, Oracles and Magic among the Azande.* Oxford: Clarendon Press.
1940   *The Nuer: the Political System and Mode of Livelihood of a Nilotic People.* Oxford: Oxford University Press.

Fajans, Jane
1993a   "Exchanging Products: Producing Exchange." In *Exchanging Products: Producing Exchange* (Jane Fajans, ed.). Oceania Monographs, University of Sydney, Pp. 1–14.
1993b   "The Alimentary Structures of Kinship: Food and Exchange among the Baining of Papua New Guinea." In *Exchanging Products: Producing Exchange* (Jane Fajans, ed.). Oceania Monographys, University of Sydney, pp. 59–75.
1997   *They Make Themselves: Work and Play among the Baining of Papua New Guinea.* Chicago: University of Chicago Press.

Faraone, Christopher, and Dirk Obbink (eds.)
1991   *Magika Hiera: Ancient Greek Magic and Religion.* New York: Oxford University Press.

Fenton, William N.
1942   "Songs from the Iroquois Longhouse." *Smithsonian Publication* 3691.
1946a   "An Iroquois Condolence Council for Installing Cayuga Chiefs in 1945." *Journal of the Washington Academy of Sciences* 36:110–27.
1950   The Roll Call of the Iroquois Chiefs: A Study of a Mnemonic Cane from the Six Nations Reserve." *Smithsonian Miscellaneous Collections* 111 (15): 1–73.
1971   "The New York State Wampum Collection: The Case for Integrity of Cultural Treasures." *Proceedings of the American Philosophical Society* 115 (6):437–61.
1978   "Northern Iroquois Culture Patterns." In *Handbook of the North American Indians,* volume 15, Northeast (W. Sturtevant and B. Trigger, eds.), pp. 296–321. Washington, D.C., Smithsonian.
1985   "Structure, Continuity, and Change in the History of Iroquois Treaty Making." In *History and Culture of Iroquois Diplomacy,* (Francis Jennings, William Fenton, Mary Druke, and David Miller, eds.) pp.3–36. Syracuse: Syracuse University Press.
1998   *The Great Law and the Longhouse: A Political History of the Iroquois Confederacy.* Norman: University of Oklahoma Press.

Ferguson, James
1985   "The Bovine Mystique." *Man* (n.s.) 20:647–74.
1988   "Cultural Exchange: New Developments in the Anthropology of Commodities." *Cultural Anthropology* 3:488–513.

Finley, Moses
1974   *The Ancient Economy.* Berkeley: University of California Press.

Firth, Raymond
1940   "The Analysis of Mana: An Empirical Approach." *Journal of the Polynesian Society* 49:483–512. (Reprinted in *Tikopia Ritual and Belief.* London: Allen & Unwin, 1967.)
1959   *Economics of the New Zealand Maori.* Wellington, New Zealand: R. E. Owen.
1964   "The Study of Values by Social Anthropologists." In *Essays on Social Organization and Values* (London: Athlone Press), 206–24.

Ford, Clellan S.
1941   *Smoke from Their Fires: The Life of a Kwakiutl Chief.* Hamden, Conn.: Archon.

Foster, Michael K.
1974   "From the Earth to Beyond the Sky: An Ethnographic Approach to Four Longhouse Iroquois Speech Events." *Canadian Ethnological Service Paper* 20. Ottawa: National Museums of Canada.
1985   "Another Look at the Function of Wampum in Iroquois-White Councils. In *History and Culture of Iroquois Diplomacy.* (Francis Jennings, William Fenton, Mary Druke, and David Miller, eds.), pp.125–142. Syracuse: Syracuse University Press.

Foster, Robert J.
1985   "Production and Value in the Enga Tee." *Oceania* 55:182–96.
1990   "Value without Equivalence: Exchange and Replacement in a Melanesian Society." *Man* (N.S.) 25:54–69.
1992   "Commodisation and the Emergence of *kastom* as a Cultural Category: A New Ireland Case in Comparative Perspective." *Oceania* 62:284–94.
1993   "Dangerous Circulation and Revelatory Display: Exchange Practices in a New Ireland Society." In *Exchanging Products: Producing Exchange* (Jane Fajans, ed.), pp. 15–31. Oceania Monographs, University of Sydney.
1995   *Social Reproduction and History in Melanesia: Mortuary Ritual, Gift Exchange, and Custom in the Tanga Islands.* Cambridge: Cambridge University Press.

Foucault, Michel
1972   *The Archaeology of Knowledge* (A. M. Sheridan-Smith, trans.). London: Tavistock.
1977   *Discipline and Punish: The Birth of the Prison* (Alan Sheridan, trans.). New York: Pantheon Books.

Fournier, Marcel
1994   *Marcel Mauss.* Paris: Fayard.

Gane, Mike
1992   *The Radical Sociology of Durkheim and Mauss.* New York: Routledge.

Gasche, Rudolphe
1972   [1997] "Heliocentric Exchange." In *The Logic of the Gift: Toward an Ethic of Generosity* (Alan Schrift, ed.), pp. 100–20. New York: Routledge.

Gathercole, Peter
1978   "'Hau,' 'Mauri,' and 'Utu'." *Mankind* 11:334–40.

Gauchet, Marcel
1997   *The Disenchantment of the World: A Political History of Religion* (Oscar Burge, trans.). Princeton: Princeton University Press.

Geary, Patrick
1986   "Sacred Commodities: the Circulation of Medieval Relics." In *The Social Life of Things: Commodities in Cultural Perspective* (Arjun Appadurai, ed.), pp.169–91. Cambridge: Cambridge University Press.

Geertz, Clifford
1973   *The Interpretation of Culture.* New York: Basic Books.

Gell, Alfred
1993   *Wrapping in Images: Tattooing in Polynesia.* Oxford: Clarendon Press.
1998   *Art and Agency: An Anthropological Theory.* Oxford: Clarendon Press.
1999   *The Art of Anthropology: Essays and Diagrams.* London School of Economics Monographs on Social Anthropology, volume 67. London: Athlone Press.

Geoghegan, Vincent
1987   *Utopianism and Marxism.* London: Methuen.

Gewertz, Deborah
1983   *Sepik River Societies: A Historical Ethnography of the Chambri and their Neighbors.* New Haven: Yale University Press.

Godbout, Jacques T., and Alain Caillé
1998   *The World of the Gift.* Montreal: McGill-Queen's University Press.

Godelier, Maurice
1977   *Perspectives in Marxist Anthropology.* New York: Cambridge University Press.
1978   "'Salt Money' and the Circulation of Commodities among the Baruya of New Guinea." In *Perspectives in Marxist Anthropology* (M. Godelier, ed.). Cambridge: Cambridge University Press.
1986   *The Making of Great Men: Male Domination and Power among the New Guinea Baruya.* Cambridge: Cambridge University Press.
1996   *L'Enigme du don.* Paris: Libraire Arthéme Fayard. (Translated as "The Enigma of the Gift" University of Chicago Press, 1999)

Goldenweiser, Alexander A.
1914a   "On Iroquois Work 1912." In *Summary Report of the Geological Survey Branch of the Canadian Department of Mines for the Calendar Year 1912* (Ottawa), pp. 464–75.
1914b   "On Iroquois Work 1913–14." In *Summary Report of the Geological Survey Branch of the Canadian Department of Mines for the Calendar Year 1913* (Ottawa), pp. 365–372.

Goldman, Irving
1970   *Ancient Polynesian Society.* Chicago: University of Chicago Press.

1975   *The Mouth of Heaven: An Introduction to Kwakiutl Religious Thought.* New York, John Wiley and Sons.

Graeber, David
1995   "Dancing with Corpses Reconsidered: an Interpretation of Famadihana (in Arivonimamo, Madagascar)." *American Ethnologist* 22:258–78
1996a   "Beads and Money: Notes toward a Theory of Wealth and Power." *American Ethnologist* 23:1–32.
1996b   "Love Magic and Political Morality in Central Madagascar, 1875–1990." *Gender and History* 8(3):94–117.
1997a   "Manners, Deference and Private Property: The Generalization of Avoidance in Early Modern Europe." *Comparative Studies in Society and History* 39(4):694–728.
2001   *Catastrophe: Magic and History in Rural Madagascar* (unpublished manuscript).

Graf, Fritz
1997   *Magic in the Ancient World* (Franklin Philip, trans.). Cambridge: Harvard University Press.

Graves, Robert
1964   *Man Does, Woman Is.* Garden City: Doubleday Press.

Gregory, Christopher A.
1980   "Gifts to Men and Gifts to God: Gift Exchange and Capital Accumulation in Contemporary Papua." *Man* (n.s.) 15 (4):626–52.
1982   *Gifts and Commodities.* New York: Academic Press.
1983   "Kula Gift Exchange and Capitalist Commodity Exchange: a Comparison." In *The Kula: New Perspectives on Massim Exchange,* Cambridge, Cambridge University Press.
1996   "Cowries and Conquest: Towards a Subalternate Quality Theory of Money." *Comparative Studies in Society and History* 38 (2): 195–216.
1998   *Savage Money: The Anthropology and Politics of Commodity Exchange.* Amsterdam: Harwood Academic Publishers.

Gudgeon, C. M. G.
1905a   "Mana Tangata." *Journal of the Polynesian Society* 14:49–66.
1905b   "Maori Religion." *Journal of the Polynesian Society* 14:117–30.

Gudgeon, Thomas Wayth.
1885   *The History and Doings of the Maoris: From the Year 1820 to the Signing of the Treaty of Waitangi in 1840.* Auckland: H. Brett.

Guthrie, W. J. C.
1971   *A History of Greek Philosophy.* Cambridge: Cambridge University Press.

Hale, Horatio E.
1883   *The Iroquois Book of Rites.* Philadelphia: D. G. Brinton. Reprint 1965, Toronto: University of Toronto Press.
1885   "The Iroquois Sacrifice of the White Dog." *American Antiquarian* 7:7–14.
1895   "An Iroquois Condoling Council." *Transactions of the Royal Society of Canada,* 2d ser., 1, no. 2: 45–65.

Hallowell, A. Irving
1960   "Ojibwa Ontology, Behavior, and World View." In *Culture in History: Essays in Honor of Paul Radin* (Stanley Diamond, ed.), pp. 19–52. New York: Columbia University Press.
1967   "The Ojibwa Self in its Behavioral Environment." In *Culture and Experience,* pp. 172–82. Philadelphia: University of Pennsylvania Press.

Hallpike, C. R.
1979   *The Foundations of Primitive Thought.* Oxford: Clarendon Press.

Hammel, George R.
1983   Trading in Metaphors: the Magic of Beads. In *Proceedings of the 1982 Glass Trade Bead Conference.* (Charles Hayes, ed.). Rochester, New York: Research Records 16, Research Division, Rochester Museum and Science Center.
1987   "Mythical Realities and European Contact in the Northeast During the 16th and 17th Centuries." *Man in the Northeast* no 33:63–87.
1992   "The Iroquois and the World's Rim: Speculations on Color, Culture, and Contact." *American Indian Quarterly,* Fall 1992, pp. 451–69.

Harris, Marvin
1979   *Cultural Materialism: The Struggle for a Science of Culture.* New York: Vintage Books.

Hart, Keith
1986   "Heads or tails? Two Sides of the Coin," *Man* 21 (4):637–56.
2000   *The Memory Bank: Money in an Unequal World.* London: Profile Books.

Heidenreich, Conrad E.
1971   Huronia: A History and Geography of the Huron Indians 1600–1650. Ottawa: Ontario Ministry of Natural Resources.

Hertz, Gilbert
1907   *"La Prééminence de la main droite: étude sur la polarité religieuse."* *Revue Philosophique* 68: 553–80. Translated (by Rodney Needham) as 'The Pre-eminence of the Right Hand: A Study in Religious Polarity' in *Right and Left: Essays on Dual Symbolic Classification* (R. Needham, ed., 1973). Chicago: University of Chicago Press.

Heusch, Luc de
1998   "The Symbolic Mechanisms of Sacred Kingship: Rediscovering Frazer." *Journal of the Royal Anthropological Institute* (n.s.) 3:213–32.

Hewitt, John N.B.
1889   "New Fire among the Iroquois." *American Anthropologist* 2:319.
1892   "Legend of the Founding of the Iroquois League." *American Anthropologist* (old series) 5 no2: 341–52.
1895   "The Iroquoian Concept of the Soul." *Journal of American Folklore* 8:107–16.
1903   "Iroquoian Cosmology: First Part." *Annual Report of the Bureau of American Ethnology for the years 1899–1900.* Washington, D.C.
1910a   "Wampum." In *Handbook of the American Indians North of Mexico* (F. W. Hodge, ed.), pp. 904–09. Washington, D.C.: Bureau of American Ethnology, Bulletin 30.
1910b   "White Dog Sacrifice." In *Handbook of the American Indians North of Mexico* (F. W. Hodge, ed.), pp. 939–44. Washington, D.C.: Bureau of American Ethnology, Bulletin 30.
1910c   "The White-dog Feast of the Iroquois." *American Anthropologist* 12:86–87.
1928   "Iroquoian Cosmology: Second Part, with Introduction and Notes." *Annual Report of the Bureau of American Ethnology for the Years 1925–1926,* pp.449–819. Washington, D.C.

Hewitt, John N. B., and William Fenton
1944   "The Requickening Address of the Iroquois Condolence Council." *Journal of the Washington Academy of Sciences* 34, no.3, pp. 65–85.

Hickerson, Harold
1960   "The Feast of the Dead among the Seventeenth-Century Algonkians of the Upper Great Lakes." *Ethnohistory* 62: 81–107.

Hobbes, Thomas
1651   *Leviathan.* Harmondsworth, UK: Penguin, 1968.

Hogden, Margaret
1964   *Early Anthropology in the 16th and 17th Centuries.* (Philadelphia, University of Pennsylvania Press).

Holmes, William
1883   "Art in Shell of the Ancient Americans." *Second Annual Report of the Bureau of American Ethnology 1880–1881*:185–305.

Hubert, Henri
1925   "Le système des prestations totales dans les Littératures Celtiques." *Revue Celtique* 42:330–35.

1934   *The Greatness and Decline of the Celts.* London: Kegan Paul, Trench, Trubner & Co.

Hunt, George
1906   "The Rival Chiefs." In *Boas Anniversary Volume: Anthropological Papers Written in Honor of Franz Boas.* New York: G. E. Stecher & Co.

Iteanu, André
1983a   *Le ronde des échanges: de la circulation aux valeurs chez les Orokaiva.* Paris: Atelier d'Anthropologie Sociale, Maison des Sciences de l'Homme.
1983b   "Idéologie patrilinéaire ou idéologie de l'anthropologue?" *L'Homme* 23(2):37–55.
1990   "The Concept of the Person and the Ritual System: An Orokaiva View." *Man* (n.s.) 25:35–53.

Jacobs, Wilbur
1949   "Wampum, the Protocol of Indian Diplomacy." *William and Mary Quarterly* 6:596–604.

Jameson, Frederick
1981   *The Political Unconscious: Narrative as a Socially Symbolic Act.* Ithaca: Cornell University Press.

Jamous, Raymond
1981   *Honneur et Baraka: les structures sociales traditionelles dans le Rif.* Paris: Atelier d'Anthropologie Sociale, Maison des Sciences de l'Homme.

Jennings, Francis
1976   *The Invasion of America: Indians, Colonialism, and the Cant of Conquest.* New York: Norton.
1984   *The Ambiguous Iroquois Empire: The Covenant Chain Confederation of Indian Tribes with English Colonies from its beginnings to the Lancaster Treaty of 1744.* New York: Norton.

Jennings, Francis, William Fenton, Mary Druke, and David Miller
1985   "Glossary of Figures of Speech in Iroquois Political Rhetoric." In *History and Culture of Iroquois Diplomacy.* (Francis Jennings, William Fenton, Mary Druke, and David Miller, eds.), pp.115–124. Syracuse, NY: Syracuse University Press.

Joas, Hans
1996   *The Creativity of Action.* Chicago: University of Chicago Press.

Johansen, J. Prytz
1954   *The Maori and His Religion.* Copenhagen: Munksgaard.

1958   *Studies in Maori Rites and Myths.* Historisk-filosofiske Medelelser 37.
            Copenhagen.

Jonaitis, Aldonis
    1991   "Chiefly Feasts: The Creation of an Exhibition." In *Chiefly Feasts: The
            Enduring Kwakiutl Potlatch* (A. Jonaitis, ed.). New York: American Mu-
            seum of Natural History.

Jones, Pei Te Hurinui
    1995   *The Traditional History of the Tainui People.* Auckland: Auckland Uni-
            versity Press.

Josephides, Lisette
    1983   "Equal but different? The Ontology of Gender among the Kewa." *Ocea-
            nia* 53:291–307.
    1985   *The Production of Inequality: Gender and Exchange among the Kewa.*
            London: Tavistock Publications.
    1991   "Metaphors, Metathemes, and the Construction of Sociality: A Critique
            of the New Melanesian Ethnography." *Man* (n.s.) 26:145–61.
    1995   "Replacing Cultural Markers: Symbolic Analysis and Political Action in
            Melanesia." In *Cosmos and Society in Oceania* (Daniel de Coppet and
            André Iteanu, eds.), pp. 189–212. Oxford: Berg Press.

Kan, Sergei
    1989   *Symbolic Immortality: The Tlingit Potlach of the 19th Century.* Washing-
            ton, DC: Smithsonian Press.

Kapferer, Bruce
    1976   "Introduction: Transactional Models Reconsidered." In B. Kapferer
            (ed.). *Transaction and Meaning: Directions in the Anthropology of Ex-
            change and Symbolic Behavior.* Philadelphia: Institute for the Study of
            Human Issues (ISHI).

Keane, Webb
    1994   "The Value of Words and the Meaning of Things in Eastern Indonesian
            Exchange." *Man* (n.s.) 29:605–29.
    1997   *Signs of Recognition: Powers and Hazards of Representation in an Indone-
            sian Society.* Berkeley: University of California Press.
    1997a   "From Fetishism to Sincerity: on Agency, the Speaking Subject, and
            their Historicity in the Context of Religious Conversion." *Comparative
            Studies in Society and History* 39:74–693.

Kelly, Leslie G. (Te Putu)
    1949   *Tainui: The Story of Hotoroa and his Descendants.* Wellington, N.Z.: The
            Polynesian Society. Polynesian Society Memoir No. 25.

Kirk, G. S.
1962   *Heraclitus: The Cosmic Fragments.* Cambridge: Cambridge University Press.

Kluckhohn, Klyde
1949   "The Philosophy of the Navaho Indian." In *Ideological Differences and World Order* (F. S. D. Northrop, ed.), pp. 356–84. New Haven: Yale University Press.
1951a   "Values and Value-orientations in the Theory of Action: an Exploration in Definition and Classification." In *Towards a General Theory of Action* (T. Parsons and E. Shils, eds.), pp. 388–433. Cambridge: Harvard University Press.
1951b   "A Comparative Study of Values in Five Cultures." Foreward to *Navaho Veterans, a Study in Changing Values,* by Evon Z. Vogt. *Papers of the Peabody Museum of American Archaeology and Ethnology,* 41, no.1, v11-ix. Cambridge: Harvard University.
1956   "Towards a Comparison of Value-emphases in Different Cultures." In *The State of the Social Sciences* (Leonard White, ed.). Chicago: University of Chicago Press.
1961   "The Study of Values." In *Values in America* (Donald Barrett, ed.), pp. 17–45. Notre Dame: University of Notre Dame Press.

Kluckhohn, Florence, and Fred Strodtbeck
1961   *Variations in Value Orientation.* Evanston, Illinois: Row, Peterson.

Kobrinsky, Vernon
1975   "Dynamics of the Fort Rupert Class Struggle: Or, Fighting with Property Vertically Revisited." In V. Serl and H. Taylor, eds., *Papers in Honor of Harry Hawthorne,* pp. 32–59. Bellingham: Western Washington State College.

Kopytoff, Igor
1986   "The Cultural Biography of Things: Commoditization as Process." In A. Appadurai (ed), *The Social Life of Things: Commodities in Cultural Perspective,* pp. 64–94. Cambridge: Cambridge University Press.

Lacan, Jacques
1977   *Écrits: A Selection.* New York: Norton Press.

Leach, Edmund
1954   *Political Systems of Highland Burma.* Cambridge: Cambridge University Press.
1982   *Social Anthropology.* Oxford: Oxford University Press.

Levi-Strauss, Claude
1949   *Les structures élémentaires de la parenté.* Paris: Presses Universitaires de France. (English version: The Elementary Structures of Kinship. Boston, Beacon Press, 1969.)

1950   "Introduction à l'oeuvre de Mauss." In *Sociologie et Anthropologie*. Paris: Presses Universitaires de France, pp. i-liii.
1958   *Anthropologie structurale.* Paris: Plon.
1962   *Totemism.* Beacon Press, Boston.
1966   *The Savage Mind.* Chicago: University of Chicago Press.
1975   *La voie des masques.* Paris: Flammarion (translated as *The Way of the Masks.* Seattle: University of Washington Press, 1982).
1988   *The Jealous Potter* (Trans. Bénédicte Chorier). Chicago: University of Chicago Press.

Liep, John
1990   "Gift Exchange and the Construction of Identity." In *Culture and History in the Pacific* (Jukka Siikala, ed.), pp164–83. Helsinki: The Finnish Anthropological Society.

MacCormick, G.
1982   "Mauss and the 'Spirit' of the Gift." *Oceania* 52:286–93.

MacGaffey, Wyatt
1994   "African Objects and the Idea of the Fetish." *Res* 25:123–31.

Malinowski, Bronislaw
1922   *Argonauts of the Western Pacific: An Account of Native Enterprise and Adventure in the Archipelagoes of Melanesian New Guinea.* Studies in Economics and Political Science, no. 65. London: Routledge.
1935   *Coral Gardens and their Magic: A Study of the Methods of Tilling the Soil and of Agricultural Rites in the Trobriand Islands.* London: Allen & Unwin.

Maning, F. E.
1863   *Old New Zealand.* London: Bentley.

Martien, Jerry
1996   *Shell Game: A True Account of Beads and Money in North America.* San Francisco: Mercury House.

Marx, Karl
1846   [1970] *The German Ideology.* New York: International Publishers.
1857–8   [1973] *The Grundrisse.* New York: Harper and Row.
1858   [1965] *Pre-Capitalist Economic Formations* (Jack Cohen, trans.). New York: International Publishers.
1859   [1970] *Contribution to the Critique of Political Economy.* New York: International Publishers.
1867   [1967] *Capital.* 3 volumes. New York: New World Paperbacks.

Masco, Joseph
1995   "It Is a Strict Law that Bids Us Dance: Cosmologies, Colonialism, Death, and Ritual Authority in the Kwakwaka'wakw Potlatch, 1849 to 1922." *Comparative Studies in Society and History* 37:41–75.

Mauss, Marcel
1920   "Les idées socialistes. Le principe de la nationalisation." Chapter of an unpublished book on the history of the nation-state. In *Écrits Politiques: Textes réunis et présentés par Marcel Fournier.* Paris: Fayard, 249–266.
1921a "Pour les bolchevistes." *La Vie socialiste,* 30 April 1921, p. 3. In *Écrits Politiques: Textes réunis et présentés par Marcel Fournier.* Paris: Fayard, 405–406.
1921b "Une forme ancienne de contrat chez les thraces." *Revue des études grecques* 34:388–97. In *Oeuvres* III:35–45.
1922   "La vente de la Russie." *La Vie socialiste* 18 November 1922, pp.1–2. In *Écrits Politiques: Textes réunis et présentés par Marcel Fournier.* Paris: Fayard, 472–76.
1923   "L'obligation à rendre les présents." Compte rendu d'une communication présentée à l'Institut français de l'anthropologie. *Anthropologie* 33:193–94.
1924a Response to a communication by A. Aftalion, "Les fondements du socialisme." *Bulletin de la Sociéte française de philosophie,* 24. In *Oeuvres* III:634–38.
1924b "Gift gift." *Mélanges offerts à Charles Andler par ses ams et ses élèves.* Istra, Strasbourg, pp. 243–247. In *Oeuvres* III: 46–51.
1925   "Essai sur le don. Forme et raison de l'échange dans les sociétés archaïques." *Annee sociologique,* 1 (series 2):30–186.
1925a "Socialisme et Bolchévisme." In *Le Monde Slave,* Year 2, number 2, pp. 201–222. Translated as "A sociological assessment of Bolshevism," by Ben Brewster in *The Radical Sociology of Durkheim and Mauss* (Mike Gane, ed.). New York, Routledge, 1992.
1936   "Letters on communism, fascism and nazism," translated by Ben Brewster in *The Radical Sociology of Durkheim and Mauss* (Mike Gane, ed.), New York, Routledge, 1992, pp. 213–15.
1938: "Une catégorie de l'esprit humain: la notion de personne, celle de 'moi,' un plan de travail." *Journal of the Royal Anthropological Institute* 68:263–281. Translated as "A Category of the Human Mind: the Notion of Person, the Notion of Self." In *The Category of the Person,* (M. Carrithers, S. Collins and S. Lukes, eds.). Cambridge: Cambridge University Press, 1985.
1947   *Manuel d'ethnographie.* Paris: Payot.
1965   *The Gift: Forms and Functions of Exchange in Archaic Societies* (translation by I. Cunnison). New York: Norton.
1968–69 *Oeuvres.* 3 volumes. Paris: Editions de Minuit.

1990   *The Gift: The Form and Reason for Exchange in Archaic Societies.* (translated by W. D. Halls). New York: Norton.
1997   *Écrits Politiques: Textes réunis et présentés par Marcel Fournier.* Paris: Fayard.

Mauss, Marcel, and Henri Hubert
1899   "Essai sur la nature et la function du sacrifice." *L'Année Sociologique* 2:29–138.
1904   "Esquisse d'une théorie générale de la magie." *L'Année Sociologique* 7:1–146.

McCall, Grant
1982   "Association and Power in Reciprocity and Requittal: More on Mauss and the Maori." *Oceania* 52:303–19.

McKirahan, Richard
1994   *Philosophy Before Socrates: An Introduction with Texts and Commentary.* Indianapolis: Hackett Publishing.

Mead, Sidney
1969   *Traditional Maori Clothing.* Wellington: A. H. and A. W. Reed.

Meillassoux, Claude
1981   *Maidens, Meal and Money: Capitalism and Domestic Community.* Cambridge: Cambridge University Press.

Méritens, Guy de, and Paul de Veyrières
1967   *Livre de la sagesse malgache.* Paris: Éditions Maritimes et d'Outre-Mer.

Metge, A. Joan
1976   *The Maori of New Zealand: Rautahi.* Revised edition. London: Routledge and Kegan Paul.

Michelson, Gunther
1974   "Upstreaming Bruyas." In *Papers in Linguistics from the 1972 Conference on Iroquois Research.* (Michael K. Foster, ed.), pp. 36–46. Ottawa: National Museum of Man. Ethnnology Division, Mercury Series Paper 10.

Miller, Daniel
1987   *Material Culture and Mass Consumption.* London: Basil Blackwell.
1995   *Acknowledging Consumption: A Review of New Studies* (D. Miller, ed.). London: Routledge.

Mitchell, J. H. (Tiaki Hikawera Mitira)
1944   *Takitimu.* Wellington: A. H. & A. W. Reed.

Mithun, Marianne
1984   "The Proto-Iroquoians: Cultural Reconstruction from Lexical Materials." In *Extending the Rafters: Interdisciplinary Approaches to Iroquoian Studies* (M. K. Foster, J. Campisi, and M. Mithun, eds.), pp. 259–81. Albany: State University of New York Press.

Modjeska, N.
1985   "Exchange value and Melanesian trade reconsidered." In *Recent Studies in the Political Economy of Papua New Guinea Societies* (D. Gardiner and N. Modjeska, eds.). *Mankind* 15:145–62.

Morgan, Lewis Henry
1962   [1851] *League of the Ho-de-no-sau-nee, or Iroquois.* Secaucus: Citadel Press.

Munn, Nancy
1973   "Symbolism in a Ritual Context: Aspects of Symbolic Action." In *Handbook of Social and Cultural Anthropology* (J. J. Honigmann, ed.), pp. 579–612. Chicago: Rand McNally.
1977   "The Spatiotemporal Transformations of Gawan canoes." *Journal de la Société des Océanistes.* Tome 33 (March-June), 54–55:39–53.
1983   "Gawan Kula: Spatiotemporal Control and the Symbolism of Influence." In J. Leach and E. Leach (eds.), *The Kula: New Perspectives on Massim Exchange.* Cambridge: Cambridge University Press, 277–308.
1986   *The Fame of Gawa: A Symbolic Study of Value Transformation in a Massim (Papua New Guinea) Society.* Cambridge, Cambridge University Press.

Myers, Fred
1986   *Pintupi Country, Pintupi Self: Sentiment, Place, and Politics among Western Desert Aborigines.* Washington: Smithsonian Institution Press.

Myers, Fred, and Donald Brenneis
1991   "Introduction: Language and Politics in the Pacific." In *Dangerous Words: Language and Politics in the Pacific.* (Donald Brenneis and Fred Myers, eds.), pp. 1–29. Prospect Heights, Illinois: Waveland Press.

Nicolas, Guy
1991   "Le don rituel, face voilée de la modernité." *Revue du MAUSS* 12:7–29.

Nowell, Charles
1968   *Smoke from their Fires: the Life of a Kwakiutl Chief.* Hamden, Connecticut: Archon Books.

Nuckolls, Charles W.
1998   *Culture: A Problem that Cannot Be Solved.* Madison: University of Wisconsin Press.

Ollman, Bertel
1971   *Alienation. Marx's Conception of Man in Capitalist Society.* Cambridge: Cambridge University Press.

Ong, Walter
1967   *In the Presence of the Word.* New Haven: Yale University Press.
1977   *Interfaces of the Word.* New Haven: Yale University Press.

Ottino, Paul
1978   "La mythologie malgache des Hautes Terres: Le cycle des Andriamba-hoaka." In *Dictionnaire des Mythologies,* vol. 2. (Yves Bonnefoy, ed.). Paris: Flammarion.

Pannel, Sandra
1993   "'Circulating Commodities: Reflections on the Movement and Meaning of Shells and Stories in North Australia and Eastern Indonesia." *Oceania* 64:57–76.

Parker, Arthur C.
1916   *The Constitution of the Five Nations, or the Iroquois Book of the Great Law.* New York State Museum Bulletin 184, Albany, NY.
1923   *Seneca Myths and Folk Tales.* Buffalo Historical Society Publications 27, Buffalo.
1926   "An Analytical History of the Seneca Indians." *Researches and Transactions of the New York State Archaeological Association.* Rochester, NY.
1968   *Parker on the Iroquois.* (William Fenton, ed.). Syracuse: Syracuse University Press.

Parry, Jonathan
1986   "The Gift, the Indian Gift, and the 'Indian Gift'." *Man* (n.s.) 21:453–73.

Parry, Jonathan and Maurice Bloch
1989   "Introduction: Money and the Morality of Exchange." In *Money and the Morality of Exchange* (J. Parry and M. Bloch, eds.). Cambridge: Cambridge University Press.

Parsons, Talcott, and Edward A. Shils, eds.
1951   *Toward a General Theory of Action.* Cambridge: Harvard University Press.

Peristiany, J.G., ed.
1966   *Honour and Shame: The Values of Mediterranean Society.* Chicago: University of Chicago Press.

Piaget, Jean
1967   *The Psychology of Intelligence.* New York: Basic Books.
1970   *Structuralism.* New York: Basic Books.
1995   *Sociological Studies.* London: Routledge. (Originally *Études sociologiques,* Librarie Droz, Geneva, 1965).

Pietz, William
1985   "The Problem of the Fetish I." *RES: Journal of Anthropology and Aesthetics* 9:5–17.
1987   "The Problem of the Fetish II: The Origin of the Fetish" *RES: Journal of Anthropology and Aesthetics* 13:23–45.
1988   "The Problem of the Fetish IIIa: Bosman's Guinea and the Enlightenment Theory of Fetishism." *RES: Journal of Anthropology and Aesthetics* 16:105–23.
1993   "Fetishism and Materialism: The Limits of Theory in Marx." In *Fetishism as Cultural Discourse* (Emily Apter and William Pietz, eds.), pp. 119–51. Ithaca: Cornell University Press.
1995a "The Spirit of Civilization: Blood Sacrifice and Monetary Debt." *RES: Journal of Anthropology and Aesthetics* 28:23–38.
1995b "Death and the Deadened: Accursed Objects and the Money Value of Human Life." In *(Un)Fixing Representation* (Judith Farquar, Tomoko Masuzawa, and Carol Mavor, eds.). Minneapolis: University of Minnesota Press.

Polack, Joel S.
1840   Manners and Customs of the New Zealanders. 2 volumes. London: James Madden & Co.

Polanyi, Karl
1944   *The Great Transformation.* New York: Rinehart.
1957   "The economy as an instituted process." In K. Polanyi, C. Arensberg and H. Pearson (eds.), *Trade and Market in the Early Empires.* Glencoe: The Free Press.
1968   *Primitive, Archaic, and Modern Economies: Essays of Karl Polanyi* (George Dalton, ed.). New York: Anchor.

Postone, Moishe
1986   "Anti-Semitism and National Socialism." In *Germans and Jews Since the Holocaust: the Changing Situation in West Germany* (edited by Anson Rabinbach and Jack Zipes), pp. 302–14. New York: Holmes & Meier.

Pye, Christopher
1984   "The Sovereign, the Theatre, and the Kingdome of Darkness: Hobbes and the Spectacle of Power." *Representations* 8:85–106.

Quain, Buell
1937   "The Iroquois." In Margaret Mead (ed.), *Cooperation and Competition Among Primitive Peoples.* New York: McGraw Hill.

Quiggin, A. H.
1949   *Trade Routes, Trade and Currency in East Africa.* Rhodes-Livingstone Museum: Occasional Papers no. 5.

Racine, Luc
1991   "L'Obligation de rendre les présents et l'esprit de la chose donnée: de Marcel Mauss à René Maunier." *Diogène* 154:69–94.

Renel, Charles
1910   *Contes de Madagascar.* Paris: E. Leroux.
1915   "Les Amulettes Malgaches: Ody et Sampy." *Bulletin de l'Academie Malgache* (n.s.) 2:31–279).
1920   "Ancêtres et dieux." *Bulletin de l'Academie Malgache* (n.s.) 5:1–261.

Richardson, John
1885   *A New Malagasy-English Dictionary.* Antananarivo: London Missionary Society.

Richter, Daniel K.
1983   "War and Culture: the Iroquois Experience." *William and Mary Quarterly,* 3d Ser., 40:528–59.
1992   *The Ordeal of the Longhouse: The Peoples of the Iroquois League in the Era of European Colonization.* Chapel Hill: University of North Carolina Press.

Ricouer, Paul
1970   *History and Truth.* Evanston: Northwestern University Press.

Robbins, Joel
1987   "Keeping to Oneself in Melanesia: Secrecy, Not-Reciprocity, and Cultural Theory." Paper presented at the annual meeting of the American Anthropological Association, Chicago.
1994   "Equality as a Value: Ideology in Dumont, Melanesia and the West." *Social Analysis* no 36:21–70.

Rosman, Abraham, and Paula Rubel
1986 [1971]   *Feasting with Mine Enemy: Rank and Exchange among Northwest Coast Societies.* Prospect Heights: Waveland Press.

Rospabé, Philippe
1995   *La Dette de Vie: aux origines de la monnaie sauvage.* Paris: Editions la Découverte/MAUSS.

Ruud, Jørgen
   1960   *Taboo: A Study of Malagasy Beliefs and Customs.* New York: Humanities
             Press.

Sahlins, Marshall
   1972   *Stone Age Economics.* Chicago: Aldine.
   1976   *Culture and Practical Reason.* Chicago: University of Chicago Press.
   1981   *Historical Metaphors and Mythical Realities.* A.S.A.O. *Special Publication*
             no. 1. Ann Arbor: University of Michigan Press.
   1982   "Individual Experience and Cultural Order." In *The Social Sciences:
             Their Nature and Uses* (William Kruskal, ed.) Chicago: University of
             Chicago Press.
   1985   *Islands of History.* Chicago: University of Chicago Press, pp. 35–48.
   1992   "Foreword" to *Magical Arrows: The Maori, the Greeks, and the Folklore of
             the Universe* (by Gregory Schrempp). Madison: University of Wisconsin
             Press, ix-xiii.
   1995   *How "Natives" Think: About Captain Cook, For Example.* Chicago: Uni-
             versity of Chicago Press.
   2001   *Culture in Practice: Selected Essays.* New York: Zone Books.

Salmond, Anne
   1978   "'Te Ao Tawhito': A Semantic Approach to the Traditional Maori Cos-
             mos." *Journal of the Polynesian Society* 87:5–28.
   1983   *Hui.* Wellington: Reed.
   1984   "Nga Huarahi O Te Ao Maori (Pathways in the Maori World)." In *Te
             Maori, Maori Art from New Zealand Collections,* ed. Sidney M. Mead,
             pp. 109–37. New York: Harry N. Abrams.
   1997   *Between Worlds: Early Exchanges Between Maori and Europeans
             1773–1815.* Honolulu: University of Hawai'i Press.

Saussure, Ferdinand de
   1966   *Course in General Linguistics* (W. Bakins, trans.). New York: McGraw Hill.

Scarry, Elaine
   1985   *The Body in Pain: The Making and Unmaking of the World.* Oxford: Ox-
             ford University Press.
Schlanger, Nathan
   1998   "The study of techniques as an ideological challenge: Technology, Na-
             tion, and Humanity in the Work of Marcel Mauss." In *Marcel Mauss: A
             Centenary Tribute* (Wendy James and N. J. Allen, eds.), pp. 192–212.
             New York: Bergham Books.

Schrempp, Gregory
   1992   *Magical Arrows: The Maori, the Greeks, and the Folklore of the Universe.*
             Madison: University of Wisconsin Press.

Schulte-Tenckhoff, Isabelle
  1986   *Le potlatch, conquête et invention: réflexions sur un concept anthro-
          pologique.* Lausanne: Éditions d'En-bas.

Schwimmer, Eric
  1963   "Guardian Animals of the Maori." *Journal of the Polynesian Society*
          72:397–410.
  1978   "Lévi-Strauss and Maori Social Structure." *Anthropologica* 20:201–22.
  1990   "The Maori Hapu: a Generative Model." *Journal of the Polynesian Soci-
          ety* 99:297–317.

Scott, James D.
  1990   *Domination and the Arts of Resistance: Hidden Transcripts.* New Haven:
          Yale University Press.

Shell, Marc
  1978   *The Economy of Literature.* Baltimore: Johns Hopkins University Press.

Shimony, Annemarie
  1961   "Conservatism among the Six Nations Iroquois Reservation." *Yale Uni-
          versity Publications in Anthropology* 65. New Haven: Yale University
          Press.

Shirres, M. P.
  1982   "Tapu." *Journal of the Polynesian Society* 91 (1):29–51.

Shortland, Edward
  1856   *Traditions and Superstitions of the New Zealanders.* London: Longman,
          Brown, Green and Longmans.
  1882   *Maori Religion and Mythology.* London: Longmans Green & Co.

Sibree, James
  1880. *Madagascar: The Great African Island.* London: Trübner & Co.
  1896. *Madagascar Before the Conquest: The Island, the Country, and the People.* Lon-
          don: T. Fisher Unwin.

Silverman, Kaja
  1985   "Fragments of a Fashionable Discourse." In *Studies in Entertainment:
          Critical Approaches to Mass Culture.* (Tania Modleski, ed.), pp. 215–247.
          Bloomington: Indiana University Press.

Simmel, Georg
  1907 [1978]   *The Philosophy of Money*, trans. Tom Bottomore and D. Frisby.
          London: Routledge and Kegan Paul.

Siou, Georges E.
1999   *Huron-Wendat: The Heritage of the Circle*. Vancouver: University of British Columbia Press.

Slotkin, J. S. and Karl Schmidt
1949   "Studies of Wampum." *American Anthropologist* 51 (1):223–36.

Smith, Erminnie A.
1883   "Myths of the Iroquois." In *Second Annual Report of the Bureau of American Ethnology for the Years 1880–1881*, pp. 47–116. Washington, D.C.

Smith, Jean
1974   *Tapu Removal in Maori Religion*. Memoirs of the Polynesian Society no. 40. Wellington: Polynesian Society.

Smith, S. Percy
1910   *History and Traditions of the Taranaki*. Memoirs of the Polynesian Society no. 1. Wellington: Polynesian Society.

Smith, Timothy
1983   "Wampum as Primitive Valuables." *Research in Economic Anthropology* 5: 225–46.

Snyderman, George S.
1954   "The Functions of Wampum." *Proceedings of the American Philosophical Society* 93:469–94.
1961   "The Functions of Wampum in Iroquoian Religion." *Proceedings of the American Philosophical Society* 105:571–605.

Speck, Frank G.
1919   *The Functions of Wampum Among the Eastern Algonquin*. American Anthropological Association, Memoir 6.
1949   *Midwinter Rites of the Cayuga Long House*. Philadelphia: University of Pennsylvania Press.

Stallybrass, Peter
1998   "Marx's Coat." In *Border Fetishisms: Material Objects in Unstable Spaces* (P. Spyer, ed.), pp. 183–207. New York: Routledge.

Starna, W. A., and R. Watkins
1991   "Northern Iroquoian Slavery." *Ethnohistory* 38:34–57.

Stirling, Amiria Manutahi, and Anne Salmond,
1976   *Amiria: The Life Story of a Maori Woman*. Wellington: Reed.

Strathern, Andrew
1971   *The Rope of Moka: Big-Men and Ceremonial Exchange in Mount Hagen, New Guinea.* Cambridge: Cambridge University Press.
1979   "Gender, Ideology and Money in Mount Hagen." *Man* (n.s.) 14 (3):530–48.

Strathern, Marilyn
1975   *No Money on Our Skins.* Port Moresby, New Guinea: Research Unit Bulletin No. 61.
1981   "Culture in a Netbag: The Manufacture of a Subdiscipline in Anthropology." *Man* (n.s.) 16:665–88.
1984a   "Subject or object? Women and the Circulation of Valuables in Highlands New Guinea." In *Women and Property, Women as Property,* ed. Renée Hirschon, 158–75. New York: St. Martin's Press.
1984b   "Marriage Exchanges: A Melanesian Comment." *Annual Review of Anthropology* 13:41–73.
1987   "Conclusion" to *Dealing with Inequality: Analysing Gender Relations in Melanesia and beyond.* (Marilyn Strathern, ed.), pp.278–302. Cambridge: Cambridge University Press.
1988   *The Gender of the Gift: Problems with Women and Problems with Society in Melanesia.* Berkeley: University of California Press.
1992   "Qualified Value: The Perspective of Gift Exchange." In *Barter, Exchange and Value: An Anthropological Approach* (Caroline Humphrey and Stephen Hugh-Jones, eds.). Cambridge, Cambridge University Press. Pp. 169–91.

Suttles, Wayne
1968   "Coping with Abundance: Subsistence on the Northwest Coast." In Richard B. Lee and Irvin DeVore, eds., *Man the Hunter,* pp. 56–69. Chicago: Aldine.

Taïeb, Paulette
1984   "L'Oreille du Sourd." *Bulletin du MAUSS* no. 11:39–69.

Tambiah, Stanley J.
1985   *Culture, Thought and Social Action: An Anthropological Perspective.* Cambridge: Cambridge University Press.

Taussig, Michael
1980   *The Devil and Commodity Fetishism in South America.* Chapel Hill: University of North Carolina Press.
1993   "Maleficium: State Fetishism." In *Fetishism as Cultural Discourse* (Emily Apter and William Pietz, eds.), pp. 217–47. Ithaca: Cornell University Press.

Taylor, Richard
1855   *Te Ika a Maui or New Zealand and Its Inhabitants.* London: Wertheim and McIntosh.

Tcherkezoff, Serge
1983   *Le Roi Nyamwezi, la droite et la gauche. Révision comparative des classifications dualistes.* Paris: Atelier d'Anthropologie Sociale, Maison des Sciences de l'Homme.

Testart, Alain
1993   *Des Dons et des Dieux: Anthropologie Religieuse et Sociologie Comparative.* Paris: Armand Colin.
1997   "Les trois modes de transfert." *Gradhiva* 21:39–58.
1998   "Uncertainties of the 'obligation to reciprocate': A Critique of Mauss." In *Marcel Mauss: A Centenary Tribute* (Wendy James and N. J. Allen, eds.), pp. 97–110. New York: Bergham Books.

Thomas, Nicholas
1985   "Forms of personification and prestations." *Mankind* 15:223–30.
1991   *Entangled Objects: Exchange, Material Culture, and Colonialism in the Pacific.* Cambridge: Harvard University Press.

Thomas, Paul
1980   *Karl Marx and the Anarchists.* London: Routledge and Kegan Paul.

Thomas, William I., and Znaniecki, Florian
1918   *The Polish Peasant in Europe and America.* Dover: New York.

Thompson, David
1987   "The Hau of the Gift in its Cultural Context." *Pacific Studies* 11:63–79.

Thwaites, R. G. (ed.)
1898 *The Jesuit Relations and allied Documents 1610–1791,* 73 volumes. New York: Pageant.

Tooker, Elizabeth
1964   "An Ethnography of the Huron Indians, 1615–1649." *Bureau of American Ethnology Bulletin 190.*
1965   "The Iroquois White Dog Ceremony in the Latter Part of the Eighteenth Century." *Ethnohistory* 12:129–40.
1970   *The Iroquois Ceremonial of Midwinter.* Syracuse: Syracuse University Press.
1978   "The League of the Iroquois: Its History, Politics, and Ritual." In *Handbook of the North American Indians,* Northeast, volume 15 (B. Trigger, ed.), pp. 418–41, Washington, D.C.: Smithsonian Institution.

1984   "Women in Iroquois Society." In *Extending the Rafters: Interdisciplinary Approaches to Iroquoian Studies,* ed. M. K. Foster, J. Campisi, and M. Mithun, pp. 109–23. Albany: State University of New York Press.

Tregear, E.
1891   *Maori-Polynesian Comparative Dictionary.* Wellington: Lyon and Blair.
1904   *The Maori Race.* Wanganui, NZ: A. D. Willis.

Trigger, Bruce
1976   *The Children of Aatentsic: A History of the Huron People to 1660.* 2 volumes. Montreal, McGill-Queen's University Press.

Turgeon, Laurier
1992   "Les objets des échanges entre Français et Amérindiens au XVIe siécle. *Recherches amérindiens au Québec* 22 (1–2):152–67.
1997   "The Tale of the Kettle: Odyssey of an Intercultural Object." *Ethnohistory* 44 (1): 1–29.

Turner, Terence
1967   "Parson's Concept of a Generalized Media of Social Interaction and its Relevance for Social Anthropology." *Sociological Inquiry* 38:121–34.
1973   "Piaget's Structuralism." *American Anthropologist* 75:351–73.
1977   "Transformation, Hierarchy and Transcendence: A Reformulation of Van Gennep's Model of the Structure of Rites of Passage." In Sally Falk Moore and Barbara Myerhoff (eds), *Secular Ritual* pp. 53–70. Amsterdam: Van Gorcum.
1978   "The Kayapo of Central Brazil." In A. Sutherland, ed., *Face Values.* London: BBC.
1979a   "The Gê and Bororo Socities as Dialectical Systems: A General Model." In D. Maybury-Lewis (ed.), *Dialectical Societies: Gê and Bororo of Central Brazil,* pp. 147–178. Cambridge: Harvard University Press.
1979b   "Kinship, Household and Community Structure among the Kayapo." In D. Maybury-Lewis (ed.), *Dialectical Societies: Gê and Bororo of Central Brazil,* pp. 179–217. Cambridge: Harvard University Press.
1979c   "Anthropology and the Politics of Indigenous Peoples' Struggles." *Cambridge Anthropology* 5:1–43.
1980   "The Social Skin." In Jeremy Cherfas and R. Lewas (eds), *Not Work Alone.* Beverly Hills: Sage Productions.
1984   "Value, Production and Exploitation in Non-Capitalist societies." Unpublished essay based on a paper presented at the AAA 82nd Annual Meeting, Denver, Colorado. To appear in *Critique of Pure Culture.* New York: Berg Press [forthcoming].
1985a   "Dual opposition, hierarchy and value: Moiety structure and symbolic polarity in Central Brazil and elsewhere." In J.-C. Galey (ed.), *Différences, valuers, hiérarchie: textes offertes à Louis Dumont.* Paris: Editions de l'Ecole des Hautes Etudes en Sciences Sociales.

1985b   "Animal Symbolism, Totemism, and the Structure of Myth." In *Animal Myths and Metaphors in South America* (Gary Urton, ed.). Salt Lake City: University of Utah Press.

1987   *The Kayapo of Southeastern Para.* Unpublished monograph prepared for CEDI, Povos Indigenas do Brasil, Vol. VIII, Sul do Para, Part II.

1989   "A Commentary" (on T.O. Beidelman, Agonistic Exchange, Homeric Reciprocity and the Heritage of Simmel and Mauss). *Cultural Anthropology* 4:260–64.

1991   "Representing, Resisting, Rethinking: Historical Transformations of Kayapo Culture and Anthropological Consciousness." In *Colonial Situations: Essays on the Contextualization of Ethnographic Knowledge* (George Stocking, ed.), pp. 285–314. Madison: University of Wisconsin Press.

1993   "The Poetics of Play: Ritual Clowning, Masking and Performative Mimesis among the Kayapo." [To appear in Bruce Kapferer and Peter Koepping, eds. *The Ludic: Forces of Generation and Fracture.* Oxford, Berg Press.]

1994   "Bodies and anti-Bodies: Flesh and Fetish in Contemporary Social Theory," in T. Csordas, ed., *Embodiment and Experience.* Cambridge: Cambridge University Press.

1995   "Social body and embodied subject: the production of bodies, actors and society among the Kayapo." *Cultural Anthropology* 10:2.

Turner, Terence and Jane Fajans
1988   "Where the Action Is: An Anthropological Perspective on "Activity Theory," with Ethnographic Implications." Unpublished manuscript, University of Chicago.

Turner, Victor
1967   *The Forest of Symbols* Cornell University Press.

Tylor, Edward
1874   *Primitive Culture.* Boston: Estes and Lauriat.

Van Gennep, Arnold
1960   *The Rites de Passage.* Chicago: University of Chicago Press.

Vernant, Jean-Pierre
1983   *Myth and Thought among the Greeks.* London: Routledge and Kegan Paul.

Vig, Lars
1969.   *Charmes: Spécimens de Magie Malgache.* Oslo: Universitetsforlagets Trykningssentral.

Vlastos, Gregory
1970   "On Heraclitus." In *Studies in Presocratic Philosophy* (David Furley and R. E. Allen, eds.) New York: Humanities Press, pp. 413–23.

Vogt, Evon Z., and Ethel M. Albert (eds.)
1966   *The People of Rimrock: A Study of Values in Five Cultures.* Cambridge: Harvard University Press.

Vogt, W. Paul
1983   "Obligation and Right: The Durkheimians and the Sociology of Law." In *The Sociological Domain: The Durkheimians and the Founding of French Sociology* (Philippe Besnard, ed.), pp. 177–198. Cambridge: Cambridge University Press.

Vygotsky, L. S.
1978   *Mind in Society: The Development of Higher Psychological Processes.* Cambridge: Harvard University Press.

Wagner, Roy
1975   *The Invention of Culture.* Englewood Cliffs: Prentice-Hall.
1978   *Lethal Speech.* Ithaca: Cornell University Press.

Walens, Stanley
1981   *Feasting with Cannibals: An Essay on Kwakiutl Cosmology.* Princeton: Princeton University Press.

Wallace, Anthony
1956   "Revitalization Movements." *American Anthropologist* 58:264–81.
1958   "Dreams and Wishes of the Soul: A Type of Psychoanalytic Theory among the Seventeenth Century Iroquois." *American Anthropologist* 60:234–48.
1969   *The Death and Rebirth of the Seneca.* New York: Vintage Books.

Wallace, Paul
1946   *The White Roots of Peace.* Philadelphia: University of Pennsylvania Press.

Waterman, T. T.
1923   "Some Conundrums in Northwest Coast Art." *American Anthropologist* 25(4):435–51.

Weeden, William
1884   "Indian Money as a Factor in New England Civilization." *Johns Hopkins University Studies in Historical and Political Science,* 2nd series, viii-ix:5–51.

Weiner, Annette
1976   *Women of Value, Men of Renown: New Perspectives on Trobriand Exchange.* Austin: University of Texas Press.
1978   "The Reproductive Model in Trobriand Society." In J. Specht and J.P.White, eds. *Trade and Exchange in Oceania and Australia. Mankind* special issue 11.

1980   "Reproduction: A Replacement for Reciprocity." *American Ethnologist* 7:71–85.

1982   "Sexuality among the Anthropologists: Reproduction among the Informants." In F. J. P. Poole and G. Herdt, eds. *Sexual Antagonism, Gender and Social Change in Papua New Guinea. Social Analysis* special issue 12.

1985   "Inalienable Wealth." *American Ethnologist* 12:210–27.

1988   *The Trobrianders of Papua New Guinea.* New York: Harcourt Brace.

1992   *Inalienable Possessions: The Paradox of Keeping-while-Giving.* Berkeley: University of California Press.

Weiner, James
1988   *The Heart of the Pearlshell: The Mythological Dimension of Foi Sociality.* Berkeley: University of California Press.

Weiner, Margaret
1995.   *Visible and Invisible Kingdoms: Power, Magic and Colonial Conquest in Bali.* Chicago: University of Chicago Press.

Weiss, Brad
1996   *The Making and Unmaking of the Haya Lived World: Consumption, Commoditization, and Everyday Practice.* Durham: Duke University Press.

White, John
1885   "Maori Customs and Superstitions."In *The History and Doings of the Maoris* (T. Gudgeon, ed.). Auckland: H. Brett, pp. 95–225.

1887–90 *The Ancient History of the Maori: His Mythology and Traditions.* 6 volumes. Wellington: Government Printer.

Widerspach-Thor, Martine de
1981   "The Equation of Copper: In Memory of Wilson Duff." In *The World is as Sharp as a Knife: An Anthology in Honour of Wilson Duff.* (Donald Abbott, ed.). Victoria, B.C.: British Columbia Provincial Museum.

Williams, H. W.
1844   *A Dictionary of the Maori Language.* Wellington: Government Printer.

Williamson, R.
1913   "Kumara Lore." *Journal of the Polynesian Society* 22:36–41

Wolf, Eric
1982   *Europe and the People without History.* Berkeley: University of California Press.

1999   *Envisioning Power: Ideologies of Dominance and Crisis.* Berkeley: University of California Press.

Index

communism, 156
  among dukes, 214; and
  permanence, 218, 225; as original
  form of social contract, 162;
  defined, 218, 227; identified with
  familial authority, 221;
  individualistic, 159–160, 225;
  primitive, 159; within capitalism,
  227–28; *see* also Marxism, Mauss,
  socialism, total prestation
communitas, 227
condolence rituals, 128–129, 142, 143,
  145
consciousness, 58–59, 141
  of charms, 110; of self, 97; partial,
  60, 63–66; unfetishized, 248
constitutive property, *see* property,
  constitutive
constructivist approach, 78
consumption, 31–32, 96, 172, 188,
  211, 224
  as metaphor of food, 260; creative,
  26, 32, 89; fetishism and, 65;
  revival of interest in, 26, 30, 265;
  see also aristocracy, food,
  production
contracts, 9, 10, 28, 133, 236–37;
  "archaic forms of," 153, 230–32;
  economic, 153–154; rental, 219;
  social, 152–154, 162, 230, 236;
  wage labor, 228
Cook, Captain James, 187
Copalle (French portait painter), 246
coppers (Kwakiutl valuables),
  93, 117, 205, 206–209, 224, 277;
  killing of, 206–207, 209,
Coppet, Daniel de, 18–20, 226
cosmology, 17, 20, 82, 126, 127, 139,
  168–69, 187, 202, 216, 261;
  cosmological center, 204; dilemma,
  130, 171; hunting cosmology, 190,
  205, 276; origins, 185
Creator, 110, 134, 139, 140, 273
creative energies, 54–56, 68, 75, 80,
  189–90, 261, 268

creativity, 21, 24, 38, 39, 46, 54–56,
  67, 68, 81, 82–83, 128, 131, 136,
  143, 163, 167, 191, 215, 239,
  248–49, 257–61
  as element of action, 248–49;
  cultural, 148; efficacy of words,
  135; historical, 249; individual
  versus collective, 59; Kwakiutl
  theories of, 198; naturalization of,
  169, 173, 187; and pleasure,
  260–61; powers of, 172, 232, 240,
  251, 259; social, 78, 117, 133, 240,
  244, 251, 259–61; theory of, 82,
  133–34, 136, 141, 143, 198; *see*
  action, alienation, consumption,
  imagination, potential, power,
  production
crests (Kwakiutl emblematic wealth),
  193, 204, 276; defined, 195; *see* also
  heirlooms, tlogwe
critical theory, 25–26, 37, 161, 227,
  240, 256–57
  flaws in 30, 227; origins of, in
  Marx, 25, 255–56; two orders of
  59–60
crown jewels, 34, 212
culture(s), 3–4, 9, 14, 21–22, 70, 95,
  97, 131, 189, 197, 198, 199, 207,
  256, 270
  change, 147; relegated to
  consumption, 32
cursing
  Maori, 174, 177–178, 182
Curtis, Frank, 209
cynicism,
  and Bolshevism, 156; and economic
  theory, 8, 154; of King Radama,
  246; and power, 247; versus naivete,
  256–57

Dalton, George, 11
Davy, Georges, 153, 274
death, 19, 96, 97, 100, 102, 120–21,
  123, 124, 127, 137, 139, 143,
  167–68, 173, 177, 198, 231

Taussig, Michael, 264
templates, *see* value, templates
Testart, Alain, 209, 225, 277
Texans, 2–3
Thadodaho, 128–129
thanksgiving, 126, 134, 136, 140–141, 261
theological attitude, *see* religion
theory
relevance of, 20–21
Thomas, Nicolas, 263, 267
titles, 93, 121, 159, 173, 191ff
two classes of, among Kwakiutl, 196–97, 198; *see* also names and naming
Tiv (West African people), 117
tjuringas, 34
tlogwe (Kwakiutl treasures), 192, 200
see also heirlooms
tokens, 72
microcosmic, 259; of value, 75; *see* also media
Tooker, Elisabeth, 126, 133, 273
tools, heirlooms as 185
torture
of prisoners, 123–124, 127, 137
total prestation, 153, 158–160, 217
totalities
comparison between, 18; "concrete," 68, 267; imaginary, 87–88, 97, 115, 142, 227–28, 257; ; of social labor, 270; opposition to idea of, 26, 86–87; social, 31, 227, 257
trade, 145–6, 231
Transactionalism, 12, 19
transgression, 172, 188
treasures, *see* heirlooms
tribute, 6, 99, 113, 120, 130, 132, 234
tricksters, 244
Trobriand Islands (Papua New Guinea island), 175
gardening, 6–7, 34, 44, 242; mortuary ritual, 166; spells, 242, 245; kula exchange, 164–166

truth
and magic, 241–42; and science, 53
Tsimihety, 247
Turner, Terence, chapter 3 passim, 85, 259, 268, 268
critique of standard Marxist anthropology, 68–69; on egocentrism and fetishization, 64, 269; on European formal clothing, 95–96;on Kayapo, 71–75; on media of value, 78; on micrototalities, 250; on minimal units of analysis, 71, 269; on rites of passage, 62; on totality, 86–88; on value and production, 80–81; political implications of, 88
Turner, Victor, 62
Tuscarora (North American people), 272
Tylor, Edward, 97–98, 105, 121, 164, 166, 177, 239, 240, 253

unique objects, 32, 34, 75, chapter 4 passim, 131
comparison of, 223; *see* also heirlooms, Kopytoff
utilitarianism
as analytical term, 263; of Bolsheviks, 156, 163, 256
utopianism, 228, 248, 251, 278
utu (Maori concept), 171, 172, 186
see also reciprocity

value, chapters 1–7 passim
among Kayapo, 70–74, 82; as importance, 55, 251; as meaningful difference, 13–16, 43–44, 46, 67; as promise of pleasure, 9; as proportion, 42, 53–55, 67–68, 75, 250, 263; communal, 84; coppers as repositories of, 206; domains of, 17–18, 56, 106, 165; economic, 1, 5–12, 14–15, 19, 20–21, 28–29, 30–32, 42, 46, 55–56, 222, 263, 265; established through gifts, 222;